Aliens and Alienists

Aliens and Alienists
Ethnic minorities and psychiatry

Roland Littlewood & Maurice Lipsedge

second edition

London
UNWIN HYMAN
Boston   Sydney   Wellington

Published by the Academic Division of
Unwin Hyman Ltd
15/17 Broadwick Street, London W1V 1FP, UK

Unwin Hyman Inc.,
8 Winchester Place, Winchester, Mass. 01890, USA

Allen & Unwin (Australia) Ltd,
8 Napier Street, North Sydney, NSW 2060, Australia

Allen & Unwin (New Zealand) Ltd in association with the
Port Nicholson Press Ltd,
Compusales Building, 75 Ghuznee Street, Wellington 1, New Zealand

First published in 1989

British Library Cataloguing in Publication Data

Littlewood, Roland
 Aliens and alienists: ethnic minorities and
 psychiatry. – 2nd ed.
 1. Great Britain. Ethnic minorities. Mental
 disorders
 I. Title II. Lipsedge, Maurice
 616.89′00880693

 ISBN 0–04–445317–5
 ISBN 0–04–445316–7 Pbk

Library of Congress Cataloging-in-Publication Data

Littlewood, Roland.
 Aliens and alienists: ethnic minorities and psychiatry/Roland
 Littlewood and Maurice Lipsedge. – 2nd ed.
  p. cm.
 Bibliography: p.
 Includes index.
  ISBN 0–04–445317–5. ISBN 0–04–445316–7 (pbk.)
  1. Immigrants – Mental health – Great Britain. 2. Minorities –
 Mental health - Great Britain. 3. West Indians–Mental health–
 Great Britain. 4. Jews – Mental health – Great Britain.
 I. Lipsedge, Maurice. II. Title.
 RC451.4.E45L57 1989
 616.89′008′693–dc20   89–14689
                                                           CIP

Typeset in 10 on 12 point Times by Columns of Reading
and printed in Great Britain by Billing and Sons, London and
Worcester

CONTENTS

Alien 1 Belonging to another person, place or family, strange, foreign, not of one's own

  5 Of a nature repugnant, adverse or opposed to

Alienate 1 To make estranged; to estrange or turn away the feelings or attentions of any one

Alienist One who treats mental diseases; a medical psychologist; a 'mad-doctor'

(Oxford English Dictionary, 1971)

PREFACE TO THE SECOND EDITION

The invitation to prepare a second edition of *Aliens and Alienists* has inevitably prompted thoughts as to how valid now seem its arguments and conclusions. Over the seven years since the book first appeared mental health in black and ethnic minority groups in Britain has remained a salient question: a stream of papers and articles, some medical and descriptive, some polemical and angry, has continued to appear. Radio and television programmes, popular and scholarly accounts, parliamentary debates over the revisions of the Mental Health Act, local policy statements and public inquiries have all contributed to the debate on what has been called 'transcultural psychiatry'; a debate to which we ourselves have contributed, sometimes sadly, frequently angrily. Where has all this left our book?

We can only say that little of substance has been achieved since 1982. The arguments we raised then remain, certainly debated but unresolved. Despite critiques of racism in psychiatry, medical practice remains much the same: an under-representation of black mental health professionals in senior positions to be contrasted with the over-representation of black people as patients under the Mental Health Act; little or no access to psychotherapy; a continued focus on the clinical pattern of illness observed in the individual patient without any understanding of its possible social determinants; a lack of interest in the historical and social construction of contemporary psychiatry itself; and piecemeal accumulation of diverse data with no generation of testable hypotheses which might link patients' understanding of distress and their own resources to the treatment of psychiatric illness; an emphasis on hospitalized patients but not on distress as experienced in the community; avoidance of the issues of racism in mental health care provision, with few serious policy initiatives in the area of health and race; no consultation between black and minority users of the available services and the providers of those services, whether doctors, nurses or health service 'managers' (to use the currently fashionable idiom). Patients and their families remain objects of study from one perspective; from the other they are the hapless victims of racist psychiatry.

If there has been little advance in theory or clinical practice, in some areas the situation is now actually worse. Except for immigration from the other European Community countries, overseas settlement in Britain has now effectively ceased. Half of Britain's ethnic minorities are British born, no longer immigrants but Britons. To some extent, the mental health problems of their migrant parents were no surprise; if West Indians coming to Britain had high rates of schizophrenia so did white Britons who emigrated to Australia. But we can now no longer talk of the mental health of 'immigrants' as something tangential to British society. The high rates of diagnosed schizophrenia among British-born Afro-Caribbeans which were found in a number of studies last year cannot be considered as the consequence of dislocation or 'culture-conflict'. Whatever the explanation (and we have to exclude a real increase in serious psychiatric illness, not only selective medicalization and inappropriate diagnosis), they indicate a pattern existing and continuing within British social structure: not a transient colonial legacy but something integral to black–white relations now, part of a continuing pattern of racial exploitation and disadvantage which is not independent of the statistics emanating from the prison or probation services or welfare agencies.

The first edition of *Aliens and Alienists* was part of a critique of 'transcultural psychiatry' which has continued, not least among the professional members of the Transcultural Psychiatry Society. The interests of this group, of which we are members, have now shifted from an emphasis on a narrowly conceived notion of 'culture' to one on 'race'. Its academic papers and symposia have attempted to clarify the role of psychiatry in perpetuating, if not actually creating, mental illness among ethnic minorities. In our opinion, much of this critique, although valid, has suffered from a lack of proper theoretical framework, one grounded in a critical social theory which can encompass the individual experience as well as its political and biological construction. With the exception of Kobena Mercer's work (reviewed here in a new concluding chapter), we are often left with a sterile debate between the practitioners who espouse objective 'value-free' explanations of illness in the individual patient and those quasi-radical conspiracy theorists who regard any involvement, theoretical or clinical, in the area as inherently suspect. Somewhere in the middle patients survive and, it is true, useful work has been carried out regarding black representation on the Mental Health Act Commission or on improving the career opportunities for black psychiatrists.

The current *culture versus race* debate is particularly bereft of serious theory. The old Community Relations Commission style of defining 'culture' as a set of check list items of difference remains grossly prejudiced and of little analytical value, a convergent approach seeking to reduce conflict. An emphasis on 'race', however, which perceives the issue simply as a divergent power conflict between two separately defined groups, and which fails to employ a notion of 'culture' which includes the institutional politics of race and its psychological representation in the individual, whether as power, alienation or resistance, is equally lacking in analytical rigor, leaving black people as the victims of forces beyond their power. We remain convinced that our suggestions as to the interplay between external social constraints and individual subjectivities remain valid.

For this edition we have left the original text unaltered except for correcting misprints, updating some of the population figures, modifying the section on the now abolished Vagrancy Act ('Sus') and adding glosses where the new Mental Health Act differs from its 1959 predecessor. On a terminological note: the distinction between *racialism* (practice) and *racism* (theory) has been generally abandoned in favour of using the latter in both meanings. We have now followed this.

The opportunity of preparing a new edition gives us the chance to pay tribute to a neglected book of which we were ignorant in 1981 – John Royer's *Black Britain's Dilemma* (Roseau, Dominica, Tropical Printers, 1977). In this humane and careful book he presents many arguments with which we are concerned here. Royer, a West Indian psychiatrist, places considerable emphasis on religion as a system of understanding and creating personal identity. *Aliens and Alienists* was sometimes criticized for its emphasis on religion and 'otherwordly' experiences as if we assumed, tacitly or otherwise, that we took these as maladaptive or even pathological. We would emphasize again that these are the modes by which many, perhaps most, people in the world interpret and experience serious mental illness, reflecting complex local psychologies of selfhood, autonomy, causality and power. To denigrate the individual's religious perspective as simply 'lacking in insight', whether we do this for reasons of biomedical positivism or vulgar Marxism, is to ignore both the intellectual elegance of religious explanation and its historical role in maintaining black identity in the face of European oppression, not to mention its pragmatic function in generating organizations which have taken on more overtly political concerns. The understanding of patients' explanatory models (as Arthur Kleinman has called them) is fundamental to any attempt to provide appropriate and equal care. It might be noted that so far neither biomedicine nor political theory have been able to provide any understanding of serious mental illness that makes sense in anybody's everyday language. Nor can they separately.

Our psychiatric colleagues however were less concerned with political theory in the book than with what they took as a distorted account of the experiences of minority patients who entered British psychiatric institutions.[1] Others pointed out that things were just as bad for white indigenous patients. Suffice to say that in our account of situations like that of Calvin Johnson (Chapter 1) we described particular patients we knew and events we ourselves observed, indeed participated in. We do not believe they are untypical of current practice in 1989.

FROM THE PREFACE TO THE FIRST EDITION (1982)

. . . As we examined the relationship between culture and mental illness, it became clear that they were already closely associated but in a rather unexpected way: the everyday life and customs of minority groups in Britain and America had been frequently characterized by politicians and doctors as pathological in themselves. . .

It became clear that to look upon 'culture' simply as a confusing factor in a value-free pursuit of scientific medicine was nonsense. The mental health of Africans and Asians has been a political question since the eighteenth century. The solution did not, however, lie in simply explaining certain patterns of mental illness as political prejudice: if failure to diagnose depression in West Indian-born patients was a consequence of prejudice, we had to explain why among West Indians in Britain the suicide rate was much lower than among other groups. Ethnocentrism lay not merely in mistaking the social for the biological (or the reverse) but in a complex and often unclear series of assumptions linking the two. While certain stereotypes were valid – Irish men and women in Britain for example did have a serious problem with alcoholism – we had to look at how these stereotypes originated and how members of ethnic minorities constructed their lives within them. We needed a type of analysis which would enable us to consider culture, experience and behaviour together at the same level – that is, the symbolic. And this was the province of social anthropology rather than psychiatry.

Although both anthropology and psychiatry originated in the study of people designated as *aliens*, they can offer a sensitive awareness of the relationship between observer and observed. While we have tried to situate our own theories within the relativistic framework we have applied to others, we are still white, male, middle-class doctors discussing the private experiences of patients who are frequently black, female and working class – part of what Michel Foucault calls the monologue of reason about madness.

To discuss the psychological adjustment of ethnic minorities is to underline yet again the popular conception of them as being primarily a *problem*. To criticize a stereotype is always in some measure to reiterate it. All individuals derive their personal identity from belonging simultaneously to quite different groups: ethnic, religious, professional and political. To single out the mentally ill immigrant – the doubly alienated – as if this is their sole possible identity is not to say that such an alienation is other than an alienation imposed by ourselves. It should become clear that when we talk about 'the illness', 'the patient', 'the immigrant' or 'the disadvantaged' we are not suggesting that these are the ideal questions, merely that these are how they are conceptualized both by society and by the individual concerned. When we talk of mental illness we are talking of the psychiatrist. When we talk of the black we are also talking of the white.

This is not a handbook. We have not produced a list of the various psychological difficulties of all ethnic minorities in Britain. Nor have we provided a glossary to a series of 'when is a delusion not a delusion?' questions; to attempt to delineate the boundaries of normality and abnormality in a rapidly changing community is anyway a doubtful enterprise. What we have tried to develop is a theoretical framework within which the involved worker can begin to make his own judgements.

Rather than offer an initial theory which is then applied in different situations, we first present the practical problems and then look at the value and limitations of various approaches to them. In Chapters 9 and 10 we develop a tentative model for looking at two rather general (and unfashionable) questions: the nature of cultural reality in mental illness and the problem of individual experience in anthropological theories.

Although the patients we talk about come from a variety of ethnic groups, we concentrate on West Indian and Jewish immigrants and their families. Other communities – Africans, Asians, Cypriots, Irish – are presented in less detail and some, such as the North Americans (the eighth largest national immigrant group in Britain), are ignored altogether. We look particularly at patients from the Caribbean, partly because of our own experience and also because we think that their crisis is the most acute and that the questions we have to consider are clearer. Cultural differences between pre- and post-migration society are not reliable predictors of subsequent difficulty and British Asians have perhaps fewer questions of identity and a greater correspondence between subjective and objective reality than do the Afro-British. The unfortunate term 'cultural schizophrenia' has been applied to groups in transition between two cultures. Schizophrenia is regarded by psychiatrists as a fragmented rather than a dual personality and if we must use mental illness as a metaphor for society, then maybe it is the West Indian rather than the Asian community which has been in a state of 'cultural schizophrenia'.

An assumption which runs throughout this book is that the expression of mental illness, while it may not always be valid communication to others, is still a meaningful reaction on the part of the individual to his situation. Another recurrent theme is the rather obvious point that the appreciation and even the conceptualization of psychological difficulties can take place only within the set of available beliefs and assumptions which are offered by one's cultural milieu – a set of assumptions which in this case involves the dominant as well as the minority culture, the doctor as well as the patient.

The fact that our explanations are drawn from social anthropology, history and the sociology of knowledge rather than from the physical sciences is not to say that mental illness is only a social phenomenon. It should become clear that we regard this as an unproductive question: mental illness is rooted both in biology and in culture, in the individual and in society. What is important is not whether mental illness should be regarded as a biological or as a social phenomenon, or whether a particular individual is 'really ill', but how different levels of interpretation interact and how they are derived from each other. The question is not whether a patient is 'orientated to reality' but to which reality and why.

While emphasizing the importance of subjective experience we do not use psychological explanations for social events. The primary reason for racism is not to be found in unhealthy or illogical thinking but, quite simply, in institutions which for some make a great deal of economic sense. Racism is not a disease but part of a political system.

Relativism is unfashionable at present. Confidence in our ability to understand and change ourselves has been replaced by a retreat to containment and isolation, a 'return to standards' and 'objective measures'. After a brief experimental period in the 1960s, psychiatrists have returned to their traditional role as custodians and dispensers of drugs and other physical treatments. We believe that the demonstration of the subjective nature of much that we take for concrete is more urgent than ever at a time when we are again concerned with controlling others, while simultaneously surrendering control over ourselves to such mystical concepts as monetarism or sociobiology. To mistake social and political models for reality is to constrain ourselves by apparently external events which are merely the expression of our own current insecurities.

These recent concerns have been characterized by a confusion between the social and the biological: skin pigmentation, a biological fact, is associated with certain existing political relationships and then extrapolated back into a fanciful biology to generate the idea of 'race'. Sociobiology takes isolated examples of animal behaviour, tags them with the name of a human institution and then informs us that this institution is the product of a biology from which we are helpless to escape. As we attempt to show, the shift from social to pseudo-biological explanation (a shift which psychiatry by its concerns on the social-biological interface is uniquely equipped to bear) is a characteristic of times when the symbolic power of decaying institutions loses its hold and they are re-established by tying social relations in a new way to universal personal experiences. The transitory and elusive become fixed to legitimate our concerns. Choices become destiny. Psychiatry, like religion or like racism, can serve as a phenomenon of this type.

Our great debt is to those patients whose lives we have laid bare and who, in addition to their other difficulties, were prepared to investigate with us the basis of our therapeutic relationship. With many this has become too personal to discuss in a book, but their ideas are to be found throughout. The histories we discuss are factual, with altered names, places and dates, and occasionally with changes of occupation and minor details, to preserve confidentiality.

ACKNOWLEDGEMENTS

We are grateful to the Editor of the *British Journal of Medical Psychology* for permission to reprint a large portion of a paper originally published as 'Anthropology and Psychiatry – An Alternative Approach'; the Editors of the *Bulletin of the Royal College of Psychiatrists* to reprint parts of 'Ethnic Minorities and the Mental Health Act: Patterns of Explanation' and 'Community Initiated Research: Psychiatrists' Conceptualisations of Cannabis Psychosis'; the Editor of *Social Work Practice* for part of 'Towards an Inter-Cultural Therapy: Some Preliminary Observations'; and to the following for permission to make substantial quotations: Allen & Unwin Ltd for the passage on p. 138 from B. Parekh's *Colour, Culture and Consciousness* (1974); Laurence Pollinger Ltd for the passage on p.155 from D.H. Lawrence's *Psychoanalysis and the Unconscious* (Heinemann, 1923); and Chapman & Hall Ltd for the passage on p.169 from Evelyn Waugh's *Decline and Fall* (1928).

We have benefited from discussing chapters of this book with colleagues in the Department of Psychiatry at St Bartholomew's

Hospital, Guy's Hospital, the University of the West Indies, Colombo University, Beijing University, Birmingham University, the Transcultural Psychiatry Society, the British Medical Anthropology Society, the Department of Social Anthropology of the London School of Economics, the Departments of Psychiatry and Anthropology at University College London, and the Institute of Social Anthropology in Oxford. We owe a particular debt of gratitude to Murray Last for his encouragement of a new edition. Various chapters have also been criticized by Chimen Abramsky, Sourrangshu Accharya, Victor Adebimpe, Edwin Ardener, Michael Beaubrun, Ranjit Chandrasena, Jacques Charles-Nicolas, Audrey Coulson, John Cox, Armando Favazza, Cecil Helman, Clifford Geertz, Bruce Kapferer, Jafar Kareem, Britt Kause, Jeanette Kupfermann, Murray Last, Ioan Lewis, Godfrey Lienhardt, Liliane Lipsedge, Jenny Littlewood, Kobena Mercer, H.B.M. Murphy, Rodney Needham, John Orley, Rosine Perelberg, Raymond Prince, Tim Rackett, Philip Rack, Nick Rose, Lawrence Ward, Bernard Wasserstein, James Watson, William Wedonoja and Michael Wood, and by numerous other colleagues, patients and members of community and religious groups. Errors of fact and interpretation are of course our own.

NOTE

1 A preface is not the place to engage in endless post hoc justifications. The reader interested in the debates in *Race and Class* and the *Transcultural Psychiatric Research Review* can scan the items listed in the references to the concluding chapter under Murphy 1982, Littlewood 1983a, Black Health Workers and Patients Group 1983, Littlewood 1984.

CHAPTER ONE

ETHNIC MINORITIES
AND THE PSYCHIATRIST

MEDEA: Come, I'll ask your advice as if you were a friend,
Not that I hope for any help from you; but still,
I'll ask you, and expose your infamy. Where now
Can I turn? Back to my country and my father's house,
Which I betrayed to come with you?

Euripides, *Medea*
(trs. Philip Vellacott, Penguin Books, 1963, p. 32)

CALVIN JOHNSON

Calvin Johnson left Jamaica and came to live in London twenty years ago. His father, a mason, died soon after Calvin left, but his mother still lives in the family home in Spanish Town, near the capital Kingston, with his sisters. Family life was harmonious, but as a boy Calvin was always getting into trouble at school. Although intelligent he never seemed to concentrate on anything for very long. He was teased by teachers and pupils for being long and thin, which made him look older than he was; he always seemed to stand out. Calvin responded by getting into fights at the slightest provocation and was eventually expelled when he was twelve.

He then left home for some time and went to stay in Kingston with one of his mother's brothers. He discovered the local library and read voraciously, achieving a broad but rather idiosyncratic general knowledge. Eventually, at his uncle's insistence, he became apprenticed to a carpenter. To everyone's surprise he immediately took to his work and soon gained a reputation as a friendly and skilled craftsman. Carpenters were plentiful in Kingston however, and, with a slump in building, Calvin was often out of a job. He decided to emigrate, and with the support of his family started to save. The year before he left, he married

Alice. She is the opposite of Calvin, dull where he is bright, prosaic where he is imaginative, careful where he is sometimes over-hasty. But both are ambitious: indeed she seems to have seen in Calvin a chance to leave Jamaica and settle in Britain.

Things went badly from the beginning. Calvin had not arranged a job before leaving and had to work as a cleaner in a factory. As a skilled worker he became rather depressed about this. Alice, to her annoyance, was forced to work as well. They nagged each other. Calvin felt she was 'acting superior' with no reason. Alice was exasperated by what she saw as his indolence. Three children were born and married life continued in a setting of muted hostility.

The Johnsons live in the two ground-floor rooms of a Victorian terraced house in South London. They share a kitchen on the stairway and the outdoor lavatory with four other families. Fellow Jamaicans live in most of the other houses along the road; in each there are three or four households and the neighbourhood has a rather run-down air. Gates and fences are missing, pavements are broken and the gardens are usually just flattened earth with piles of rubbish and disintegrating cars. Focal points for the street are the local market a quarter of a mile away, the Pentecostal chapel round the corner and an illegal drinking club in a basement. Although structurally unsound, the houses are carefully decorated inside. Each household is clearly separated into living and 'reception' rooms. The casual visitor is struck by the constant activity: neighbours are visiting each other, children play on the pavement, women are singing in the yards, men are mending cars in the road and a group of teenagers sit on the walls discussing, as elsewhere, music, money, sex and the future.

Three years ago Calvin had saved enough to be able to go on his first visit back to Jamaica. While he was there he had a strange experience: he heard a voice from God which told him to read certain verses in the Bible. With divine inspiration he was able with some difficulty to interpret their meaning. Having learnt that meat was sacred food reserved only for the saints, he became a vegetarian. At the same time he became a Rastafarian. On returning to London he began to have doubts about the whole business, but he now thinks these doubts were prompted by the Devil.

Later in the same year he went to his local post office with his daughter Victoria to cash a postal order – advance payment for a job he was to start later that week, replacing some floor boards in a near-by house. Disturbed by Victoria's latest school report and an argument he had had with her teacher, Calvin was feeling rather irritable and tense: after some weeks without work the offer of a job was particularly important. He signed the form, but after examining it the cashier told him to wait and went behind a partition. A quarter of an hour later he re-appeared with three policemen who rather abruptly asked him how he got the postal order. Humiliated and angry, Calvin tried to walk out of the post office with his daughter, but was pulled back. Completely losing his temper, he lashed out, hitting a policeman more by chance than intention, and was promptly arrested. Victoria, the cashier and a small group of bystanders watched silently. While struggling, Calvin took out of his pocket and waved a 1966 shilling which he always carried with him: 'The sun was shining on it as if the lion would step out. I began to sing "The Lord is My Shepherd". The police said "You black bastard - you believe in God?" They took me to a mad-house – Oh God, since when are we religious mad?'

After some weeks in a psychiatric hospital the charge was withdrawn and Calvin went home; the postal order had been cleared but the job was now lost. In the course of the next year his relationship with the local police was tense. He was arrested for assaulting his two cousins while he himself pursued an unsuccessful case against the police for assault with the help of a community legal aid centre. Calvin became well known at the local magistrates' court and his quarrels with the police became a vendetta.

While remanded on the assault charge he was seen by the prison psychiatrist: 'This man belongs to Rastafarian (*sic*) – a mystical Jamaican cult, the members of which think they are God-like. This man has ringlet hair, a goatee straggly beard and a type of turban. He appears eccentric in his appearance and very vague in answering questions. He is an irritable character and he has got arrogant behaviour. His religious ideas are cultural. He denied any hallucinations. He is therefore not schizophrenic at the moment. He came to England in 1961 but he has obviously been unable to adjust to the culture of this society. He tells me that he would like to be repatriated to his homeland and I am of the opinion that this certainly would be a most desirable outcome because if he continues to live in the United Kingdom there is no doubt that he will be a constant burden to society.'

We first met Calvin after he came to the hospital where we worked, admitted under Section 136 of the Mental Health Act. Using this provision, the police can take anyone they feel to be in need of psychiatric attention from a public area 'to a place of safety', which usually means a psychiatric hospital. This time the trouble had started after Calvin had been smoking cannabis and arguing with Alice. Normally it had little effect on him apart from inducing a mild euphoria, but 'This time round I let it all out. I told my probation officer I would do something. I knew what I was doing but I couldn't stop. I wasn't mad.' The police were called by neighbours after he had thrown the family pans and an oil stove out of his window. Seven policemen eventually got him to the local hospital, where the Indian doctor on duty noted: 'He was lying in the lift with two policemen on top of him. The patient was unkempt with long matted hair, talking in broken English and was difficult to follow. He frequently mentioned Christ and lions. There were ragged lacerations on his hands where he had been handcuffed. Probably a relapsed schizophrenic. Observe carefully.'

A West Indian nurse had visited his wife earlier that week after Alice Johnson had become concerned about her husband's increasingly aggressive behaviour. Alice said that she had escaped being knocked about only because he was still on probation. The nurse also saw Calvin: 'Overactive but did not feel ill. He felt God had been using him to try and put the world right. I would say he is very mad and I think a lot of this is due to smoking marihuana.'

His wife told us that she thought he had been well until the first episode with the police. Since then he had become increasingly irritable and had even hit her twice. Unlike Calvin, she dated his religious interest to the post office incident. He insisted on reading the Bible to the family, particularly the Book of Revelation, with his own interpretations and talked continuously of the importance of the date of 'the beating' – 7 July. Alice did not feel he was mentally ill and was anxious for him to leave hospital 'after his aggression was cured'.

When we talked with him the morning after he was admitted, Mr Johnson was obviously humiliated by the events of the preceding day, but attempted to conceal this behind an infectious humour. He said the police had probably beaten him up only because he struggled; although they were racially prejudiced against black people in general, he did not think they had picked on him personally. He explained to us how God talked through him. Perhaps he really did have some special mission, but he was not quite sure. After the usual blood tests and X-rays and further discussion between his wife, the doctors and the probation officer, Calvin went home with an offer of another talk the following week.

He did not take up that appointment – or others – and we next met a year later in almost identical circumstances. This time the admitting psychiatrist felt the diagnosis was 'mania or marihuana psychosis'. The police had been called by a traffic warden who complained that Calvin was now claiming to be Jesus: 'The police are still beating me, they have given me a terrible beating. I keep running from them. I am very much afraid of the police. My father told me to stay away from the police when I was young because they are not nice. They are going to put me into prison. No trouble till they beat me up. I think the whole world has come to an end – the prophecy has been fulfilled. A man is a weakness against his whole self – I see the testing in my heart. He loves us all – a man can break the Devil – we are all Jesus if we live the life. If you know God you feel things inside you: I hear voices and I get visions every night. When I close my eyes I see a light.'

We did not feel that he needed to be in a hospital and he returned home to his family.

ETHNIC MINORITIES IN ENGLAND

Before trying to understand what has been going on between Calvin Johnson and the medical profession, we must take a brief look at the background of the two groups involved – the ethnic minorities and the psychiatrists. Is this sort of situation a common experience for members of ethnic minorities?

Most members of minority ethnic groups[1] are recent immigrants to Britain together with their descendants. In this book we are principally concerned with immigrants from Europe and the Third World rather than with immigrants of white British origin such as Australians or New Zealanders. The minorities comprise a wide variety of quite different groups. There is certainly no single 'immigrant culture', although they do face similar problems of cultural adaptation and economic insecurity. Some, such as the half a million Polish-born, have been settled here for many years. Those from Asia and the Caribbean are more recent immigrants. Since the 1960s the migration of people from the New Commonwealth has dropped and has been almost exclusively of the spouses and children of immigrants already settled here [229]. The number of other ('foreign') immigrants has, however, continued to rise [192]. The total number of people entering the country each year is usually substantially less than the number leaving [305]: immigration from the Commonwealth has only twice in fifteen years been greater than the emigration to the Commonwealth. Table 1 shows what percentage of the total population migrants form.

Although 'immigrants' are generally conceived of as non-white, we can see that a significant proportion of them come from Europe and North America. There are nearly as many immigrants from Italy and Poland together as from the Caribbean. 'New Commonwealth immigrants' – those from Commonwealth

Table 1   Immigrants in England and Wales
                 (% of total population)

(a)	*'Internal migrants'*	
	Scotland	1.59
	Northern Ireland	0.44
(b)	*Commonwealth migrants*	
	India	0.64
	Pakistan and Bangladesh	0.27
	West Indies	0.48
	Africa	0.35
	Cyprus	0.14
	Other New Commonwealth	0.28
	Old Commonwealth	0.30
(c)	*Other countries*	
	(largest groups)	
	Irish Republic	1.38
	Germany	0.30
	Italy	0.21
	Poland	0.21
	USA	0.20

Old Commonwealth figure from the Office of Population Censuses and Surveys, 1980 (306); Figures for Africa, Cyprus and other New Commonwealth countries calculated from Commission for Racial Equality, 1978 (78); other figures from Cochrane, 1977 (72). Pakistan is of course no longer in the Commonwealth.

countries attaining independence since the war – are usually 'non-white': the expression is an official euphemism for immigrants popularly perceived as 'black' or 'brown'.

The table does not show the numbers of the descendants of immigrants who have been born in Britain. There are for instance half a million British Jews, many of whose parents and grandparents came here earlier in the century. By 1985 there were 2.2 million people including immigrants whose ethnic *origins* were in the New Commonwealth or Pakistan. 48 per cent of them were born here [304].

Seventy per cent of British Jews live in London, as do over a third of the Irish and more than half of New Commonwealth migrants [304]. Only half of the total population live in large towns, compared with 90 per cent of West Indians and 80 per cent of Asians [315]. Local sex ratios vary – a higher proportion of West Indians in London than elsewhere are women because of the type of work which is available.

The different migrant groups have brought with them a diversity of cultures. Some of these persist; others are discarded. Previous knowledge of British society varies from Caribbean countries familiar with English names, places and history, to Asian communities with quite different patterns of social structure and language. While the East Europeans were drawn from communities with virtually total literacy, two thirds of Indian villagers cannot read or write [226]. In the Caribbean, where 70 per cent of the population are not born to formally married couples, the typical family unit has been described as the mother and child with the father rather loosely attached to them [394]. Indian immigrants have usually brought with them a tight knit family kinship system based on *jatis* or sub-castes, in which a dominant male member heads each family.

While some immigrants to Britain, such as the East Europeans, originally lived in towns, New Commonwealth immigrants usually come from villages, often in particular areas (such as the Punjab and Gujarat) which have a tradition of migration to Britain. Some immigrant groups were already minorities before they came to Britain – East African Asians, European Jews and the ethnic Chinese of Vietnam.

The major reason given for migration from the Caribbean has usually been economic instability and unemployment because of reliance on a single industry, sugar, followed by the passing of the McCarran Act in 1952 which reduced West Indian migration to the United States. Up to a third of the citizens of some small islands now live in Britain [420]. In India, pressure on the land, population growth and unemployment also resulted in immigration as an urgent necessity. Political and racial persecution are now seldom the reason for migration; since the Polish, Jewish and Ukrainian migrations of two generations ago, the only large groups of exiles have been the East African Asians, Vietnamese and Latin Americans. Apart from the Jews there has been little immigration solely for religious reasons since the Huguenots. Other big groups include students, especially from West Africa, who have settled here, and soldiers and prisoners who remained after the Second World War, in particular Poles and Italians.

The reasons for inviting immigrants to Britain in the 1950s and 1960s were economic. Many groups were selected for specific jobs: a large proportion of the Filipinos in London were recruited by one agency as domestic servants and nursing aides. London Transport conducted recruiting trips in the Caribbean. The textile and transport industries throughout Western Europe required labour on a large scale; the size of the industrial labour force had decreased relative to the total population and upward social mobility left a need for unskilled labour. This was rationalized in terms of humanitarian motives and the obligations of the ex-colonial power. Although this was sentimentally important the underlying reason was always the need for unskilled labour [64].

The ideal of the 'Commonwealth citizen' has been gradually eroded as its meaning became economically and politically clear. It had effectively disappeared when the 1981 Immigration Act introduced the racial categories of 'patrial' and 'non-patrial'. The current Nationality Act is based on these immigration categories. The possession of British passports now makes it *more* difficult for East Africans to visit relatives in Britain than if they have Kenyan passports. Many immigrants wanted to become British rather than remain as migrant workers, and their conditions of social and economic life are often less restricted and vulnerable than those of migrant workers in France and Germany. The belief that it is possible to become truly British – and its frustration – may however cause a different type of stress. New Commonwealth immigrants are not particularly secure: deportation orders are most frequently served on migrants who come from New Commonwealth countries [300].

The identity the immigrant eventually assumes will be one

which is in part shared by all immigrants. In part it will be shaped by particular cultural values modified by his or her own experiences.

In Chapter 6 we consider in greater detail the conditions of life in Britain for minority ethnic groups. There is now abundant evidence that they have proportionally more low-paid jobs and unemployment, more substandard housing and poorer physical health than do the general population. Through these and through countless everyday situations runs the experience of racism.

THE PSYCHIATRISTS

What about the doctors who are concerned with mental health? Are their backgrounds and education likely to make them particularly sympathetic to psychological difficulties in ethnic minorities?

Psychiatrists are of course doctors and will have spent at least six years studying and practising general medicine among a variety of patients. Medical students are, however, drawn from a limited social stratum. The Royal College of Surgeons observed a generation ago that medicine would 'lose immeasurably if the proportion of such [privately educated] students in the future were to be reduced in favour of the precocious children who qualify for subsidies from Local Authorities and the State purely on examination results' [352]. Although psychiatrists are less conservative than their colleagues, it would be surprising if psychiatry did not continue to display the attitudes of a privileged minority, less than 3 per cent of whom are drawn from unskilled or semi-skilled families. Over a fifth of all medical students are themselves the children of doctors and they are drawn unevenly from around the country.

Medical students, then, do not bring to their medical education a cross-fertilizing diversity of social backgrounds. They soon discover that the emphasis of a doctor's training is on physical facts: it is only in the last few years that a small amount of social science has been offered halfheartedly in the undergraduate curriculum. Modern medicine values the scientific rather than the empathic approach. Empathy and a less authoritarian relationship with the patient are reserved for those conditions such as mental illness where the doctor has less confidence that he has effective technologies; an informal relationship between doctor and patient implies that the illness has a poor prognosis [154].

The first person the immigrant meets when seeking help for emotional difficulties is usually the general practitioner. While his knowledge of human problems may well be extensive he is unlikely to know much psychiatry. In the late 1960s, seven out of twelve London teaching hospitals had no full-time psychiatric teaching staff; training for most GPs consisted of a perfunctory visit to a rural mental hospital and the 'demonstration' of interesting patients in the classroom. Few doctors wish to be psychiatrists, and the speciality is not held in high esteem in the medical establishment. Psychiatrists are seen by medical students as unstable and confused [48], and as working in the least desirable speciality after dermatology [334]. Medicine has been described as a scientific parvenu, anxious to discard those mystical elements which remind it of its own disreputable past [3], and to be interested in the insane is still regarded as faintly suspect. A professor of surgery recently stated that British psychiatry was a haven for 'misfits and incompetents' [12].

Only 7 per cent of newly qualified doctors think of psychiatry as an attractive career, and less than one in twenty of trainee specialists are psychiatrists [357]. The status of mental health is reflected in the proportion of the NHS budget devoted to it which had dropped below 8 per cent by the mid-1970s, although half of all hospital beds are occupied by the mentally ill. The lucrative and secret 'distinction awards' are given to 25 per cent of psychiatric consultants but to 73 per cent of thoracic surgeons [41].

The modern psychiatrist is a descendant, not of the psycho-analyst, but of the nineteenth-century mental asylum keeper. As treatment for physical illness became increasingly effective, the mentally ill – incurable – were lodged in large purpose-built hospitals. Each was governed by the superintendent, a paternal-istic figure whose popular image has been described as both divine and satanic: divine because of his power over the sick and satanic because of his demonic knowledge [139]. The physical coercion of the pre-psychiatric era was replaced by moral authority: the ideal psychiatrist, like the ideal colonial official or plantation owner, was a 'father to his children'. Cures could occasionally be effected by his 'presence'.

The current reputation of the psychiatrist is still rather Faustian. The image of the benign physician alleviating mental distress has been assailed by claims that he merely penalizes alternative behaviour in the name of medicine; by criticism of the role of psychiatrists in colonial wars and in controlling dissent in the Soviet Union; by doubts about the use of psychiatric drugs by doctors in prisons and the humanity of such psychological techniques as the Special Control Units [38, 68, 85, 126].

Psychiatrists, however, regard themselves as more radical than other doctors: 70 per cent of a sample of British psychiatrists are agnostics or atheists and half of those who are politically committed support the Labour Party [414]. American psychiatrists are also relatively left-wing and they are less authoritarian than other physicians; they also rate the aesthetic rewards of their job higher than the financial ones [341]. Of all medical specialities they are the most liberal on such questions as abortion (gynaecologists being the least). Only a third of American psychiatrists would however 'admit blacks to close kinship by marriage'. Psychiatric treatment in America is related to the doctor's political opinions; authoritarian psychiatrists use drugs and electro-convulsive treatment, while the liberals prefer psychotherapy [341].

As a scientist the psychiatrist will try to make unbiased observations and an accurate diagnosis, and to offer the correct treatment. He will also perhaps attempt to understand the patient's illness and to sympathize with disturbing experiences. Until recently, because of his inability to help his psychotic patient, all the conscientious psychiatrist could do was to try to classify the symptoms. This inability to affect the course of severe mental illness was punctuated at intervals by exaggerated claims from psychoanalysts and others to cure a variety of social ills. An American neuro-surgeon who stated that a large proportion of urban 'disturbances' were the result of brain disease was promptly offered a half-million-dollar grant [68].

Since the discovery in the 1950s of powerful psychoactive drugs – the 'major tranquillizers' – the psychiatrist has for the first time been able to effect changes in those patients who have severe (psychotic) mental illness. With rare exceptions, there has been a concurrent decline in interest in the meaning of psychosis for the patient. The emphasis in the examinations for membership of the Royal College of Psychiatrists (which influences the reading and orientation of the future specialists) is on biology and genetics rather than on the social sciences. The new psychotherapies, such as family therapy or encounter groups, have been devised for those with the less serious psychological disturbances. With the psychoses, the psychiatrist has usually found it more profitable to concentrate on diagnosis and physical treatment.

IMMIGRANT PSYCHIATRISTS

One factor which might perhaps mitigate any psychiatric ethnocentrism is the large proportion of junior psychiatrists in Britain who are themselves immigrants, particularly from the New Commonwealth [81]. (By contrast, in the United States, where psychiatry carries a greater prestige, fewer than 2 per cent of psychiatrists are black compared with 12 per cent of the general population [433].) Foreign-born doctors have never been popular with the medical establishment. In the 1930s the British Medical Association opposed the admission of more than a tiny number of Jewish doctors who were refugees from the Nazis. The President of the BMA told the Home Secretary that 'the number that could usefully be absorbed or teach us anything could be counted on the fingers of one hand' [419]. A large proportion of British-born psychiatrists are now, however, members of the Jewish minority, particularly at the prestigious Institute of Psychiatry.

Immigrant doctors are not evenly distributed in the hierarchy: 57 per cent of psychiatric senior house officers (the most junior grade) were born outside Britain [43] but only one out of every eight recently appointed consultants [44]. A not uncommon situation is the Indian junior psychiatrist attempting to interpret the experience of an East European patient to a white British consultant on the basis of reports made by Malaysian or West Indian nurses. Four fifths of overseas psychiatrists in training come from developing countries where the provision of psychiatrists is very different from Britain; 64 per cent come from the Indian subcontinent but only 4 per cent from Africa (including South Africa) and Latin America.

Compared with their British-born colleagues, they are older, less likely to have accepted their present post for its training or research facilities, and unlikely to be trained in psychotherapy. As a concerned professor of psychiatry observes, they are orientated to a biological interpretation of mental illness, go into psychiatry after failing to get jobs in general medicine and seldom return home to practise psychiatry [60]. Many came to Britain to take exams and stayed on after they failed [392]. While two-thirds of recently appointed senior registrars (the post below that of consultant) in mental subnormality were from overseas, there were none in cardiology or general medicine [180].

Like many of their patients then, some psychiatrists are themselves immigrants, yet they find themselves defining normality and abnormality in Britain. Since they might have to cope with difficulties of language and custom and different doctor/patient and doctor/nurse relationships, it is perhaps understandable if they avoid looking at mental illness from a psychological or social perspective which might well be threatening to their own adjustment [310]. 'Few foreign graduates succeed in acquiring a firm grasp of the contending theories of personality development and fewer still progress to a real competence in group or individual psychotherapy' [60]. Overseas trainee psychiatrists seldom complain publicly of overt racial prejudice in the profession, but their colleagues say of them that over a fifth have language difficulties and a fifth have 'cultural difficulties' [43].

The pass rate of psychiatric trainees from the New Commonwealth countries in the qualifying exam in psychiatry is half that of those born in Britain [336]. This probably reflects their jobs in the isolated and less popular speciality of mental handicap. Of recent consultant appointments in psychiatry, overseas doctors were nearly twice as likely to be offered a job in this field as in general psychiatry [351]. Only 13 per cent of junior overseas psychiatrists work in the prestigious teaching hospitals, with their well-equipped libraries and other facilities [45].

DOCTOR AND PATIENT

The meeting between psychiatrist and patient does of course involve two people who have their own particular expectations. If the situation is familiar to them, they will probably make an effort to live up to the other person's expectations [154].

We have seen that the psychiatrist is likely to regard psychiatric illness as he does physical illness. He also has less clear expectations of how the patient is likely to behave and what, in different societies, the limits of normality and abnormality are. In addition to his background and training, the psychiatrist's attitude to the minority patient will be formed by his own personal problems, conscious or unconscious racist assumptions and the particular setting in which the two meet. He is, amongst other things, an employee of the state and responsible to it for maintenance of its beliefs and disposal of its funds [252].

Patients too have their expectations: to be sick in our society offers us freedom from many social obligations and from responsibility for the illness, but it presumes a desire to get well and a motivation to ask for medical help [313]. The extent to which a patient sees himself as ill and in need of treatment varies with his culture. What may be endured in India requires therapy in New York. What is insane behaviour in Barbados may not be in Jamaica. Acceptance of the role of a mental patient depends on our beliefs about the nature of mental illness and whether any stigma is associated with it. Psychiatrists are rare in developing countries and admission to a mental hospital is an uncommon – perhaps unheard-of – event. There is one psychiatrist in Britain for every twenty thousand people compared to one for over a million in Nigeria. The immigrant family may be hesitant about agreeing with a doctor who tells them that their relative is mentally ill. They may not even see the problem as a medical one: the patient may come from a rural community in which all Western medicine is regarded with distrust. Many societies carry out similar religious healing ceremonies for both physical and emotional distress and do not make the Western separation between the two.

The immigrant patient may well see the psychiatrist as a doctor rather than specifically as a psychiatrist. Not burdened with European folk-lore about psychiatrists (and endless cartoons of bearded doctors sitting next to patients on couches), he looks for themes familiar to him from his experiences with other doctors and hospitals: the ward with its rows of beds and quiet discipline, the uniformed nurses and white-coated doctors; authority, certainty, a minimum of questioning and immediate treatment. Ironically these are the very aspects of medicine which psychiatrists are discarding, in the belief that they may actually perpetuate psychological difficulties [440]. As psychiatry has sought to relinquish the magical symbols of medicine, many of these have been confusingly adopted by other professions: porters, clerks and domestic staff may now wear the clinical white coat [154].

A common mode of arrival of minority patients at a hospital is to be brought in by the police under Section 136, like Calvin

Johnson (see p. 4), often at night [258]. Does the psychiatrist see himself as an ally of the police or the patient, or perhaps of both? Is his overriding reaction to dispose of the problem as soon as possible and get back to bed?

To observe another person is always to some extent to diminish their individuality – especially in a hospital interview. For the patient the stress of the interview is increased when the doctor starts by talking privately with the police who are waiting on the ward, taking them aside, reading the admitting form and glancing periodically at the patient. If he then dismisses the police, greets the patient, shakes his hand and talks to him as if he is about to explain this embarrassing situation, the doctor will soon find himself in a difficult position. The patient sees a friend and confides his denunciation of the police to him while the doctor listens patiently. The psychiatrist is then startled by a request from the patient to return home. He feels irritated – the patient has taken advantage of his kindness. With the police gone, the nurses will be reluctant to help him to restrain a person he may now believe to be in urgent need of medical attention; their looks suggest he has made a fool of himself and wasted their time; he cannot persuade the increasingly anxious patient even to continue to talk to him. The patient begins to realize that the doctor has not really been sympathizing with him and that he has other plans. The doctor changes: his tones becomes hectoring and tense, and he provides increasingly unpleasant arguments for the patient to stay.

In the end the patient is sedated with the help of the nurses or dishonestly promised that he will be allowed home in the morning. In either case, he feels betrayed – he is not going to be so trusting again. Since his attempt at understanding the patient produced an unsatisfactory result, the psychiatrist also decides not to waste time talking next time. No more messing about – in future he will sedate the patient straight away. He rationalizes this by saying that it is not fair to the patient to deceive him and that it is easier anyway to talk the next morning, when he will be able to listen to a comfortably sedated patient with their respective roles clearly defined and his own anxieties diminished.

A black patient brought to a psychiatric ward by the police will regard the whole business with suspicion, if not panic. He is puzzled by the doctor's insistence that he is there to *help*. The doctor's behaviour does not bear this out. If the patient is, like Calvin, in the hospital because of behaviour associated with unusual religious experiences, he may wonder whether the doctor thinks these are 'genuine experiences'. If the doctor says they are, he is placating the patient, who realizes he is lying – why otherwise would he keep the patient in hospital? If the doctor ventures a medical explanation of the phenomenon the patient knows he has no chance of a fair hearing – the doctor will continue to try to persuade him to accept his own interpretation.

However sympathetic he may be initially to a patient who is anxious to spread the news of his divine mission, the psychiatrist will soon change. He must observe the patient and 'take a history' in accordance with the expectations of medical practice and the watching nursing staff. He tentatively suggests the patient is ill. If the patient disagrees, wakes the other patients or throws things about the ward, the doctor writes down 'no insight' and moves, reassured, into his more rewarding decision-making role.

Whatever interest doctor and patient may take in each other, the confrontation is limited by time. The interview is limited to a few key questions. The doctor wants to know whether the voices talk among themselves or talk directly to the patient. Such a question seems irrelevant to the patient. He is initially concerned with whether they are going to harm him. Why is the black patient feeling so suspicious? Maybe the police and the hospital are behaving in this extraordinary manner because they have a grudge against him. How widespread is this conspiracy? How much will it be wise to say to the doctor? The psychiatrist is meanwhile looking for such 'first-rank symptoms of schizo-phrenia' as whether the patient experiences his thoughts being controlled by external influences. If these are found, the patient's own explanation of his situation can again be dismissed. He is now firmly told he is sick and must have some medicine; patient and doctor have achieved their definitive roles.

The patient is told he must stay in hospital, he is asked to strip and the doctor examines him physically. The psychiatrist may be unsympathetic and harsh and he may make the wrong diagnosis, but by tradition he must on no account miss any physical illness. Further reduced to an object, the patient lies there as the doctor applies various instruments and listens and peers. The doctor gives instructions and leaves; the patient tells the nurses his age, address and occupation and accepts sedation for the night. The black patient may be reassured by the fact that the nurses, who are frequently also black, accept without‵ question the medical definition of his experience. Often he is not.

Until both doctor and patient can agree on common ground, there is unlikely to be a basis for friendship or even an acceptance of help. At present this tension is resolved only when the patient accepts the doctor's view of the situation and entirely rejects his own. Over the next few days responsibility is gradually withdrawn from the patient: for his liberty, his clothes and his beliefs [156, 374, 440]. His most popular move will have been to present a typical symptom to the doctor, resulting in swift and standard procedures to deal with his condition and a lessening in uncertainty for the staff. His further progress depends on the rapidity with which he accepts the new concepts and opportunities open to him.

An immigrant patient who has had many admissions to mental hospitals will have been given repeated explanations that he is not entirely responsible for his actions. The doctor should not then be surprised to find that the patient will not take any further responsibility for his problems and that he now passively expects the doctor to find him a job and accommodation and to solve his various domestic difficulties. The psychiatrist is confirmed in his belief that one of the effects of mental illness is a long-term loss of initiative and motivation. Unless he offers the unlikely option of psychotherapy, the psychiatrist now steps back and explains that medicine is not the solution to all problems but only those accepted by the patient as divine intervention, spirit possession or sorcery. Psychiatry thus deals with that part of the immigrant's experience which originate in his original society but not with those related to problems in Britain – discrimination, housing and unemployment. It de-Caribbeanizes and de-authenticates him. While depriving the patient of much of his tradition, it does not seem to offer much in return.

THE RASTAFARIAN

Let us look again at what happened to Calvin Johnson. We have already suggested that mental illness is closely tied to culture and religious beliefs. We know that he was a member of Rastafari. Can knowledge of Rastafari alter our understanding of his situation? Who are the Rastafarians? [24, 62, 219, 297, 436.]

Millennial prophecies about a return to Africa were circulating among the black churches of Jamaica in the 1920s. The black nationalist Marcus Garvey announced that an African king was about to become the saviour of the oppressed black people of the Caribbean and the United States. The movement itself began with the news, a few years later, of the crowning of Haile Selassie (Ras Tafari) as Emperor of Ethiopia, the ancient black kingdom which had never been colonized by Europeans.

The Rastafarians, a number of separate groups, are the largest (with over 100,000 members) and most characteristic of the indigenous Caribbean religions – and the one least influenced by Christianity. They believe that Haile Selassie is God and various of their leaders have also claimed divinity. Adam and Christ were black. The black people are the chosen race, but because of their sins they were enslaved and exiled by the Europeans. Redemption and a return to Africa are however at hand. They share with other sects an interest in numerology and the Book of Revelation, from which are drawn the titles of the Ethiopian kings: 'King of Kings, Lion of the Tribe of Judah.'

Rasta men exclude their women or 'queens' from decision-making and value them principally as followers and mothers. Family life is highly regarded. Abortion and contraception ('the white man's plan for black genocide') are abhorred. Suspicious of establishment doctors and hospitals, many believe that 'no death is natural'. Illness is universally treated with *ganja* (cannabis) – 'the herb' – which is smoked, eaten and drunk: a source of nutrition, entertainment and revelation. Alcohol is avoided and some Rastas follow dietary restrictions similar to those of Judaism. Many are vegetarians. They also avoid food prepared by non-members. To outsiders their most distinctive characteristics are their uncombed beard and hair ('dreadlocks'). They frequently work as artisans and craftsmen, and a highly praised Rasta virtue is 'art' – the ability to perceive the real and the authentic behind conventional appearance and to communicate this to others.

The movement, originally drawn from the dispossessed Jamaican peasantry and working class, is now found in different forms in other Caribbean islands, New York and London. At different periods it has passed through various phases – immediate expectations of semimiraculous transport to Africa followed by withdrawal to communes, punctuated by the occasional uprising. This history is reflected in the current Rasta groups. Some are principally religious, and a Rasta delegation to

Ethiopia engaged in heated discussion with the Ethiopian Orthodox church over the divinity of the Emperor. His subsequent death did little to diminish their faith. The Ethiopians sent a mission to Jamaica which opened churches and conducted Amharic language classes but met with mixed success. Separatist Rastafarians maintain a militant anti-white position which critics say verges on racism. (Garvey, an admirer of the Ku Klux Klan, is supposed to have regarded himself as the first fascist.) Perhaps more common is a diffuse humanism, in which each individual is valued for his own qualities, with increasing contact with non-Rastas and the development of a loosely Marxist perspective: 'If a man be as black as night, his colour is in our estimation of no avail if he is an oppressor and destroyer of his people' [24].

Rastafarians have had poor relations with 'Babylon', the Jamaican establishment, in particular with the police, partly because of their cultivation of cannabis and their ostentatious rejection of middle-class goals, but also because of an associated criminal group – 'the rudies'. Leaders of attempted revolts were executed or 'taken to gaol on sedition or to the asylum for lunacy . . . The wider society associated Rastafarianism with madness' [297].

Since 1966, when a rather bemused Haile Selassie visited the Caribbean to a tumultuous welcome from the Rastafarians, they have been taken up and patronized by the middle-class elite and the Jamaican political parties and 'assimilated . . . into the mainstream of thought on black power and majority control' [297]. There was even an unsuccessful move in the Jamaican Parliament to replace Queen Elizabeth by Emperor Haile Selassie as Head of State. The influence of the American Black Power movement persuaded many Jamaicans to see in the Rastas an authentic black culture: Rastafarian clothes, language and hair were adopted by the intellectuals. Rasta music in its commercialized form – reggae – is now well known. Traditionally avoiding conventional politics, the movement has become increasingly radical; Rastafarians mobilized to protect the revolutionary government in Grenada.

Although unenthusiastic about West Indians coming to Britain – 'Repatriation [to Africa] not migration' – there are large numbers of Rastas in London, particularly since the tour of the singer Bob Marley in 1975. It would be a mistake to see them as being merely a religious sect. Their analysis of the historical relations between black and white is accepted by many young

British blacks who have taken as badges of black identity reggae, dreadlocks and the Rasta colours – 'the gold of the Jamaican flag, the black of Africa, the green of fertility and red for the blood of the martyrs'.

INSANITY OR MEANING (OR BOTH)?

Knowing a little about Rastafari, the white psychiatrist can perhaps develop some understanding of Calvin Johnson's behaviour which might otherwise have seemed a little bizarre: his perception of his experiences in religious terms, the emphasis he placed on the lion on his 1966 coin when he was in a crisis, and the significance for him of 7 July (the seventh day of the seventh month, celebrated by many mystics such as the Essenes). His attitude to hospitals and the police seems reasonable, given the history of the Rastafarians and the experience of ethnic minorities in Britain.

His story leaves us, however, with some problems. In the rest of the book we shall be looking at them in some detail, but for the moment we shall content ourselves with briefly sketching them.

If we can show that the beliefs of someone who is possibly mentally ill are in fact shared by many other people does this *explain* them? If insanity is conventionally regarded as meaningless, have we then shown that Calvin is not psychologically abnormal? How common anyway are Rasta beliefs among West Indians? Calvin's religious experiences and his use of cannabis are not of course limited to his sect – are they more abnormal if they occur outside a church?

When we consider whether Calvin is mentally ill we are of course making certain assumptions about *normality*. Taking his actions altogether, are they abnormal in Britain – or in the Caribbean? Even if we decide that we really know what is normal behaviour in both situations, he is not just moving from one to the other – he is a member of part of one existing in the other. Black people in Britain, even more than other minorities, are regarded by the majority as a separate group, whatever their own aspirations to assimilate have been. It is clearly difficult to define normality in a community which is undergoing rapid change and trying out different methods of adaptation. The obvious solution is to ask Calvin's wife and friends. Alice Johnson in fact did not say her husband was mentally ill but she did complain that he was violent towards her.

To accept that different communities have quite different expectations of normality carries certain implications. If we say, for instance, that a particular religious experience is abnormal, we are saying that societies in which it is a common experience contain a large number of unbalanced people or even that these societies are in some way unbalanced altogether. Evangelical and charismatic churches offer West Indian immigrants in Britain a degree of continuity with the Caribbean, a feeling of being part of British culture and, most importantly, a sense of community and meaning in their lives [215]. If white British society regards many of them as unbalanced for engaging in such practices as 'speaking in tongues',[2] this is a serious blow to the credibility of such an adjustment.

We may in fact doubt that a society composed of unbalanced people can actually exist. It is common in Southern Europe and the Third World to accuse neighbours of practising witchcraft. Is this a sort of cultural paranoia which can be treated [234]? Or is it only abnormal if immigrants from these communities express the same beliefs here? Is it abnormal even then?

If we assume that the behaviour of someone who is considered insane in Britain, say an Italian immigrant with religious visions, is none the less normal because he comes from a society in which such behaviour is acceptable, we run into another difficulty. Not all Italians (or West Indians) are religious, nor do they all have experiences such as possession by the Holy Spirit. Adopting the values of a new society involves discarding the old: a continued expectation of supernatural events in the everyday world is hardly likely to facilitate integration into an industrial society. Discarding 'superstitions' enables the successful immigrant to measure his integration against his 'primitive' compatriots'. Modern medicine encourages us to regard emotional difficulties as illnesses rather than as spiritual questions. The immigrant nurses who saw Calvin Johnson were convinced that he was insane. Who are white English psychiatrists to tell them that their fellow countryman was merely exhibiting 'native' beliefs?

Frantz Fanon has described how black West Indian colonial officials working with the French in Africa returned home with exaggerated stories of the primitiveness of the Africans [127]. Unlike the French, they were unable to relax their official stance with Africans: 'Between whites and Africans there was no need of a reminder: the difference stared one in the face. But what a catastrophe if the West Indian should be taken for an African!' – or for a black nurse or doctor to accept such a bizarre behaviour as normal. For black nursing staff and relatives, a patient from their country with traditional beliefs may be a serious threat to their own assimilation.

Calvin Johnson's wife said he had been aggressive and had beaten her twice. To what extent should such behaviour be a concern of doctors? Was he more aggressive than other members of his community? We may decide that, even for people subject to very considerable stress, wife-beating is pathological or, on the other hand, that West Indians generally beat their wives and one should not, therefore, be very surprised. In either case, ignorance and prejudice simplify the doctor's problems but bring little assistance either to the individual or to his family. To ignore the question altogether leaves the possibility of very real stress being ignored. The violence was, after all, the problem which worried Alice Johnson.

Different societies have their own way of describing what we usually call mental illness. It may be thought of, as it is by most psychiatrists, as analogous to physical illness or it may be perceived as a religious phenomenon – spirit possession or the consequence of witchcraft – or even in terms of abnormal or anti-social behaviour. It is possible that when Mrs Johnson asked us to 'treat' her husband for violence she was talking about something like middle-class ideas of psychiatric illness; 'mental illness' for her might well have meant something quite different – perhaps epilepsy or a brain tumour.

Why do different societies have different concepts of mental illness? Is it that non-Europeans fail to recognize something which is quite obviously there? Or is 'mental illness' really a cultural idea, like spirit possession or witchcraft? If the latter is true, what do concepts of mental illness in our own society imply? What sort of function do they have?

Calvin Johnson described how at times he had been entered by God. Is this related to the classical schizophrenic experience of being controlled by some outside force? In urbanized individuals both in the West and the Third World this psychotic experience is described in terms of machines, but rural communities use the idiom of spirit possession [89, 234, 404]. If spirit possession is a normal experience how can we tell the difference? Are there 'non-cultural' markers of mental illness like blood tests? Can we say when a belief becomes a delusion?

How seriously did Calvin take his religion? He was not brought up as a Rasta and seems to have undergone a rather sudden conversion about which he later developed doubts. Are conversion experiences healthy? Do religious beliefs precipitate mental illness or can they help the individual to become better adjusted? If, as we have suggested, Rastafari is a black response to the experience of white domination, would not political action have been a more appropriate response for Calvin? Or even depression? Is it possible that religion and mental illness may both be alternative responses to the same situation?

We may wonder whether the sort of physical conditions Calvin was living in may not themselves cause psychological problems. If this is so we could predict that ethnic minorities are likely to have a lot of mental illness. Are the stresses of actual migration – the change of lifestyle and the problems of a new language – likely to lead to mental illness? Would it really be best to repatriate mentally ill immigrants, as the prison doctor believed? What are the consequences of exposure to racism for mental health? Psychiatry may be able to tell us something more about racism: is it itself a sort of delusion?

Calvin's fear centred around the police. Is it reasonable to say he was paranoid? Were his feelings of persecution out of proportion to his experiences and were they very different from those of the rest of the black British community? Not all black people in Britain react as Calvin did. Does this invalidate his beliefs or is it possible that the only people who can articulate the most pressing preoccupations of their community are those we conventionally describe as insane?

Before his second admission to hospital, Calvin had been smoking *ganja*. Cannabis is extensively used in Britain and many other countries without apparently causing harmful effects. Users claim that it is preferable to cigarettes or alcohol. For the Rastafarians it is a ritual drug of primary importance, although Jamaicans believe, on little evidence, that it leads to violence [297, 355]. Some Caribbean and Indian studies suggest, however, that cannabis may sometimes cause auditory hallucinations and feelings of persecution [162]. One doctor who saw Calvin suggested his problem was 'marihuana psychosis'. On the other hand we have seen that much of his behaviour and beliefs were an intelligible response to his situation. Does the possibility of their being precipitated by cannabis make them any less meaningful?

Many of these questions seem rather academic. We may wonder how necessary it is to concentrate on the exact definition of normality. Is it really necessary to decide whether Calvin is schizophrenic (insane) or has a 'situational reaction' precipitated by cannabis and emotional stress – or indeed whether he has any psychological problems at all?

The answer is certainly important for Calvin. Even if psychiatrists consider that he did not have an illness, his actions resulted in significant distress to his family and himself, and laid him open to prosecution for 'breach of the peace' and assault. If doctors place responsibility for his actions back on Calvin (on the grounds that they were probably intelligible, given his situation), society will punish him, since psychiatry has restored his responsibility.

We may of course feel that this would be preferable to being treated in a psychiatric hospital. But what if Calvin had the type of experiences conventionally called mental illness – such as schizophrenia? Is psychiatric diagnosis merely an elaborate charade of social control carried out in the name of medicine? Is it really concerned with helping people with psychological difficulties? Could it be both?

Calvin Johnson himself clearly thought that the less he had to do with psychiatrists the better. He was admitted to a mental hospital because other people thought he was insane: the police, his neighbours, a traffic warden. Their assumption was confirmed initially by psychiatry but then rejected.

How likely are doctors to interpret behaviour as insane? In America the diagnosis of mental illness has often been merely a rubber stamp on decisions made by the police or the courts [374]. Doctors in general usually assumed the presence of illness until disproved [374]. British psychiatrists, however, usually delay a diagnosis until they have unequivocal signs of mental abnormality [211]. A video film of Calvin talking with us about his experiences was shown with his agreement to a group of neurologists – doctors with some interest in psychiatry from the biological point of view. The film was of poor quality and the most noticeable features were Calvin's 'dreadlocks', his conviction that God was working in him, his vigorous gestures and rather inappropriate good humour. These doctors all considered him mentally ill. In contrast a group of psychiatrists thought the film merely showed someone rather eccentric.

One cannot understand mental illness in ethnic minorities by looking only at the patients, and in this chapter we have also paid some attention to the doctors. Is it possible to avoid on the one hand undirected empathy and inaccurate observation, and on the other sterile labelling and the medicalization of everyday problems? How easy is it to look at the behaviour of someone from another culture and at the same time try to experience their reality?

Psychiatry requires a detailed and sensitive knowledge both of language and subtle non-verbal behaviour. Discrimination against immigrant doctors and psychiatry's low status within medicine seem to have resulted in psychiatric hospitals being staffed by psychiatrists many of whom are themselves immigrants and who would prefer to be working in another branch of medicine. Although it might be hoped that the shared experience of prejudice and migration would lead to a sympathetic understanding of the emotional difficulties of immigrant patients, overseas doctors and nurses are offered little chance of exploring their own experiences and are attracted perhaps to an approach based on medical treatment alone.

We have briefly touched on the expectations and stresses of migrants coming to Britain. Already we are in a position to predict that some of their major emotional difficulties may be associated with discrimination. Before looking in detail at these, we shall have a look at *racism* itself and see that not only have medicine and psychiatry invariably been associated with it, but that they have provided it with some of its most powerful arguments.

NOTES

1 *Ethnic group* is an intentionally vague or general term used to avoid the false objectivity of *race*. The ethnic group may be a nation, a people, a language group, a sociologically defined so-called race or group bound together in a coherent cultural entity by a religion. (Modified from English and English [117].)
2 Although common in British evangelical groups since the seventeenth century [187], this experience is now unusual outside the Pentecostal churches (see p.177).

CHAPTER TWO

MEDICINE AND RACISM

And the determination of my biology no longer imprisoned
by a facial angle, by the texture of hair, by a nose sufficiently
flat, by a sufficiently melanian tint, and the niggerness no
longer a cephalic index, or a plasma, or a soma, but
measured with the compass of suffering.

From 'Memorandum on my Martinique' in *Cahier d'un
retour au Pays Natal*, Aimé Césaire, trs. Lionel Abel; quoted
in *From the Green Antilles*, ed. Barbara Howes (Souvenir
Press, 1967).

Two types of 'outsiders' – the mentally ill and non-Europeans –
have been referred to as *aliens* – people set aside by various
theories as being basically different. Whatever these theories
specified in detail, two similar conclusions have invariably
emerged:

(a) The outsiders are deficient in some particular characteristic.
(b) Being deficient they have to be spared the stresses of
responsibility.

The paths of the non-European and the mental patient continually
cross and sometimes run together. The same theories are used to
keep them alienated. We even find them described as manifestations of the same phenomenon. As the black immigrant has been
the popular paradigm of the immigrant, so have the relations
between black people and white medicine been the most
characteristic of the association between science and social
control.

THE ALIENS

Every society has its own characteristic pattern of normative behaviour and beliefs. It has therefore to solve the threat not only of antagonists external to the group but also of those inside who may be deviant. If accepted patterns are to be seen as normal, we need a theory of abnormality. The solution is to *include* both normal and abnormal inside the dominant beliefs.

However we conceive of our group, whether a class, a nation, or a race, we define it by those we exclude from it. These outsiders are perceived as different from ourselves. They may have different languages, different customs or beliefs. They may look different. We may even regard them as sick or as sub-human. However we define them we perceive them as an undifferentiated mass with no individual variations.

Outsiders always pose a threat to the status quo. Even if they are not physically dangerous, they are threatening simply because they are different. Their apartness is dangerous. It questions our tendency to see our society as the natural society and ourselves as the measure of normality. To admit a valid alternative is already to question the inevitability of our type of world. We forget that the outsiders are part of our definition of ourselves. To confirm our own identity we push the outsiders even further away. By reducing their humanity we emphasize our own.

In times of conflict or competition we are even less able to recognize the other group as being made up of distinct individuals. In a wartime report the anthropologist Gregory Bateson suggested that 'since all Western nations tend to think and behave in bipolar terms, we shall do well in building American morale, to think of the enemy as a hostile entity. The distinctions and gradations which intellectuals prefer are likely to be disturbing' [27].

Successful belief systems pre-empt the possibility of change by apparently describing all possible alternatives in the restricted form of the outsider. He is always necessary: he is part of our beliefs and his presence legitimates our institutions. He is the model for all challenges to the accepted order.

Outsiders' characteristics must be contrasted unfavourably with our own. They are nature: we are culture [247]. Excessive cruelty and sexuality is attributed to groups which are technologically less developed than ourselves (too little discipline), while the technologically more advanced are seen as mindless automatons (too much discipline). Some groups are paradoxically both. We delineate the features of the outsider and avoid seeing ourselves in this mirror of our own deficiencies; his evident peculiarities become the scale by which we measure our own conformity. To many communities, including Europeans, the outsider appears dirty and bestial, aggressive but matriarchal, treacherous but stupid, and frequently with an enormous sexual appetite [203]. Some societies perceive their neighbours as cannibals or witches or lunatics – the standardized nightmares of the community.

Outsiders in our midst have also to be identified and isolated. Because they are so close and yet are difficult to distinguish they may be even more dangerous than the outsider from abroad: heresy and witchcraft are contagious. Immigrants, like psychiatric patients, were once ritually washed and examined on their arrival [156, 302].

If we cannot clearly perceive the outsiders, we are likely to require complicated technologies for detection. Accusations of witchcraft occur when the relations between people are ambiguous [121, 264]. Racist ideas in America came to full theoretical development only when slavery was ending. German anti-semitism was directed against the hidden outsider who lay concealed within. Official racism in Britain worsened as immigrants have become British rather than consenting to remain migrant labourers.

The term 'alien' refers us both to the geographical outsiders, the foreigners, and to the outsiders in our midst, including the psychiatrically ill. Both internal and external aliens have a role in our society: they demonstrate to the average individual what he should avoid being or even avoid being mistaken for – they define for him the limits of his normality by producing a boundary only inside which can he be secure. Abusive terms for other groups – honkies, queers, niggers, nutters, gorgios, goys – are used particularly inside our own group to reassure our companions and ourselves of where our loyalty lies. We remain on guard externally and internally. The mentally ill inside our society are conceived of as in a state of chaos and non-meaning; even if we do not see their rejection or inversion of the dominant values as deliberate, they serve as a model for such a rejection; homosexuals are a threat to security.

The actual identity of the outsider may change. War between

European nations has usually resulted in black-white differences being shelved and 'our blacks' being accorded a temporary white status [126]. Michel Foucault suggests that in the early medieval period in Western Europe the lepers were the victims of this terror of internal contagion; attention then shifted to those with venereal disease, and later the mentally ill. The leper house became the psychiatric hospital [139].

Because on cold examination the outsider seldom offers a real physical threat to the community, it has been suggested that his major function is to promote individual rather than social adaptation. Psychoanalysts suggest that we always need outsiders to act as scapegoats for our personal shortcomings. We 'project' on to them impulses which we find unacceptable in ourselves. If it were not for the outsiders we would be decent and pure; they will contaminate us all with their uncontrolled violence, madness and sex. The outsider is mysterious, irrational and abnormal, but however repulsive he may be we risk finding him dangerously attractive: we are always menaced by our projected impulses. Although deficient in moral qualities, he has an athletic sexual performance and will eventually overcome us by sheer re-productive capacity [184, 203].

To say that all societies use an 'Us/Them' distinction to legitimate their institutions is not to say that the outsider is merely the transient victim of an inevitable psychology. Projection is a mechanism, not an explanation. 'They' may be a very real physical presence whom we need to control. As we shall see, the rhetoric of the American War of Independence had to advocate freedom for the white settlers and deny it to the black slaves. This was achieved by ascribing to blacks a different biology. This solved the immediate contradiction, legitimated their exploitation and provided a model for the later theory of eugenics which was directed at the problem of the poor white and the mentally ill. (Although we have referred to the outsider as 'he', similar arguments to those described in this chapter serve the sub-jugation of women.)

Alternatively the outsider may be seen as a threat only in as much as the qualities ascribed to him are in themselves a real threat. Minority ethnic groups in Britain have been accused of spreading epidemics (the Asians), pimping (the Maltese), smuggling heroin (the Chinese), subversion (the Irish) or treason (the Jews) [419, 420]. Their churches and associations were accused of spreading ideas subversive to their newly adopted country. Student radicalism is blamed on foreign students, and British trade-unionists who have emigrated to Australia are accused of spreading 'industrial unrest'. In addition to providing a model of 'not-us', the outsider offers a convenient solution to any current problems. To dehumanize minorities facilitates their removal or unemployment in periods of economic recession [153] and also provides an immediate (but false) solution to other problems located in the majority community.

White stereotypes of the West Indian picture him as feckless and stupid (assimilating him to the previous stereotype of the Irishman), while in New York the West Indian immigrant is known as the 'Black Jew' because of his astute business acumen. In Britain he is regarded as uninterested in education even though a primary reason for migration from the Caribbean was the better educational opportunities believed to exist in Britain [420]. We may get paired stereotypes: too clever, keep to themselves (Jews, Asians); not clever enough, don't keep to themselves (Irish, West Indians).

How is the outsider identified and isolated? We can distinguish between biological differences such as skin colour, and cultural differences like religious beliefs. At different periods the majority culture has been likely to penalize one rather than the other. Current discrimination in Britain is directed towards skin colour rather than towards nationality, language or religion. Indeed 'immigrants' are conceived of as usually black, although in recent years the number of New Commonwealth immigrants has been less than that of those from the Old Commonwealth and other countries [305]. Even a touch of the outsider is contagious – we refer to 'a touch of the tar brush', not of the 'white-wash'; the children of black West Indians and white Britons are 'black'. In the colonial period much legal argument centred on how close an African ancestor a European could have and still remain 'white'; opinion settled for one great-grandparent or even great-great-grandparent [203]. Colour is not universally associated with ethnic prejudice. In Switzerland, where to be black is to be associated with the prestigious international organizations in Geneva, prejudice is largely reserved for the unskilled Southern European migrant worker [64].

The most obvious marks of discrimination – skin colour or

mental illness – are those the individual can do least about. A member of a religious minority, such as the Jehovah's Witnesses, who cannot be immediately recognized as such, is usually one who has made a deliberate decision to adopt a particular belief and life-style. Membership of a 'racial' or a pathological group is a status ascribed by others, while a religious identity is achieved by the individual. Descendants of past immigration who have no visible differences of colour may become indistinguishable from the general population unless, like the Jewish community, they are set apart by their religious beliefs.

The outsider who tries to pass for a member of the majority culture, whether he is an immigrant or psychiatric patient, will usually attempt to conceal his past and deliberately to appear part of the dominant group. Foreigners can, with some difficulty, become 'naturalized' . Blacks can try to 'pass'. Signs of outsider status, whether skin pigmentation, accent or culture, are a *stigma* [155]. The outsider is always conscious of a precarious identity. When rejected he may attempt to reaffirm or rephrase his original identity: 'queers' become 'gays', black becomes beautiful, and psychosis becomes rebellion.

Sometimes the inferiority of the outsider is no longer self-evident, either because the facts are too obviously at variance with our theories or because we lose faith in a particular type of rationalization. We then cast about for new systems, new sanctions and new explanations. We may draw upon any type of theory, theological, psychological or biological, to restore the natural order: ourselves at the top, the outsiders underneath. The State of Alabama, seeking a new legal weapon in its effort to preserve segregation in the 1950s, funded a 'scientific study aimed at proving Negroes are mentally inferior to whites' [314]. If scientists can demonstrate that the outsiders, whether foreigners, immigrants or the mentally ill, are in some fundamental way *different* from us, it will be evident that they have different needs from us and we must accordingly treat them differently and keep them separated – or alienated.

MEDICINE AND INSANITY:
THE DISCOVERY OF MENTAL ILLNESS

During the medieval period in Europe insane people appeared to have been relatively free to wander about where they wished [139]. They were also free to suffer and to remain uncared-for; unless the insane were dangerous, they were of no concern to others. Foucault used the imagery of the Ship of Fools to suggest that they were forcibly driven out of the community and entrusted to sailors, who were paid to leave them in a distant city. When detected, other boatmen were bribed and they continued their goal-less pilgrimage [139]. In a similar way, Americans last century believed that it was the official policy of Europeans to send their mentally ill as immigrants to the United States [302].

These wanderings resemble the difficulties of our own chronically mentally ill who pass through a repeated cycle of psychiatric hospitals, prisons, hostels and lodging houses. As we expel them from one temporary institution to another, we too wonder at the curiously unsettling nature of mental illness. It was once believed that there was a parallel between the restless and shifting seas and insanity. The continual changes encountered in travelling were mirrored in the apparent inconsistencies of the disturbed mind. Because they lived near to the oceans the English were believed to be especially liable to mental abnormality. Sea travel was recommended as a treatment for depressive brooding, and in hydrotherapy mental patients were subject to a variety of treatments which demonstrated the affinity of insanity for water [389].

The enclosing of agricultural land and other economic changes associated with the development of early capitalism created a wandering population of dispossessed peasants, and a consequent increase in unemployment, vagrancy and theft. At first these people were likely to be accused of heresy or witchcraft and dealt with accordingly [139, 264], but the solution eventually adopted in France was to confine together all those who were 'idle': mentally ill, delinquents, unemployed and petty criminals. Within this large group no distinction was made between those we would now regard as actively criminal and those who were merely socially embarrassing because of their abnormal mental state.

By 1800 the new European science of psychiatry began to draw precisely this distinction. The nineteenth-century word for a psychiatrist was the *alienist*, the one who was designated as an intermediary between the social world and the world of the mentally ill, who defined the relations between the two or who, in other words, was the agent of their alienation. He identified the mentally ill, segregated them, and, if possible, later reintroduced them into the community. Science, not religion, determined what were acceptable thoughts within the heads of the average citizen. Reason instead of faith became the new measuring stick. Just as 'we appoint officers of public health whose business is to hunt out fever and contagious maladies, the offspring of ignorance and neglect, and to trace them to their lair, and strangle them at birth . . . let us think . . . how the same principle may be applied to diseases of the mind' (quoted in Rosen [345]).

The new concept of mental illness developed as part of the ideology of the French and American revolutions. Curiously, it was attributed to these very changes. Pinel, who was accused by the Committee of Public Safety of hiding their enemies among his patients, blamed an increase of psychosis on the revolution itself. Benjamin Rush described 'revolutiona' – a hypochrondriacal illness found during the American revolutionary war among people excessively concerned with property, prestige and social changes: inflation was the major cause. Mental illness was blamed on the French Revolution by conservative alienists, while radicals emphasized the psychopathology of the monarch [1, 194]. In the 1850s a thesis was presented at Berlin University on 'democratic disease': mental illness was blamed on the 'pressure of modern life', faster travel and the greater scope offered to 'individual fancies'. French psychiatrists suggested that the English were particularly prone to mental illness because of the disappointments associated with financial speculation and the disturbing effects of religious freedom [345].

'The vicious effeminacy of manners', the increased social collisions between people who no longer knew their place, greater opportunities and correspondingly greater disappoint-ments, accidents, increased sexual indulgence and 'abundant sources of moral agitation' in the cities were contrasted with the state of the 'contented peasantry of the Welsh mountains' and the 'wilds of Ireland' and the slaves of the West Indies: 'the finer the organs of the mind become by their greater development . . . the more easily are they disordered. We seldom meet with insanity among the savage tribes of men' (quoted in Rosen [345]). Because peasants had simple beliefs, they had brief 'uncomplicated attacks' of madness [140].

MEDICINE AND SLAVERY:
THE DISCOVERY OF RACE

When first contacted, the indigenous peoples of the lands colonized by Europeans were curiosities – they were presented at court, exhibited and occasionally married. The appearance and customs of Asians and Africans were explained by the different climate – the tropics turned one black – and by their ignorance of Christianity [203]. Colonization and slavery were justified by right of conquest and the belief that slaves were the losers of tribal wars whose lives had been generously spared. They were not originally regarded as naturally inferior [92, 203].

The blacks did have one strange characteristic: they did not apparently become insane. This claim was brought back from Tahiti by Bougainville, was popularized by Rousseau and remained a part of psychiatric theory till recently. Only in a state of primitive simplicity, with none of the cares and duties of civilization, could man be truly happy. The Greeks had believed there was no illness before Pandora opened her box, and Freud suggested that neuroses were caused by the restraints modern civilization imposed on biological drives. More recently the modern European family has been held responsible for schizophrenia. Tuke and Pinel suggested that mental illness was a type of damaged sensibility, the result of our separation from nature. Clearly here was good reason not to overload the lucky native with responsibility. Apart from the obvious political advantages of such a theory for the European, it provided a satisfying answer to any vague promptings of guilt he experienced; he himself was being punished by the mental ill health which inevitably accompanies the discharge of high duties . . .

The idea that the primitive could not become mentally ill evolved into the idea that in some sense he was already ill [407]. The African was simultaneously 'a child, an idiot and a madman' [203], Kipling's 'half devil – half child'. Primitive religion was 'organized schizophrenia', magic the 'pathology of culture', the savage an 'obsessional neurotic'. Native healers were epileptics, hysterics or neurotics. The mentally ill shared the primitiveness of tribal men. In mongolism, the non-European was likened to the subnormal. If the insane regressed to a primitive state of mind because of the stresses of society, the blacks were already there. Among them madness was, as it were, spread out thin – their normal condition. At the least his illnesses were simple: 'The morbid mental phenomena of an insane Australian savage will of necessity be different from the morbid phenomena of an insane European, just as the ruins of a palace must be vaster and more varied than the ruins of a log hut' [269].

Because they were nearer to nature, psychotics and primitives were both resistant to hardship. Pinel described a Scottish farmer 'with the physique of Hercules' who had the reputation of curing mental illness: 'His method consisted in forcing the insane to perform the most difficult tasks of farming, in using them as beasts of burden, as servants, in reducing them to an ultimate obedience with a barrage of blows at the least act of revolt' [139]. When non-Europeans and the mentally ill clearly did demonstrate intellectual capabilities, these merely represented even worse *moral* deficiencies: 'excessive cunning' and 'mischievous brute-like intelligence', as the psychiatrist Maudsley described his patients' attributes [388]. If the language of one form of degradation is inappropriate, another is used.

When there is a wide gulf between ourselves and the outsiders, complex theories are unnecessary. For the mentally ill however, who had only recently been distinguished from the common criminal, elaborate and sophisticated theories were rapidly established. In the case of the non-European, the distinction was initially clearer; his inferiority was culturally and morally apparent and complex theoretical underpinning was unnecessary.

By the 1800s exploitation of the African was however being widely questioned. Benjamin Rush, the pioneer American psychiatrist and a signer of the Declaration of Independence, suggested that claims to European supremacy were 'founded alike in ignorance and inhumanity'. Slavery in the United States and the West Indies needed more sophisticated arguments than that it was an institution which offered opportunities for a Christian education [203]. Missionaries (who had anyway in the Caribbean been denied access to the slaves) were blamed for slave revolts: spiritual equality could apparently suggest the idea of political equality. As the number of free blacks gradually grew, the churches instituted segregation. Slaves who became Christians had originally been freed; this soon proved uneconomical. In 1792 the Church Council in Cape Town agreed, as had churches in the Caribbean and United States, that black Christians could be slaves. Preachers combed the Bible for suitable texts in support of slavery, and lawyers created a complex literature on its constitutional sanction. Appeals were made to the book of Genesis: blacks were believed to be the descendants of Ham, who had been cursed by his father Noah for seeing him naked. Theologians and anthropologists debated the possibility that black and white had been separately created [203, 399]. If the slave was ethically and morally equal to his master, the new theory of legitimation had to be based on his only difference: the biological fact of skin pigmentation provided the basis for the scientific theory of *race*.

Racial rather than cultural differences were now used as the justification for slavery. What was this new idea 'race' and how were racial differences conceived?

The high esteem in which science was held in the nineteenth century led to a variety of biological explanations. The fact that the slaves were now free (and had potential access to a similar environment) meant that justifications for oppression had to be couched in constitutional and genetic explanations rather than in those of culture and environment; the very possibility of change was now denied. Some years later the same thing happened to the other outsiders: the European middle class ceased to improve their economic position and, as in the 1970s, a crisis of faith signalled the end of optimism in the treatment of mental illness [388]. The danger was seen as excess, a loss of self-control (as in masturbatory insanity), or biologically inevitable. Psychiatrists such as Henry Maudsley advocated selective breeding as a solution to mental illness.

Following the work of Linnaeus, attempts were made to classify all plants and animals, including humans. The biological relationship between white and black was debated. The black was described as a type of ape, the product of sexual union between whites and apes, or a type of degenerate white [203]. Black albinos presented a problem: it was eventually decided that they were blacks who had degenerated even further [203]. There was speculation on the practicability of interbreeding apes and black people. The assumption that the 'primitive' occupies a position between the apes and Europeans is still found in sociobiology – the theory that social behaviour can be largely explained by biological concepts such as aggression or territoriality. The concept of the Great Chain of Being arranged all living organisms in a hierarchy in which the white was the perfect creation. This idea was consolidated in the later theory of evolution. Darwin and Malthus replaced God as the authority; in an age of enlightenment only science could rationalize inhumanity. Biblical exegesis was replaced by measurement.

To treat humans as objects required objective theories: in 1788 appeared an approach which later became popular – the weighing of brains [412]. 'Both Europeans and Americans sought in the nineteenth century development of somatometry [the science of comparative body measurements] a scapegoat for individual conscience. They saw the function of statistical somatometry as a means of gratifying the desire for certainty. They would allow the purely statistical experimental and "uninvolved" discipline of somatometry to justify an a priori judgement. Then, too, any such investigation that proved the Negro, Indian, Malay or Mongol to be below the Caucasian in the scale of civilization would again justify the new colonial policies as well as separating the races. It was a circular proof seeking to justify what nearly everyone already accepted as true' [174].

The use of scientific ideas was frequently bizarre: discussing the advantages of castrating black people, one writer observes that 'a few emasculated Negroes scattered around through the thickly-settled Negro communities would really prove the conservation of energy' (quoted in Haller [173]). The US Senate in 1914 decided that cocaine was the cause of rape by blacks, while their psychological difficulties were caused by 'sexual ruminations' and a 'shut-in personality' [433].

Slaves had been found to be prone to particular mental illnesses – *drapetomania*, characterized by the irresistible urge to run away from the plantations, and *dysaesthesia Aethiopica*, or rascality [407]. Emancipation was, however, apparently no answer:

Enlarged freedom, too often ending in licence, excessive use of stimulants, excitement of the emotions, already unduly developed [could only lead to insanity. The blacks] are removed from much of the mental excitement to which the free population . . . is necessarily exposed in the daily routine of life, not to mention the liability of the latter to the influence of the agitating novelties of religion, the intensity of political discussion . . . They have not the anxious cares and anxieties relative to property. They were taught from infancy obedience and self-control . . . The cause of insanity and other diseases with them now, from which they were exempted in slavery, is the removal of all healthful restraints that formerly surrounded them.

In 1957 psychiatrists suggested that mental illness among blacks in the USA was due to an interest in politics: the black was 'constantly stirred up by his needs, as well as by the propaganda of his leaders and by the communists' [437]. Blacks were regarded as a physiologically different race from whites. Beyond skin colour the difference included body odour, the speed of conduction of nervous impulses and the quantity of grey matter in the brain. 'Even the negro's brain and nerves, the chyle and all the humours are tinctured with a share of prevailing darkness' (quoted in Thomas [407]). Black men were believed to produce black semen. The success of silk manufacture in America was doubted because 'the smell from the Negroes would be offensive to the worms' [203].

The medical profession repeatedly pointed out that as scientists only they were qualified to pass comment. A doctor from the deep South even remarked that 'the pecularities in the diseases of Negroes are so distinctive that they can be safely and successfully treated . . . only by Southern physicians' [407]. Science had finally proved that while whites alone could possess determination, will power, self-control and reason, the blacks loved 'melody and ostentation' but lacked judgement. Sometimes the black was discovered to have increased sensitivity, at other times decreased sensitivity. The theories were often contradictory but always demonstrated the superiority of the whites and the impossibility of the blacks improving on their own (biological) deficiencies. Links between science and politics were close. Some professors of anatomy (the key discipline for the racial theories) were members of white suprematist organizations. The Association of American Anatomists asked all doctors to 'keep a careful record of all variations and anomalies' between black and white [173].

The favourite measurements included the facial angle (associated with popular beliefs about the presumed intelligence of the owl and the elephant, two creatures with a large facial angle) and a variety of cerebral dimensions. One study compared the brain weight of eminent white individuals with that of other races and species [174]. Top came Turgenev with 2,012 grams, followed by Cuvier with 1,830, a certain General Bill Butler at 1,758, Thackeray with 1,658, Zulu 1,050, Australian 907, Gorilla 425, Chimpanzee 390. A lawyer from Philadelphia 'demonstrated the sanity of an individual according to the dimension of head hairs submitted to his trigometer . . . Seizing time by the forelock' he built a theory of hair classification which 'led him to seek out a new reason for the National Crime of enslaving the negro-man' wrote a critic of his 'New Science to Sustain Slavery' [174].

A study in East Africa in the 1930s suggested that black brains were far smaller than white brains; in fact they were barely above 'the lowest weight compatible with the human mind of the lowest type' [418]. The adult black brain weighed the same as that of a white child of seven or eight. The brains of Africans who were over forty-five appeared senile, demonstrating the strain of European education on the native mind. Photographs clearly showed the increase in the proportion of 'undifferentiated' and 'immature' nerve cells. (The language used is revealing.) Some layers of the African brain were larger than those in Europeans – these were the layers supposedly devoted to the instincts of appetite and sex. The paper was received with acclaim; it was

> relevant and simplifying [to the] difficult labours [of the colonial administration]. If to the lack of durability, numerical deficiency of neurones is added, the outlook is black indeed . . . Wishful thinking on all native questions must vanish from today before *scientific thinking* and mental hygiene must take its place as the premier public health problem in Kenya . . . The real danger arises when there occurs the mind of a child of six in the body of a man of twenty.[1]

One doctor remarks that in thirty-two years in Africa he has never met an African with normal European intelligence: the premature closure of the sutures of the skull prevented the brain of the black from developing fully.

This type of theorizing could not offer any hope that environmental change could bring equality. Even the earlier theory of phrenology (the science of 'bumps on the head'), which had justified the 'natural distribution of labour', had suggested that different social and economic conditions could affect human faculties [382].

As races 'ascend up the evolutionary ladder' the extent to which the lower jaw stuck out was reduced and the weight of the abdominal organs shifted from thorax to pelvis. The much-reported large genitals of blacks reflected those 'sexual extremes [which] belong to the age of awakening consciousness or nascent intelligence'. However, nature would punish such a phenomenon – 'the abuse of the organs of reproduction will certainly result in their becoming functionless'. The 'furor sexualis' of the black was not entirely biological, however, but was partly the result of 'frequent changes in social and commercial status of the negro race'. Culture was intrinsically enmeshed in biology. The educated French black was *évolué* (evolved). Although the underlying message was always the same, interpretation shifted from simply advocating the irreversibility of biological factors ('what was decided among prehistoric protozoa cannot be changed by act of Congress') to practical criticism of moves towards racial equality: 'It is gross folly to attempt to educate both [black and white] on the same basis. When education will reduce the large size of the negro's penis as well as bring about the sensitivity of the terminal fibres which exist in the Caucasian' there might be equality (quoted in Haller [173]). Education was not the answer – 'a classical education for a negro whose proper vocation is raising rice or cotton or garden truck, is as much out of place as a piano in a Hottentot's tent' [173].

Sometimes the explanations were genetic or anatomical, sometimes social or political. All agreed on the same course of action, namely to continue as before: 'A child should be allowed to develop in sympathy with the race trend.' There is of course no evidence that there are any significant differences between blacks and whites, whether in brain size, the quantity of grey matter or any other similar measures [412]. In any case there is no correlation between brain size and intelligence: Cromwell's brain was more than twice the size of that of Anatole France [160]. The brain of modern Europeans is smaller than that of the Eskimo or of their Neanderthal ancestors, neither of whom it seems were more (or less) intelligent [284].

Another immutable difference was provided by the theory of instincts: McDougall pointed out that the instinct of submission was more fully developed in the black race [407]. Aversion of one race for the other was natural and healthy – Houston Stewart Chamberlain observed that small children automatically started crying if a Jew came by, even though they had previously never heard of Jews [30].

SEX AND STATISTICS

Of impeccable scientific respectability was the new discipline of statistics. In 1840, the directors of the US Census pointed out in advance how useful it was going to be for comparisons between black and white [95]. The results were alarming for the opponents of slavery. In the North, the (free) blacks were seven times more likely to be mentally ill than the whites. In Louisiana only one in 4,310 slaves was mentally ill. Such were the bad effects of freedom that in Maine one in fourteen blacks was mentally ill. Slavery clearly benefited mental health. Further investigations, however, showed that there were peculiarities in the figures – one town in Maine with a population of only three blacks had six mentally ill blacks. Extensive falsification was found and the statistical method fell, for a time, into disrepute [95]. When psychiatric hospitals were first built for the blacks, however, the apparent sudden increase in insanity was taken as evidence of the deleterious psychological effects of liberty [314]. Statistical and genetic theories are still prominent in theorizing about 'race'. Lamarck's theory whereby characteristics acquired during life are transmitted to later generations suggested that people who lived in the colder northern countries became more vigorous than those in the indolent tropics. On the other hand, natural selection (which became politically popular in the theories loosely called Social Darwinism) claimed that Europeans were 'fitter' because in a tough climate only the strongest survived to reproduce: colonists employed it to explain why whites in a savage environment did not immediately become savages themselves [399].

The diversity of human societies was attributed to racial differences. All humans are related genetically and we all therefore have greater or lesser degrees of relatedness with other people. There is no obvious point at which we could draw a line and say 'this but not that group of people constitute a race': we can have five hundred races or five – or one. In fact human variability is most usefully described by mapping separately different characteristics rather than by trying to impose formal boundaries [160]. Different measuring sticks, which have included skin colour, facial structure, blood group and even copulatory position, produce different patterns of relatedness. The degree of conviction with which these differences are regarded as biologically significant appears to depend on the climate of political opinion. There is no universally valid way of classifying people. If skin colour is emphasized, the tribal Japanese Ainu are placed in the same group as the European, while blood groups suggest affinities between Indians and Hungarian gipsies.

Emphasis on the supposed sexual characteristics of non-white races led to an interest in 'cross-breeding', as it was called by analogy with the farm-yard. Ambiguity is frightening; that the clear boundary established between black and white could be blurred by inter-racial love and thus by children of mixed parentage was particularly threatening. Until 1967, seventeen American states had laws against intermarriage. A new technical language developed to control 'miscegenation',[2] utilizing such apparently precise terms as half-bred, hybrid, mulatto and octaroon. Curious as such expressions might now appear, such theorizing is fundamental to current racial classification in South Africa: exact measurement and the analysis of the clustering of such characteristics as width of the nostrils and distance between the eyes.

Once the belief in definitive racial groups was established with their particular social characteristics, and individuals could be reliably ascribed to one or the other, the effect of 'cross-breeding' could be studied in detail. Post-mortem examinations showed that while the brain weight of the 'full-blooded Negro' was five ounces below that of the white, 'slight intermixtures' of white ancestry in the black tended to 'diminish the negro brain from its normal standard'. Intermarriage in the British Empire led to epilepsy and crime: 'The Bastard – a mixture of white and black blood – normally seems to present all the worst characteristics of both races, and so degraded is the position he occupies that he is compelled to associate still with his coloured half-brothers' [164]. To the black who knew his place some type of primitive dignity was conferred – immunity from care or mental illness. If he was the offspring of 'inter-racial breeding' he was condemned to insanity and crime. In popular literature the villain was the 'half-breed' [399]. In fact only about a fifth of 'black' Americans do not have any white ancestors [185] and in the Caribbean perhaps even fewer. Such theories still have some currency. Prejudice against the children of intermarriage is frequently greater than against the 'pure black' [339]. A London doctor in 1980 announced that he tells his black patients that mixed marriages 'would put back genetics a thousand years' [123]. A recent textbook of physical anthropology suggests it is more 'natural' to have sex with members of one's own ethnic group: inter-ethnic sex is usually avoided by one's sense of smell [21]. Until recently in many American states it was illegal to *advocate* intermarriage [284].

Genetics had the advantage of combining a fascination with the fantasized sexual characteristics of the non-white with an apparently rigorous scientific methodology. Frequent emphasis was placed both on the supposedly large size of the black penis and its frequent use. The slaver who advertised the 'hot constitution'd ladies' in his cargo [407] freely offered black women to white men while 'the gross clasps of the lascivious Moor' presented a danger to white womanhood. Jefferson described love between blacks 'as more an eager desire than a tender delicate mixture of sentiment and sensation'. The deliberate destruction of family life among black slaves was inevitably accompanied by a discovery of their 'natural' sexuality. For the white male 'white women are for marriage, mullatoes for fornication and Negresses for work' (quoted in Davis [92]). In Caribbean islands such as Barbados, where there were many white women, sex between the slave and her white master was not encouraged, but it was accepted in Jamaica, where white women were in short supply [92].

Castration was frequently practised on slaves for a variety of trivial offences [203]. As Fanon suggested, it appeared that there would be no room for anyone else in the cathedral if three blacks inside it had erections. Fear of being overwhelmed by the outsider has often resulted in anxiety over the reproductive capacity of immigrants and the mentally ill. Americans of English ancestry were concerned that 'Jews and the foreign-born and the poor' were particularly fertile and would swamp 'the American type' as Theodore Roosevelt called it. In an attempt to render the black 'docile, quiet and inoffensive' an Atlanta medical journal offered a paper on 'Castration Instead of Lynching'. Economic considerations prevented a solution of the 'black problem' by repatriation: '3,000,000 workers form too valuable an economic factor to be eliminated unless the race problem is too dangerous to the State and there is no possibility of solving it in any other way' [173].

Since before Cicero warned Atticus not to buy British slaves because of their stupidity, foreigners have traditionally been considered less intelligent than the native rulers [30]. Dominant groups manage to do well at measures which they consider significant. Traditional intelligence tests made no allowance for cultural differences in motivation and perception. (Dakota Native Americans, for example, do not volunteer the correct answer to a problem unless they are convinced that everybody else knows it and will not be offended by their answering.)

The psychological tests used to screen army recruits during the First World War demonstrated the superiority of the Nordic over Alpine, Mediterranean over Negro 'types'. Differences between European ethnic groups are no longer taken seriously, but we are still left with one large division: that between white and black. Jensen suggests that there are two types of intelligence – creative intelligence, typical of whites, and rote intelligence, typical of blacks. Lest we think he is being purely academic, he warns of 'the dangers of current welfare politics unaided by eugenic foresight' [199].

Modern psychological justifications of racism are beyond the scope of this book and we refer the reader to Kamin's *The Science and Politics of IQ* [206]. However, we would point out that popular statements which aver that one group is 'more intelligent' than another assume that, given the same environment, one group of people have a greater natural (genetic) endowment than does another. But black and white do not live in the same environment in Britain or America. If blacks are discriminated against to a significant extent, then any such statement is meaningless. To resort for a moment to the analogies of the laboratory psychologist, we can breed two populations of animals, one of which is very good at performing a particular task and one of which is very bad. However, in a poor environment both groups perform badly, and in a good environment the gap between the two groups is diminished [88].

After the abolition of slavery, the blacks in America became a 'problem'. Theories of white supremacy came under attack. John Stuart Mill wrote that 'of all vulgar modes of escaping from the considerations of the effect of social and moral influences on the human mind, the most vulgar is that of attributing the diversities of conduct and character to inherited natural differences' [281]. Attempts were now made to send the freed slaves back to Africa.

One of the stranger beliefs about the 'black problem' was that it would somehow go away by itself. In the late nineteenth century, research involving census data, prison mortality rates and insurance company reports concluded that the inevitable deterioration of the black race removed from their natural habitat would result in their *becoming extinct* [407]. No longer protected by the beneficent institutions of slavery, the blacks were now exposed to the full rigours of 'race struggle'. At the same time another group of aliens were also conveniently fated to disappear by their very nature. Morel's degeneration theory of mental illness suggested that successive generations became neurotics, psychotics and finally infertile subnormals.

SCIENTIFIC RACISM IN EUROPE

In nineteenth-century Europe, as in the colonies, science supported the assertion of the natural superiority of one group or another (usually the Anglo-Saxon [30]). Depending on where the boundaries of countries happened to lie at a particular time and on current political considerations, the theories were subject to rapid change. Initially racial differences had been used to describe the pattern of class relations within a society. In France, for instance, the peasants were supposed to be descended from the Alpine people while the aristocrats traced their origins back to the Franks. After the national defeat of 1870 French scientists reclassified the Germans as Slavs and developed the doctrine

'Celtism', which sanctified the alliance with Britain. During the Second World War, the German anthropologist Gunther and 'Inspector-General of Mental Training' Rosenberg gave the Japanese Nordic ancestry [30], reminiscent of their present status in South Africa as 'honorary whites'.

Anatomical racial experts such as Broca and Ammon were able to distinguish no less than thirty-four distinct shades of skin colour. Physical anthropology – the study of variations in the human body – degenerated into a search for pre-existing 'pure' races [431]. 'Somatometrists in Europe and America experimented with measurements of skull shape, language, hair pile, skin colour, temperament and political belief in order to determine the reality and ranking of dozens or hundreds of stocks' [174]. Among the instruments devised were the craniograph, the occipital goniometer, the *cadre à maxima* and the micrometric compass. Broca's museum contained five hundred skulls: he accumulated by his death over 180,000 measurements. Noses were allocated to such categories as leptorrhines (thin ones with narrow nostrils) and platyrrhines (flat with broad nostrils).

It was suggested that there were distinct European races – Nordics, Alpines, Celts and others; this distribution accounted for the major linguistic and cultural patterns in Europe. For the Frenchman of 1873 'the native or acquired difficulty among the Germans of getting the nervous centres of the medulla oblongata to carry out the orders of the cerebral cortex regarding syllabic sound production – they say fa and pa for va and ba – is a pathological fact still observable in our own day' [30]. Gobineau believed that the despised South Europeans were of black ancestry and Benjamin Franklin maintained that the English were the only true white race [203]. Kretschmer suggested that certain races were prone to particular patterns of mental illness related to their body measurements. Chamberlain believed that Teutons could always be recognized because of their inherent characteristic of 'loyalty'.

Biological characteristics were believed to determine the destiny of nations in the struggle for supremacy. The anti-Semite Lapouge wrote in the 1880s: 'I am convinced that in the next century millions will cut each other's throats because of one or two degrees more or less of cephalic index' [30]. He was right, not because anatomical differences determined human behaviour, but because people believed they did.

The Nazis applied the scientific method to the question of race with the greatest enthusiasm. Eminent physicians, including internationally recognized authorities on such questions as blood groups,[3] evolved complex systems of racial classification and assessment, involving especially designed instruments (such as calipers for measuring the width of the nose) and graphs of the normal distribution of individual physical characteristics, complete with their limits of statistical error. The later 'genetic experiments' of the concentration camps were suggested by Herman Gauch, who wrote in 1933 in *New Foundations for Research into Social Race Problems*: 'If non-Nordics are more closely allied to monkeys and apes than to Nordics, why is it possible for them to mate with Nordics and not with apes? The answer is this: it has not been proved that non-Nordics cannot mate with apes' [30]. German women who associated with immigrant workers were sent to the camps [64].

Although we now tend to regard the Nazis as the major exponents of selective breeding (eugenics), they were only carrying to a logical conclusion racist opinions commonly held throughout Europe and America before the Second World War. In the nineteenth century, Engels had described the Irish as an incompetent race [116] and Marx wrote of a colleague, 'It is now quite clear to me that as shown by the shape of his head . . . he is descended from the negro . . . The importunity of the fellow is also negroid' (quoted in McLellan [265]).

The biological solution to the contradictions of slavery was a trial run for the application of medicine to other social problems. With the idea of 'race' clearly established, Lombroso was able to suggest that law should be based on biology and not 'antiquated notions of natural reason or Christian morality' [160]. Biological problems required biological solutions – sterilization, castration or physical elimination. Eugenic attempts to remove the unemployed or tubercular 'unfit' were not confined to reactionaries: indeed among the most enthusiastic advocates were the statisticians and psychologists associated with the Fabian Society [166]. The pioneers of intelligence tests were frequently associated with this type of policy [206]. As unlikely a body as the English National Council of Labour Women passed a resolution calling for the sterilization of 'defectives' [172]. A report prepared in 1922 by the Psychopathic Laboratory of the Municipal Court of Chicago recommended a draft law empowering the State

Eugenicist to sterilize 'potential parents of socially inadequate offspring' [172]. The socially inadequate included all psychiatric patients, delinquents, the inebriate, the deaf (including those with seriously impaired hearing), the homeless and those with chronic infections.

In 1910 a report of the Committee of the (British) Eugenics Society maintained that unemployment was genetically determined: the unemployed 'was born without manly independence and is unable to do a normal day's work however frequently it is offered to him' (quoted in Haldane [172]. During a period of unemployment a Canadian businessman offered to pay his workers to be sterilized: several accepted. An American judge ordered one Chris McCauley, who had been accused of burglary, to be sterilized, remarking, 'This man, about thirty-five years of age, is subnormal mentally and has every appearance and indication of immorality. He has a strain of negro blood in his veins, and has a disgusting and lustful appearance' [172].

REPRESSIVE BENEVOLENCE:
THE DISEASE OF DISADVANTAGE

With the defeat of the Nazis, racio-genetic explanations of social characteristics were for a time discredited. No longer could patterns of family organization or mental breakdown be traced to racial differences in the brain. Although 'kinkiness' of hair was still associated with infrequency of depressive episodes [137], the theory of the 'black brain' was replaced by that of the 'black family'. But even in the 1960s the cruder type of biological explanations continued to be used by the medical profession: 'Some . . . physicians who have had extensive experience treating Negroes consider a serious suicidal attempt to be *prima facie* evidence of white ancestry' [322].

The same economic conditions persisted. The essential contradiction of the labour market – the ideology of free labour with the need for a reservoir of disposable labour – was solved in a new way. The discredited authoritarianism was replaced by non-coercive control which turned the black into a passive consumer of sociological and psychiatric expertise. The Eugenics Societies were succeeded by the Mental Health Movement.

Opponents of racism had previously tried to show black people as innocent but sick. The liberal Benjamin Rush regarded blackness as a type of attenuated leprosy [401]. Like leprosy, it was characterized by apathy, 'morbid insensitivity of the nerves and strong venereal desire'. The black was not merely treated as a leper: he was one physically. He should thus be treated with the compassion and care usually given to the sick, but he should be sexually segregated. Because the leprosy was congenital rather than contagious he could still be safely employed as a domestic.

By the 1950s the black was seen as socially rather than biologically disadvantaged. Black family life was described as 'tenuous, insecure and precarious', and yet its most enduring and stable figure was criticized as dominant and overpowerful: the 'matriarchal' black mother appeared. The psychodynamic theory that depression is related to the real or threatened 'loss of a love object' was used as an explanation for the finding that American blacks from the deep South were less likely to be depressed than those who came from the North: as the Southern blacks had fewer material possessions they had less to lose and 'never became depressed' [322].

The characteristics the black inherited were now 'attractive' ones – he was a natural musician and athlete, was loyal and capable of hard work, and so on. Blacks were not slow to point out that this stereotype was merely a revival of the primitive at a pre-intellectual stage of development: the large number of German composers was not usually attributed to German 'natural rhythm'.

The black came to be seen as a victim of racism: his family life – 'a tangle of pathology' – was the result of discrimination and slavery 'so severe and absolute that it moulded the Negro's character into a submissive, child-like "Sambo", whose traits resembled those of the victims of Nazi concentration camps' [92, 286]. The common West Indian and black American domestic pattern of serial monogamy without legal marriage was attributed to slavery, even though in the course of this century a progressively *smaller* proportion of black women have married [433]. The immediate political situation was avoided by emphasizing the 'legacy of slavery'. The self-image of black children who did not associate with whites was found to be more positive than that of those who did; black men expressed a preference for a spouse lighter coloured than themselves. The poor opinion blacks had of themselves was explained by their historical failure to compete with whites, rather than as a result of continuing discrimination. The black was still inferior, but he was now 'culturally deprived' rather than lacking a stage of brain development. His failure to achieve fluency in 'standard English' or to adopt middle-class patterns of child discipline were seen as impoverishment [71]. The culture of poverty became a poverty of culture.

The question for black immigrants and other ethnic minorities becomes one of whether the attributes of status and power in white society, a particular way of life and type of education, are merely the trappings of prestige (in which case they can be ignored and an alternative 'black' cultural style pursued) or whether they are essential tools to achieve power (in which case 'black identity' has to some extent to be sacrificed). How far can power be achieved with the preservation of a minority culture and to what extent is the minority culture merely the culture of losers? Particular patterns of perception (which we know vary from one culture to another) or linguistic facility may be associated with successful adaptation, not because they are in themselves necessary to succeed but because they are the characteristics of the group which has traditionally held power [71].

The 'characteristics' of minorities which are studied are usually negative ones. It is difficult to find mention of black Britons in the media without the assumption of some type of 'problem' [316]. No one has attempted to explain the low rates of suicide and alcoholism in West Indians in Britain while much has been written on their rates of delinquency. In a period of greater toleration of a range of sexual behaviour and demands to alter radically western family structure, black women are regarded as 'promiscuous' rather than as courageous pioneers. Serial monogamy is regarded less as a pattern in itself than a continued failure to reach the goals of white middle-class marriage [253]. In the last century general paralysis of the insane (a late sequel to syphilis) was attributed to social stress; the infrequency of it in Africa was attributed to 'the simple life of these natives: no cares and no struggle for existence such as is found in European cities' [164]; Krafft-Ebing lamented the association of 'civilization and syphilization'. When the venereal origin of general paralysis was established there was no flood of papers extolling the hygienic advantages of African family life. Mental illness was instead attributed to the fact that Africans practised masturbation – a habit 'the natives are addicted to' [164]. In a period when homosexuality was both a disease and a sin, the apparent absence of it in Africa was a triumph, not of morality, but of 'unrestrained sexual instincts'. Even 'perversion' conferred prestige.

Laudable characteristics are always qualified: 'In a certain proportion of this class [people of mixed black and white ancestry] ethical feelings are developed, moral irregularities are not condoned and an *exaggerated* self-respect developed' [163] (our italics). Even apparently understandable psychiatric reactions are not really valid: 'Whilst it is the rule to find in the negro race vague ideas of persecution, poison and influence, it is quite rare for a *reasonable* basis for such beliefs to be expressed or for these ideas to be built up into a *logical* system' [163] (our italics).

STEREOTYPES AND SCAPEGOATS: THE DISEASE OF RACISM

As the apparent inferiority of black people was now a syndrome blamed on past racism, prejudice itself became an illness. Discrimination was now psychologically abnormal behaviour. Racism was a delusion [329, 433]. It was part of a syndrome including anti-semitism, anti-feminism, anti-homosexuality and a fondness for punitive measures [421]. 'Super-patriots' were identified who projected their unacknowledged fears and wishes on to other ethnic groups. Xenophobia suggested a *morbid* fear of foreigners, by analogy with insect phobias or agoraphobia. The percentage of prejudiced individuals in Britain was found to be 27 per cent in 1968 [343]. Prejudiced individuals were those who used such 'unhealthy' ways of thinking as *stereotyping* – the assumption that all members of minority groups were of the same type and lacking in individuality, together with a selective emphasis on their less desirable characteristics – and *inconsistent value judgements* – in which minority groups were simultaneously perceived as both seeking power and looking inward [151]. A popular psychology textbook explains 'prejudice' by looking at the personalities of racially prejudiced female college students: they are found to be highly conforming, self-centred, with above average respect for their parents, a tendency to neatness and a lack of sensuality [186].

While these descriptions are true of individuals within a society and are useful for comparing one person with another, they fail to explain why a society as a whole may be racist. Racist attitudes may be manifest as a highly articulated set of beliefs in the individual, but they are also found in less conscious presuppositions, located in society as a whole [203]. Prejudice is a mechanism, not an explanation: one can be prejudiced against cigarette smokers without denying them political rights; racism is the quite specific belief that cultural differences between ethnic groups are of biological origin and that groups should be ranked in worth.

While previously racism had been supported by medicine, it was now explained as the disease of certain pathological white individuals [433]. What the theory did not explain was how society as a whole could be racist if only a section of it suffered from this delusion. Racism is not a disease or a delusion, for in a racist society such beliefs are highly adaptive. In a racist society the racist is the *normal individual*. To single out the most prejudiced, those who most accurately reflect the social view, and to call them mentally ill, is to find a scapegoat. We excuse ourselves by using the very mechanisms for which we condemn the racist. Everybody who benefits by racism in a racist society is, in some measure, a racist.

Certain personality configurations can, it is true, be highly regarded in a particular society. The significance of 'prejudiced individuals' may lie, not in their individual power, but in the way they serve as a model. It has been suggested that our own society particularly values the 'authoritarian personality' we have just described [2].

Racism is seldom a coherent set of beliefs, and we can find it not only in the deliberate actions of overt racists (active racism) but in its latent form; in, for example, the less conscious avoidance of non-Europeans in employment and housing (aversive racism). Aversive racism is manifest by the absence of its subject: to take an American example – the Golden Age of the United States is found in the Western. One of the major protagonists of this period is, however, conspicuous by his absence: the black [223]. The whites, having (temporarily) solved 'the black problem' by the Civil War, were able to turn their aggressive energies to the Far West. The problem returned, but fantasy was able to recapture that brief period when moral doubts about American society were concealed by an exuberant confidence in the westward expansion. The extermination of the Indians, unlike slavery, could be seen as heroic. They were conceived of as 'worthy opponents'.

This noble savage stereotype persisted throughout the period of degradation of the black: it was given to nations whose martial powers was respected by the Europeans – the North American Indians, the Zulu and the Maori. The 'Hamitic' hunting peoples of East Africa were considered superior to the agricultural 'Bantu' [381].

Psychoanalytic interpretations rest on a belief in the formative role of early childhood. Racism has been interpreted as a sequel to the time when a young child first learns to control its bowels. This 'anal phase' is characterized by an emphasis on control, a balance between input and output, the development of a clear boundary between self and excrement, and a preoccupation with dirt. Anthropologists too have pointed to the relation between category formation and dirt ('matter out of place' [104]). We have seen that prejudice can be regarded as the projection of our own unacceptable desires on to scapegoats. An accident of skin pigmentation allowed the European to use this early anal experience as a metaphor for later political realities: the black is equated with faeces, with the dirty part of ourselves. Clean/Dirty parallels White/Black, Us/Them.

The 'anal personality type' is characterized by identification with the parents, with rigidity and a denial of sensuality, very similar to the concept of the 'prejudiced personality' which was arrived at through experimental psychology. He is the petit bourgeois, the frustrated little man who identifies with his superiors, denies his own wishes and projects them on to a group he considers beneath him. Wilhelm Reich suggested that the roots of fascism were to be found in this type of personality configuration [338]. The unpleasant part of ourselves is located in other groups: Jews and Asians crave power and influence, while the Irish and West Indians are bestial and stupid. Such stereotypes are common in bar conversations or in lavatory graffiti (a suitable place if we accept the psychoanalytical theory).

There are associations with other body zones. Fears of being swallowed up by the blacks are represented in an endless series of cartoons of missionaries in cooking pots. We have already considered the fantasy of the black penis: as sensuality is denied in the white, the white woman is placed on an asexual pedestal out of its reach [184].

It has been suggested that modern European society is particularly liable to this type of mental splitting and projection [223]. Not merely has science legitimized racism in certain particulars, but the whole nature of the scientific enterprise has perhaps contributed to its possibility. The fragmentary, empirical nature of our theorizing leads to that split between idea and feeling which was carried to its conclusion in Auschwitz or in the slave trade; legal argument long centred on whether non-Europeans should be regarded as people or as objects [203].

Emphasis on the hidden fantasies of a racist society, unlike empirical psychology, involves every white in a responsibility for racism and a responsibility for self-examination. There are, however, certain dangers in the psychoanalytic approach:

(i)   It is assumed that psychological mechanisms, derived from universal childhood experience, actually generate racism (rather than perpetuating it in each generation). Race riots have been attributed to 'father hatred' [398] and minority groups are seen as victims of 'displaced' aggression.[4]

(ii) We are still left with a need for economic and political understanding to explain why in a particular society racism exists and functions. The difference between overt and latent racism is the difference between those who see themselves as in direct economic competition with, and in close proximity to, ethnic minorities (the working class in Britain) and those who benefit from the presence of immigrants and can afford to live in more affluent conditions. When an Institute of Race Relations survey revealed that the working class were particularly (overtly) prejudiced, it argued that this was an 'educational problem'.

(iii) Emphasis on latent racism and the unconscious guilt associated with it leads to a situation where aggressive racism may be seen as healthy and even preferable to the strategies of liberal aversive racism [223]. Psychoanalysis returns us to the problem of the healthy racist in a racist society.

RACISM AND PSYCHIATRIC TREATMENT

Theories of racial supremacy had their impact even inside the mental hospitals. In America, not only were black patients segregated from the white, but among the whites themselves some groups (usually the Irish) were also kept apart. Until the Civil War black mental patients were kept in prison. If close association of the races was believed to be harmful to the community as a whole, how much more so would it affect the precarious balance of the emotionally disturbed: 'The natural antagonism of the races is opposed to the course [of integrating hospitals]. It would be mutually prejudicial to both whites and blacks, but especially to the former, were the two blended in one asylum.' In 1948 the President of the American Psychiatric Association was still officially opposing the desegregation of psychiatric hospitals [90, 407].

In America there is a very wide variety of psychiatric facilities depending less on medical condition than on income, ranging from the state asylums, which have a larger proportion of involuntary patients, to private out-patient psychotherapy and daily psychoanalysis. Patients of the same social class as the physician are more likely to receive psychotherapy than physical treatment for the same problems [190]. Different ethnic groups do not have the same access to a range of facilities. In all types of government institutions, medical and penal, there are disproportionately more non-whites than whites [433]. For similar types of childhood delinquency, the social standing and affluence of white American parents enable them to have their children diagnosed as 'troubled' (and given psychotherapy), while black children are 'troublesome' (and sent to a reformatory) [407].

In Los Angeles 11 per cent of white psychiatric patients but only 3 per cent of black patients are seen more than ten times in the clinic. Not surprisingly, American psychiatrists with a high 'ethnocentricity' rating themselves are less likely to accept patients from minority groups. The diagnosis of psychosis is more frequent in black Americans than among whites; even taking only those patients with a diagnosis of psychosis, a higher proportion of blacks are hospitalized than whites [433]. Compared to a similar group of white patients, black patients are more likely to be given powerful anti-psychotic drugs and less likely to be in psychotherapy [75]. They are also more likely to be detained in mental hospitals against their will.

White professionals say that psychotherapy with black clients is not very successful [165, 363]. The blacks demonstrate their hostile aggression to the white therapists by coming late, 'acting out', missing appointments and by silence during the sessions. The 'primitive character structure' of the black apparently makes psychoanalysis unsuitable. (It is anyway available to disproportionately fewer in the black population for financial reasons.)

Psychoanalysis was based on the bond between patient and physician, independent of the social context in which this relationship occurred. It was initially able to ignore cultural differences between the two because both came from essentially the same social milieu. Attempts by the client to raise cultural questions were interpreted by the analyst as moves to avoid an emotionally significant relationship between them. Given this deliberate avoidance of the question of social roles, it is easy to see how a patient from an ethnic minority or a colonized society was perceived as childlike in the therapeutic context: the relations of colonial psychiatrist and colonized individual were already perceived in parent–child terms. Analysts examined the dreams of black Americans and found that 84 per cent of them were 'simple childlike wish-fulfillment dreams' [255]. Jung, talking of his postulated cultural strata in the mind, said that the Negro 'has probably a whole historical layer less'. He warned white Americans that 'living with barbaric races exerts a suggestive effect on the laboriously tamed instinct of the white race and tends to pull it down' [407].

In South Africa, medical facilities are segregated according to the racial categorization which each individual carries on his or her identity card. All life, economic, social and sexual, is determined by 'scientific' allocation of race, although the exact boundaries of the different groups vary depending on political circumstances: in the 1930s it was estimated that between a third and a half of the 'whites' were of 'mixed descent'. After the Nationalist Party came to power in 1948 the suicide rate doubled among black Africans. There are no black psychiatrists in South Africa according to a recent report by the World Health Organisation [446]. A certain proportion of the psychiatric services are, as in the United States, designed to make a profit. However, these are not private facilities for the whites but for the blacks; an arrangement involving private profit-making institutions, contracted by the government and advised by an Army Medical Corps brigadier, caters for the black mentally ill [282]. The 10,000 patients in these institutions are all involuntary patients. None of them has a full-time doctor, conditions have been described as overcrowded and degrading, and treatment consists solely of drugs and maintaining the building. The patients' labour is subcontracted to other companies. An editorial in the *Lancet* suggests that changes in the law have opened the way to 'pass-law' offenders being placed in these institutions [236]. The Mental Health Amendment Act of 1976 provides for one year's imprisonment for publishing uncensored information about psychiatric services in South Africa or taking photographs of the patients or institutions.

Is there any bias in the provision of mental health services to different ethnic groups in Britain? There are few private psychiatric facilities here compared with the United States and we might expect a more equitable distribution of services. However, we know that even within the National Health Service there are differences in the facilities offered to different classes. A report by the Royal College of General Practitioners in 1977 showed that GPs spend 50 per cent more time with middle-class patients than they do with working-class patients. Immigrant patients, dissatisfied with their treatment in the NHS, appear to be increasingly turning to private doctors [424].

If we take class and age differences into account, are there any differences in treatment offered to blacks and whites in Britain? No one has yet looked at this methodically. Although less likely than the British-born to see a GP for psychiatric reasons, West Indian men are more likely to be admitted to psychiatric hospitals [72, 317]. Psychotic black patients are twice as likely as British-born and white immigrants to be in hospital detained involuntarily, 'sectioned' under the Mental Health Act [259, 361]. Four out of ten of them in one study were involuntary patients at some point in their admission [258]. Asian-born patients in Britain are also more likely to be involuntary patients in psychiatric hospitals and less likely to refer themselves [318]. A study of the use of psychiatric facilities in a London hospital over a three-week period suggested that immigrant patients, both black and white, are particularly likely to refer themselves to hospital as emergencies but they are less likely than the British-born to attend appointments booked for them [262]. Black patients are more likely than white patients to see a black member of the psychiatric team and to see a junior rather than a senior doctor. When differences in diagnosis are allowed for, they are still more likely to receive the powerful phenothiazine drugs and to receive electro-convulsive therapy. A large proportion of Jewish patients receive convulsive treatment; this is, however, related to a greater incidence of depression among Jews.

Racism in psychiatric treatment may occur in many forms. Overt discrimination in Britain is rare, perhaps because of the considerable number of psychiatrists and psychiatric nurses who are themselves members of ethnic minorities. Members of minorities are less likely to get the more 'attractive' type of psychiatric care such as individual or group therapy because they are regarded as not meeting the 'ideal' criteria for psychotherapy (including the type of problem or middle-class mode of describing their feelings) which are traditionally associated with the best response to this type of therapy in Europe. What is particularly lacking is the commitment of psychotherapists to work with ethnic minorities.

Between a white doctor and a black patient the colour difference may be either exaggerated or it may be ignored. Exaggeration is likely to lead to stereotypes of 'West Indian psychosis' and neglect of individual emotional difficulties unrelated to discrimination. A sympathetic doctor may see his patient as so scarred by racism as inevitably to be a passive victim with no secure identity and little self-respect; he may then bend over backwards to support him, to avoid any guilt the patient brings out in *him*. Underestimating the difference in culture by the white psychiatrist leads to an avoidance of the problems of discrimination and to a lack of sensitivity in understanding non-medical approaches to emotional difficulties.

The meeting of a white patient with a black psychiatrist produces a *status contradiction* for the doctor. Patients and relatives have to reconcile their rather different attitudes to immigrants and to doctors. In our experience they are often patronizing, feel they are getting second-class treatment and complain to a white psychiatrist that a black doctor cannot understand them or even has too many problems of his own to be helpful.

Status contradiction also occurs with black patient and black psychiatrist. The mutual awareness that both are immigrants is usually concealed beneath class and professional differences. The patient regards the doctor as really 'white', while the psychiatrist, often from quite a different society from the patient, agrees with his white colleagues that psychotherapy with a working-class patient (not of course a *black* patient) is rather unrewarding. The patient suspects that an English doctor might have helped him more. Neither recognize themselves in the other.

To draw some conclusions from this chapter, we have seen that ethnic relations have been looked at with the aid of psychological and psychiatric theories in three ways:

(i)   Blacks are physically and mentally inferior and should be treated accordingly.
(ii) To be black is to be the innocent victim of racism. The characteristics of being black are those of an illness which cannot, however, be cured.
(iii) Racism is part of a pathological personality pattern.

Racism is explicit in the first explanation, latent in the second and obscured in the third. Racism is neither a science nor a disease but a set of political beliefs which legitimates certain social and economic conditions. It is pointless to ask which is primary – prejudice or exploitation. They developed historically together, each validating the other.

We shall now look in detail at one particular psychiatric theory which justified political domination: the strange belief that only Europeans could become depressed.

NOTES

1 Even today textbooks of physical anthropology classify certain ethnic groups as *paedomorphous* – the fully developed adult resembles ancestral larval forms 'except in the maturity of their reproductive organs' [21]. The human life-cycle is a pervasive metaphor: mental retardation and psychopathy are conventionally regarded as 'arrested development'.
2 The word (which was originally a hoax), although derived from *misc-* (mix), carries of course the connotation of *mis-* (undesirable). Similarly, the redundant term *subculture* (a division of a culture) implies 'beneath culture' (cf. *subhuman*).

3 Hitler called intermarriage between Jew and Gentile 'blood poisoning'. Blood is a popular racist theme: Rosenberg said, 'I believe that this recognition of the profound symbolism of blood is now mysteriously encircling our planet, irresistibly gripping one nation after another' [284].

4 In the case of the individual racist we can, however, show how institutional prejudice may be used to solve personal problems. For a summary of the various explanations of racism and the extent to which they are compatible see Le Vine and Campbell [244].

CHAPTER THREE

THE QUESTION OF BLACK DEPRESSION

Naturally most of the race are care-free, live in the 'here and now' with a limited capacity to recall or profit by experiences of the past. Sadness and depression have little part in his psychological makeup.

> W.M. Bevis, 'Psychological traits of the Southern Negro with observations as to some of his psychoses', in the *American Journal of Psychiatry*, Vol. 1, 1921, pp. 69–78

The experience of depression is familiar – we can all share to some extent someone's unhappiness or despair. It might be assumed then that depression can be easily recognized in all communities. But, precisely because sadness or happiness are everyday occurrences, we already have available cultural mechanisms for understanding them, for modifying them and for incorporating them into our social life. It seems possible that certain patterns of depression are specifically found in industrialized societies. The apparent total absence of depression among the subject peoples of the colonial empires was used to justify the assumption that Africans and Asians were incapable of examining their feelings, had difficulty expressing their emotions and were less likely to have a distinct personality. In this chapter we shall look at some of the difficulties involved in comparing mental experiences of people in different societies and then look at a young student from West Africa who became depressed while studying in Britain.

COLONIAL PSYCHIATRY

Medical theories of racial differences did not play an important part in the justifications for colonization in Africa and Asia.

'Most characteristic of the African native are his lack of apprehension and inability to visualize the future, and the steadfastness of his loyalty and affection' [263]. Such assertions demonstrated a paternalistic security in British cultural superiority (in spite of occasional lapses at the beginning of this century into talk of blood and destiny), rather different from the desperate attempt of whites in America and the Caribbean to ward off the abolition of slavery and black equality. There was, however, a certain ambivalence about whether it really was desirable for the black man to acquire British culture: 'there is no class . . . which is less welcome to the lay Englishman than the "black white man" who has abandoned his racial integrity and is quick to learn European vices' [263]. Kipling regarded the Indian as a colt; when educated he became a mule [399].

French and Portuguese colonial policies in particular emphasized cultural rather than biological distinctions. When their colonies became in theory 'overseas territories' of the metropolitan country, the blacks could become 'French' or 'Portuguese' by a tortuous acceptance of European language and culture, a process aptly described by Frantz Fanon as 'colour blindness'. In the British colonies, segregation was instituted supposedly for non-racial reasons. In his textbook of imperial administration *The Dual Mandate in British Tropical Africa*, Lord Lugard recommended that colonial towns should have 'a segregation of standards, and not a segregation of races' [263]. In practice, land, work, entertainment and sport were segregated in the whole of British Africa until the 1950s.

Some settlers, however, did believe in biological differences. In a recent book, J. C. Carothers repeated his earlier assertions that 'the African mind' has peculiarities all of its own [58]. Carothers, who was castigated by Fanon for his earlier description (in a World Health Organisation report) of Africans as 'lobotomized Europeans', was a psychiatrist and prison medical officer in East Africa. As author of the government White Paper *The Psychology of Mau Mau*, he had suggested that the Kikuyu had an insecure identity and needed firm direction [339]. Pointing out now that the 'popular stereotypes . . . are by no means false', he recapitulates the old studies on skull size, brain cell type and intelligence tests together with new data from the Director of the South African 'National Institute for Personnel Research'. The African, he concludes, has difficulty using symbols or differentiating conscious from unconscious processes, lacks both general principles and a developed superego, and does not see himself as having sustained responsibility for his own actions. Dr Carothers maintains that the adult African persists in patterns of thought appropriate to a European child: 'European and African cultures are not parallel and the African is persisting in a pattern which European man has passed beyond' [58]. French psychiatrists in Africa had suggested that 'the Algierian has no cortex; or more precisely, he is dominated, like the inferior vertebrates, by the diencephalon' [126].

Mental illness in the colonized population was frequently attributed to physical illness or social transition. Accurate estimates of the prevalence of mental illness was difficult. When the first mental hospital was opened in Madagascar, the locals brought in their psychiatrically ill relatives; previously, said the French doctors, they had been killed. A common sequence was that initially no mental illness was found by the white doctors, but later it was remarked that violent explosive reactions (classified as schizophrenic or by local names) were common while depression was rare. These transient psychoses were 'attributed to the limited development of the African brain' [217].

As more psychiatric facilities became available in the colonies, the absence of mental illness was recorded less often. It was realized that better facilities enabled more emotional difficulties to come to light. To determine accurately the exact numbers of people with psychological difficulties or illnesses is difficult even in Britain. Few of the early colonial psychiatrists admitted, as did James Donald in 1876 in the West Indies: 'To institute any comparisons between this country and England of the proportion of insane relative to the population is difficult, owing mainly to the fact that in many cases national peculiarity is mistaken for mental derangement, and also because of our ignorance of the constitution of the inhabitants' [102].

Services for the mentally ill were rudimentary. The few government psychiatrists practised in large prison-like institutions situated near the capital [150]. The mentally ill were brought to the hospital by their relatives. Like mental asylums in Europe of the same period, they were overcrowded and understaffed, offering only rudimentary treatment, usually of a physical nature. Even now many of these hospitals are run without doctors by locally recruited nurses, usually untrained, who, with a paramilitary uniform and ranks such as 'Petty Officer', are little more than guards. At the time of independence few colonial territories had medical schools (there were three in black Africa). New Guinea has had psychiatric services of any type for only twenty years.

Mental hospitals were places where Africans were taken because they were 'mad' and this madness was recognized by the fact that they were violent and antisocial. They were not expected to be treated, and if they recovered this was a matter of chance; recovery was expected to be transient. Many of the mental health ordinances of this era imply a similarity between the 'lunatic and the criminal'. [150]

As late as the 1930s psychiatrically ill Africans were placed in prison [159]. At a period when all mental patients were certified, this certification could only be done by a military doctor [159]. Transcultural psychiatry was

based on work carried out by a host of short-term visitors to Africa with varying ideological and theoretical positions, psychoanalytic, anthropological, sociological and descriptive. This has resulted all too frequently in a wealth of data about some strange ritual of an obscure tribe, analysed with style and erudition but without comment on general trends particularly as they relate to the more mundane aspects of clinical psychiatry. [150]

In the newly independent countries of the Third World, although industrialization, rural development and malnutrition pose greater problems than mental illness, there has been a steady development of psychiatric facilities. The all too commonly adopted solution has been to seal away the mentally ill in large psychiatric hospitals on the European model. New ideas pioneered include collaboration with traditional healers (in Ghana they are organized into a union with official recognition and a training programme) and the establishment of therapeutic communities based on small villages.

MELANCHOLIA

The notion that non-European societies had no emotional disorders at all had been largely abandoned by the beginning of this century. Psychiatrists, however, have continued to believe that such cultures have their own unique patterns of mental illness. These differences were believed to be related to characteristic patterns of child-rearing or particular cultural values. Kraepelin, the originator of the concept of dementia praecox (later called schizophrenia), found that depression was rare in Java [224]. Depression was believed to be rare among American blacks and Africans until the 1960s [327]. Suicide was also thought uncommon. (In fact suicide had been a frequent occurrence among black slaves and Amerindians [92, 450].) Earlier this century one out of every hundred thousand Africans ended his or her life – a tenth of the British figure. When suicide did occur it was supposed to be the socially accepted solution to particular problems, as in Japan or the Pacific island of Tikopia, rather than the despairing act of an isolated and unsupported individual, as it was conceived of in Europeans [31, 135].

The reported suicide rate of most immigrants in Britain is greater than that of the British-born. An exception to this appears to be the Caribbean-born community: the suicide rate of West Indian men is 85 per cent that of the general male population; for West Indian women it is nearly half that of other women (Table 4, p. 92). Depression is still diagnosed less commonly among West Indian and Asian patients in psychiatric hospitals than among the British-born although this does not reflect the actual occurrence of depression in the community [54, 72, 74].

Depressive illness was found to be particularly frequent among some European communities such as the Jews and the Protestant Hutterites of the northern United States [112]. Depression was said to require a degree of introspection and verbalization; it was the malady of a more mature and sophisticated society [407]. Blacks could not experience melancholy because they had a simpler brain: they were incapable of blushing, not because of their skin colour but because of their mentality [389]. The prevailing stereotype was of a happy-go-lucky, feckless child of nature, with irrepressible high spirits, unburdened by the heavy responsibilities of civilization, with little self-control and an apparently boundless sexual appetite [407]. To the psychiatrist it appeared that 'the negro mind does not dwell upon unpleasant subjects: he [sic] is irresponsible, unthinking, easily aroused to happiness, and his unhappiness is transitory, disappearing as a child's when other interests attract his attention. He is happy-go-lucky not philosophical. His peculiar mental attitude is not the result of a knowledge that his poverty, his social position, his unhealthy and cheerless surroundings cannot be bettered, therefore are to be borne cheerfully: but that of a simple nature which gives little thought to the future and desires only the gratification of the present. Responsibility is accepted thoughtlessly and is readily laid aside; its weight is not felt nor does it occasion any anxiety. The simplest amusements distract him, and he gains pleasure from occasions which should rather give rise to sadness. Depression is rarely encountered even under circumstances in which a white person would be overwhelmed by it. The expression of suicidal ideas is seldom heard, and suicide is an extremely rare occurrence in the negro race, though it is not unknown: indeed, within the past year a negro patient in this institution committed suicide . . .' [163].

If the black was less burdened mentally he could bear a heavier burden physically: 'deeply embedded in European consciousness is the idea that individuals who suffer melancholia are especially sensitive and intellectually aware' [327]. The belief that intellect and responsibility entail depression has been common since the Romantic period, with its emphasis on the terrible price to be paid by melancholic genius and morbidly heightened sensitivity. Depression was the result of the higher biological and social role of the white man; it became a symbol of his responsibility and superiority. Even in the seventeenth century, depression implied refinement, as Ben Johnson tells us in *Every Man in His Humour*.

The black in the British Empire was regarded like the Afro-American as cunning and infantile but faithful and superstitious and insensitive to pain [399]. Black West Indians, said the Jamaican historian Edward Long, carried out their work 'perhaps no better than an orang-outang might, with a little pain, be brought to do' [284].

The black man did not even possess an individual mind but shared a communal mind, attuned to the elementary collective consciousness of his tribe [250]. He was supposed to make little distinction between himself and the outside world; he believed his actions caused thunderstorms and his life was determined by the stars. Like a child he believed the world revolved around him. Mental illness in his case was not the inwardly directed disturbance of a finely attuned mechanism, as it was for the white, but an undifferentiated 'primitive psychosis' usually involving violence against his fellow.

Emotional difficulties which in the civilized led to self-doubt and questioning apparently passed unnoticed by the primitive or caused *conversion hysteria*, the mimicking of physical illnesses such as paralysis or blindness. Conversion hysteria is traditionally believed by psychiatrists to be the expression of mental conflicts which have not been verbalized or consciously appreciated. The civilized man assimilated and worked through his conflicts while the primitive split them off and dissociated himself from them. While anxiety and fear were common among the British soldiers in India, Indian soldiers under the same conditions developed hysterical reactions; they appeared to deny their fears [432]. Such studies were used to demonstrate 'the traditional oriental concern with loss of face' in contrast to the supposed capacity of the European to deal with unacceptable feelings rationally.

A limited vocabulary of self-exploration has also been said to be characteristic of working-class Europeans. Depression following a specific stress was found to be common among the middle classes in America, while the lower classes had hypochondriacal complaints, malfunctioning bowels and diffuse pains in their limbs accompanied by a general worry that there was something wrong with their body [190]. The middle classes gave a specific reason for their depression, while the working class were seen as being unwell in a rather 'non-specific' manner. 'Hypochondriacal compaints' are often associated with a stereotype of other cultural groups: the English traditionally regard the French as obsessed with their livers and their digestion.

The more accurately other societies are observed the greater the extent to which depressive illness is discovered. Why did the earlier studies suggest that depression was uncommon among non-Europeans? We shall look at three possibilities:

(i)   Depressive illnesses did occur but they were not noticed.
(ii) Depression was missed because it didn't appear to the Europeans as depression.

(iii)   There has been a real change and depression is now more common.

(i)   *Why depression may have been missed*
Severe depression is commonly found among people later in life. The populations of the developing countries have a different age structure from Europe: fewer people survive to reach late middle age because of disease and malnutrition. Since a small percentage reach the age of greatest risk of depression, the community as a whole will show few examples.

Different types of abnormal behaviour have different effects. The vagrant psychotic in Britain wandering about and talking to himself is certainly seen as ill, but no one is likely to call an ambulance. Deviant behaviour which does not break the law (although it may well break unofficial rules of normative conduct) is not in Britain a cause for alerting social agencies unless the individual is seen to be in immediate physical danger. Behaviour characterized by physical violence, assaults or destruction of property (that is to say deviant behaviour of an *overactive* rather than *underactive* type) is likely to lead to help being sought: the community cannot attempt to cope with this behaviour as they might with depression and withdrawal. If the community has to be disrupted to the extent that a policeman is called and the patient is sent many miles by difficult transport to a distant mental hospital, he has to have made quite a nuisance of himself. If a community has few psychiatric facilities, they are likely to be allocated to those people whose emotional difficulties are the most conspicuously deviant and whose behaviour is the most disruptive. In view of the primitive conditions of the colonial hospitals, admission was dreaded, and it was probably easier for a depressed person to avoid admission and persuade the community to look after him than it was for a patient whose mental illness was more disruptive or embarrassing [150]. 'In the Caribbean, while schizophrenia is regarded as supernatural, depression is natural' [213]; it may thus be tolerated as part of everyday life.

Certainly fewer West Indians than whites are admitted to hospital in Britain with depression, but to interpret this fully we need to know more about the attitudes of both blacks and whites towards mental illness, mental hospitals and psychiatry, how they perceive depression and when and how they find it necessary to consult a doctor. Recent studies in America and Africa suggest that, not surprisingly, black people do get depressed. With better hospital facilities and less blatant racism, they are more likely to seek medical advice and less likely to be cared for by their community alone [327].

(ii) Different types of depression

Depression may be missed if we always look for it as it appears in Europe.

One of the characteristics of depression in Britain is *guilt*: mildly depressed people are often self-critical and likely to blame themselves for having become ill. A more severely depressed patient often believes that his illness has brought terrible shame on the family or even that he has committed unspeakable sins which will be punished with eternal damnation. These awful crimes are often of a trivial nature. St Augustine appears to have gone through an emotional crisis in which he became excessively preoccupied with his childhood stealing of apples [14]. Only with recovery from depression do these peccadilloes recede into their usual perspective. Some cultures, such as the Christianity of Augustine's time, permit such morbid emotional experiences to be integrated into everyday beliefs. Delusions of guilt are particularly characteristic of European societies [293]. They are now less common in Europe than they were fifty years ago, perhaps owing to the declining hold of religious belief [243]. We know that social expectations can modify even the most vivid fundamental experiences; in West Africa depression of even a mild type may be associated with hallucinations, a type of experience which may be a cultural norm in certain societies, in particular crises or in certain religious settings [444]. In Europe hallucinations are traditionally associated with schizophrenia although they can occur at other times.

A society may use physical illness as a model for emotional experience and pay particular attention to such changes in bodily feelings as 'butterflies in the stomach', 'lumps in the throat' or the loss of energy which occur in depression. A study of black and white psychiatric patients suggested that the black patients were less likely to experience isolated feelings of anxiety, depression or irritability as separate experiences [240]; the assumption was that blacks experience these three states as more similar to each other than do whites. An emphasis on dividing subjective states into a variety of verbal categories is not of course a mark of superiority, only of a particular mode of perception. It is anyway not limited to the Western middle class: some Australian aborigines have an extensive lexicon of grief and depression ranging from disappointment to extreme melancholy [285].

What use do we make in practice of distinctions between tension, disquiet, stress, anxiety, nervousness and agitation? The three French concepts *anxiété*, *angoisse* and *inquiétude* are described in everyday English by the single idea *anxiety*. The Gestalt school of psychiatry believes that depression is in fact due to losing touch with bodily feelings by undue emphasis on verbalization. Every culture structures its experiences with the available cultural tools and even the experiences of psychosis can be expressed in terms of religion, family or social conflicts [427]. Black immigrants feel that 'the emotional life of the Western man, and more particularly of the Englishman, lacks the depth and intensity of for example the Asian or the African' [310].

A member of an ethnic minority group in Britain knows that his doctor is something to do with hospitals, medicines and physical illnesses, and may feel that the best way of communicating with him will be to talk his language of bodily complaints. Like the psychoanalyst, however, he may personally think it more significant that he dreamt he had intercourse with his sister. A language of pains and malfunctioning organs will prove to be easiest for both patient and doctor to talk together; the one will be as little interested in the dream as the other is in distinguishing anxiety from depression. Recent studies of depression in Asian and African patients suggest that Indian patients are likely to be agitated and have bodily complaints. Africans also have physical complaints and are less likely than the British to have suicidal or guilty thoughts [35, 405].

Frantz Fanon eloquently describes the immigrant in Europe who, lonely, bewildered and cut off from his cultural roots, appeals to the initially sympathetic white doctor [127]. A vague series of physical symptoms seems to evaporate with the doctor's questioning and probing; the patient grows more nervous and the doctor irritated. In despair the patient seeks different doctors, anxiously trying to convince them of *something*. The medical community builds up its picture of the inarticulate black malingerer: the 'North African syndrome'. In Britain Asian women are allocated the similar 'Begum syndrome' [147].

Depression, then, is recorded by psychiatrists only if patients actually complain of it by name or if they have delusions of guilt, both highly culture-bound values. Can we say that depression exists without being recognized by name? One solution is to see if there is a bodily change in depressive illness which can then be measured in different communities without needing to use words. We could see how this overlaps with culturally recognized states in different languages. We do find a pattern of physical symptoms in depression: sleep disturbances such as waking early in the morning, constipation, loss of energy and lassitude, difficulty in concentrating, loss of appetite and decreased sexual desire. Most of these symptoms were originally called neurasthenic. In Europe they are associated with subjective depression, which is recognized as such by the patient. If we use these measures of depression, we find that there are often approximately equal numbers of depressed people in different countries [405]. Symptoms very similar to these were recorded in Africa and Australia in people dying of 'Voodoo death' (who often indeed demonstrated a considerable degree of guilt [270]).

What appears to have happened is that doctors did see patients with these 'physical' complaints, but put them down to physical causes such as malnutrition and ignored the possibility of depression. It is of course much easier when confronted with difficulties of people emotionally distant to understand them in organic terms. As we have seen, foreignborn psychiatrists in Britain may initially feel safer with biological rather than sociocultural explanations. In Britain, old people who are depressed are likely to be seen as physically senile [349].

Is it meaningful for us to talk of 'depression' if it is not verbalized as such? If we use only physiological measures such as heart-rate, the electrical conductivity of the palms or the flow of blood in the arm (which all alter in different emotional states), we find that they do not differentiate between emotional states even as different as fear and anger. Depression seems to require words to describe it. 'Emotions' tend to assume bodily changes which alter the way we appreciate the outside world [28]. More 'cognitive' states of mind (such as feelings of persecution) appear even less likely to have physical concommitants.[1]

(iii) *Are patterns of depression changing?*
Patterns of mental illness can change. The suicide rate among

blacks in New York is higher than it is for whites [182] and guilt is found among depressed blacks as often as among depressed whites [413]. Depression is now commonly reported in the Caribbean and Africa (indeed it is *more* common than in London [309]) and the mass suicides at the Peoples' Temple in Guyana appear to have put an end to the myth that only whites kill themselves [66]; this episode has however been described as mass hysteria, as opposed to such 'heroic' suicides as Masada. It is possible that depression may be associated with prestige. Self-determination results in greater self-esteem [327]. Earlier theories had suggested that because Africans did not become anxious, they were incapable of responsibility. It seems more likely that they were not made anxious through responsibility because they never had the opportunity. More 'western' services alone do not necessarily mean that we find more depression: the current South African opinion is that subjective depression is rare among blacks [49]. It is significant that two of the features of 'primitive depression', agitation and paranoia, are commonly found in depression in an isolated and disadvantaged group in British society – the aged.

MARGARET OKUNDE

Migrants pass from one set of cultural values to another. We shall now look at how different types of mental illness can be attempts at solutions of a single problem.

Margaret was born in northern Nigeria, the youngest child (and the only daughter) of six. Her father was the local village schoolmaster. Although their community was traditionally Islamic, in the near-by provincial town Christian Nigerians from other regions mixed freely with Moslems. Both groups were discarding their traditional way of life in favour of a Western urban life-style. The typically strict family atmosphere was relaxed a little for Margaret, who was spoilt, treated as irresponsible, but allowed her own way on most matters.

Her father's friends were the head of the local dispensary, the government health inspector and neighbouring teachers. Conversation at home centred on the political future of the country, on government public health campaigns and on expanding education programmes. Little attention was paid to Islamic precepts but much to the prestige conferred by degrees, diplomas and doctorates. Margaret was allowed to participate in the men's discussions, a sign of the family's urban aspirations, but a scandal to the neighbours. Her elder brothers all passed through secondary school and went on to become teachers and local government officials. One went to university. The family had expected that Margaret would marry locally and settle down near her parents (her father was sixty when she was born). However, eight years before we first met her, when she was nineteen, Margaret decided that she too wanted a career and that a modern woman should have a training and responsible job in her own right before marrying.

After a lot of discussion it was agreed that Margaret could continue her studies in England as she wished, although she had passed in only two out of her eight school subjects. Her brothers agreed to contribute, although by now they were bringing up their own families. Margaret felt very conscious of the sacrifices everyone was making for her. She arrived in London, enrolled at a college of further education and found a place in a student hostel. The plan was that she would take some more 'O' levels, qualify as a clerical civil servant and, after some experience, return home and settle down; she would be the first woman in her community who had studied away from home, her independent status would be assured and no husband would dare banish her to the kitchen. She would be able to teach the other women 'to be modern' and help establish services such as child health centres.

The studies did not go very well and by the time she was twenty-three Margaret had passed only three more exams, in biology, government and public administration. Her father died and her mother went to live with an older sister. The family home broke up but her brothers continued to support her, not without appeals to her to hurry and finish her studies. One of them came to work in London. Margaret decided that she was not studying properly because of the noise in the hostel and moved into a flat. The next year she fell in love with a fellow Nigerian student and they started living together. James wanted to get married, but Margaret, still valuing her independence, was anxious to complete her studies first. Her brother was furious over the affair and a family quarrel was only just avoided; he promised not to let the relatives in West Africa know.

The year after, a baby girl was born and immediately fostered out so that Margaret would continue her studies. James was unhappy about this and Margaret accused him of wanting to satisfy his 'African feelings' by having her bear his children and cook his food for him while he gained 'Western prestige' as an architect. His studies were going better than hers and he accused her of jealousy. They moved from their flat to a bedsitter so as to afford the fostering. The next year Margaret had a miscarriage three months before her next set of exams; she failed in all subjects. She became depressed and found it increasingly difficult to study. Her boyfriend said she was depressed because she was guilty about her daughter. Her brother said she was depressed because she had disgraced the family. Her general practitioner said she was depressed about her exams and gave her Valium. Her relationship with James deteriorated. She began to have difficulty concentrating and wondered what was interfering with her mind. Could it be that he was in some mysterious way preventing her from studying so she would have to stay at home and cook for him? He laughed at her when she suggested it and pointed out she seemed to be getting rather 'African' ideas herself. She began to feel nervous when walking down the street. People seemed to be talking about her and his colleagues started to look at her in a rather peculiar way.

Her doctor started her on some different tablets and, feeling better, she decided to leave the room and her boyfried and start by herself again. She packed her belongings and went to see her brother. He said there was not enough space for both her and his family. Not being able to afford a hotel and not finding any cheap accommodation, she returned to the bedsitter. Her boyfried was still out of the house, and deciding she had totally ruined her life and let her family down she took her remaining tablets. Her suicide attempt failed.

Two days later, her boyfriend phoned the general practitioner to ask him to take Margaret to a psychiatric hospital as Margaret had, he said, become insane. She spent her first day on the ward running about and tearing her clothes off, singing at the top of her voice, with a terrified look in her eyes, and occasionally making rather ineffectual assaults on the other patients and nurses. However, after a few days she seemed to be more happy in hospital and told us that she would now be safe: James had put spells on her so that people would hate her, he had poisoned her food and killed her baby. Evil forces sent by a *babalawo*, a sorcerer employed by James, were 'keeping her primitive' and preventing her from achieving her final diploma; she could hear them telling her what a bad mother she had been and how they were going to torment her. Margaret denied their accusations and said she was being tormented without justification. The voices stopped within a few days of coming into hospital and she regained her normal composure although still complaining of her lover's schemes. She still had difficulty in thinking, talking to others and relating to the other patients. She felt she was irritable and had no energy. She refused an offer of psychotherapy when she left the ward, saying that her problems came from outside herself and she was sure that she could obtain her diploma at the next attempt. She said she did not feel guilty about the baby, which had arrived because of her boyfriend's wish to have a family. To our surprise she wanted to return to him, although still accusing him of witchcraft. He told us that he saw no difficulties between them except that Margaret would not look after the baby and complained about cooking for him.

It seemed clear that James was trying to get the best of both worlds. He certainly refused her the right to continue her studies, and in spite of his protestations of being 'progressive' persisted in trying to force her into a domestic role against her obvious wishes. Was he practising witchcraft on her? We were not sure but, on balance, felt it was unlikely. It may be argued that he was only treating her as most men treat women in Britain, but for Margaret the situation was a conflict between Britain and Africa, between 'modernity' and 'primitivism'.

We wondered how clear Margaret was about her own motives. In spite of her denial of guilt (or indeed any responsibility for what had happened) she was unhappy about her relationship and her little girl. She was also very conscious of her responsibilities to her family. She underestimated the difficulties of the studies but, having made more and more compromises with her own beliefs and upbringing, had concentrated all her energy on becoming 'qualified' to the exclusion of other interests and experiences. Both of them had difficulties in evolving a life-style out of the available patterns of the two cultures. They would perhaps have benefited from marital therapy with a British and an African therapist. They refused the offer and we don't know whether Margaret will succeed in her ambitions, whether she will modify them or whether she has started a career as a mental patient, explaining her failure as due to 'witchcraft' or maybe 'depression'.

We felt we had a reasonable understanding of her difficulties because we had time to get to know her well. If the doctor was ignorant about her society, her ambitions and experiences, then her arrival at the hospital with apparently bizarre behaviour, hallucinations and accusations of persecution would probably have led to a diagnosis of schizophrenia. It is interesting that Margaret initially tried to adjust to her difficulties by a pattern characteristic of British culture, complaining of depression to her relatives, visiting her general practitioner, taking tranquillizers and even an overdose. It seems that when these failed, she developed an acute psychotic reaction, not uncommon in African society [259]. It is ironic that she used an 'African' explanation for her difficulties in moving to a European society. With the norms of expected behaviour in the hospital and the support elicited by her original mode of coping (depression), she soon again became typically depressed. It is rare for patients from a rural environment in the Third World without Margaret's educational aspirations to show initially 'European' modes of coping. Only after they have been in hospital on many occasions do explanations in terms of witchcraft give place to self-referrals with depression [259].

THE SICK ROLE

Whether depressed people go on to take their own lives depends on the support offered by their community and also how their status as a sick person is recognized. Some approaches to the depressed person may help to make sense of his or her situation and perhaps make it more bearable. The recognition of a certain status (such as being the victim of a witch) entails treatment including attention and support. Among fundamentalist sects, depression may be regarded as a divine test, a trial sent, like the sufferings of Job, to test the individual's capacity to maintain faith in the Deity [112]. Each culture uses what we call mental illness for its own purposes and the symptoms are moulded accordingly (see Chapter 9). The Malay who threatens to run *amok* and the Latin American peasant with the *susto* anxiety reaction are both using ways of dealing with tension acceptable to their own society [217].

Psychiatrists conceive of severe depression as due to a chemical disturbance of the brain. Although this point of view relieves the patient of personal responsibility so that effective anti-depressant drugs may be taken, it does deprive the individual experience of any meaningful significance, possibly leading to greater isolation. Depression involves the whole person and cannot be split off like a broken arm.

Suicide itself can be encouraged as an acceptable means of dealing with certain situations, as in Japan, where feelings of guilt are uncommon in depression [293]. In different societies

> suicide . . . may be a light matter, the recourse of anyone who has suffered a slight rebuff, an act that occurs constantly. It may be the highest and noblest act a wise man can perform. The very tale of it, on the other hand, may be a matter for incredulous mirth, and the act itself impossible to conceive as a human possibility. Or it may be a crime punishable by law or regarded as a sin against the gods. [29]

If it seems obvious to us that suicide should be regarded as the consequence of an illness – depression – we should remember that it is less than thirty years since it was a crime in Britain: the survivor of an overdose of drugs might awaken to find a policeman by the bedside.

Social expectations of the way sick people behave have an effect on the way illness is expressed. We found that on the Caribbean island of Antigua the accepted picture of the insane individual is someone who is *dangerous*. Over 80 per cent of the psychiatric patients in the hospital were taken there by the police, while in neighbouring Guadeloupe, where the typical mental patient is popularly seen as someone who creates a public disturbance but who is not necessarily dangerous, less than a quarter of the patients are involuntary. There are approximately equal rates of admission in both islands, but Guadeloupe has greater psychiatric resources – more doctors, clinics and qualified nurses. Where there are few facilities, it seems that to gain access to them one has to pose a threat to the community. There were no significant differences between the ˙patients of the two countries once they were in hospital. The 'dangerous mental patient' is a culturally patterned sterotype to which the patients initially conform and is not just the consequence of different illnesses or delayed treatment. In this case limited medical resources influence the character of mental illness via communal beliefs rather than by directly causing more serious illness. When both the services provided and the beliefs about mental illness come to resemble those of the industrialized countries, we would expect that the patients more and more frequently demonstrate 'Western' patterns of psychological disturbance.

Twice as many black psychiatric patients as white in Britain are involuntary (p. 57). Apart from medical insensitivity or prejudice we must consider the possibility that the patients have not adopted the white British way of 'going crazy'; West Indian patients are said to be more 'disturbed' on admission to hospital than are whites [361]. This is not to say that it is simply the consequence of their background: black Americans have to show greater mental disturbance than do whites before they are referred to a doctor [377], and a similar pattern may occur in Britain for the Afro-Caribbean community.

GUILT, AGGRESSION AND SOCIETY

Other social features may influence patterns of mental illness. We have seen that in industrialized societies *guilt*, a cultural variable, is common in people who are depressed. Do societies which encourage guilt have high rates of depression? The Protestant and Jewish religions in particular have been singled out as conducive to guilt: they are associated with quite a high frequency of depression [132, 293]. However, West Indians, with low reported rates of depression in Britain, are more likely to belong to a fundamentalist Protestant church than is the average white Briton. It is difficult to say how religious beliefs can focus attention on guilt – perhaps by an emphasis on personal responsibility and salvation. In North Africa two thirds of depressed patients in one study felt guilty: guilt was not, however, found to be related to religious belief but to the degree of literacy [114].

It has been suggested that some cultures educate children by 'shaming' techniques and others by 'guilt-inducing' methods [99].

'Guilt-inducing' societies would be likely to have a greater amount of depression than shaming societies. All cultures, however, probably use both methods to a greater or lesser extent. Among the British, guilt-inducing methods seem to be concerned with sexual matters: while obligations to parents are encouraged by shaming techniques; in Japan the reverse is true [99, 207].

There is some evidence that depression may result from the inhibition of aggressive responses to frustration [210]. It has been suggested that children who have been disciplined by punishment tend to direct their aggression outwards and hold others responsible for any difficulties they later encounter (the seeds of paranoia), while children from whom affection is systematically withdrawn are likely to hold themselves responsible (the seeds of depression). The so-called 'Victorian' Caribbean family has thus been held responsible for the comparative frequency of paranoid reactions among West Indians. Paranoia is, however, as we shall see in the next chapter, a common response in any disadvantaged or isolated group, including linguistic and ethnic minorities and the deaf. Witchcraft beliefs have been said to facilitate paranoid thinking by enabling individuals to blame others when things go wrong [234]. Aggression is thus diverted on to others and the individual himself does not feel responsible and is hence not likely to become depressed. However, witchcraft beliefs are compatible with a strong cultural encouragement of the experience of guilt, as they were in seventeenth-century Puritan England [291]. In Ghana, where depression and suicide are not uncommon, women frequently become depressed and *accuse themselves* of being witches [131], and although rural communities in the Sudan 'believe in the evil eye [they] generally appear to feel that suffering is due to some fault of theirs' [122]. It has been suggested that guilt is encouraged in Ghanaian society by the abrupt weaning of children and in holding the individual accountable for his actions to a greater extent than in neighbouring West African communities [425]. It may be that historically witchcraft beliefs in the form of self-accusations were a prelude to the development of guilt [291]. Belief in witchcraft and witchcraft accusations are not necessarily a very emotional matter anyway: they can be a mundane, almost banal, way of regulating everyday affairs [121].

The idea of internally and externally directed aggression has been used to explain the relationship between homicide and suicide in different cultures and at different periods. Suicide is rare in wartime when killing others is socially acceptable. The psychoanalytical idea that there is a 'quantity' of aggression which can be released on different objects is supported by the finding that in Britain a third of murderers go on to kill themselves.

Fanon describes the common jibe of the French in Algeria that the Arabs were too busy killing each other to be responsible: they had a cultural 'need for blood' and, having no inner life, killed other people rather than themselves when depressed. There was, however, a drop in intra-communal violence when the Algerians started fighting against the French [126]. To distinguish societies simply by whether they employ inwardly or outwardly directed aggressive strategies ignores the difference between aggression which is directed against one's own community and aggression directed against another group (and the possibility that this might change). There is a difference between violence as a simple release of aggression and violence as a motivated means to another end. Childbattering has recently been found to be less frequent in Northern Ireland than in England [181]. Generalizations about 'violence' which consider it only as the release of aggression ignore the social dimension in favour of a rather mechanistic theory.

We cannot generalize about why some ethnic groups have a low suicide rate without a knowledge of their previous cultural norms, techniques of education and the interplay within the family between different types of parental role, parental dominance and family size. Patterns of behaviour learnt in one particular cultural situation can be displaced into another system. Black patients in London (such as Beatrice Jackson – p. 227) who develop acute psychotic reactions as a result of racism or personal difficulties direct their resentment (in the form of paranoid delusions involving witchcraft) not against representatives of white society such as the police but against their own black neighbours. As this anger dies away they become depressed; the hospital situation appears conducive to aggressive feelings being turned inwards.

It would be surprising if different rates of depression could easily be related to a single variable. If capitalism is associated with the subjective experience of depression it is not easy to explain the link. Possibly the work ethic makes an individual feel a valid and significant individual only in relation to his productivity. The universal physical features of depression, disturbed sleep, loss of energy and difficulty in concentration, might lead to a lowered capacity for work and thus a subjective feeling of personal worthlessness. Unemployment is certainly associated with depression [324].

In this chapter we have begun to see how mental illness has to be understood against particular patterns of coping. Rudimentary services lead not merely to underestimation of the extent of psychological difficulties but actually seem to influence the way these difficulties occur. Each society is likely to encourage a characteristic patterning of mental illness. While we cannot rely on the universal value of one particular way of describing emotion, we cannot depend either upon physical measurements. Reported subjective experiences have always to be considered in relation to the available cultural ways of perceiving the world and to the particular social organization of a community.

While emphasis on internal mental states is not limited to Europeans, the way emotions are expressed and recognized does vary with culture. We have seen how difficult it is to decide even so simple a question as whether another person is 'depressed'. Among the ways societies appear to influence the expression of sadness are the emphasis placed on guilt and the way one is expected to deal with hostile feelings.

NOTE

1 We have here considerably simplified the old question of the external validity of internal mental states, and their relation, if any, to physiological changes. For a more detailed account of these questions see the essays in Gustafson [171]. Part of the problem is that 'depression' refers to A, the name of a subjective mental state familiar to all of us in this society, but also to B, the name of a pathological state of mind (or mental illness) in which depression A appears to be a predominant feature. It is possible that depressive illness B does not in fact inevitably involve subjective depression A, which is a particular *social* concept used to explain it. In this case the name 'depressive illness' is rather a misnomer. Even if we are considering only the subjective state A, the fact that we have a name for it suggests that it is really qualitatively different (as we appear to appreciate it). What is

the relation of this hypothetical state to the verbal structuring of our experience? What would we feel if we did not have the word? We can side-step the question if we say that 'emotion words' such as depression are nouns which only suggest entities while they really refer to tendencies which manifest themselves predominantly externally (including physiological changes) [362]. If we look at external behaviour only, we can avoid the whole problem of the 'real nature' of these mental states which we are trying to translate into other cultures. In practical psychiatry, however, we are concerned with the empathic understanding of another in his terms and the necessity of correlating this with the experience of others. We return to the necessity of 'translation' whether this is logically acceptable or not.

CHAPTER FOUR

MENTAL ILLNESS AMONG IMMIGRANTS TO BRITAIN

HAMLET: Ay, marry, why was he sent into England?
FIRST CLOWN: Why, because a' was mad; a' shall recover his
wits there; or, if a' do not, 'tis no great matter there.
HAMLET: Why?
FIRST CLOWN: 'Twill not be seen in him there; there the men
are as mad as he.

Hamlet, Act V, Scene 1

Moving from one society to another caused emotional difficulties
for Margaret Okunde. In this chapter we shall look at some of
the different ways migration is believed to be related to mental
illness. So far we have been largely concerned with migrants from
the New Commonwealth, but we shall see that there are
psychological problems involved in moving from one European
country to another and even in moving about inside the same
country.

Is migration always followed by emotional difficulties? Are
they related to the stresses of migration itself or do they occur
because the sort of people who migrate are unstable? Are
migrants liable to any particular type of psychiatric illness? How
important for their adjustment are the reasons which led them to
move and the types of communities they form afterwards?

MIGRATION AND MENTAL ILLNESS

Even when immigration is encouraged for economic reasons,
attitudes to newly arrived foreigners are ambivalent. While their
labour is welcome, migrants are expected to conform to the
customs of their new country as soon as possible. The country of
adoption, especially at times of crisis and insecurity, may doubt

the ability or even desire of the immigrants to become full citizens.

Countries such as the United States, whose development depended on continuous migration, were always concerned about the type of immigrant they were getting. Only poor, disadvantaged and exiled people migrated: would they be able to adapt? As early as 1648 immigrants had to show they would not become 'public charges' [302]. In the 1840s an American anti-immigration movement persuaded the government to see how many immigrants had ended up in the state mental asylums. The numbers were far greater than might have been expected, and it was suggested that some European countries were deliberately using emigration to get rid of their mentally ill. Some doctors felt that America had been flooded with 'the scourings of Europe with their vicious inheritance because the character of the government and institutions of the United States is such as to attract the Paranoiacs, since they are fertile project makers, and see in the United States a great field for all their projects' (quoted in Ødegaard [302]).

By 1882 psychiatrically ill people were prohibited from migrating to America: anyone in whom mental illness was detected within a year of arrival was liable to deportation. Later, this period was extended to three years providing it could be shown 'that the illness was caused by events or conditions prior to migration'. That has been the nub of the question ever since. In contemporary Britain mentally ill (and homosexual) immigrants are denied entry.

Certain groups of immigrants in various countries are more likely to be treated for psychiatric disorders than non-immigrants. Is this because: (a) potentially mentally ill people are more likely than others to migrate (the selection hypothesis)? Or because (b) the process of immigration itself causes mental illness (the stress hypothesis)?

Doctors initially favoured the first suggestion: immigrants came from 'tainted' stock. Each country contributed its own particular taint: the Irish were liable to 'terminal dementia', the Germans and Scandinavians to depression, Jews to 'hidden sexual complexes', while West Indians in New York were prone to delusions of persecution [302].

By the beginning of this century America had extended the ban on immigrants who were mentally ill to exclude alcoholics, psychopaths and people over the age of sixteen who were illiterate [302]. Within a few years immigrants were admitted only in proportion to the numbers from the various countries of origin already settled in the United States. Medical and psychiatric controls were thus an intermediate step between a period of comparatively unrestricted immigration and restrictions on what were overtly political grounds. Explanations of the mental ill-health of immigrants as the residue of 'tainted stock' were abandoned when it was found that the rate of mental illness in the children of immigrants to America was intermediate between that of their parents and that of the population as a whole [368]. Interest turned instead to the difficulties experienced by settlers in a new country – poverty, a different society with new values and norms, and often a new language. Perhaps the stress of migration caused mental illness?

Travellers, the isolated and the uprooted were believed to suffer from a disorder known as *Nostalgia* [346]. It was first described during the Thirty Years War in the seventeenth century among Spanish soldiers in Flanders who had little prospect of leave. The symptoms included dejection, fever, palpitations and anxiety. The patient recovered on being sent home. Each episode was brought on by memories of home; among Scottish soldiers it was precipitated by hearing the bagpipes. Nostalgia seemed to be related to the culture of origin: soldiers from the Swiss pastoral area of Appenzell were more susceptible than those from commercially minded Glarus. Nostalgia was observed during the Retreat from Moscow, among the Swiss mercenaries of the Papal Guard and even as late as the American Civil War. It then seemed to vanish. Incidentally no one had thought to look for it among the uprooted black plantation slaves. We know, however, that those West Indian slaves who were brought from Africa were more than twice as likely to be psychiatrically ill as those born on the plantations [149].

The first systematic attempt to investigate the rival merits of the 'selection' and the 'stress' hypotheses was that by the Norwegian psychiatrist Ødegaard [302]. He looked both at Norwegians who had emigrated to the United States and at the Norwegian population in Norway. Schizophrenia appeared more common in those who emigrated. He suggested that this was because people who were liable to become ill were the ones who were most likely to migrate (the selection˙ hypothesis).

He came to this conclusion for two reasons. Few immigrants became mentally ill in the first year after migrating, when stresses might be expected to be greatest; and examination of the hospital notes of the migrants who became ill suggested that they had always had a rather unusual personality. According to their relatives they had been sensitive people, out of touch with the world, yet they were restless and ambitious and despised 'the bird in the hand'.[1] It now seems, however, that most people who become schizophrenic have not had a previous abnormal personality [434]. The other point – that stress is greatest immediately after migration – is debatable. Because we cannot easily define, let alone measure, this type of 'stress', it is difficult to be certain. It is possible that the pressures on a migrant are greatest, not immediately after a change which has been anticipated and prepared for, but after some years of settlement if it has become clear that the new life in the adopted country has fallen short of expectations.

IS THERE AN 'IMMIGRANT MENTAL ILLNESS'?

If there is a characteristic type of psychological difficulty repeatedly found among migrants, it seems likely that the stress of immigration itself plays an important and specific part in their breakdown. If, on the other hand, migrants are liable to the same patterns of illness as the pre-migration population, the fact of migration itself may be less important. Is there any evidence of such an 'immigrant breakdown syndrome' similar to the old idea of Nostalgia?

It seems unlikely. Immigrants tend to develop broadly the same type of psychological difficulties as do their relatives back home and the natives of their country of settlement: depression, anxiety and the more serious mental illnesses such as schizophrenia or manic-depressive psychosis. There does not seem to be a separate type of illness to which immigrants are more liable because they are immigrants.

The mental illness of immigrants, however, often takes on a *persecutory* aspect. Paranoid reactions have been noted in many groups of migrants, including West Indians in Britain and the United States, German-speaking servants in England in the 1920s, Arab immigrants in France, European immigrants in

Australia, post-war refugees in Norway and Poles, Hungarians, West Africans and Ceylonese in Britain [259]. In a group of 250 psychotic patients in our own hospital, we found that no less than 56 per cent of those who came from New Commonwealth countries had some type of persecutory delusion. They believed they were the victims of a plot by their neighbours, that they were being accused of spying or that witchcraft was being practised against them. In the same study, European immigrants from Italy, Cyprus and Germany were unlikely to have beliefs of being persecuted, even those who had come to Britain as refugees. It seems possible then that a cause of feelings of persecution is colour prejudice. Perhaps 'delusions of persecution' are merely a strong reiteration of the experience of discrimination. West Indians in the Caribbean, unlike those who emigrate to Europe or America, are not normally likely to develop feelings of persecution. In fact delusions of persecution in the Caribbean are only common among the *white* minority, who often have complex paranoid beliefs concerning race, colour and ethnic identity [427].

To become suspicious is of course a natural response to situations in which one is unclear about what is going on or why certain things are happening to one. An explanation for paranoia in immigrants may be the difficulty of speaking a new langauge [5]. This did not seem to be the case with our own patients, as those who were most likely to develop feelings of persecution were those who presumably had the greatest facility in speaking English – the West Indians and Africans. European immigrants were not especially paranoid. It may be that an important influence on the development of suspicion is not total ignorance of English so much as having to use a different style of English in which one's expectation of being understood is not fulfilled. Another group of people who have high expectations of communication but meet difficulties in practice are the deaf, who are also particularly liable to develop paranoid illnesses.

An illness involving delusions of persecution was said to occur specifically in immigrants – the 'aliens' paranoid reaction' [218]. This was a short-lived episode lasting a few days in which a rather confused and bewildered patient became increasingly suspicious and then terrified, engaging in bizarre behaviour in public such as stripping off clothes and conversing with various hallucinatory voices. (A similar illness – 'jungle madness' – was seen among

Europeans in the tropics.) This type of reaction often has a religious flavour and contains elements related to the pre-migration culture, such as a confession that certain cultural rules have been broken and a belief that someone is practising witchcraft [259]. These reactions often seem to be precipitated by specific situations such as losing a job or news from home. Margaret Okunde and Beatrice Jackson are patients with this type of reaction (pp. 72 and 227).

Such acute psychotic reactions are not really specific to immigrants. Although rare now among European-born people, they were common last century, particularly in rural areas. Although the stresses of immigration may well bring them on and give them their characteristic paranoid flavour, they are perhaps patterns of emotion response found in predominantly agricultural countries which have been brought along with other aspects of the patient's culture. They are common in the Third World and may be a cultural alternative to such English practices as child abuse or taking drug overdoses. These acute episodes, although often repeated, are not followed by any serious long-standing psychological deterioration.

Psychiatric patients from Eastern Europe in Britain have often been said to have *personality disorders* [288]. It is possible that they have a personality characterized by excessive 'individualism' which initially had led them to prefer a capitalist country but which in fact is still maladaptive in Britain. The concept of a 'personality disorder' is, however, rather dubious. It is not really an illness, is diagnosed on rather loose grounds and often represents a breakdown of communication between patient and doctor rather than a general inability to cope adequately with everyday life.

PATTERNS OF MIGRATION

The first studies to weigh the 'selection' as against the 'stress' hypothesis attempted to answer questions about the effects of migration in general. They looked at refugees, political dissidents and economically motivated migrants, European and non-European migrants all together as one general category. The motivations, stresses and supports of a Scotsman who comes to London to work and later has a drinking problem are, however, unlikely to be those of a Polish post-war refugee who enters hospital with a diagnosis of schizophrenia.

Ødegaard compared two types of *internal* migration within Norway [13]. He found that people who settled in the capital were more likely to develop mental illness than those who had been born in Oslo, while those who moved to a rural area had fewer psychiatric difficulties than the country population. Black Americans who were born abroad (external migrants) had less mental illness than did internal black migrants [266].

Different migrating populations have diverse resources and a different ability to cope with the stresses encountered. It is unlikely that there will be a simple relationship between migration and mental illness which holds good for all types of migration.

IMMIGRANTS TO BRITAIN

Most studies on the psychiatric disorder of immigrants to Britain have been based on hospital records. The most comprehensive of these is an analysis of all people who were admitted to psychiatric hospitals in England and Wales at the time of the 1971 Census. Table 2 shows the comparative rates for the larger immigrant groups.

Table 2   Country of birth and mental hospital admission (per 100,000 population of each ethnic group)

	Men	Women	Both sexes
England and Wales	434	551	494
Scotland	712	679	695
N. Ireland	1391	1102	1242
Irish Republic	1065	1153	1110
West Indies	449	621	539
India	368	436	403
Pakistan	294	374	336
Germany	356	513	439
Italy	272	400	340
Poland	610	790	704
USA	359	576	473

Source: Cochrane 1977 (72). Rates are age/sex-adjusted for the population over fifteen years old (England and Wales 1971).

There are clearly considerable differences between minority groups. A man from Northern Ireland is five times more likely to enter a psychiatric hospital than a man born in Italy. West Indians are more likely to be admitted than the English-born, while Indians and Pakistanis (who include immigrants from what is now Bangladesh) are less likely. There is certainly no particular excess of hospital admissions among New Commonwealth immigrants compared to those born in England. The most striking difference is between the immigrants from Scotland, Northern Ireland and the Irish Republic contrasted with those from Europe and other overseas countries. Only immigrants from Poland had a rate of admissions for mental illness which was also more than a third above the native level.

Other studies have found a low rate of mental illness among immigrants from Cyprus and Malta but a particularly high rate among West African immigrants [18, 361]. The rate of schizophrenia in migrants from West Africa between the ages of twenty-five and thirty-five has been calculated at nearly thirty times that of the native British population. In the 1950s it was suggested that perhaps a quarter of Nigerian students in Britain had serious psychological difficulties [235]. According to the last census, in the borough where we were working there were forty-

Table 3   Country of birth and mental hospital admissions for schizophrenia and alcoholism

| | Alcoholism | | Schizophrenia | |
	Men	Women	Men	Women
England and Wales	28	8	87	87
Scotland	218	46	90	97
N. Ireland	349	69	96	160
Irish Republic	265	54	83	254
West Indies	14	7	290	323
India	34	9	141	140
Pakistan	10	14	158	103
Germany	23	3	99	130
Italy	4	2	71	127
Poland	33	9	189	301
USA	49	38	76	133

Source: Cochrane 1977 (72). Rates are of admission per 100,000 population over fifteen years old (England and Wales 1971). Schizophrenia here includes schizo-affective and paranoid psychoses; alcoholism includes alcoholic psychosis.

five people who came from a smallish African country; without exhaustively checking the hospital records we found that at least nine of them were among our psychiatric patients.

Total numbers of psychiatric patients like these do not tell us in detail the types of problems and illnesses for which the patients are admitted to hospital. Some ethnic groups seem much more liable to one difficulty than another.

We can see from Table 3 that there are twenty-five times as many men admitted from Northern Ireland with *alcoholism* as there are from the Caribbean, and eighty-seven times as many from Italy. On the other hand West Indians more than any other group seem likely to have *schizophrenia*. Twenty-five per cent of male psychiatric patients from Northern Ireland are having treatment for drinking problems compared with only 3 per cent of West Indian men. While half all male patients from Pakistan are treated for schizophrenia, this is true for less than 10 per cent of Irish male patients. Both the 'internal migrants' from Scotland and Northern Ireland and those from the Irish republic (who might be considered to have some similarity to the internal migrants in terms of history, language, culture and proximity) appear to have high rates of alcoholism compared with the immigrants from the New Commonwealth countries.

If we look at *suicide* (Table 4) we find fewer differences between the different groups. All ethnic groups except American men and West Indians appear to be more likely to kill themselves than the general population. *Attempted suicide* is less common among West Indians in Britain than for the general population, but is more common than in their country of origin [52, 53].

There does not then seem to be a common pattern of psychiatric problems among immigrants. There is certainly no evidence that 'immigrants are likely to become mentally ill'. Each ethnic group seems to have its own characteristic pattern of difficulties.

PITFALLS OF STATISTICS

There is no perfect way of finding out the extent of psychological difficulties among any one group. The figures we have quoted – the numbers of people admitted to psychiatric hospitals – probably conceal a number of inaccuracies. Not all psychiatrically

Table 4   Country of birth and suicide

| | Standardized Mortality Ratio | |
	Men	Women
All countries	100	100
Scotland	138	145
Ireland (all parts)	154	149
West Indies	85	60
India and Pakistan	100	122
Germany	177	239
Poland	221	207
USA	98	198

Source: Cochrane 1977 (72). Figures are estimated suicides (including official suicides, undetermined suicides and accidental poisoning) in England and Wales, by country of birth, for men and women over twenty.

ill people are in a psychiatric hospital at a particular time and many may never be, particularly if their problems are the less disabling emotional difficulties such as mild depression or anxiety. Migrants from some countries may tend to be treated for the consequences of alcoholism in a general medical ward rather than a psychiatric hospital. Whether people are admitted to hospital depends on the facilities offered, how serious the condition appears to be to the patient, his family and his doctor, and also the amount of support the community can offer. Recent studies show that native-born American whites are more likely to use private psychiatric facilities than immigrants or blacks; as statistics from private clinics are not often included in surveys, these patients are 'lost' for our figures and the white American-born group appears to have a lower rate of mental illness [433].

West Indian patients are said to have a more 'disturbed' illness when they are admitted; as not all people in Britain who have a psychotic illness actually see a psychiatrist [384] it is likely that disturbed rather than withdrawn patients are preferentially admitted. There may then appear to be more West Indian psychotic patients.

Our knowledge of mental illness in immigrants in Britain is based almost entirely on those who have contacted psychiatric services. Before we rely on admissions to hospital as a valid indicator of the amount of mental illness in a particular group we must take into consideration the number of beds in different areas, the legal and administrative procedures for admission, the distance of the hospital from the community, discharge policies, the availability of outpatient, private and community facilities, and how our particular population views mental illness.

We must also see if the time likely to be spent in hospital alters the chance of patients being there while a survey is conducted. American blacks for instance spend longer in psychiatric hospitals than do whites, while in a study of patients with severe (psychotic) illnesses we found that some black patients were likely to stay in hospital for only three weeks compared with fourteen weeks for similar white patients: a 'spot check' at any time would be less likely to find black patients [259]. Those groups which are likely to have a larger number of patients re-admitted in a single year (perhaps because of lack of community support) are likely to have inflated numbers of patients with psychiatric difficulties which usually need repeated admission over the year. Scots, for instance, may be only two times more likely to be alcoholic than the English, but if alchoholics are admitted to hospital for treatment three times as often as other patients, then the total number of admissions of Scotsmen with alcoholism in a year will suggest that the difference is much greater.

Newly arrived immigrants are usually young adults. Certain patterns of psychiatric disorder, such as schizophrenia, are found to occur particularly in this age group. If we fail to allow for the different age structure of the immigrant population we will find much higher rates of these illnesses. According to the 1971 Census, while 59 per cent of the New Commonwealth-born Britons were between the ages of fifteen and forty-five, only 37 per cent of the population as a whole were in this age group. We are likely to find that newly arrived groups have few of the illnesses associated with old age: taking the number of patients with the organic psychoses (which are found most commonly in old age) the study we have quoted showed that the rate in the English-born was apparently twenty times that in the West Indian-born [72]. Certain emotional difficulties may be more common among men than women, among single people or in one social class rather than another. We have to make a similar allowance for these differences: immigrants are usually more likely to be men, single and working-class than the population they settle amongst.

Most studies of mental illness in ethnic minorities have been in inner urban areas, areas characterized by widespread poverty, overcrowding and a proliferation of lodging houses and hostels. These are the areas traditionally associated with high rates of mental illness among the native British, both because of the effects of such conditions and – especially – because chronic psychiatric patients tend to be forced into them (see Chapter 6). Immigrants, on the other hand, live in these areas because of lack of capital and because discrimination makes more desirable areas difficult to enter. Any tendency for the immigrants to develop mental illness will be underestimated if we compare them with the native British in an inner-city area who have a higher than average rate of illness.

THE DIVERSITY OF IMMIGRANT GROUPS

To talk of 'immigrants' as if they comprise a single group is fallacious. How much do the Irish who have come to work in London have in common with the Bengalis? Even immigrants from the same country come from a variety of different cultural and religious groups. Table 2 shows the rates for German-born patients, but nearly a third of these 'Germans' have British-born parents; they are the children of servicemen and their wives who were stationed in Germany [72]. To what extent can we even include together in a single group of 'ethnic' Germans such different people as wartime refugees and more recent immigrants and students? A high proportion of the 'Indian' patients in our own hospital came from the Bombay Jewish community.

The Caribbean islands are not a single cultural entity. Some, such as Trinidad, have an important Asian component, both in terms of culture and descent. Some British ex-colonies, such as Dominica and St Lucia, are partly French in language and culture. West Indians in Britain often prefer to live with fellow islanders than with 'West Indians' in general. A nursing colleague from Barbados once told us how he was asked for advice about a West Indian in Croydon who was causing a great deal of ill-feeling by keeping his neighbours awake all night with shouting and music. He had answered half-seriously that it sounded as if the man was insane – but maybe he was just a Jamaican!

Jamaicans in their turn distinguish themselves from 'small islanders'.

Different islands in the West Indies may have different patterns of stress and adaptation. The percentage of psychotic patients with paranoid psychoses is six times as great in Trinidad as in Jamaica, that of alcoholism four times [353]. We have found that West Indians from Jamaica are slightly more likely to be admitted to hospital in Britain with a psychosis than are those from the other islands.

Who migrates?

Immigrants come to this country with a variety of expectations which are met in different ways, and these are probably reflected in the patterns of illness [368]. There was *less* serious mental illness among refugees in displaced persons camps in Europe after the Second World War than among the same immigrants when they had settled later in Britain [288]. Not all the Hungarians who came to Britain in the 1950s were political refugees; for many the events of 1956 were an opportunity to come to the West for personal or economic reasons. Those who were politically motivated were less likely to become mentally ill subsequently [279].

Certain types of migration are easier than others. West Africans (who initially had family or government support to study here) and Scots, two groups who perhaps have less difficulty than others in coming to England, both have *high* rates of mental illness. Asians in Britain, who have great difficulties to overcome before migrating and the biggest change to make when they settle, appear to have comparatively little mental illness. Differences in life-style will be greater for Asians than for West Indians and least for the Scottish and the Irish. On the other hand Asians may be prepared for the biggest changes and so are less susceptible to 'stress'. When migration is difficult, only the most determined and resilient are likely to migrate. Also, the bigger the improvement in living standards, the more easily does the immigrant bear conditions which would perhaps seem intolerable to a native.

Thus both 'stress' and 'selection' may play some part. It is difficult to say whether the intention to return home after a period in England is important; both West Africans and Poles who intended to return but are prevented from doing so, either by delay in passing examinations or by politics, have particularly high rates of psychiatric difficulties. Although few Asians do eventually return to the Indian subcontinent, most believe that they will do so: this has been called 'the myth of return' [8].

Language difficulties do not seem to be significant in all groups. Italians and Poles have quite different rates of admission to psychiatric hospitals. Although the ability to speak English may be reflected in easier communication, it may offer a greater access to psychiatric services and thus an increase in recorded mental illness. For the Italians, migration was always difficult. They had to wait a considerable time for vouchers but, once here, were usually able to find work in catering with fellow Italians [420].

The Polish community
Polish immigration has certain unusual aspects. The Poles nearly all came to Britain between 1939 and 1950, political exiles from the Nazis and the Russians, and included a particularly high proportion of men. Many had been professionals, military officers or civil servants, but they could only find work in Britain in unskilled jobs [420].

From the beginning they had well-organized facilities, a 'government in exile', Polish-language newspapers and schools, Polish Roman Catholic parishes and youth clubs. Like the Ukrainian exiles (who have recently been in conflict with the Vatican on this issue) their churches represent a good deal of political and nationalistic feeling. Their arrival was not welcome to British workers, who regarded them as potentially antisocialist if not actually fascist. Their politics have remained strongly nationalist, even in the second generation, and there is a continuing sense of involuntary exile [420]. Soon after their arrival, Polish men were found to be five times more likely to be admitted to a psychiatric hospital than were men in the general population [288] and they still appear to have an above-average rate of mental illness (Table 2, p. 89). A study of Polish psychiatric patients in Bradford suggests that, like black immigrants, they are particularly likely to have delusions of persecution [189].

Gender and stress
Stress among immigrant communities in Britain may be un-

equally distributed between the sexes. For some it may be the isolated woman who remains at home all day with the children, lonely and friendless, who is the one with the most difficulties. In another group it may be the men who spend their working life isolated by language in a large factory. Table 2 suggests that in all groups except the Scots and Northern Irish it is women who are most likely to be admitted to psychiatric hospital. This is also true of the English-born population. (The life expectation of being admitted to a psychiatric hospital in Britain is 11 per cent for men but 17 per cent for women.) In most groups about a third more women are treated in hospital for psychiatric difficulties than men. It is likely that Scottish and Irish men are more isolated and likely to be single and living in lodging houses than are foreign-born migrants and are thus more vulnerable. However, a large number of them appear to be chronic alcoholics who have been able to 'drift' to England with comparative ease.

West Indian women, unlike Asian women, are likely to make the decision to come to Britain themselves and are often isolated and self-supported. Those Spanish women who go to Geneva to find a secure job before their husbands give up their work in Spain are particularly likely to become mentally ill [64]. In the Caribbean women are more likely to be unemployed than men [15]. Probably the same is true here. West Indian men in Britain appear to have wider and more effective ties with others outside their families than do the women [32].

The difference between male and female admissions does seem larger for West Indians than for most other groups (Table 2). However, while male British-born whites are more likely to consult their doctor about psychiatric difficulties than are West Indian men, the reverse is true for women [317].

Time in Britain
How soon after migration is the risk of mental illness greatest? If stress really is important for breakdown, it is likely that the longer the time the migrant stays in Britain, the longer his or her goals remain unfulfilled and the greater the realization of failure. For serious psychiatric illness the West Indians are likely to have been in Britain for more than five years when they first become ill, unlike other immigrants. Whilst the West Indian patients have been in Britain for ten years on average, for West Africans the interval is three years [259, 361].

It is possible that stress plays a more important part in the illness of West Indians while West Africans are 'selected'. Different groups may, however, be liable to stress at different periods. Arab immigrants to France appear to have two peaks of maximum breakdown, at three years and nine years [321]. Immigrants to Australia from Western Europe are most likely to become mentally ill in the first year after migration; those from Southern Europe become ill later [288]. West Africans in Britain are predominantly students who intend to stay for a short period only, and perhaps are susceptible to early frustration. West Indians may be prepared for a longer struggle, intending to settle, and realize their failure only after some years. Possibly immigrants from urban areas or with middle-class aspirations are likely to become ill earlier.

Cultural change

Immigrants to Britain bring with them psychological responses to difficulties characteristic of their community. Social roles which are potentially stressful in the pre-migration culture may nevertheless have certain supports which disappear on migration. The traditional tension between mother-in-law and daughter-in-law in India is buffered by the women of her extended kin group in a way which is impossible in Britain. In a new environment new resources may however be found: the traditionally 'passive' Asian women have taken a leading role in the strikes at Imperial Typewriters and Grunwick.

Migration may provide certain advantages in coping with psychological difficulties. We do not know why the rates of alcoholism among West Indian men in Britain are low compared with Scots in England. Both groups of migrants come from societies which have long had serious drinking problems [22]. In the Caribbean island of Antigua one in five psychiatric admissions is for alcoholism (and three out of five in the neighbouring French island of Guadeloupe) as compared with one in thirty-three admissions for West Indians in England. It is possible that those West Indians who do drink heavily cannot save enough money to emigrate to Britain. However, the life-style of West Indians in Britain may offer certain advantages in avoiding alcoholism. These might be different patterns of drinking, of recreation or of reducing stress.

One advantage of living in Britain is that there are fewer

mental illnesses of physical origin such as malnutrition or infection. Nearly half of all psychiatric patients in Jamaica have associated physical illnesses [51]. The physical health of immigrants is, however, poorer than that of the general population, and it is possible that a proportion of their mental ill health can be attributed to organic factors, including dietary deficiencies, which could be easily remedied.

Pattern of community in Britain
The size and distribution of minority communities in Britain probably influences the amount of community support available. The smaller Polish groups in Britain after the war had more mental illness than the larger ones [288]. Larger communities offer the advantage of shared experience, a variety of sources of support and the chance to preserve a greater part of the home culture. French-Canadians appear to have higher rates of psychological disturbances than English-speaking Canadians only in situations where they are in a minority [290]. On the other hand the scattered Chinese community in Britain does not seem to have a particularly high level of illness.

Expectations and experience
Even isolated individuals can function adequately if their expectations are met and they enjoy a certain degree of economic and psychological security. European missionaries in China were more likely to break down than those in Africa. In China they encountered a powerful urban culture which was able to challenge their beliefs and teaching. In Africa, as part of the dominant political structure themselves, there was less reason for them to doubt their own values [323].

People who migrate for financial reasons usually have high expectations. European migrants to Australia with professional qualifications had a comparatively high rate of mental illness when recognition of their qualifications was delayed [229]. While Asians usually experience a rise in socio-economic status relative to their original position, West Indians may actually experience a fall. Job difficulties are particularly great for those West Indians with the highest educational qualifications [391]. In Jamaica educational advantages are much more significant than skin colour in obtaining a good job: not so in Britain.

The community response

The different ethnic communities in Britain have different attitudes to mental illness. The threat of repatriation may be a considerable bar to their seeking psychiatric aid, or indeed to recognizing difficulties. Asian women in Britain appear to have a low incidence of mental illness. It is often suggested by white doctors that this is because when they break down the family tolerates them at home without consulting a doctor. Incapable of leaving the house they assist with domestic tasks. However the admission rates for Asian men, who usually work outside the family and are the chief economic support of the family, are even lower.

People with severe mental illness in Britain may not always see a psychiatrist [384]. However, even if the family structure of West Indians was such it could never cope with schizophrenia and all schizophrenic West Indians were invariably admitted to hospital, this would still not appear to account for the much greater proportion of West Indians in psychiatric hospitals with this diagnosis: three times that of the English-born. Different patterns of experiencing and expressing distress, including depression, alcoholism and delinquency, may however be just different responses to a very similar situation, and may in fact be to some extent 'chosen' by the individual or his society (see Chapter 3). In Tristan da Cunha in the 1930s there was an epidemic of hysterical convulsions among women. In the 1960s, when the population was temporarily evacuated to England because of a volcanic eruption, it was these same women who were most likely to seek medical attention for physical complaints [332]. It seems likely that they were prone to have psychological difficulties of some form; Britain offered a 'medicalized culture' which enabled them to structure their difficulties in terms of physical illness.

Is it possible that the immigrant groups who appear to have little mental illness have instead high rates of some other types of deviant behaviour? A study of different ethnic groups in Birmingham [233] showed in fact that the pattern of crime was similar to that found in mental illness: compared with the general population, the Irish were over-represented, the Asians under-represented and the West Indians about the same. Crime statistics are, however, as fraught with difficulties as those of mental illness: ethnic groups who aspire to a middle-class life-style might engage in concealed 'white-collar crime', such as tax evasion, which is not reflected in police or legal records.

While emigration is frowned upon in some countries (such as France), in many it has become an important and valued part of the economy through the remittances which the emigrants send home. Between 1946 and 1960, a third of the population of the West Indian island of Montserrat emigrated. One in six Cypriots now live in Britain. Even countries which depended upon emigration may regard it with misgivings. Although Asians value the economic benefits of emigrating to Britain they are still wary of British customs in matters such as sex and alcohol. Some West Indians believe that since migration to Britain started there has been increased quarrelling and loss of community spirit [420]. It is possible that in those communities in which migration is not especially approved of, it may itself be a form of deviance.

Repatriation
Do mentally ill immigrants return home? Could this be the explanation of the apparently low rates of psychiatric difficulties among Asians? We do not know. Although the threat of repatriation hangs over the heads of those immigrants who become mentally ill and who are non-Commonwealth immigrants or Commonwealth 'non-patrials', comparatively few have been actually repatriated under the Mental Health Act (less than ten per year) [259]. However, mentally ill immigrants are often encouraged to return home 'voluntarily'. This is perhaps in the belief that the illness is caused by the stresses of migration and that the patient will recover back in his original country.

One in seven re-admitted psychiatric patients in Jamaica are immigrants who have returned from Britain [50]. These patients had become ill after emigrating to Britain but they became *worse* after returning home. Most had never married and on returning to the Caribbean remained solitary and isolated. A doctor who has worked with them emphasizes how the family sacrifice involved in emigration and the expectations of success contribute to the subsequent stigma when the emigrant returns as a mental patient [50]. Some immigrants who maintain close links with their country of origin may have low rates of admission (Italians), but others have high rates (Irish). Those for whom returning is the most difficult, the Poles, have a particularly high rate.

A MULTIPLICITY OF EXPLANATIONS

There appears to be no single explanation for the different rates of mental illness applicable to all minority groups. Some features seem more significant in one group than another. The Irish, for instance, while liable to some degree of discrimination, have fewer language difficulties and are not discriminated against on the basis of colour. The problem lies in deciding which of the possible difficulties are significant for a particular group. One solution is simply to add together all the difficulties each group experiences and to see if the final 'score' bears any relation to the rates of mental illness. The contribution of five different items has been assessed – lack of community integration, status isolation (an atypical mixture of different statuses such as being a black professional), experience of discrimination, the under-reporting of illness and the possibility that the immigrants were mentally ill before coming to Britain. The total scores seem to reflect the relative frequency of mental illness in different groups [19].

West African students seem particularly liable to a variety of disadvantages. Apart from the usual stresses of life in Britain for foreigners – the food, the weather, the experience of the 'typical British personality', discrimination, and economic and legal difficulties, they have middle-class aspirations, are likely to be older than other students, they are socially and sexually isolated and less prepared for the demands of their course [7]. Failure to qualify often results in the withdrawal of their grant or family support, and they then try to work and study simultaneously. Many of them, like Margaret Okunde, also have children [420]. It is common for a woman in West Africa to work while being a mother, and most women, even though they may have followed their husbands to Britain, are also likely to be studying or training.

We have seen in this chapter how difficult it is to find out exactly how common mental illness is in different immigrant groups. We have previously seen that mental health statistics have been distorted for political ends and how easy it is to jump to erroneous conclusions.

What firm conclusions can we come to? For the number of figures we have employed, surprisingly few. It appears that there is no characteristic mental illness specific to immigrants. Some immigrant groups seem to have more illness than the British-born population; some have less. This appears to be related to the different patterns of migration – who migrates, and why they do so. The two explanations – *stress* and *selection* – have a different relevance for different groups.

Those communities which have a low rate of mental illness – the Indians, the Chinese and the Italians – have certain features in common: great determination necessary to migrate, migration for economic reasons and an intention to return home, little attempt at assimilation and what can be described as 'entrepreneurial' activity. The groups with the most difficulties – the internal migrants, the East Europeans and the West Africans – appear quite dissimilar. Serious mental illness does not seem to be related to refusal to assimilate. If anything, cultural similarity to the white English-born population is associated with high rates of mental illness (the West Indians and the Irish). Social status and economic status in Britain by themselves do not seem relevant; but those immigrants who are likely to have declined in status after migration – the Poles and West Indians – appear to have high rates of mental illness.

Mental illness appears to be found most frequently in those immigrant groups who are forced migrants and those who have a comparatively easy voluntary migration, and least commonly in those who have a difficult voluntary migration plus lower expectations.

In this chapter we have tended to assume that if immigrants were fit when they migrated but later became ill, this was a direct consequence of the act of migration itself. But as a nineteenth-century psychiatrist pointed out: 'When an attack of insanity takes place, and we look among the occurrences of the past life for the cause of so singular a phenomenon, we seize on the most prominent or peculiar, and easily persuade ourselves that we have found the object of our search' [333]. We shall try to consider some of the other likely causes of mental ill health in ethnic minorities settled in Britain. But first we shall look at the limitations of an aspect of medicine we have regarded rather uncritically in this chapter – the psychiatric diagnosis.

NOTES

1   It has recently been suggested that one of the historical consequences of mental illness has been to stimulate human migrations [324].

CHAPTER FIVE

A DIGRESSION ON DIAGNOSIS

A man who spent 18 months in a disused sewer in the grounds of a mental hospital has been given a temporary home in a hostel in Southampton. Now Knowle hospital is to hold an inquiry into why Mr C. P, aged 44, was refused treatment as a long-stay patient. Mr P said yesterday he knows the answer himself. 'I know I'm not mad . . . but I do need help. I found it very confusing with one psychiatrist saying I was schizophrenic and another telling me that I was definitely not.'

Guardian, 16 June 1979

LABELLING AND DIAGNOSIS

In looking at the relative numbers of people with psychiatric problems from different minority groups, we have suggested that the differences may be partly due to the way doctors perceive their patients. For instance the frequency of alcoholism and the comparative infrequency of schizophrenia found amongst men who come to Britain from Eire (Table 3, p. 90) is probably related to the fact that many Irish men who develop schizophrenia may also drink heavily. When symptoms of schizophrenia and alcoholism are both present, the English doctor selects the diagnosis of alcoholism alone because of the way he tends to perceive Irish people [20].

Let us look at two serious mental illnesses – schizophrenia and the affective psychoses (the severe disturbances of mood which include mania and depressive psychosis). Affective psychoses appear more understandable than schizophrenia because the delusions are congruent with the patient's prevailing mood, and the doctor can more easily imagine himself in the patient's position than he can with schizophrenia [198]. Among white

English-born men, admissions for schizophrenia are twice as common as for the affective psychoses; among West Indian men they are ten times as frequent (Table 5). We can also compare the total for both these psychoses with the total for the milder psychological disturbances, the neuroses (such as panic attacks, obsessional thoughts or phobias). While for English men and internal migrants, psychoses are twice as common as neuroses, among Asian and European migrants they are five or six times as common, and among West Indians they are sixteen times as common [72]. This may mean that, for the same sort of problem, a diagnosis of psychosis (or more specifically of schizophrenia) is given more readily to members of some ethnic groups than to others. In Israel the disadvantaged Oriental Jews are three times as likely to be diagnosed as having schizophrenia than an affective psychosis: for the European Jews the two conditions are diagnosed equally frequently. We have seen that non-Europeans were initially believed to have bizarre and incomprehensible mental illnesses. Is it possible that high rates of schizophrenia really mean little more than poor communication between patient and doctor? Perhaps the mental patient does not have a distorted relationship with reality so much as an inability to present his experiences and difficulties to the psychiatrist in a form the latter can understand?

The whole process of diagnosis in psychiatry has been criticized, originally by psychoanalysts and more recently by sociologists. Picking a single label is felt to lead to a dehumanized and isolated conception of the individual with a totally inadequate picture of his or her feelings and experiences. A diagnosis can tell us nothing about why a particular patient came to see us, what they feel about their problems, what their other difficulties

Table 5 Rate of mental hospital admission per 100,000 of the male population over fifteen years old

	Schizophrenia	Affective Psychosis
Men born in England	87	45
Men born in the West Indies	290	30

Source: Cochrane 1977 (72).

and assets are, or indeed what sort of person they are.

Critics say that even if a diagnosis could reflect the whole of an individual's personal experience, the act of pigeon-holing is still invalidating. A bad prognosis becomes a self-fulfilling prophecy: once we diagnose schizophrenia (traditionally an illness associated with relatively little chance of complete recovery) the patient conforms to our expectations because of the way we respond to his label. That psychiatric labels certainly are demeaning is indicated by their frequent use as terms of abuse: hysterical, psychopathic, schizoid, paranoid. We shall see how even whole societies have been described in this way. If mental illness is indeed no more than social labelling then the whole business of diagnosing mental 'illness' is something similar to witch-finding [401].

To be described in anyone's shorthand is demeaning. Doctors are resented for their habit of referring to patients as 'the interesting liver' or 'the ectopic in the next bed'. With specifically emotional difficulties the reduction of a complex series of problems and experiences to an 'anxiety state', or worse, to a 'personality disorder', becomes even more dehumanizing.

DAVID SHARP

David is a seventeen-year-old son of West Indian immigrants who came to London from Montserrat soon after he was born. His father used to be a train driver on the London Underground but he has not been able to work for some years because of a chronic kidney problem. Having previously had few interests outside his job, Mr Sharp has now become bored and despondent, and lies on a sofa at home for most of the day. He has lost his previous enthusiasm for life and looks far older than his forty years. The family is kept going by Mrs Sharp, who works at night as a 'fluffer' on the Underground, cleaning machinery. Returning at dawn, she prepares the family breakfast, sends the two younger children off to school, persuades David to pay another fruitless visit to the Job Centre and jollies her increasingly bitter husband into helping her with the housework. Recently, even her apparently unlimited energy appears to be flagging and she has begun to wear an anxious look.

Over the last year David has become increasingly withdrawn.

He no longer sees his old friends and spends long periods alone, locked in his bedroom reading science fiction comics and performing a variety of private religious rituals. His door is adorned with a series of elaborately decorated crucifixes. The Sharps' greatest concern was David's increasing arguments with them, which ended with him shouting and running out of the room. Their general practitioner suggested they should bring him to see us. David came up to our clinic a few times, both by himself and with his parents. He was a rather shy and reserved boy, continually apologizing for bothering us, but blaming his parents for not leaving him alone.

In the letter we wrote to the Sharps' family doctor we suggested that David's adolescence and unemployment seemed to be bringing out into the open family difficulties which had previously been hidden. We advised both the doctor and family that his parents were encroaching on his privacy and that he could only get back at them by withdrawing into himself or getting in a rage. We did mention, however, that David was reacting rather unusually to the family situation and suggested the possibility that his curious rituals might be early signs of a schizophrenic illness.

The Sharps continued to come and see us, but the family atmosphere did not improve. After a few months their general practitioner retired and we were requested by his partner for a report on our 'schizophrenic patient'. A week later, a family argument resulted in David hitting his father. Mr Sharp wanted to throw him out of the house, but his mother insisted on calling a doctor. We were phoned that night and asked if we could admit a 'violent paranoid schizophrenic'.

Both the general practitioner and ourselves were to blame. A tentative medical hypothesis can never be the explanation of a whole set of personal and family problems. We were wrong, not in suggesting that David might be developing schizophrenia, but in failing to offer to both the Sharps and their doctor adequate ways of coping with the family difficulties which did not stigmatize David as the person responsible. This is so whether he was likely to develop schizophrenia or not. We managed to persuade the Sharps that David did not need to come to hospital. The family atmosphere has improved considerably with joint family interviews, and David is now able to stand up to his parents without anybody getting upset. He has still not been able to find work, but spends part of his time at a local community bookshop helping to produce a radical black newspaper. His curious rituals have disappeared and he has found a girlfriend.

Psychiatrists defend the practice of diagnosis by pointing out that without some sort of abstraction and classification of psychological difficulties, we can never find out their cause or do anything about relieving them. Without accurate figures we cannot assess the needs of minority groups or provide the necessary services. This book could have been composed solely of a series of case histories of patients, but some sort of classification would still have been necessary to suggest whether they were a representative sample or to show how a particular problem is related to being a member of an ethnic group.

If someone consults us complaining of seeing white mice running about on the floor when she drinks heavily, while another person tells us that after her husband died she has been seeing him around the house, it is helpful to have some sort of cataloguing system which tells us what each hallucination might indicate. If we encourage the woman with delirium tremens to talk about her hallucinations without offering her physical treatment, we will probably soon kill her; while to give drugs to the widow rather than help her mourn her husband would be, at best, grossly insensitive.

Nor is the diagnosis of schizophrenia merely futile labelling. Many psychiatric reactions of ethnic minorities which superficially resemble schizophrenia may be best helped by psychotherapy, but they are usually diagnosed as schizophrenia and then treated with drugs. If we say that patients like Calvin Johnson or Margaret Okunde are schizophrenic when they are not, we are subjecting them to unnecessary long-term medication, the stigma of mental illness and a self-perception as an invalid. If, on the other hand, we fail to recognize schizophrenia, we have again misinterpreted our patient's experience and possibly condemned him to a gradual process of emotional deterioration, with its harmful effect upon his personality, family and livelihood. Although we may postulate an alternative society in which the reaction we call schizophrenia may be a path to enlightenment, in our society it is a horrifying experience.

It is essential for the psychiatrist to be able to distinguish between serious mental illnesses which, although they may have social precipitants, are not self-limiting and situational reactions (like Calvin Johnson's) which can be explained best in social or political terms. With the short time devoted to each psychiatric patient (about sixty minutes per patient each year by each consultant), 'diagnostic error' in minority patients deserves some consideration.

Although preoccupation with cataloguing a person's experience can be dehumanizing, this is not inevitable: some of the profoundest interpretations of the experience of insanity, such as those of Karl Jaspers and Ludwig Binswanger, were based on simple descriptions of the patient's experience, uncluttered by any particular theory [198, 271]. Sympathetic awareness of a patient's experiences is the fundamental first step to understanding them and to helping them. To use a diagnosis is to try to condense the vast amount of information we find out about someone: their life history and their personality, their difficulties and how they get on with others, how we think they have coped and how they will manage in the future. It does not assume that the problem has a single cause (whether we favour biological or social explanations) or even that it is an isolated entity. For a recent defender of the classification of psychological illness, diagnosis is always 'a hypothesis to be tested and refined' [68].

People have characteristics which they share with all other human beings, characteristics which they share with some other people, and characteristics which are unique to them alone. Diagnosis deals only with the second of these; it is meaningless if we assume it can also refer to either of the others [211].

Supporters of psychiatric diagnosis have, however, often been a little disingenuous in their attempts to refute its abuse. They usually assume that the process of diagnosis can be separated from social considerations and that 'misdiagnosis' is the failure to do this [439]. At the same time they accept that such an abstraction from the social context is itself dehumanizing. They feel that the use of diagnosis simply to control deviant behaviour is regrettable but suggest this is because of inadequate psychiatric facilities [68]. Given our tendency to simplify and concretize concepts, it is inevitable that we will use a shorthand intended for explaining a particular behaviour as a substitute for understanding another human being.

We have also seen that diagnoses such as depression can be used to legitimate social control. Once patients are given a psychiatric diagnosis this of course determines to a great extent their future life, employment opportunities, housing and the extent to which they are considered responsible for their actions [155].

Whatever the medical justification, the frequent diagnosis of alcoholism in Irish patients or schizophrenia in black patients reinforces our popular stereotypes, stereotypes which ultimately perform certain social functions. Mental illness itself is less a 'thing' located in the individual than a concept which both explains and controls relations between individuals (see Chapter 9).

THREE SIMILAR DIFFICULTIES

We shall now look at three ethnic minority patients who were all given the same diagnosis, and see how this may reflect rather different situations.

Rama Roy died earlier this year from a perforated stomach ulcer. He was fifty-one and had lived alone for some years in a lodging house. Mr Roy had been born into a wealthy middle-class family of Indian origin which had settled in South Africa. His father was a lawyer and an important figure in the local Hindu community. Rama, educated at private schools and at London University, was ambitious. He initially hoped to go into politics and joined the South African Indian Congress, but then left for post-graduate study in economics in the United States. After four years' work with the United Nations Commissioner for Refugees, he went home to find that his family had decided to go back to India. Rama returned to Europe and worked in various international organizations in Geneva, marrying a Swiss girl and settling in Paris. His wife's family wanted him to convert to Roman Catholicism, but he refused. The marriage soon deteriorated. He began to feel that he no longer belonged to any particular community and even the international ideals of the United Nations had become increasingly meaningless. To cope with the various diplomatic functions and parties he was expected to attend, he started to drink heavily. Within a few years he was regularly consuming two bottles of whisky a day. At the same time he began a rather desultory study of Indian philosophy. His work gradually deteriorated and he divorced. During a brief visit to his parents in Bombay he remarried and returned to Geneva with his Indian wife. Still dissatisfied, he then moved to London, and for the first time began to have difficulty finding a good job. His wife was unhappy and went on a visit to Bombay with their young daughter. She did not return, and Rama, continung to drink heavily, eventually decided to obtain psychiatric advice.

Rama appeared divided between two societies – Europe and India of which he had little direct experience. While frequently mentioning his Indian heritage, he had no contact with other Indians in Britain and maintained a completely Western life-style. He was a rather pleasant but diffident man with an affected, world-weary air. Although he came into hospital to try to cut down his drinking, he never participated in any activities and failed to turn up for appointments which were arranged to help him to find a job or accommodation. He was always apologizing for putting us to any trouble and was fond of engaging in rather vague 'intellectual' conversation. The next time he was admitted to hospital was at the insistence of his landlady after he had started vomiting blood and had refused to eat for several days. Once on the ward he stopped drinking and agreed to most of our suggestions without enthusiasm. Declining psychotherapy, he repeatedly affirmed that he had made a mess of his life. He was not suicidal but appeared content in a rather listless way to continue drinking, quite aware of the deteriorating state of his health.

James McDonald came to London from Aberdeen. His father was a heavy drinker, impulsive and often violent. James had two brothers and a sister, all of whose marriages have ended in acrimonious separations. The family life at home was disorgan-ized and they had few social contacts, James's father eventually quarrelling with all his friends. As a labourer in a period of widespread unemployment, he was even less successful than others in finding work. James himself left school barely able to read after years of truanting which had been tacitly supported by his parents, and worked spasmodically as a ship's steward and a crane driver in a quarry, with some rather minor involvement in dealing in stolen cars. A small man with a congenitally dislocated hip, he was a passive hanger-on to various groups who met in the local pub, the butt of their jokes, a nervous and depressed person, uncertain of himself, with few strong convictions or interests. He derived a certain amount of satisfaction from the transient loyalties engendered in planning petty crimes in the rather sordid hotels and bedsitters which had become his home. James was always the loser, the one who got caught, the one who couldn't hold his drink. His rather dreamy acceptance of life and its insults was punctuated by rare outbursts of rage which usually resulted in him making a fool of himself: it was safer to just exist without responding.

James never really understood why his wife married him. Nor, according to her accounts, did she. She said the marriage had been a disaster from the beginning. Amongst other difficulties James was virtually impotent. He was frequently drunk, often hitting her and then bursting into tears. In Scotland he went to see his doctor after recurrent episodes of blurred vision, headaches and dizziness; he had occasional black-outs and twice fractured his skull. Several times his wife and he split up, only to come together again for brief periods. In an attempt to make a fresh start they came to London, but this ended in a final separation and divorce. James told us that his wife had been constantly unfaithful to him and only came back to him when she in her turn was discarded. He last saw her and their daughter two years ago when he went to her flat at Christmas with presents for them. Half drunk, he made a plea for yet another reconciliation but was turned out by her boyfriend. He was admitted to hospital that evening after being found in the street, crying and banging his head against a wall. He came into our hospital on six occasions, each time after drinking bouts had ended with an epileptic fit or an overdose of drugs.

In therapy it became clear that whilst James had a poor opinion of himself he blamed his wife for all his troubles: like everybody else she too had used him for her own purposes. He was good at getting to know people superficially, being obsequious to the staff and ingratiating with the patients. However, he never became particularly involved with anyone's problems, or indeed his own. He came to the hospital sporadically, attending group and occupational therapy without much enthusiasm and launching, when prompted, into an interminable description of his life. His behaviour changed when he started drinking and he frequently phoned us up, demanding new tablets and threatening to kill himself unless we found him better accommodation. It was difficult to help him to plan his life, every suggestion rapidly proving fruitless, and we became reconciled to offering help only in the major crises. He was found one weekend in a coma in his lodging house and died shortly afterwards. He had drunk about eighteen pints of beer and taken a bottle of aspirins. We never knew how seriously he wanted to die: an acquaintance who had seen him the day before said he had not seemed depressed.

Yvonne Clarke was born in London during the war. Her father was a black American airforceman who later settled in England and her mother was a young Irish art student. Yvonne grew up on the edge of London's artistic fringe of small theatre clubs and pub entertainers, part of a happy and rather disorganized family. Her father died of problems related to drink when she was about ten and her mother returned to Ireland with the children. Yvonne came back to London when she was sixteen after a broken affair. We did not discover exactly what happened, but she has hinted to us rather mysteriously about 'perversions'. She has had only unsatisfactory relationships since then and talks of sex with distaste. She occupies a large 'shabby-genteel' flat in Bow, and has a facility for landing rather interesting jobs, such as doing clerical work for a publisher of occult literature. Her flat swarms with a large variety of injured animals which she is always finding in the streets. Last year the children next door painted racist slogans on her wall; she reacted by a chilly silence in public but confessed to us that the episode had made her considerably nervous.

Yvonne has been drinking heavily since she returned to London. She drinks in bouts, not touching alcohol at all for about two years and then going on a month-long carouse of port and barley wine, drinking herself unconscious every night at home. She was eventually admitted to hospital with hallucinations and in very poor physical health. We have recently become increasingly worried because in between her bouts she remains rather withdrawn and suspicious, engaging in frequent quarrels with her neighbours over her animals, and has been accusing them of 'tapping' her electricity meter.

She has no friends and seldom sees her brothers, who also live in London, because 'they are alcoholics too'. Yvonne is intelligent and articulate, engaging with enthusiasm in any conversation, quick to make up her mind and scornful of other opinions. Her views are a blend of humanity and violence: she 'would kill anyone who hurts animals'. Her language is a little grandiose and exaggerated and, like many of her interests, appears frozen in the mode of about twenty years ago. Fiercely independent when she comes into hospital she makes a point of proclaiming herself an alcoholic and goes round persuading the other patients to 'confess' their difficulties. She gives long speeches on the decay of morals and talks with despair of the human race.

Rama, James and Yvonne all appeared to come to England less for economic reasons than as a solution to personal difficulties. For all three migration to London was comparatively easy: Rama appeared here on yet another stopping-off point in his search for a secure cultural identity; for James, London was a new chance to patch up his marriage; while for Yvonne it was a return to the place of her idealized childhood and a refuge from an unpleasant experience. For none of them does the move appear to have been a very happy choice.

The difficulties each experienced and their responses to them are similar enough for us to call them all alcoholics. This diagnosis does tell us about these features which they are likely to have in common: isolation and gradual social deterioration, poor physical health, a feeling of hopelessness and a mistrust of others, difficulty in defining and living a meaningful existence, loss of interest in the company of others and some of the risks they run – serious physical illness, depression and suicide. The diagnosis does suggest what their different situations may lead to and how we might best help them.

Each of the three, however, has clearly a unique personality. They all arrived at their heavy drinking from different directions and for each person it solved temporarily different problems. Not all the features typically associated with alcoholism were present in all three: no one else in Rama's family was a heavy drinker, for instance, whilst Yvonne does not seem to have lost her enthusiasm for living.

DIAGNOSIS ACROSS COMMUNITIES

Psychiatric diagnosis has been criticized by doctors themselves, not because it is theoretically unjustified, but because it often does not work in practice. Psychiatrists, it has been said, seldom agree on a diagnosis anyway and, compared with physical medicine, the diagnoses do not prove very useful either in recommending a particular treatment or deciding what course the illness will take [274].

Disquiet has been raised by the ease with which people can acquire such labels as 'mentally ill' or 'schizophrenic'. In a well-known American study, some researchers arrived separately at a psychiatric hospital each claiming to be hearing hallucinatory voices, falsifying their names and profession but otherwise responding to questions truthfully. After a cursory examination most of them were diagnosed as schizophrenic and admitted to the hospital [347]. In another research project clinical psychologists and psychiatrists were shown a videotape of an actor who had been 'trained to be normal'. One group of them overheard a high-prestige figure declare the man to be psychotic: only 8 per cent of this group decided that he was mentally normal, compared with 57 per cent of those who saw the tape without hearing the accompanying suggestion [406].

A study in which patients were given separate interviews by pairs of doctors showed that in only about two thirds of them did both doctors agree on the diagnosis [227]. One reason for diagnosis is to collect together certain patterns of behaviour into useful categories so that psychiatrists from different countries can compare different rates. Will this always be fruitless because of the different way we look at people?

American doctors have appeared more likely than British doctors to regard people as mentally abnormal [211]. The British psychiatric tradition views the individual from outside, only scoring him, so to speak, when he appears very different from other people. The pervasive influence of psychoanalysis in the United States, however, resulted in an attempt to peer inside and perceive more diffuse and hypothetical malfunctioning. The American tradition minimized the difference between the sane and the insane, but at the cost of including larger and larger numbers as abnormal. One patient was considered to be psychotic by 33 per cent of the American psychiatrists who saw a video film of him but by only 3 per cent of the British doctors [208].

American psychiatrists were particularly likely to find *thought disorder* and *passivity*, two of the abnormal experiences which are traditionally associated with a diagnosis of schizophrenia, although they are often defined rather vaguely. The word 'passivity' may be used in everyday language just to mean 'passive' but in psychiatry it refers to a serious disturbance between the boundaries of the self and the outside world in which one experiences one's will, thoughts, actions or emotions as being those of an external power. If we recorded this every time someone said that they felt their life was controlled by others we should end up with so many schizophrenic people that most of us would qualify as insane at sometime.

The concept of schizophrenia in the United State has traditionally been considerably broader than in Britain, with the result that many more people have been given this diagnosis. A study which compared groups of psychiatric patients in New York and London found that while 34 per cent of the patients in London had a diagnosis of schizophrenia, no less than 62 per cent of the sample in New York were given this diagnosis [86]. This was not due to a different pattern of illness in the two cities: psychiatrists using an agreed mode of interviewing and arriving at a diagnosis reduced the percentage in New York to 29 per cent and increased the London percentage to 35. Over 60 per cent of the American patients to whom the project teams gave a diagnosis of neurosis, depression or personality difficulties had been diagnosed by their own doctors as schizophrenic.

If psychiatrists disagree among themselves to this extent, even when they speak the same language and come from a very similar society, we may wonder what happens when they are trying to recognize problems in patients from a different society with a different native language. Spanish-speaking patients in New York have more symptoms when interviewed in English than when interviewed in Spanish, even when the psychiatrists use a special rating scale [267]. This may be partly because what is quite a natural characteristic when speaking an unfamiliar language – slow speech with long pauses between words – is also a symptom of depression. However, these patients were rated as abnormal on all types of symptoms. The social class and colour of the doctor may also affect the communication of problems. Patients are most likely to explore their feelings if the therapist is similar to them in ethnic group and class background [57].

How relevant are the British diagnoses for minority ethnic groups? In a review of this problem, we found that the doctors who had worked with minorities varied in their opinions [259]. Few of the studies had used a standardized interview. One author suggested that as many as 85 per cent of the West Indian patients had 'an atypical reaction'; others said there were no differences from white British-born patients. The concept of 'atypical psychosis' – atypical that is for the classical European tradition – is not often used in Britain. In a reaction against an earlier generation of psychiatrists who enthusiastically discovered a host of bizarre syndromes all over the world, most atypical psychoses are now included in certain rather broad categories of illness such as schizophrenia which are presumed to have a biological component and to occur in most cultures. 'Atypical' features are regarded as merely local variations of the basic illness pattern.

We have found that certain features which are comparatively rare in British-born psychiatric patients are not uncommon in patients born abroad: 40 per cent of patients with severe (psychotic) mental illness who had been born in the Caribbean or Africa structured their illness in terms of a religious experience, compared with 20 per cent of white patients born in Britain [259]. Twice as many black patients had had their diagnosis *changed* in the course of their psychiatric career, suggesting either that British doctors found it difficult to diagnose them or that the patients did not easily fit into the 'classical' categories. Using a standardized interview technique we found that many patients who were given the diagnosis of schizophrenia had short-lasting acute psychotic reactions of the type we described on p. 87. ⌐

How applicable are European categories of mental illness to other societies? Since 1961 the World Health Organisation has been conducting a study in nine countries (Britain, Colombia, Czechoslovakia, Denmark, Taiwan, India, Nigeria, the Soviet Union and the United States) to see whether there really is an illness called schizophrenia in different cultures and whether the local psychiatrists agree on its criteria [445]. This study found that in all these countries there was a group of patients who had a similar cluster of symptoms to schizophrenic patients in Britain.

Two countries, however, had a much wider concept of schizophrenia which included more patients. These countries were not, as might be expected, developing countries, or even countries with similar social systems, but the Soviet Union and the United States, two countries whose psychiatric practices have been particularly criticized [439]. The reason for the differences probably lies in their theoretical approaches to mental illness (and their large and influential psychiatric establishments). We have already seen that the American approach minimizes the differences between normality and abnormality and attempts to understand mental illness in terms of mental processes which are found in all people. The Russian approach (or at least that prevailing in Moscow, where the study was done), like the American, does not concentrate on the actual symptoms: it emphasizes the consequences of the illness and how the individual may best be reintegrated back into society [38, 216]. It is ironic that these theoretically humane approaches, both emphasizing an optimistic attitude to schizophrenia – its intelligibility and the possibility of social acceptance (as opposed to the more medical emphasis on biological and genetic aspects in Britain and other countries) – have in fact led to a large number of apparently normal 'schizophrenics'.

Does the fact that the World Health Organisation found a similar pattern of schizophrenia in quite different countries suggest that schizophrenia is a universal phenomenon, independent of culture and probably with a biological basis? It is possible that the patients in the study did not really come from widely differing societies: they lived near university psychiatric hospitals where 'Westernization' might well have produced similar patterns of psychological difficulties. In addition psychiatrists from different countries have often studied in the same psychiatric tradition or even at the same universities. They may thus fit any abnormal behaviour into similar patterns. What we have yet to do is to take 'non-Western' concepts of mental illness and to try to validate them on a 'Western' population using traditional healers.

One of the most exciting aspects of the WHO study has been the two-year follow-up [370]. This showed that however important particular symptoms might be for the actual diagnosis of schizophrenia, they were not related to the prognosis. Social isolation, single marital status, an unfavourable environment and a poor sexual adjustment were characteristic of patients who had a poor outcome, not the type of delusions or hallucinations. The prognosis was also related to the *country* where the patient lived: in Europe and America patients were more likely to be still sick two years after the first study than were patients from developing countries. While we cannot say that schizophrenia is a 'Western illness' or that the European colonists were accurate in describing societies without mental illness, it does appear that a culture may be important in producing *chronic* mental illness. There is a certain amount of evidence that societies with little Westernization have lower prevalence rates of schizophrenia [415, 295]. Some types of schizophrenia may well start as a transient psychological disturbance of biological origin whose persistence as a mental illness is due to social attitudes which do not accept certain abnormal experiences as valid, together with failure to integrate the experiences of the individual into those of the community [87].

ELIZABETH AHYI

Psychiatry tends to look at mental illness in two rather different ways. We can study the person as he appears to others and explain illness as if it were a thing which happens to one by analogy with physical disease. In this case we emphasize the biological and genetic contribution to the experience. Alternatively we can try to look at the illness from the point of view of the person experiencing it – as a fundamental disturbance of the whole individual in relation to the reality of his community.

The difference between the two approaches is the difference beween *explaining* and *understanding* [198]. They are different ways of approaching any relationship with other people. Both are essential if we are to try to understand or alleviate psychological difficulties. Psychiatry without explaining becomes a mishmash of subjective theories, the patient a battle-ground for the ego trips of various charismatic theorists; while psychiatry without understanding becomes a dehumanizing technology, differing from veterinary science only in its choice of subject.

The last chapter and this have considered the importance of objective measures – looking at the patient from the outside. The experiences of Calvin Johnson and Margaret Okunde (pp. 1 and 72), on the other hand, were briefly considered from their own point of view. Unfortunately if does not follow that appearing to understand someone's situation in this way will lead to the patient's automatic recovery. Social circumstances may be impossible to alter. In addition psychotic illnesses often have a momentum of their own which is independent of the precipitating situation.

Elizabeth Ahyi is Nigerian. Her family are wealthy and westernized and in close contact with a local Methodist mission near Lagos. After her father's death, her mother remarried when Elizabeth was about ten and she was sent to a boarding school. She saw little of her family for the next few years but passed her exams at school easily and began to work in another part of the country as a secretary. There she met her husband, Jonathan, who was planning to come to Britain to study law. His father was a powerful local figure, a landowner and the owner of several stores.

Elizabeth and Jonathan married and came to London, Jonathan to study and Elizabeth to work in the Overseas Department of the BBC. Jonathan's brother and his wife Alice were already here, and the two families pooled their resources to buy a house in Camden Town. After Elizabeth had a son, she became depressed and did not return to her work. Her doctor offered her anti-depressants, but she became worse and was eventually admitted to our hospital.

We discovered that the two brothers quarrelled frequently and that Alice had spent some time that year in a psychiatric hospital with a diagnosis of schizophrenia. In spite of the brothers' quarrels, Elizabeth felt that Jonathan showed more loyalty to his brother than to her. She happened to see a letter which hinted that Jonathan's family had been against him marrying her. The couple stopped having sex. Elizabeth suspected that Jonathan had found a girlfriend in his college: he denied her accusations. Elizabeth devoted herself to her son. She found difficulty in accepting the domestic habits of the other three; she found them 'primitive and dirty – typical of their part of Nigeria'. She was often frightened by Alice bursting into the living-room and screaming at her hallucinations and the two women continually argued about their domestic responsibilities. Soon after she became depressed Elizabeth was sexually assaulted by a hair-dresser. Jonathan failed an exam and had to repeat a year's study.

When we met Elizabeth, she was quiet and withdrawn. After a few days she told us she was hearing voices: she could hear Jonathan's brother accusing her of witchcraft and his old father, back in Nigeria, calling to her telling her that she had ruined his son's life. She herself wondered if the two brothers were practising sorcery against her. Her brother-in-law had been burning incense in his room, and she had found some strange books there. She could also smell soap, hair oil and shampoo. Her illness and the preoccupation with hair appeared to be an understandable response to her background and situation. Alice's hallucinations seemed to be providing Elizabeth with a model for solving her domestic difficulties – a solution which allowed Jonathan to abandon her without feeling responsible. We offered these ideas to both husband and wife. The voices soon stopped, and after a few weeks' rest in hospital Elizabeth returned home to her baby, cheerful and confident. Over the next few months we discussed with the Ahyis the possibility of their living away from the other couple as the relationship between the two brothers, and the repeated episodes with Alice, seemed to precipitate Elizabeth's depression. But to move was impossible: both brothers had used all their money buying the house. Relations between Elizabeth and Jonathan improved all the same, and for a year everything appeared reasonably well.

Elizabeth then became depressed again in exactly the same way. This time she stayed in hospital for some months. She was soon admitted again – and again. She started hearing us making comments about her appearance and strangers giving her bizarre instructions about washing her baby's hair. Her hallucinations were mingled with other sounds: inside the noise of passing cars were voices accusing her of trying to kill her son. Evil spirits passed comment on her appearance and a television announcer passed cryptic messages to her. At first we thought her worsening condition was due to domestic difficulties, but on talking to everybody it appeared that there actually had been less tension in the house. Elizabeth and her husband appeared to be getting on fairly well. Jonathan had dropped his girlfriend and took time off from his studies, which were now going well, to look after her. During joint interviews he no longer appeared to try to invalidate her statements. Elizabeth herself confirmed that all was well at home, but we did still wonder why her husband was himself getting on better as she became ill. Her mother came to London, stayed for some time and then took Elizabeth back to Nigeria. During her year there the voices continued.

Jonathan's brother has left the area and divorced Alice, who has now been in a psychiatric hospital for over a year. Elizabeth waits at home wondering if she will follow. Despite a considerable amount of supportive psychotherapy with the Ahyis, the voices continue. Elizabeth has heard them every day for some years; she is woken up by them; they leave for some time to return suddenly and accuse her in the street or in the shops; sometimes they keep up an unidentified murmuring in the distance. Unlike many patients who begin to treat their hallucinations with indifference, Elizabeth's personality and emotions have remained unchanged. The voices startle and terrify her every day. She telephones us at night in a panic asking what to do. By offering her medication and by constant reassurance and encouragement, we think we have been able to prevent institutionalism and long-term damage to her personality. Elizabeth has been able to stay at home and even to work for short periods. She still has her friends, her interests and her family. Her son is now six. He tells us he wants to become a doctor.

Whether we believe that schizophrenic illnesses like Elizabeth's are essentially a social experience or a biochemical abnormality, they do involve psychological changes which do not respond simply and immediately to an altered social environment. Social milieu is of fundamental importance and the liberalization of mental hospitals has contributed to a more humane and stimulating atmosphere, and a better recovery rate. We also know that the relapse rate of schizophrenia is probably related to the emotional atmosphere of the patient's family [417]. But this is not to say that environment is the sole cause or the sole means of treating schizophrenia. After a certain point, serious mental illnesses have a momentum of their own and they cannot be modified easily by a change of atmosphere or by psychotherapy.

This does not mean that the illness is a meaningless experience, but it does suggest that one of the ways of helping psychotic patients is with medicines such as the phenothiazine drugs as well as psychotherapy. Like all drugs they can have unpleasant side-effects, occasionally of a chronic and irreversible kind. Although their use should be limited to *conditions where there is no other effective treatment*, they can be and frequently are misused by the medical profession.

Whether we employ medical diagnosis constructively or

whether we use it as an excuse for our inability to understand patients from ethnic minority groups (or even to justify racism), it is only useful in those psychological difficulties which show a clear break between normality and abnormality. We shall now turn to look at the less serious but none the less significant responses to racism and poverty, and the conflicts between immigrants and their children born in Britain.

CHAPTER SIX

THE PRICE OF ADAPTATION

O Natty, Natty
Natty 21,000 miles away from home
O Natty, Natty
And that's a long way
For Natty to be from home
                Bob Marley and the Wailers, 'Natty Dread', 1974

Many immigrants have psychological difficulties which do not usually result in admission to hospital: the depressions and anxieties caused by settling in a new country, the frustrations and loneliness induced by racism and the inevitable clash of values. Such difficulties are usually regarded, not as mental illnesses, but as problems of adaptation – problems which require social and political action rather than the intervention of psychiatrists or psychologists. The experience and perception of mental illness are, however, invariably bound up with cultural and political assumptions and, at the same time, poverty, disadvantage, cultural change and the tensions between generations take their toll of the individual's mental health.

There is a fair amount of 'hard' data on such questions as hospital admission or unemployment, but we have little information on life satisfaction or general well-being. This is partly because of their elusive nature. It is difficult to conduct a conventional survey to look at them and the doctor can usually find out more from the novels and poetry written by members of other ethnic groups and by living and working together with them.

Chapter 4 looked at mental illness in immigrants in relation to the characteristics which they bring with them and whether they are especially vulnerable people. Migrants, however, respond actively to their experiences after they have arrived. They become to a greater or lesser degree part of the general population, and the problems they eventually face are to a considerable extent problems which are also shared by other disadvantaged groups. But we shall start by looking at some long-term difficulties which are the specific consequence of one particular type of immigration. Then we shall consider the available evidence for the effects of social and economic status and life experiences on mental health, and finally see how different ethnic minorities have devised their own solutions.

THE SURVIVORS

A high proportion of Jewish immigrants are of course the survivors of Nazi persecution. Abraham Bernstein was born in Germany, the eldest son of a Polish bookbinder. Shortly after the Nazis came to power his father was arrested. He was eventually deported to Poland when Abraham was aged eleven. The family never saw him again. Abraham recalls a childhood of poverty and terror. The community's synagogue was destroyed and they were forbidden to work. Abraham's school was closed and he spent his days scavenging for food for his mother and brothers. Their wealthier Jewish friends or those with relatives abroad were able to leave Germany for Britain and America. The Bernsteins remained. Abraham thought of trying to make his way abroad but realized he could not leave his family. A few of their neighbours moved to another area and tried to pass as Gentiles: they were arrested. The initial violence abated and the family settled down to an impoverished and apathetic wait. Eventually they were taken to a camp on the Polish border where they existed for months in a stateless limbo. In 1938 Abraham was brought to England by a charitable organization and was taken in and educated by a Jewish family. All his relatives disappeared without trace.

Abraham is now fifty-nine. He works as a taxi driver. Although he still lives in the Jewish area of North London to which he came as a boy he feels little identity with it. He seldom attends the synagogue and has not claimed any reparations from the West German government. Isolated episodes of anti-semitic graffiti or abuse leave him apparently untouched. He is unconcerned with the resurgence of racist beliefs or with the political situation of Israel.

For many years Abraham has had chronic insomnia and he lies awake tormented by painful memories. When he does manage to fall asleep he dreams almost nightly about fragmentary incidents of mob violence. He is always anxious and apprehensive and is startled by any unexpected event or sudden noise. He finds it difficult to cope with stress of any type: he cannot stand up for himself in arguments with the boss of his taxi company. He dislikes working at night but rather than say so he takes his taxi home or drives endlessly around the streets avoiding any potential fares.

Abraham experiences the curious phenomenon of *survivor guilt* – a vague pervasive conviction of having done something wrong and shameful. He frequently reproaches himself for still being alive when so many others have perished. It has been suggested that survivor guilt acts as a kind of testimonial: 'By continuing to suffer himself the survivor seems to be trying to provide an enduring memorial to his slaughtered friends and relations' [67]. Abraham does not consider his guilt a medical problem and appears to find it inconceivable that he should not suffer in this way.

Abraham's wife Rachel has suffered even more intensely, as she spent a year in a concentration camp. Her experience has been reflected in the way she has brought up their children. She feels unable to respond to them emotionally while at the same time she has an over-protective attitude and an urgent need continually to give them food. Their grown-up children still live at home, and the daughter, who has refused many opportunities to marry, seems unlikely to leave. Their mother constantly fears that some terrible fate awaits them and lives in expectation of a return of anti-semitic terror. She has recurrent dreams in which the children are trapped with her in the camp. She gets up repeatedly in the night to make sure that they are breathing.

Other groups of exiles are the South-East Asian refugees and the 28,000 Asians with British passports who were expelled from Uganda in 1972. The East African Asians spent long periods in resettlement camps before finding employment and accommodation. Most of them resisted attempts at 'dispersal' and, against strong local opposition, chose to live in areas such as Leicester where East African Asians had already established themselves. It is too soon to say what the psychological effects of forced migration for this community will be in the long term. 'Survivor guilt' is unlikely, as nearly the whole community left together. At the same time a violent disruption of settled life, an unwanted displacement and the status of being regarded by the host community as an unwelcome problem (with their own Resettlement Board) have taken their toll of a community previously well-known for its initiative [225]. Although most of them hold British passports it has been clear to them that few regard them as 'British'. The heads of most households are now aged over forty; a majority have at least one family member who is either sick, disabled or retired [80].

SOCIAL CONDITIONS AND MENTAL ILLNESS

The majority of post-war immigrants to Britain came specifically for economic reasons – to provide a better standard of living for themselves and their families than was possible at home. Their two immediate needs were jobs and housing. Work and accommodation were also the major points of competition and possible conflict between immigrants and the local population.

It was inevitable that economically motivated migrants should settle as near as possible to their place of work during the period of high employment opportunities in the 1950s. Immigrants from the New Commonwealth and Pakistan have on the whole followed in the footsteps of earlier working-class migrants such as East European Jews and the Irish immigrants of a hundred years ago as regards areas of settlement and type of work. They tended to settle in inner-city areas such as Tower Hamlets, Lambeth and Islington in London. Jobs were available only in those urban areas where the housing shortage was already acute. With the exception of the medical profession (nearly half of hospital doctors are immigrants) and nurses (15 per cent of London nurses are immigrants), migrants were employed in manual occupations [226]. The jobs usually taken by recent immigrants were unskilled work in the garment trade, catering and public transport: jobs characterized by insecurity or low wages and inferior status.

The inner urban areas where they live are marked by poor-quality housing and the outward movement of the economically more successful. A high proportion live in private rented accommodation and many of the homes are overcrowded and lacking in basic amenities. Racial discrimination by landlords was a major factor which originally forced immigrants to settle in decaying urban zones: the display of 'no coloureds' signs was not prohibited until the Race Relations Act of 1968. Ethnic segregation within these areas is most common for the Pakistani community, followed by Indians and then West Indians [202].

The Community Relations Commission said in 1977 that

the urban deprivation and social disadvantage experienced by ethnic minorities differ from those of other residents in urban deprived areas, in degree, in kind, in their causes and consequences. Ethnic minorities are more likely to be socially disadvantaged and multiply-deprived than the rest of the population, they experience distinctive clusters of multiple deprivation, and a major cause of their deprivation is the racial discrimination which they face. [82]

There is now abundant evidence that material and environmental deprivation is experienced by ethnic minority groups. The West Indian community in particular experiences overcrowding and shared dwellings, lack of amenities, high unemployment and low family incomes.

The national census in 1971 amply documented disadvantage in housing, unemployment and family life. Seventy per cent of the ethnic minority population were concentrated in only 10 per cent of enumeration districts. These particular districts contained nearly three times the average proportion of British households that shared or lacked hot water, twice as many which shared or lacked a bath and nearly three times as many above the statutory overcrowding level. Twice as many immigrant families did not have exclusive use of all basic amenities, half as many lived in local authority accommodation and twice as many lived in private furnished accommodation. If they did obtain a council house or flat, black immigrants were twice as likely to live in high-density pre-war council estates. While less than 1 per cent of households in the general population were in shared dwellings without exclusive use of either cooking stoves or sinks, 8 per cent of New

Commonwealth families lived in these conditions. Twice as many West Indians as members of the general population did not have exclusive use of bath, hot water and inside lavatories. The Inner London Education Authority has found that three times as many West Indian children as white children are likely to experience multiple deprivation as judged by living in lower-working-class homes with large families and qualifying for free meals.

The proportion of West Indians who were out of work at the time of the 1971 Census was twice as high as for the total population and still is in 1989; while the total numbers of unemployed doubled between November 1973 and November 1975, the unemployed numbers of minority ethnic groups increased four-fold. Men from the New Commonwealth earned less in professional, white-collar and skilled manual work than British-born men of their own age and in the same level of job. Job levels held by black men are lower than those of white men who have the same educational qualifications [152].

The most comprehensive review of the living conditions of West Indian and Asian immigrants is the survey summarized in *Racial Disadvantage in Britain* by D.J.Smith [391]. This shows that they have inferior jobs, are less well paid and have poorer housing than the general population. The report also presents evidence of discriminatory practices in recruitment for jobs and by private landlords. A study which used actors to apply for accommodation and work conclusively showed that colour was more important in discrimination than 'foreigness'. Black council tenants were paying about the same rent as white council tenants in spite of their inferior accommodation. Private tenants from minority groups were paying much higher rents than white private tenants, again despite marked inferiority in the quality of the accommodation.

Ethnic minorities share their surroundings and living conditions with socially disadvantaged white groups in our society, including the poor, the aged and those who are physically handicapped. Can we then expect them to have higher rates of illness because of this? To what extent does social environment cause illness? There are no simple measures of social environment; among those which have been used are poverty, residential area, social isolation, social class and unemployment.

An American Congressional report has suggested that unemployment leads directly to higher rates of suicide, mental hospital admissions and serious physical illness [124, 409]. Physical illness shows widespread variations in different classes: the difference in the Standardized Mortality Ratio between classes I and V is four-fold for pneumonia, six-fold for bronchitis and seventeen-fold for otitis media [94]. Infant mortality in Merthyr is double that in Oxford. This is in part due to occupational differences – bronchitis is associated with outdoor work. Medical services for working-class areas are however worse in terms of the number of hospital beds, doctors and nurses. The availability of good medical care appears to be negatively correlated with the need for it – the 'inverse care law' [179]. According to the Merrison Commission on the NHS, the gap between facilities offered to the working class and the middle class is widening.

Because of their cramped living conditions, young black children are likely to have frequent accidents at home, especially burns [450]. Industrial accidents are common among Asian immigrants because of their unfamiliarity with heavy industry, language and training difficulties, and the fact that they work long hours in industries which already have high accident rates [449].

Poverty and mental illness have often been observed to co-exist, but it is difficult to see exactly how they are interrelated. Where there is economic and social deprivation there always appears to be a disproportionate amount of psychiatric illness. The deprived urban areas of London consistently display a higher proportion of patients than do the more prosperous regions [431]. For example Stepney in East London has a hospital discharge rate of 19.8 patients with schizophrenia per ten thousand adults compared with only 7.3 for suburban Enfield. There is a significant association between the number of patients discharged from hospital and unemployment, frequency of overcrowding and overall population density.

A variety of psychological difficulties appear to be most common among the socially isolated and among those who are unmarried, particularly unmarried men. Numerous studies have confirmed that schizophrenia is particularly common in poor, 'socially disorganized' and overcrowded inner-city areas and among unskilled manual workers [177, 190, 442]. Suicide is commoner in areas characterized by social disorganization and social isolation [365]. Social isolation may however be common in middle-class areas [177] and manic-depressive psychosis, usually a less incapacitating illness than schizophrenia because of its better outcome, seems either to be more common in affluent areas or is evenly distributed in all social classes [177, 385]. The classic study of Faris and Dunham in 1939 showed that first admission rates to hospital for severe mental illness were highest in the central slum sections of Chicago and decreased progressively as one moved outwards to the more prosperous suburbs [129].

It was believed a hundred years ago that mental illness among the lower social class '. . . lies behind and is anterior to their outward poverty' [197]. Faris and Dunham, however, claimed that it was social disorganization which led to intrapsychic disorganization: 'The result may be the lack of any organization at all, resulting in a confused, frustrated and chaotic personality . . . It is just this type of unintelligible behaviour which becomes recognized as mental disorder' [129].

Fifty years ago, then, mental illness was seen as the consequence of environmentally induced stress. But could the high rate of schizophrenia in poor neighbourhoods be partly due to people who were already ill coming to live here? There is some evidence to support this suggestion: schizophrenia seems to occur equally among the different social classes, but, possibly because of the stigmatization of mental patients, together with their less efficient social functioning, they migrate to cheap lodging-house districts, perhaps attracted by the anonymity characteristic of such areas [177]. This process has been termed by psychiatrists 'social drift'.

People with incipient schizophrenia seem to be more likely to go into or remain in low-status occupations [109, 157, 303]. If we compare the social class of schizophrenic patients with that of their fathers at about the same age, the patients sometimes appear to have moved down the occupational scale before they first see a doctor [157]. Schizophrenic men may achieve less than we might predict from their school performance or their father's occupational status; there is often a decline in occupational level after the onset of the illness [37, 108]. Other studies have, however, suggested that there is no social drift by schizophrenic patients, and that they do not move down the social scale [190].

It is possible that moving to run-down areas has accelerated the process of mental illness in people who may be vulnerable. We cannot clearly show that the later development of schizophrenia was due to the same mental state as the initial move. Immigrants

do not of course 'drift' into these areas: they are forced to live in
them, and it has been suggested that the social isolation
characteristic of lodging-house areas may lead to schizophrenia
when the isolation is determined by factors outside the individual's control [128].

Reliance on hospital statistics is not enough. We have seen that
the use of certain diagnostic categories reflects ethnic stereotypes,
and the same applies to social class: psychiatrists give a diagnosis
of psychosis more readily to working-class patients [249].
Neurosis may appear to be common among the middle classes
only because professional people are more likely to request
treatment for such difficulties.

One of the most thorough attempts to look for a relationship
between social environment and mental health has been a
detailed comparison between the Isle of Wight and an area of
Inner London [358]. This study avoids the distorting effect of
hospital statistics and differentiates the movement of patients to
poor areas from the pathological effect of living in such an area.
Psychiatric difficulties among children are twice as common in
Inner London as in the Isle of Wight, and anxiety and depression
among adults are also considerably more prevalent in the city.
'Social drift' can be excluded as a cause of psychiatric problems in
children since these problems are as common in children who
have been raised in London as it is in those who have moved
there with their families. Similarly, 'out-migration' – the healthy
moving out of the city (the opposite of 'drift') – has not occurred.
The high prevalence of difficulties in London ten-year-olds is
related to the fact that more London families suffer social
disadvantage; depression is more common in working-class
mothers, and since psychiatric difficulties in mothers impair their
relations with their children, the children are affected indirectly
by the family's social circumstances.

STRESS AND SOCIAL CHANGE

Psychiatric illness may be directly associated with social environment. A study which shows that working-class women with young
children in London are four times more likely to suffer from
depression than middle-class mothers concludes: 'Depression . . .
is fundamentally related to social values since it arises in a

context of hopelessness consequent upon the loss of important sources of reward or positive value' [46].

How does being working-class cause one to be depressed? It could be that working-class women have to put up with greater stresses, or alternatively that they are in some way more vulnerable to stress. Interviews with over five hundred women in Camberwell showed that depression follows the experience of loss or severe disappointment ('life-events') or hardships continuing for at least two years, such as damp and overcrowded accommodation and insecurity of tenure [46]. Life-events are class-related: 'A middle-class woman has a close to zero risk of eviction . . . The working-class woman is not only subject to a higher frequency of the same kind of event that the middle-class woman experiences, but also has an overlay of specifically "working-class" events' [47]. Although working-class women experience them more frequently, life-events by themselves only partly account for the difference in depression in the two classes. Those women who become depressed are those who also have certain 'vulnerability factors' which make them more likely to break down in the face of hardship or loss. These vulnerability factors include lack of close ties with a husband or boyfriend, early loss of their mother, having three or more young children at home and being unable to find a job. They are all more common in working-class mothers.

The impact of social change is a particularly stressful life-event, and for first-generation ethnic minorities adaptation to a new community after migration is probably the major event of their lives. The impact of social change can be observed most easily in small Third World communities which are changing rapidly and which are small enough for us to survey the whole population and not just those who come to a psychiatric hospital. We shall briefly look at two examples from West Africa and India.

The Tallensi are a farming people in Ghana. They were traditionally divided into clans each derived from a founding ancestor. Society is polygynous and organized in separate homesteads. Daughters leave home to marry husbands from a different clan. Family life is warm and the children are integrated into everyday adult life; each child, in addition, to blood relatives, has classificatory 'brothers, sisters and fathers' of the same lineage group. Maternal uncles provide an indulgent adult who compensates for the stricter role of the father. Physical punishment of the children is rare and weaning is gentle; there is little concern in the community with witchcraft or sorcery, and 'natural' death is blamed on the ancestors rather than, as with some societies, on neighbours (see Chapter 7). Individual moral failings are recognized without a strong sense of guilt or sin: suicide is rare. *Galuk* or insanity is caused by the ancestors and is characterized by sudden wild and confused behaviour which may turn to violence. It is treated with herbal infusions: if these are unsuccessful the patient is kept attached to a log in the centre of the homestead. The Tallensi are quite open about the presence of *galuk*, but an affected person is considered incapable of marrying or of assuming communal responsibilities.

The anthropologist Meyer Fortes visited the Tallensi in the 1960s, thirty years after his first visit [138]. In the interval the population had grown, schools had been built, people were leaving the community to work elsewhere and the gradual introduction of a cash economy permitted the purchase of bicycles. Fortes found that the Tallensi now had many more chronic patients in their homesteads than previously. These patients had become ill after events associated with cultural transition such as visits to the urbanized south of the country. The local healers reported that their traditional methods no longer worked in treating *galuk*.

In India, the caste system offers us a variety of social groups, living in the same area and with broadly the same cultural assumptions, but under quite different pressures. Among the castes of an Indian coastal village are the Brahmins, the Bants and the Mogers [61]. The Brahmins, who have a patrilineal (father-descended) system, are the traditional landowners and priests: they have a disproportionately large representation on the village council. They are the richest and most educated group. The Bants, peasant cultivators, and the Mogers, fishermen, both trace their descent through the mother. In these two groups children are brought up by the mother's brother, but this is slowly changing under government influence to a patrilineal system in which descent is traced through the father and in which the children are brought up by him. As a result Bant and Moger households now show a variety of intermediate patterns. The children are caught between two adult male authority figures, the father and the mother's brother.

All three castes are Hindus but each tends to worship a particular group of gods. The Brahmins have the highest ritual status, with the Bants second. The Mogers, who come much lower down the religious pecking-order, have recently become richer than the Bants. The Bants have the highest frequency of psychiatric symptoms: their privileged position next to the Brahmins is threatened by the increased wealth of the Mogers and in addition they are in the process of changing their family structure. The Mogers too are changing, thanks to their improving economic situation, but for them it is apparently less stressful. Minor psychological symptoms amongst both Bants and Mogers are more frequent in those who are changing to the patrilineal system, but psychosis is most common among the Westernized Brahmins.

Different groups may experience quite different events as stressful. An American study distinguished between significant life-events in two groups – non-Hispanic whites and the Americans of Asian, African and Hispanic origin. For the first group the death of a loved one, marriage and a first job seemed especially important, while the others appeared more affected by a new love, a new friend or a new job. Although poor housing, discrimination and unemployment underlie the illnesses of many black patients in Britain, few complain specifically about them to their doctors. The first hospital referral usually follows an event which epitomizes their attempt at making a new life in Britain: children in trouble with the police, failure to pass an exam, eviction or the visit of a relative from their home country.

Are those members of ethnic minority groups who become mentally ill under greater strain than those who do not? Skilled Greek workers in Germany who are not able to use their skills have an above-average rate of psychosomatic illness. A majority of the Spaniards in Geneva who had emotional problems had been working in uninteresting, badly paid and unpleasant jobs, while in 90 per cent of mentally ill Algerians in Paris the illness was related to job difficulties [64].

West Indian patients in Britain who become psychiatrically ill have experienced significantly more chronic environmental stresses such as overcrowding, poverty, poor accommodation, insecurity of tenure and a long working day than have English patients [19]. However, they have suffered no greater hardships than those West Indians who are not ill. Mental illness in West Indians may be the consequence, not of external problems, but of the chronic stress caused by competing for upward occupational mobility in a social system which ostensibly encourages all its members to strive but in which this mobility is largely blocked by racial discrimination [276].

West Indians had, by and large, failed to be socialized in the predominant norms prevailing in the English working class, norms which suggested that if one had working-class origins, occupational striving would be of little avail. Many Afro-Britons are in what we might describe as a 'double-bind' relationship with society . . . He must strive, but he may not succeed. [19]

RESPONSES TO RACISM

Since the nineteenth century, when *The Times* stigmatized Irish labourers as indolent and Charles Booth declared Jewish immigrants deficient in social morality [226], the public response to ethnic minorities has become a little less crude, although certainly no less prejudiced. Immigrant groups are subject to discrimination in housing and employment, in education services and in everyday inter-personal relations. How does the experience of racism affect the psychological adjustment of minority groups?

We have seen that the housing of ethnic minorities is substandard. They occupy the transitional zones of towns, areas which are falling into disrepair and scheduled for eventual demolition, in accommodation which has rudimentary sanitation and cooking facilities. Black migrants live in areas where their white neighbours are the socially inadequate and the socially disdvantaged: the poor, the old and the physically and mentally handicapped. In the early 1960s only 11 per cent of privately let property was both advertised and did not specifically exclude coloured people. In spite of the various Race Relations Acts, extensive prejudice continues amongst private landlords, local authorities and housing agencies. As late as 1971 the House of Lords could decide that a local authority's rule that an applicant for accommodation had to be 'British' was not discriminatory.

The newly arrived immigrant may not at first realize he is discriminated against. According to a PEP report, few recent immigrants complain of discrimination in housing, either because it is not immediately apparent or perhaps because they avoid exposing themselves to an awareness of it.

Employment is the area in which immigrants soon recognize unequal treatment – over a third feel they have been personally discriminated against [79]. While only one in four West Indians who had professional jobs before migration obtained similar work in Britain [152], industrial managers regard blacks as less skilled than whites [449]. Black workers are employed only if the job is menial, or if there is a shortage of labour, the filter being covertly operated by receptionists, clerks and gatekeepers rather than being explicit company policy. Again, the Race Relations Acts appear to have limited effect: of the 298 applications to industrial tribunals in 1978 which were concerned with discrimination in employment only twenty were successful [76].

Apart from discrimination in the search for accommodation and work, black immigrants are also the victims of racially motivated violence. The intensity and frequency of these assaults tend to fluctuate. Peaks of violence have coincided with inflammatory oratory such as the speeches on immigration by Enoch Powell. In the 1970s the marches and rallies of the National Front were followed by a series of attacks on Asians. About one-fifth of all the indictable assaults reported to police in Tower Hamlets for the first six months of 1977 were against Asians, who represent only one-fourteenth of the population of the borough [410]. Given the increasingly common feeling among migrants that the police are not concerned with their interests, even this figure is likely to be an underestimate.

The immigrant is continually under the threat of deportation. Hotels and factories are raided on 'fishing trips' for illegal immigrant workers and even hospital records are not immune from Home Office scrutiny. Immigrants who have been in Britain for less than five years can be deported if their husbands or parents are deported or if they are convicted of a crime which could be punished by imprisonment. Immigrants could also be deported under Section 86 of the Mental Health Act if medical advice suggests 'it is in their interest'.

Prejudice is experienced not only in major issues of economic survival but in everyday life:

Racism is not confined to the public realm; it appears in countless small ways as well. A white couple with many children is said to have a large family, whereas a similarly situated black couple is said to breed like rabbits. White immigrants to Britain, who have always out-numbered black immigrants, are said to come in 'large numbers', while the blacks come in 'hordes' or 'waves'. Middle classes living together constitute a suburb, miners a community, and the immigrants a ghetto. Racism appears in the way the immigrant is cheated by, say, a shop assistant as if honesty in her view was not to be practised with respect to him; it appears in the way promises given to him are broken as if promises given to a black man are not binding; it appears in the way he is gratuitously insulted as if his feelings deserved no consideration; it is expressed in his social ostracism, in the way his favours are taken for granted and those by the white man to him considered to require more than equal in return, in the way his social graces and intellectual skills are treated as unusual in 'someone like him', in the perverse glee taken in not being able to spell or pronounce an immigrant's name correctly, in petty abuses over the fence, in refusing to take him seriously on any question, in accusing him of having a chip on his shoulder when he refuses to be patronised, in expecting him always to be smiling and polite in apparent gratefulness for the privilege of being allowed to appear in the white man's presence . . . Such instances are all individually trivial but can be cumulatively shattering and general enough to make an immigrant's life unbearable. If he ignores them, he is in danger of losing his self-respect and dignity; if he reacts to them on each occasion, he is in danger of getting consumed by the fire of his rage. [310]

Prejudice is not merely experienced as an external constraint; it becomes part of the self-image of the immigrant – a self-image which is defined by others. He must achieve success within the stereotype offered to him. The American or West Indian black is faced with the ironical fact that he can only succeed as a boxer or musician: 'Reggae assaults the primitive brain stem where emotions originate' [24]. When he values spontaneity over calculation he admits he has no future. A patient of ours with a psychosomatic complaint was the only black teenager amongst a group of friends at a technical college. Disliking music of all types himself, he was constantly questioned about black music by his companions. He pretended to be a reggae singer and was driven to complicated stratagems to avoid being heard. He benefited by confirming the majority view: he was for them a predictable and 'safe' immigrant. We have occasionally been asked to help young black men who have white girlfriends and who are totally unable to live up to the sexual demands which the couple's joint fantasies have generated.

Since immigration is a comparatively novel experience for Britain (unlike the United States, where 'immigrants' are not conceived of in quite the same way as a separate group), the immigrant is subject to a stereotype of himself or herself as embodying a variety of undesirable characteristics. Even his minor crimes such as motoring offences are recorded on a Special Branch register [111]. Until recently age was determined on entering the country by X-rays of the bones, 'marital status' by vaginal examination. The specific country of origin is of little importance. Even though only one-third of immigrants in the 1970s were not white, the use of 'immigrant' in a newspaper headline invariably means a black, usually West Indian [64]. The black presence in Britain is an 'invasion', a metaphor both of cancer and human enemies [395].

As children have been born to West Indian and Asian immigrants in Britain there has been a shift to describing members of these ethnic minorities as 'black'. 'The black immigrant comes to feel less like a West Indian in English society and more like a black man in a white society' (quoted in Watson [420]). The term 'immigrant' is still used, particularly if the transitoriness or undesirability of their being in Britain is being emphasized. The children of West Indian parents are still termed 'immigrants.' The black Briton, then, is identified with the 'black' of the Third World, whose 'value' was made plain in the reporting of the uprising in southern Zaire, where the fate of a small group of whites was continually headlined in the press, with hardly a mention of the massacre of thousands of blacks or indeed the cruelties of the Zaire government, against whose policies the uprising was a reaction.

The individual in cultural transition can usually choose from a variety of identities, identities which may be primarily political, religious or professional. For the immigrant to Britain from the

New Commonwealth, even though he may trace descent from both black and white ancestors, one identity only is offered and that is 'black'. And 'black' is a synonym for trouble [316]. While the white lives in 'cramped conditions' or 'cannot find a house', the black is 'overcrowded'. He is defined as a problem, a nuisance or a failure, in terms of unemployment, disdvantage, delinquency, educational subnormality – or mental illness. Contact with him is reserved for those who deal with crime or sickness – but even for them he is specially troublesome: a Conservative party spokesman on health recommended extra financial incentives to those GPs who 'suffered' from a high proportion of immigrant patients.

Ethnic minorities of course do have some health and personal problems which are related to their pre-migration culture or to that of their parents. For example the use of lead in some ointments which have been used by Indian parents around the eyes of their children may be injurious to their health. The significant fact is that all his problems are located in the immigrant or in his culture rather than in political or economic conditions in Britain. Most immigrants who have tuberculosis did not bring it with them to Britain – they acquired it here [64]. Not surprisingly, single migrant males provided a large proportion of the cases of venereal disease in the late 1950s and early 1960s; as households were set up, this diminished [64]. Assigned a marginal place in a non-egalitarian society, the difficulties of the immigrant are seen as a function of his biology or his deliberate refusal to live up to 'British norms' [64].

Probably the most popularized health problem of minorities has been that of rickets among Asian children. Although of course a very real illness, the concentration on rickets to the exclusion of other health hazards illustrates a variety of popular preoccupations: uncommon in the pre-migration society (in a state of nature under the tropical sun), it is now common, not just because of the lack of sun in Britain but because phytic acid present in chapattis prevents children absorbing vitamin D from milk (something unpleasant in their own food prevents their children from enjoying the natural goodness available in Britain) and causes rickets (an unpleasant disease which stunts them and which we thought had disappeared last century). A nice tidy problem: the solution – education of the immigrant.

With an economic recession, immigration has been halted on

economic grounds, but for the immigrant doctor the problem has been located as one inside him. A decision by the medical profession to reduce the number of doctors employed in the Health Service has been achieved partly by reduction in the numbers of projected places available at medical schools. At the same time there has been a sudden 'concern over standards' and more stringent controls have been placed over the entry of immigrant doctors. There is in fact no evidence that these doctors are any better or worse than they have been in the last thirty years.

How do members of ethnic minorities react to their difficulties? A study in Birmingham looked at minor emotional difficulties in immigrants from Asia, who were compared with British-born whites, matched for age and sex [74]. The migrants tended to have fewer emotional difficulties, and were more likely to be in employment and to have had a stable employment history. They felt they were less likely to have had their life disrupted in the preceding year by stressful events than were the non-immigrants. On the whole they were better off than five years previously. They had found things in Britain to be at least as good as expected and often better. Few of them complained of prejudice – one-third had experienced it in employment but less than one in twenty from the police.

Compared with immigrants from India, those from Pakistan had a lower symptom score, were less likely to report prejudice and were more likely to feel they were better off than previously. It is possible that the Indians had been relatively better off before migrating and were thus less likely to have improved their economic position. Islam has also proved more resilient in Britain than has Hinduism, which is primarily an Indian national religion.

It appears that some groups of immigrants, then, are certainly not dissatisfied with having migrated to Britain. This survey was, however, limited to Asians in one particular area. They were compared with British-born whites of an inner-city district who might reasonably be expected to feel less satisfied with their life than the general population, since 40 per cent of the inner-city group were unemployed. The pattern of life satisfaction and symptoms is likely to be quite different when contrasting ethnic groups in different areas. A survey conducted in Southall in the 1980s might have come to rather different conclusions.

We cannot assume that racism is the major difficulty which members of ethnic minorities consciously articulate. A survey some years ago suggested that the aspect of Britain with which West Indians were most discontented was the weather [91]. Depression is more common among the West Indian community in Birmingham than it is amongst white British-born or Irish, but the major reasons given for depression by the patients are problems with children, which are four times as common as for the whites, and marital difficulties, which are twice as common [54]. For someone who moves to another society and hopes to become part of it and who arrives to identify with its citizens, to be consciously aware of rejection may be so threatening that it can be initially articulated only in other terms, such as those of religious or family identity.

The reaction to stress depends largely on the original intentions of the community – whether they intend to settle or whether they are sojourners who hope eventually to return home. Close contact with the pre-migration society may offer an alternative identity to that of 'immigrant'. The Chinese in Britain maintain close ties with their original community in Hong Kong, of which they are still considered to be indispensable members [420]. Most return to 'sterling houses' built with money sent back over the years from Britain. Some areas in Hong Kong exist largely on remittances, and generous contributions are also made to schools and community centres. Gujarati, Hindu and Sikh men were soon joined by women from their home areas, and Pakistani men, who usually emigrated later, have now accumulated enough money to follow suit. Political events at home still set up reverberations in the immigrant community: the exiled President Makarios made a major appeal from the pulpit of the Orthodox church in Camden Town. Identity with the home country may be articulated in less conscious ways: during the Algerian war the crime rate rose among Algerians in France and then declined after their country had achieved independence from France.

Close ties with the country of origin are characteristic of the sojourners – in particular the Asian, Cypriot and Turkish immigrants. In many cases the return is continuously delayed and many accept that they will probably remain in Britain [8]. Many Greek Cypriots who came to Britain as sojourners now regard themselves as exiles; their homes in Cyprus now fall in the

Turkish occupied zone. The major difficulties for these groups are the acceptance of life in exile, the gradual relinquishment of traditional patterns and conflict between the first generation, often wary of British customs, and the second generation, who are born here and frequently see themselves as British.

The Jewish community has always been divided between those who wanted to assimilate and those who saw in Britain a country in which they could establish isolated centres of traditional life. A group of Orthodox Jews in Manchester has applied to the city council for permission to establish an *Eruv* – an area of the city which the community of ten thousand can consider as a privileged domestic space, unhindered by conventional restrictions [168].

The situation of the West Indians has been the reverse of that of the Asian and Cypriots, for whom 'home' is their country of birth. The Caribbean migrant came to Britain, the 'historico-cultural navel of the West Indian society' [188], as if he were coming home – to a society of which he regarded himself as an integral part. His school was dominated by textbooks written in England, his career by the Oxford and Cambridge Examination Boards, his town by English place names and monuments to English admirals. He is told, however, that his arrival means that 'our nation has never faced a greater danger' [409]. The response of the first generation to rejection was to reassert in a rather different way their initial British and Christian values – a way which may be typified by Pentecostalism: the substituted goal of 'white' Christianity, unlike the real British goal of economic success, is attainable. This attitude has been characterized by radical blacks as 'colour blindness' or an attempt to achieve invisibility. The response of many of the second generation has been only partly a return to traditional values, as these traditional values are conceived of as already white. They have established a new identity which is in part drawn from Caribbean culture and in part from their experience in Britain – a process which has been called *ethnic redefinition*. The adoption of some of the values and beliefs of the Jamaican Rastafarians (Chapter 1) has provided an identity which is specifically that of being black in Britain today: Babylon is no longer the Jamaican establishment but Britain. 'Home' is now Africa or a fabled Ethiopia. They identify not with white Britain but with Zimbabwe and Soweto. At the same time they have gained a critical perspective on the identity of their parents, an identity which is, in a sense, included in their own [379].

Ethnic redefinition is a reassertion of the values of a disadvantaged or stigmatized group analagous to the women's movement or to 'coming out' for the homosexual. It contains not only a reasserted identity but an explanation of the original stigmatization; it thus deals explicitly with the attitude of the dominant group and offers an explanation for it. It is not a retreat into a ghetto but is directly concerned with the majority culture: not only have many young whites been deeply influenced by Rastafarianism, but a number, particularly girls with black boyfriends, have actually joined it. In a similar way the proselytizing branch of Hasidic Judaism, the Lubavitchers, have converted a number of non-Jews, no mean achievement given the roots of this sect in traditional Eastern European Jewish religion and custom [231].

Because black ethnic redefinition is a redefinition against the assumptions of white society, it is in a large measure still defined by these stereotypes. Rather than deny the stereotype validity, redefinition accepts it and gives it a positive value or plays rather uneasily with it, challenging white society with a mirror of its own prejudices. It is not so dissimilar to the reverse process – the desperate denial of the stereotype at all costs. Sartre suggests that the French Jew lets himself be poisoned by the racist stereotype: in deliberately avoiding acting in accordance with it he robs himself of his own authenticity. His conduct is continually overdetermined from outside [371]. Ethnic redefinition may provide a secure identity in the face of continual invalidation, but it is an identity still conceived of in terms of the dominant culture: the identity of the Briton who happens to be black is primarily *that of a black*.

The history of the self-image of the Asian, Cypriot or Turk has not simply been a movement towards a British identity. He has sometimes undertaken moves towards white British society similar to that of the West Indian and carried out a similar withdrawal. In this case it has been a withdrawal to a *reassertion* of his original culture rather than the creation of a new identity.

Ethnic redefinition or reassertion is not always simply a response to prejudice: Sikh men started to wear their turbans in the early 1960s only after some years in Britain and when their wives came to join them. The aspects of the original culture which are most rigorously reasserted are usually those which are considered fundamental to the continuation of boundaries internal and external to the community. Sexual politics inside and the spectre of intermarriage outside are the key problems which face both Jewish and Asian groups in the attempt to avoid assimilation. Asian men with families are anxious that their daughters should have a British education and are prepared for a limited degree of assimilation, but they are reluctant for them to go to mixed-sex schools. For some immigrants, reassertion of traditional values may occur only after personal disaster. The reasserted pre-migration identity appears firmly rooted, while to attempt to move continually towards affluence and partial assimilation is always precarious, liable to be threatened by a major setback.

THE OZCHELICK FAMILY

Zafer Ozchelik is now seventeen. She came to England from Turkey with her parents when she was two. She has two older brothers and an older sister. Her father, Gulden, arrived from a small Anatolian village with little money and with no relatives here. He settled with his family in Islington and worked for five years in a local factory, accumulating enough capital to launch a small grocer's shop. This prospered as more Turks and Turkish Cypriots settled in the area. He moved to larger premises, opening a café and then a dry-cleaning business.

The four children went to the local school together with white children born in Islington and other immigrant children from the Caribbean and Ireland. In the evening and at weekends they helped in the shop. The mother first worked in a local clothes factory but, as they became more prosperous, she stayed in the shop. Visits back to Turkey encouraged their fellow villagers to come and settle in the same area. Gulden arranged their passages, found them work, and, because of his prosperity and success, became the recognized head of the small community. Then the family moved to a residential suburb in South London. Zafer finished her schooling privately and the family began to lose contact with their relatives in Islington and Turkey, visiting rarely but continuing to send presents and support them financially. A substantial gift helped to establish a mosque, but no one in the family visited it after the inauguration. Most of their new neighbours were English and the boys adopted middle-class interests and ambitions. Sometimes betrayed by their name or slight accent they were embarrassed when asked where they came from; usually they passed as English-born.

Zafer was hoping to go to a secretarial college when, owing to the simultaneous failure of various financial enterprises, her father was declared bankrupt. Their lifestyle became severely restricted and the two boys started work in a local bank. Gulden became very depressed and lost any interest in business. With the help of the relatives in Islington who had not been affected by his collapse he was able to continue living in the same house, but he did not return to work and spent his day wandering around the house lamenting. No encouragement from his family seemed to help. He lost his place as leader of the immigrants from his village, less because of his financial straits than because of his apathy. He was treated by the family doctor for stomach pains and an ulcer, for heart trouble and depression.

Gulden began to attend the mosque and found some consolation in the religion he had long ignored. He started telling the family that their misfortune was the result of their forsaking Islam. He forbade the boys to drink and family arguments developed whenever they went out in the evening. He considered going back to Turkey but was unable to face returning as a failure. The children were not impressed by his new convictions and still considered themselves English. The mother intervened between the boys (who privately said that their father had become senile because of his disappointment) and Gulden, who, although increasingly reclusive, had become domineering inside the family. He planned to establish a branch of one of the Turkish Islamic fundamentalist parties among the London Turks but made little practical attempt to achieve this.

We met Zafer one afternoon in the casualty department of the local hospital where we had been called by the doctor on duty. She had been brought in by car apparently while having a fit. She was sitting in a chair, her eyes wide open, staring blankly in front of her through her tears. She didn't want to talk at first, but gradually, with help from her brothers, we were able to find out what had happened. Her elder sister had married, glad to leave the tense atmosphere of the house. Zafer was forbidden to go to the secretarial college even though her brothers offered to pay, and was increasingly restricted to the house. Gulden said he was looking for a husband for her; Zafer was outraged but there was little she could do. Her mother, anxious to salvage something from the collapse of their hopes, advised her not to precipitate an argument while her father was still unwell. The brothers coped by avoiding him as far as possible. That afternoon, with the help of the boys, Zafer had ventured to visit their cousins. Her father had found out and followed them in a rage, burst into the house and, finding them dancing to records, had punched the boys and their cousins and tried to pull her out by the hair. He had been restrained and partially calmed down while her brothers took Zafer home. She sat in the car, huddled up and shaking, and then had the 'fit'.

A failure by English values as he conceived them, Gulden had attempted to return to the pre-emigration style of life which he had previously renounced, but his children were unable to follow him. They were able to get some sense of security by an increasingly *greater* affiliation to British society which was threatened by their father's movement in the opposite direction. Luckily this family appears to be benefiting from family therapy. We hope that in time the father will be able to see his return to traditional values as not necessarily the best solution for the children, while they will be able to accept that their family do not all have to try to be as 'English' as possible.

FAMILIES AND CHILDREN

It is difficult to generalize about the difficulties faced by the younger members of ethnic minorities, not only because of the diversity of cultures in which they are growing up (and children before they go to school may have few contacts outside their immediate family) but because they may or may not be immigrants themselves. West Indian and West African children have often come to Britain with their parents when young, or followed them later; many West Indian children have been born here and been sent back to the Caribbean for some years; some children have been born here and have remained here except for brief visits 'home', like many Asian and Cypriot children.

What is the effect of immigration on young children? Children of West Indian immigrants to Britain who have been born in the

Caribbean have been compared with those born in Britain [360]. Although they had had quite different life experiences (those born in the Caribbean being more frequently separated from their parents and those born in Britain more likely to be cared for by non-relatives), the two groups of children showed little difference in their emotional adjustment. The authors of this study point out, however, that the children who were born in the West Indies emigrated to Britain when they were quite young; emigration in adolescence might well be more traumatic.

Compared with adults, children are seldom admitted to psychiatric hospitals and they tend to have quite different problems. Looking at the figures we have suggests that the pattern is similar to that of adults (Table 2, p. 89). West Indian-born children are admitted more often than British-born children, Asian children less often [73].

Studies of immigrants' families have tended to divide them up into two broad groups: Asian and European families, whose major problem is seen as that of moving from one culture to another and whose problems are *external* to the family, and West Indian families, whose difficulties are seen as located somehow *inside* the family itself.

Perhaps because they appear most likely to achieve financial security, Asian families are described as supportive and as offering their children a passport to success in Britain. Their fault is considered to lie in their being *too* self-contained and too constricting and in not being prepared to adjust to British life – criticisms levelled at immigrant Jewish families earlier this century. For Asian children, going to school is often a traumatic break with family life; their culture and language are not taught and are not usually regarded as additional skills to be valued, or else they are placed in 'Asian' schools. Parents have high and sometimes unrealistic expectations of academic performance. The assumption is that Indian or Pakistani children come from a family group not so dissimilar from that in Asia. In fact Asian family life in Britain is often radically different from the pre-migration society: women frequently work outside the home in opposition to the traditional pattern.

This move away from tradition to a more individualistic pattern of life is symbolized by the question of 'arranged marriages' [205]. British-born South Asians have to negotiate their way between the contrary views of màrriage as a contract between two families which is arranged by parents on the children's behalf and the idealized Western model of free choice of partner and intimate courtship [23]. The traditional family approach to marriage is still usually followed, despite dramatic reports of rebellion [435]. While arranged marriages apparently remain generally acceptable and successful, Asian girls are having an increasing influence on the actual choice of partner and are likely to persuade their parents to select a partner who has lived in Britain for some time.

The problems of West Indian children are seen by white professionals not as in the transition from one culture to another but as located within the family they are born into: black households in Britain and America often centre round the mother; the father is relatively peripheral and may live alone or with his parents. This matricentral family is criticized as matriarchal and thus pathological – 'a deviation from the norm', 'disorganized', 'irregular' and 'unstable' (e.g. Moynihan [286]). It has, however, been suggested that the tendency to see the black family as deviant is due to a confusion between the *household* – the actual people living together in close proximity in the same domestic group – and the *family*, which also has financial, legal and emotional bonds but which may not be located in a single place [69, 394].

The 'basic human social unit' is not the 'nuclear family' (father, mother and child) but mother and child [142]. While whites view with equanimity patterns of marriage which seem totally at variance with British norms[1] when they are located overseas, they are likely to be critical of 'non-standard' patterns in their midst. The Asian family is not considered pathological, because it includes what they term the nuclear family.

West Indian families may also appear to be more dysfunctional than Asian families because of a 'high visibility' of family difficulties. The young West Indian girl who becomes pregnant or who develops a liaison undesirable to her parents may be able to leave home easily, while a deviant Asian girl is 'contained' within the family. She is seen as a threat to the family *honour* (such as the Gujarati *izzat* code) and must be concealed. The West Indian girl is seen as contravening a *moral* code and her pregnancy may be regarded by her parents as the first step on an irrresistible downward path: it is often followed by attempted suicide [53].

There is no valid reason for regarding a matricentral family taken on its own terms as pathological [283]. The 'Victorian' discipline of young West Indian children as perceived by distressed white liberals is probably the functional result of young children in the Caribbean taking on what whites might see as parental roles towards their younger siblings. Not to mention the colonial legacy.

That the West Indian family is not pathological for individuals inside is not to say that it provides the best opportunity for responding to prejudice and discrimination outside. In fact its very origin is in the historical relation of the West Indian to the white. Slaves in the Caribbean were forbidden to marry. Their children were the property of the slave owners and fathers had no parental rights or duties. The mother assumed the major responsibility for bringing up her children. After emancipation marriage remained an ideal associated with property and social status. Formal marriage was postponed until the couple could set up an independent home, when the husband could support the family financially. Children born before the establishment of a permanent union would therefore tend to be cared for in the setting of a matricentral household. To some extent the postponement of marriage until economic security has been achieved continues in Caribbean society today, but West Indian immigrants are increasingly adopting the pattern of earlier marriage.

The matricentral family in Britain produces certain difficulties, but these are difficulties of transition, as for the Asian community, and not difficulties due to the nature of the family itself. In the West Indies older female relatives are often available to provide skilled childrearing while the mother is out at work. In this country she frequently does not have this form of support. A high proportion of patients with acute psychotic reactions are mothers struggling to bring up children single-handed in adverse conditions. Compared to English working-class women, more West Indian mothers work full-time, partly to pay for more expensive accommodation. They are forced to make use of child-minders and the children may thus be adversely affected by lack of stimulation and play. West Indian parents are able to afford fewer toys for their children than are white parents and have less time to spend playing with them [360].

Some young West Indian children have developed a syndrome similar to that of autism; they are apathetic and withdrawn and often fail to learn to speak. Over four-fifths of a group of these children had mothers who were severely depressed over social difficulties and who also felt guilty at not being able to provide their children with a suitably stimulating environment [325].

West African parents with a totally different set of cultural assumptions often foster their children out to white foster parents for long periods; although this is believed to be an educational advantage, it frequently causes difficulties for the children, not only in choosing between two sets of parents but in choosing between a black and a white identity [364].

Many of the difficulties faced by black children are not problems in the family but are located in the relations of these families to the outside world. A comparison of black and white families in London showed that a greater proportion of black parents held unskilled or semi-skilled jobs, although both groups had similar levels of educational achievement [360]. They were twice as likely to be overcrowded and were more likely to lack such basic amenities as hot water, lavatories and kitchens. The mothers worked longer hours, and 60 per cent of them had five or more children compared with 30 per cent of the white group. More of the children had been in care or looked after by other relatives. The quality of family relationships was as good as for white children and there was no difference in the number who had mentally ill or criminal parents. This study concluded that both groups had a very similar family pattern – a nuclear family of stable marriage with a father who was included in the family: the black family in this instance was no more matricentral than the white family.

These West Indian children were more self-reliant than the white children, were expected to help more in the home and were more restricted in their social activities. Their educational level was poorer, especially those who had been born in the Caribbean rather than in Britain. Black children on the whole are no more likely to have psychological difficulties than white children or to have behavioural difficulties at home [359]. Where they do seem to differ is that their conduct at school is worse; the authors suggested that this is related to their lower educational attainment, the disparity between strict discipline at home and a more liberal atmosphere at school, racism in the schools and the fact that they attend poorer schools. A more recent study has suggested, however, that the behaviour of West Indian children at school is no worse that that of white children [73].

Education is the principal way for the children of immigrants to overcome social and economic disadvantage, but there are particular difficulties for the dialect or Creole speakers from the Caribbean. Like white working-class children they are taken to be less competent in standard speech than the middle classes.

Security is a consonance between personal experience and the world of others and the West Indian child finds himself defined as black in a white world by a white language. Unlike an Asian child, he is not at first conscious of cultural transition – he is, after all, 'at home'. Language 'difficulties' in West Indian children are the expression of traditional linguistic patterns rather than 'inability to speak English'. Instead of describing them as failing by speaking substandard English we could consider them as discriminated against for using a different language [71]. Spoken language is the mode of communication between ethnic minorities and the representatives of the establishment, including doctors; their 'normality' will be highly dependent on this variable. Language difficulties seem to contribute to employment difficulties, but they are difficult to separate from the effects of prejudice [390].

A disproportionately high number of children of West Indian origin are placed in schools for the educationally subnormal or in the lower streams of comprehensive schools. In the 1970s, 34 per cent of the educationally subnormal school population in the Inner London Education Authority Area were children of immigrants, although they constituted only 17 per cent of the total school population. Eighty per cent of the ESN immigrant children were of West Indian origin. It has been suggested that many West Indian children of average and even above-average ability are assigned to these schools on the basis of unreliable testing [71]. Newly arrived children may be tested when still in a state of 'culture shock', and black children often achieve lower scores when tested by a white psychologist. American studies suggest that such conventional measures of intelligence as conceptual abstraction and verbal syntax are closely related to class and economic status.

English teachers may have negative and self-confirming expectations of the school performance of black children. The performance of West Indians in London schools is significantly poorer when children are told their intelligence is being measured

and that the test is to be administered by a white experimenter
[421]. Assessment of scholastic performance has frequently failed
to take into account significant differences between the structure
of Creole and standard English.

The psychological difficulties of older children fall into two
general types: those which were already present when they were
younger and which persist – these are usually related to family
problems; and those which are new – their origins usually lying
outside the family. Black adolescents have been likely to leave
school early and look for a job rather than attempting to acquire
further education. Their experience as young adults is a
confirmation of their experiences as children. Unemployment
among young black workers rose by 450 per cent between
February 1974 and February 1977 compared with an increase of
150 per cent of the population as a whole.

In November 1976, 40 per cent of young people under eighteen
who were registered as unemployed in Lambeth were black [84].
Youth Employment Officers systematically underestimate the
intelligence of black school leavers when interviewing them, and
a detailed study of school leavers carried out in Lewisham in 1977
[77] showed that black teenagers were three times more likely to
be unemployed; those who did find a job had taken longer to get
it, made more job applications and attended a greater number of
interviews than their white contemporaries. The black school
leavers had searched for work at least as hard as the white but
even so had been less likely to find the kind of work they had
hoped for and were less satisfied with their jobs. Two-thirds of
the unemployed black adolescents felt that they had probably
been discriminated against by employers. 'I phoned and they said
"come in"; when I came in they said the job had gone. when I
got home my cousin phoned them up and they said yes there was
a vacancy' [77].

A common experience for black teenagers has been 'sus' – the
charge of being a suspected person under Section 4 of the
Vagrancy Act 1824, which enabled the police to arrest 'every
suspected person or reputed thief frequenting or loitering about
or in . . . any street or highway, or any place adjacent to a street
or highway with intent to commit an arrestable offence'. Until its
repeal the Vagrancy Act (a successor to the Act which first
legalized compulsory psychiatric hospitalization) allowed arrest-
ing police officers not to produce any independent evidence or

show that the person suspected was 'guilty of a particular act tending to show his intent'. Individuals were thus charged and convicted of 'being a suspected person' without having committed any crime, and there was no right to trial by jury. Already in 1967 the Lord Chief Justice was anticipating an increase in court business because of the entry of immigrants 'in hosts' [167]. He has, in a sense, been proved right: the sus law was disproportionately used against young black people [191]. In 1977, 2,366 people were arrested in the Metropolitan Police area on 'sus', 1,042 of whom 'were judged by appearance to be West Indian or African' [176]. Immigrant areas have not been, however, areas of particularly high crime rates [336].

Adolescence is the period of life when one's identity is thrown into the sharpest focus. It is ideally a time when there is a reconciliation between one's identity as a child and one's identity as an adult, between one's conception of oneself and the conception offered to one by others [119]. The achievement of a valid identity and the security it brings depend upon a congruence between what one has experienced, one's self-definition and the definition ascribed by society. For the young black, adolescence is likely to be the eventual realization of failure – failure according to the criteria of white society.

NOTE

1   The white English working-class family has, however, also been described as matricentral [134], as of course are naval families.

CHAPTER SEVEN

SICK SOCIETIES

No sooner had we got used to the psychiatric quack who vehemently demonstrated the serpent of sex coiled round the root of our all actions, no sooner had we begun to feel honestly uneasy about our lurking complexes, than lo and behold the psychoanalytic gentleman reappeared on the stage with a theory of pure psychology. The medical faculty, which was on hot bricks over the therapeutic innovations, heaved a sigh of relief as it watched the ground warming under the feet of the professional psychologist. This, however, was not the end. The ears of the ethnologist began to tingle, the philosopher felt his gorge rise, and at last the moralist knew he must rush in. By this time, psychoanalysts had become a public danger.

D. H. Lawrence, *Psychoanalysis and the Unconscious*
(Heinemann, 1923; Penguin Books, 1971, p. 201)

The last chapter demonstrated two difficulties which face us when we try to assess the psychological adjustment of someone who belongs to a minority ethnic group. Both are related to the fact that his problems are defined by the majority culture.

The West Indian family, in common with families in other disadvantaged groups [34, 133], is regarded as pathological because it apparently lacks a father. The paternal role of guide and disciplinarian is assumed by others – by the magistrate, the social worker and the psychiatrist [103]. Black children are, nevertheless, well adjusted inside the family and their 'pathology' (delinquency) is directed outwards against the wider society [359]. The assumption that the family itself is maladaptive enables representatives of the majority culture to 'enter' it for the purpose of control. As with 'sus' there is concern with control and surveillance in the absence of illness or crime in the accepted sense. Delinquency and behaviour disorders are moral rather than medical concepts and they more clearly reflect normative judgements. To isolate them as illnesses existing in 'nature' facilitates and legitimates their 'treatment' [448].

We have seen that psychiatrists regard economic position, occupational status, housing and education as associated *separately* with patterns of mental illness and that minority ethnic groups are particularly vulnerable because they happen to be disadvantaged in all of these areas. Minorities are thus characterized by many independent disadvantages ('multiple deprivation') and the solution is seen as tackling each one in isolation.

For the black individual however, each disadvantage is only a partial reflection of a single ascribed status – being black. All his disadvantages are maintained by this status – a status which is a function of his relations with the majority culture – not by a series of separate failings located inside him. Even the most educated and affluent members of a disadvantaged group are not able to escape its emotional stresses [241]. All disadvantaged groups share a similar purposelessness, a loss of self-esteem and a loss of meaning in their lives, together with bitter resentment which is manifested as delinquency: a characteristic set of attitudes which is less a sickness of the mind than a 'sickness of spirit' [133].

If delinquency and low IQ scores are associated with a particular minority ethnic group, it is not because they are located in the group itself, in its biology or in its social organization [344]. Both these characteristics are almost universal among groups subject to racism by others, even when they are physically identical to the dominant groups [133].

To assess the adjustment of the minority individual we must consider him in relation to his own culture; we must try to avoid looking at isolated 'sub-cultural' patterns which are regarded as pathological by the dominant group. The rest of this book is concerned with attempting to do that. Can white psychiatry look at psychological adaptation without the bias and ethnocentrism implied in its own cultural standpoint? We shall start by looking critically at one approach to culture and mental illness – that of psychoanalysis.

CULTURE AND PERSONALITY

The psychoanalytical method which originated in Freud's clinical work at the beginning of the century claimed to offer a universal and non-judgemental method of investigation of the mind. As psychoanalysis was regarded as a psychological or even a biological theory, it was a tool independent of cultural assumptions and one which could be used to show how these assumptions arose. Culture existed to control instinctual drives. In all societies children passed through similar developmental stages; the resulting personality was a product of parental frustration, indulgence or discipline of instinctual needs at these stages. Different child-rearing practices created different personality types.

Psychoanalysis, however, was still dependent on many nineteenth-century assumptions. It suggested that there were striking similarities between early man, the modern European child, the modern 'primitive', and the insane [144]. All four were believed to use 'magical thinking' (believing that wishes could change the external world) and 'concrete thinking' (confusing an object and its representation). Like women and like criminals, they 'loved many names and liked to change them', enjoyed adornment, had a prominent abdomen and did not walk erect [160]. They could be controlled by simple tricks or an act of will [399].

Ethnographic studies were extensively used to illustrate the psychoanalytical theories of child development and of insanity; for psychoanalysis, the primitive, like the psychotic, was a child. Psychotics were believed to regress back to a point of childhood development, a point beyond which the whites' ancestors and modern non-literate communities had not evolved. Sexual urges, which were repressed in the European and could appear only in his dreams, were apparent in the day-time symbols of both psychotic and savage [238]. Differences between European and tribal man, between sane and insane, once located in an anatomical space, were now found as points in a developmental time. Every European during his life recapitulated the history of the human race [160].

Schizophrenic paintings were likened to those of the Expressionist artists who had been influenced by tribal artefacts and children's drawings. Beneath the veneer of twentieth-century man still stalked the primitive who would appear sporadically in the form of the insane. The psychotic offered to Surrealists, as the primitive had to the Romantics, a metaphor or even a model for the rejection of the contemporary family and state, of bourgeois social and sexual norms.

At about the same time, many anthropologists became committed to the concept of 'culture' – the distinctive way of life shown by a particular ethnic group or community. It was suggested, following Dilthey and Spengler, that each society has a distinctive cultural configuration which patterns life in that society and structures the thoughts and emotions of each member [29, 207, 257]. An attempt could be made to describe the personality of the average individual – the basic personality or 'national character' which would yield clues about the particular stresses on everyone in the community independently of their personal idiosyncrasies. This 'Culture and Personality' approach was particularly concerned with how the early experiences and socialization of young children were related to the communal values they would later be expected to endorse [428]. Margaret Mead contrasted different child-rearing practices in Melanesia, and Erikson analysed the childhood of European figures like Luther, Hitler and Gorky to see how representative they were of their community [119, 273]. The culture of immigrant groups was suggested to be a consequence of their patterns of weaning [287].

These anthropologists felt that by using the psychoanalytical theory of personality development they would be able to describe all societies in similar psychological terms without making value-judgements about their technological 'level' or degree of civilization. Such an approach suggested that each society must be taken on its own terms; what was normal behaviour in one community might be abnormal in another.

In perhaps the best-known of these studies, *Patterns of Culture* [29], Ruth Benedict compares three diffrent communities: two ethnic minorities in North America, the Kwakiutl Indians of the north-west Pacific coast and the Pueblo Indians of the south-west, and a colonized people living on an island east of New Guinea, the Dobuans. The Kwakiutl have a comfortable material existence – they trade with neighbouring communities using a currency of etched copper; time is passed in hunting, fishing and wood-carving. According to Benedict their representative insti-tution is the *potlach*, in which men attempt to outdo each other by offering lavish feasts and gifts: The distribution of presents has always to be repaid with interest and failure to do so results in humiliation for the recipient. Periodic contests in which possessions are destroyed are the measure of social prestige. 'Extravagant' is a term of commendation and the ideal man is one who shames others. The Kwakiutl encourage religious ecstasy and believe that 'the gift of the spirit destroys man's reason'. Even healing the sick is competitive: the successful shaman is the one who outwits his colleagues. Benedict suggests that the whole of Kwakiutl culture operates along a single emotional spectrum ranging from victory to shame.

The Pueblo Indians by comparison practise restraint and moderation. Ceremonies are sedate, sober and inoffensive. Religion, unlike that of most North American Indians, is not ecstatic. Ritual is the most important Pueblo social activity – the cults of the Masked Gods, of healing, of the sun, of fetishes, of war and of the dead. The dates of rituals are carefully calculated using a calendar. Emphasis is placed on the exact ceremonial wording, and daily conversation is largely concerned with possible mistakes in rituals. No one who feels angry is permitted to participate, and display of strong feelings is always avoided. Divorce is performed when the husband returns home and finds his possessions in a neat pile by the threshold. Wealth is less important than the performance of ritual offices, but these offices are not sought but pressed on reluctant individuals.

The third group, the Dobuans, inhabit an island of scanty resources. Benedict regards them as treacherous and lawless. Mutual hostility is the norm. Marriage is literally a physical trapping of the husband by his future mother-in-law. So suspicious are husbands and wives of each other that they live alternate years in each other's villages, during which time the spouse on alien ground is deliberately humiliated. Men and women come together only for sex; adultery is commonplace and children are bribed by one parent to spy on the other. Death is never a 'natural' event and the first suspect is always the surviving spouse. Cooking is never left unattended lest it be poisoned. As among the Kwakiutl, society is competitive, but in secret: the extent of each person's yam harvest is kept hidden. Successful gardening is the stealing of yams by sorcery: a good crop is possible only by magical theft. Beneath a superficial friendliness every Dobuan practises sorcery. Their most prized skill is sharp trading. Prosperity can only be wrung from a malevolent world by conflict.

All three societies, says Benedict, have characteristic personality traits: megalomania among the Kwakiutl, obsessionality among the Pueblo and paranoia among the Dobuans. These traits occur everywhere – in daily life, in marriage and in death. Kwakiutl marriage is a competition between the families of bride and bridegroom; it can even be performed without a bride: marriage to the left foot of the 'father-in-law' provides the opportunity for a ritual contest. While after every death the principal concern of the Dobuans is vengeance on the hypothetical killer, the rare Pueblo murderer is initiated into a special society and treated as a bereaved spouse.

The extent to which an individual conforms to the basic personality of his society is taken by Benedict as a measure of his normality. Thus people whose personality is particularly attuned to that of the community become its leaders. Personality traits such as paranoia may be encouraged and rewarded by some societies but regarded as dangerous deviations or even mental illness by others. To be considerate to others in a head-hunting community is regarded as insanity [273].

The psychoanalytical approach to other cultures was not limited to tribal communities. During the Cold War a profile of Russian national character was made by Benedict and Mead: Russians were found to be 'warmly human, tremendously dependent upon secure social affiliations, labile, non-rational, strong but undisciplined and needing to submit to authority' [222]. Social scientists and psychiatrists have often been employed by governments to offer military and political advice. 'Political psychiatry' in 1947 was the name given to the techniques used to select the leaders of post-war Germany by the doctors of the Information Control Division of the American occupied zone [249]. During the fifties American psychoanalysts had difficulty finding any Russians to interview and evaluated the Soviet basic personality by analysing the chess play of Russian grandmasters [222]. Erikson placed great emphasis on the Russian habit of tightly swaddling babies which resulted in 'smouldering vasomotor madness'. The Russian institution of 'a strong leader whether called Csar or Stalin' was due to wrapping children up tightly: security, children learnt, involved a loss of independence [222].

The Appeals of Communism, a study of the enemy within the gate, interviewed ex-members of various Communist Parties and decided that English-speaking Communists were mentally unbalanced:

> The American and British respondents in particular included a large proportion of emotionally maladjusted individuals who were seeking to solve their emotional problems by attacking society . . . While Communism in the United States and England may be viewed as an aberration, in France and Italy it takes on the proportions of sub-culture. [222]

While those outside were clearly enemies, those inside must be insane (p. 28). Another study suggested that 'the overall picture of Communist mentality is somewhat like paranoia (precision of sorts imposed upon a distortion of reality)' [222].

A single 'basic personality' did not always seem adequate to describe the European societies of which the psychiatrists themselves were members. Henry Dicks, a psychiatrist attached to British Intelligence during the Second World War, had been involved in political work with German prisoners. He suggested that the Soviet Union represented a conflict between the traditional Russian 'oral' pattern of behaviour of the average citizen and the 'anal-compulsive' or puritanical patterns found in the Party: 'Charisma attaches . . . to those who can demonstrate their mastery over oral gratification needs' [100]. Bateson, one of the originators of the 'double-bind' theory (according to which schizophrenia develops in response to certain ambiguous family situations), was critical of psychoanalysts who simply suggested that 'Germans are submissive' and pointed out that the same person is dominant and submissive in different situations [27]. He suggested that two patterns of paired reactions could occur – complementary patterns, in which opposing positions are taken up by two individuals in a given situation, and symmetrical patterns, in which one individual responds to the other with the same behaviour. Bateson said the British tend to use symmetrical patterns ('fair play' or 'I'll stop if you do') while the Germans preferred complementary patterns ('I can't stop fighting because I'll be finished off'). His description of the German basic personality is another variant on the 'loss of face' and 'they need strong rulers' themes.

How valid is this concept of a 'basic personality'? Psycho-analysis assumes that there is always an exact equivalence between the experiences of every individual in a society and that society's culture, but it is a simplification to say that there must always be one single ideal personality in a society. All societies comprise constituent groups, each with their own different expectations of reasonable behaviour. Minority groups generally regarded as deviant evolve their own codes of acceptable behaviour to make sense of their experiences and to relate to others. Skid-row alcoholics have their own vocabulary to distinguish the important elements in their world: characteristic ways of relating to institutions such as hospitals and the police, to type and sources of alcohol and to the random passer-by. The pattern of their lives is richer than would be implied by merely describing them as individuals who fail to accept normal social responsibilities because of periodic intoxication.

The 'culture' of a particular society tends to be a frozen abstraction of a series of events unfolding in time which is considered in isolation from other groups. We have seen that the 'matriarchal' black family is a product both of historical and contemporary black-white relations. The Kwakiutl *potlach* took its classical form only during colonial occupation.

The attempt to discover the basic personality of another society is clearly not a culture-free activity itself. Long before the advent of psychiatry, travellers had tagged other nations with single epithets - gullible, savage, childish and so forth [399]. In the sixteenth century, Italians were martial and Germans individual-istic; by the twentieth century, the reverse [284]. The Pueblo are described by Benedict as ritualistic only because their form of ritual activity is similar to European rituals of church and state: sedate, emotionally controlled and formal. Are the *potlachs* of the Kwakiutl any less ritualistic because they take place in a more emotionally charged atmosphere? It is easy to pick out as the *dominant* characteristics of another ethnic group precisely those cultural attributes which are most different from our own everyday life. The location of witches, so far from being 'paranoid', may be a humdrum everyday chore [121].

Alternatively, societies are described with concepts derived from European psychiatry: paranoia and grandiosity. These are of course terms which are derived from observations of individual psychiatric patients in Europe. Cultures which encourage psychological mechanisms in the individual which psychoanalysis regards as unhealthy (such as the paranoid 'projection' of one's own feelings on to others) are then characterized as unhealthy in themselves. If the basic Dobuan personality is paranoid by European standards then Dobuan society is a paranoid society. Individual adaptation might be regarded as relative to society, but the society itself is regarded as pathological by the values of psychoanalysis, effectively those of the European middle class [98].

The human individual and his illnesses are a pervasive metaphor for society and its 'ills'; minority groups are a 'cancer in the body politic', while the community as a whole may be 'sick' or 'dying' [395]. It is not that a frequent correspondence between individual experience and social organization occurs because the former generates the latter [287], but that social institutions employ models taken from biology and emotion for purely social concerns [296]. A sociological theory of psychoanalysis might well point out that this is exactly what psychoanalysis itself does. The eighteenth-century 'discovery' of insanity provided a model in which antagonistic political theories could be described as pathological (by Hitler) or pathogenic (by Reich and Marcuse). Mental illness itself, like sex, when 'freed' from its social constraints becomes a metaphor for liberation [85].

What is the value of the 'Culture and Personality' concept of normality? If mental illness in a particular community is the rejection of the dominant cultural pattern, as Benedict suggests, then we would expect the mentally ill in a 'paranoid society' not to be paranoid themselves. In fact the reverse is usually true. The Yoruba of Nigeria, described as 'paranoid' by a local psychiatrist, have mental patients who themselves are particularly likely to be paranoid [234]; their paranoia appears to be maladaptive even within their own 'paranoid society'. If the Japanese value docility and self-control [31], we would expect Japanese mental patients to be aggressive and uninhibited, but they are in fact quiet and restrained [118]. In a 'paranoid' society a man may, to avenge an insult, wipe out both the offender and his family; he will be rewarded with increased prestige. The actions of the man with *paranoid delusions*, however, are a threat to the whole community because of their idiosyncrasy and lack of social appropriateness.

The relativity of mental illness is difficult to demonstrate. We cannot show that the mentally ill Indian immigrant in a catatonic stupor would have been acknowledged as a saint if he had stayed in India; it appears unlikely. Chapter 9 takes this discussion of normality in society a little further. As we shall see, far from simply rejecting mental illness as its antithesis, society may structure it and use it to articulate a variety of social concerns. Psychopathology does not determine society: society limits and directs pathology for its own purpose.

PSYCHOANALYSIS AND COLONIAL PSYCHIATRY

What relevance did these psychoanalytical ideas have for the everyday practice of psychiatrists who worked with non-Europeans? Were they of purely theoretical interest?

Although written sixty years ago, B. J. F. Laubscher's *Sex, Custom and Psychopathology* is often cited as a valuable and distinguished study [237]. Laubscher, a psychiatrist working in South Africa, is clearly very involved with the Tembu people and their problems, and much of the book is strikingly humane and concerned. He makes an attempt to understand the Tembu way of life sympathetically, including the execrated 'sniffing-out' of witches, much beloved of English novelists like Rider Haggard [399]. He compares the consecrated food of the Tembu to the consecrated host of the Europeans but, one suspects, less to enhance the Tembu than to debunk Christianity. He even offers local recipes with the playful suggestion that European hostesses try them when short of ideas.

The book is profusely illustrated with photographs. The frontispiece, 'A Tembu Maiden', is a young woman wearing only a fringe of beads gazing into the distance, one nipple delicately silhouetted against the far horizon. A scene of breast-feeding is coyly subtitled 'a two year old boy stops his play for a drink'. One picture shows the author in a native court, with hat, white trousers and cigar, sitting on a chair next to the chief; the elders sit on stones, the plaintiff squats on the ground. Another group of photographs towards the end of the book shows some of his black patients, completely naked and staring bleakly at the camera in front of a tall wire fence, captioned 'Imbecile – Uncircumcised', 'Catatonic – Burst of laughter', 'Schizophrenic – Circumcised' and so on.

Laubscher describes the local healers, the Isanuses or diviners, the Amaggira, or sniffers-out, and the Amaxhwele, who are herbalists and sorcerers. He regards the Amaggira as quacks and charlatans and emphasizes their evil reputation for mutilating corpses and selling potions for unpleasant purposes. The Amaxhwele are drifters and psychopaths, frequently the relatives of his mental patients; they are motivated by a desire for sex with their numerous female followers. He has however great respect for the Isanuses, whom he considers to be a superior type of Tembu. Indeed, he believes they possess telepathic powers.

One problem for Laubscher is the local experience of *Ukutwasa*. When he hears the River People call, a Tembu becomes listless and aimless; he develops aches and pains, loses weight and suffers bad dreams; he becomes agitated and worried; suddenly he runs for the river and jumps in. Under the water he is believed to learn divination and healing. On emerging ten days later from the river he begins to practise as a healer. Laubscher finds it difficult to decide what is going on. The Isanuses, his favoured category of healers, tell him that Ukutwasa is the call for training which only they have undergone with the River People – anyone else who claims to have been 'called' is a fraud. The other healers (who are regarded as charlatans by both Laubscher and the Isanuses) also claim to have experienced *Ukutwasa*. The local population tell of people who jumped in and drowned. The psychiatric patients claim to have undergone *Ukutwasa* and the epileptics in the hospital describe the underwater world to the doctor. Laubscher eventually decides that the experiences of the Isanuses are somehow 'genuine' (but does not elaborate) while the others are deluded or faking.

The Tembu recognize all types of auditory hallucinations as *Ukutwasa* but distinguish them from the toxic psychoses of delirium or fever. They use a single descriptive category to describe both the visions of the seer and the experience of mental illness which Europeans usually distinguish as different experiences.

The title of the book is born out by detailed descriptions of sexual intercourse, initiations involving genital manipulations and Tembu sexual fanatasies and delusions. Psychoanalytical explanations are used to interpret Tembu behaviour. They project their fears on to others: hence their belief in witchcraft. Tembu women are persecuted at night by unpleasant beings who force them to have sexual intercourse. One of these spirits is a snake which, after copulating with a woman, hides in her vagina to bite the penis of the unsuspecting male. Laubscher considers this accepted belief (of both male and female Tembu) to be penis envy on the part of the woman.

Like Freud, he believes that mental illness is a regression back to childhood stages of development. The Tembu, however, as *normal* adults are less repressed than adult Europeans: they remain at a primitive level of development resembling that of a child. When they do regress in a psychosis therefore they do not have so far to regress. That is why, he says, it is difficult to tell an insane African from a sane one!

Tembu personality is described by Laubscher as characteristically 'oral': orientated to the first stage of child development in psychoanalytical theory. When food is available, the Tembu eat to saturation and they bite each other during sex. 'The mouth thus becomes as important medium for satisfying physiological and psychological needs. The native is a gluttonous eater and eats for a sense of fullness and not for the satisfaction of an appetite.' In the author's mental hospital 'reactions to food are especially sadistic and voracious when meat is served. On such days excitement and restlessness, shouts and fighting are common among the females.'

Their powerful oral instincts lead the unfortunate Tembu to steal cattle from the white ranches. They tell Laubscher that meat has become so scarce that they are able to eat it only once or twice a month. Unhappily for the Tembu their oral needs are not met with the same understanding by the white farmers as they are by the author. The local magistrates are unanimous as to the best way of stopping cattle theft: whipping. 'Natives understand and appreciate the use of force.' Laubscher himself does not approve of whipping and his solution is to regard the problem as a medical one: the cattle thieves are 'feeble-minded or psychotic persons' and should be treated accordingly.

The author believes that his psychiatric work will be useful to the colonial government. He is critical of the destruction of traditional black culture by urbanization and Christianity ('a veneer of civilization') and of the availability of alcoholic spirits (the well-known oral tendencies of the Tembu having unfortunate results in this direction). He is sympathetic to their past culture but not to their future aspirations:

He has made his jump to become emancipated in such a social setting and without the assistance of constructive organized thinking about him and for him during this transition period . . . Failure there will be, for the native is but a child amidst the complexities of Western civilization. Nevertheless it is not immediate results we seek, but the psychological effect of conditioning him to our problems as his problems, for on his co-operation depends the security of the future generations in this country of ours.

INSTINCT, PATHOLOGY AND POLITICS

The psychoanalytical approach can offer us interesting hypotheses about the stresses faced by an individual in a given community. As with its explanation of racism (p. 53) it shows us how personal conflicts may provide intense personal affects which can articulate existing social institutions. What it does not offer is an explanation of how these institutions originate or function.

While it promises a universal approach to mental illness, it in fact equates mental illness with 'regression', and non-European thought with 'unhealthy' mental mechanisms. It is easy to see how this leads to descriptions of whole societies in terms of pathology. In its attempt to provide a single unitary theory of both the individual and his society, it equates institutions such as witchcraft with paranoia (on the debatable assumption that they both employ similar mental mechanisms).

The idea that the black was childlike (and thus *unrepressed*) is held simultaneously with the belief that he is neurotic (too *repressed*) or psychotic (*regressed*) [287]. Like the cruder racist beliefs, its concepts are often contradictory, but the central theme is always the same: the pinnacle of evolution is the 'optimally adjusted personality' of the white European (preferably one who has been psychoanalysed) [98].

Psychoanalysis ignores the historical relation between societies. In its rather diluted application to the practical issues of international conflicts and war, this apparent denial of political considerations results in a clearly self-serving picture of other communities. Its study of minority groups and non-Europeans ('the care-free children of the jungle or desert') [342] again has rather predictable consequences. Conflicts between societies are reduced to conflicts between different child-rearing practices: the 'black problem' in Britain is the fault of the black parents.

While it is quite reasonable to look for associations between the socialization of instinctual drives in a particular community and the culture of that society, it is not legitimate to describe some societies solely in terms of certain drives and then say that they are *nearer* to these drives [376]. It is as meaningless to explain black culture as 'oral' as to describe Laubscher's white compatriots who buy and sell cattle as 'anal'.[1] Laubscher does not accept that both cattle ranching and rustling are social activities, a struggle to control economic resources. He does not tell us anything of Tembu history or their political relationship to the white settlers. We never learn whether they live on their traditional land and whether they work on the colonial ranches or live on their own produce. Relations between black and white are mentioned only in terms of African pathology: black culture is static, frozen, awaiting our analysis. Social change is only 'the discharge of suppressed emotion' [342].

In this study by Laubscher, perhaps the most sympathetic colonial psychiatrist, we find that the failure to use an adequate psychological or sociological theory produces a curious split. He reconciles his obvious affection for the Tembu with their degraded status by singling out a few of them as noble and heroic, the representatives of some higher tradition. (A similar idealization is found in imperial novels such as John Buchan's *Prester John* and Rider Haggard's *King Solomon's Mines*).

Such a split is not uncommon in attitudes to immigrants and other minority groups – they are regarded as living a debased version of some hypothetical superior culture which is worthy of admiration but which can only be found in the elusive few. Their degeneration is regarded, not as a function of their relations with the majority culture, but as something located in themselves. British gypsies are usually perceived in this way [40, 307]: the gypsies in the neighbouring lot are never 'real' gypsies.

NOTE

1   Black culture is of course 'oral' in a rather different sense – gospel songs, sermons and the blues – when there is no access to alternative technologies.

CHAPTER EIGHT

A PRELUDE TO INSANITY?

He was talking very excitedly to me, said the Vicar, about some apparatus for warming a church in Worthing and about the Apostolic Claims of the Church of Abyssinia. I confess I could not follow him clearly. He seems deeply interested in Church matters. Are you quite sure he is right in the head? I have noticed again and again, since I have been in the Church, that lay interest in ecclesiastical matters is often a prelude to insanity.

> Evelyn Waugh, *Decline and Fall*, 1928
> (Penguin edn, 1937, p. 73)

Ethnic minorities in Britain are not of course encapsulated groups like the once colonised small-scale communities of the Third World. Although we can use some of the methods and insights of anthropology (and be on guard against repeating its mistakes), we are not able to look at any groups in Britain as isolated entities. Relations with the dominant white group are even more important than for the Tembu.

Few migrants to Britain have come with the intention of totally assimilating. Many groups, particularly European Jews and Asians, while wishing to enter into full economic relations with the wider community, have tried to keep intact much of their traditional pattern of family and community life, language and religion. Paradoxically they are often seen as being the groups which have 'integrated' the most successfully. Psychological conflicts in these communities are frequently those of individuals moving from one well-established cultural tradition to another.

For European immigrants and their children, both Jewish and Catholic, religion is the last element of the pre-migration culture to be discarded, long after dress, language and behaviour have become those of the majority culture. For the Hasidim, the

Jewish immigrants who are the least anxious to assimilate, religious values are the centre of a highly complex set of cultural patterns by which they deliberately isolate themselves from fellow Jews and the majority culture.

For black Caribbean immigrants, excluded by racism from the possibility of assimilation (an assimilation which they always recognized as one of the objectives of migration), religion has provided the basis for a personal definition of themselves, which is opposed to that of the majority culture, and which is ethical rather than racial. West Indian Pentecostals brought with them to Britain a set of values which they believed were typically British. The realization that this was not entirely so, together with their rejection by white churches, means that Pentecostalism may now stand for a definition of first-generation 'West Indian culture'. Unlike (second-generaton) Rastafari, Pentecostalism, in spite of its apparently anti-materialist ethos, holds out to its members the possibility of ultimate acceptance by the white community. If it provides a halfway stage to assimilation, it also provides many of the beliefs and assumptions which, when inverted, become Rastafari.

In as much as it can conceive of religion ('the relatively modest dogma that God is not mad' – Madariaga) as a real phenomenon, psychiatry is generally hostile to it. Psychiatrists are less likely to be members of churches than other doctors [341] and many would agree with Freud that belief in God is 'so patently infantile, so incongruous with reality, that to one whose attitude to humanity is friendly it is painful to think that the great majority of mortals will never be able to rise above this view of life' [143].

Religious sects which, like Pentecostalism, believe in an approaching millennium are common among disadvantaged minority groups. The Seventh Day Adventists were one of the few British churches explicitly to welcome black immigrants. To non-believers these sects seem to function by offering compensation, a substitute satisfaction for their members' failure to achieve real goals: 'Being at the bottom on so many counts they are attached to the myth of the Elect and to the fantasy of reversal of roles . . .' [403].

It is popularly believed that insane people in our society frequently become very religious. Religious revivals and films have often been blamed for causing mental disorders. Evidence

in fact suggests the contrary [260]: for instance church membership and readiness to go to church in a personal crisis seem
associated with better mental health [256].

The psychiatrist acknowledges the area in which his concerns
overlap with those of the priest by seeing it as a confusion:
religious interest in a patient obscures the appropriate diagnosis
[260]. In West Indians 'mania is *complicated* with delusions of a
religious character' [102] (our emphasis). Religious beliefs are
regarded as merely one of a series of cultural values which
passively fill in the structure of a mental illness which itself results
from physical causes. While the schizophrenic last century was
preoccupied with religious questions, today the content of his
delusions is likely to be sexual [220]. The seventeenth-century
English radical Winstanley appears to have suggested something
similar; a preoccupation with religion may precipitate a crisis –
'by poring and puzzling himself in it [a man] loses what wisdom
he had, and becomes distracted and mad' – but the form the
religious expressions take appear to depend on something else:

> and if the passion of joy predominate, then he is merry and
> sings and laughs, and is ripe in the expression of his words
> and will speak strange things; but all by imagination. But if
> the passion of sorrow predominate, then he is heavy and
> mad, crying out, He is damned, God has forsaken him and
> he must go to hell when he dies, he cannot make his calling
> and election sure. And in that distemper many times a man
> doth hang, kill or drown himself . . . [443]

In this chapter we shall look at some of the 'confusions' which
can result when the psychiatrist tries to detect mental abnormality
in very religious members of minority groups.

EVADNE WILLIAMS

In our hospital, as in many others, the majority of the nurses and
domestic staff were West Indian immigrants. One Sunday
morning some years ago when on duty at the hospital, one of us
(RL) was asked by the matron to see a nursing auxiliary who,
after attending her church, had started work on the ward. She
had 'become peculiar, singing hymns loudly, neglecting her

patients but then, after telling them to have faith in her, had suddenly burst into tears'.

Forty-five-year-old Evadne Williams was born in Jamaica and had come to Britain when she was thirty, after having worked in the capital, Kingston, as a typist. She had difficulty finding work in London and, disappointed in her wish to become a secretary, worked successively as a packer in a factory, a domestic and a laundress, before eventually finding a permanent niche in the local hospital. She was well liked by her colleagues, black and white, whose only complaint was of her excessive religious zeal, which made them feel rather uncomfortable, particularly when it was directed towards the patients.

Nine years after arriving in London, Evadne Williams had joined her local Pentecostal church, which has a predominantly West Indian congregation. She remains unmarried and her social life is exclusively centred around religious activities. The highlights of her week are the five meetings of her church, a small independent sect of about thirty members, which meets in a rented school hall. Soon after joining she began to 'speak in tongues', one of the 'gifts of the Spirit' encouraged in her sect. She continued working in the hospital, apparently happy, although her only close friends were fellow members of her congregation. Evadne lives alone in a rented room, leaving it only for church or work. In spite of her enthusiasm she never takes any part in running the church or organizing activities but can always be relied on as a volunteer for street-corner testimony and evangelization. She believes that her coming to Britain was part of God's purpose to spread the gospel to a people who had forgotten it and to bring them back to Christ. Although deeply religious, she is certainly not sanctimonious and can laugh at herself and others. A travel poster in our waiting room has been embellished by her with the words 'England is not so bad after all' and she has added 'You need the Lord Jesus' to another which advertises a psychotherapy group.

When we first met I did not know she had seen a psychiatrist previously. Evadne had in fact been admitted briefly to another hospital some months before 'in a state of ecstasy'. She saw me quite happily, immediately grabbing my arm and making me sit down, but then started sobbing against my shoulder. Before I could ask what the trouble was she suddenly gave a scream and rolled over on the floor, crying out something I could not grasp.

It was difficult to understand exactly what she was saying, but her speech had a coherent rhythm, something like that of an evangelical preacher or a racing commentator [354]. Suddenly she jumped up, sat down next to me again and explained rather breathlessly and at great length that she was being unfairly treated in the hospital for spreading the word of God and that she was being martyred. Then she quizzed me on my knowledge of the Book of Revelation.

She started singing gospel hymns and, pushing me into a corner of the room, began an ecstatic dance on her own, punctuated by rousing cries of 'Praise the Lord'. She would not answer any questions and I sat by helpless, laughing when she laughed and consoling her when she cried: she was able to make me feel I was sharing her enthusiasm even if I did not really understand it.

It then occurred to me that as she was a Pentecostalist she had just been 'speaking in tongues'. She had probably been carried away during the service and the fervour generated by the 'tongues' had somehow been continuing since. With relief I suggested this to the nurses and asked them to telephone the members of her church, who would know what to do. They did not seem very convinced. I sat down and waited next to Evadne, who continued as before. About ten of her friends arrived. To my astonishment they told me this was nothing like speaking in tongues, that Evadne was 'sick in the head' and I had better give her an injection immediately. With this advice I decided that perhaps she could be psychiatrically ill after all. I offered her some medicine and she fell asleep. She has attended my clinic regularly since then, takes daily prophylactic medicine cheerfully, agrees with her church that she has had a 'break-down', continued to attend her church and during the service *still speaks in tongues*.

This episode gave rise to a number of problems:

(i) The diagnosis was made by a religious sect, not the psychiatrist.

(ii) The way I interpreted Evadne's behaviour varied with whichever model I had in my head. Her rapid staccato speech with repetition, religious content and occasional unintelligibility could be perceived both as religious fervour and 'hypomanic' speech. Even after I attended services at her church with her, I was still not convinced I could always tell the difference if it were not for the *context* in which the behaviour occurred.

(iii) It was difficult to separate Evadne's experience into the two types of experience – religion and mental illness. Could the two be perhaps the same phenomenon? Had being a member of the church stopped her from becoming ill before, or on the contrary had over-zealous participation in activities like speaking in tongues driven her to a position where even her sect saw her as ill?

(iv) It occurred to me that possibly another more 'extreme' sect might have said that Evadne's behaviour was not pathological. Maybe she was just too enthusiastic for this particular group. To protect themselves from being seen by society as deranged, her group had perhaps labelled her as ill. If this was the case, the medical profession was being used to delineate ritualistic differences between churches!

(v) What was glossolalia (speaking in tongues) anyway? To what extent was it a 'normal' phenomenon? Were charismatics mentally unbalanced?

SPEAKING IN UNKNOWN TONGUES

Speaking in tongues, or glossolalia, is believed by its practitioners to be one of the gifts of the Holy Spirit as described in the Christian Bible.[1] To many doctors it is unintelligible and meaningless gibberish [6].

It appears to be common amongst the revivalist groups which periodically emerge among the poor and disadvantaged and in periods of general religious enthusiasm, as among the Quakers during the Puritan Revolution. Comparatively rare now in European Christianity, it is still found among the Pentecostal groups. A recent revival of glossolalia, 'The Charismatic Movement', has occurred in the mainstream churches, notably among Catholics. There are now over two million practitioners of glossolalia in the United States, where the phenomenon has spread to middle-class denominations like the Episcopalians, Lutherans and Presbyterians. Practitioners say that as they are a gift from God 'tongues' cannot conflict with the Bible, although some of the seventeenth-century enthusiasts considered that such individual religious experiences transcended the authority of the Scriptures.

From the psychological point of view speaking in tongues is a trance-like condition: a dissociative state like hysteria. It is, however, highly controlled behaviour which occurs at specific points in the church service. Glossolalia includes utterances of varying lengths, sometimes lasting up to an hour. Participants report that the experience is accompanied by feelings of freedom, tranquillity and happiness. There has been controversy as to whether glossolalia has to be learnt like a language or whether it is a universal psychological response which, like a reflex, can be triggered off by the appropriate stimuli. When new members join a Pentecostal group they are encouraged to believe that they too will be able to experience the 'Second Baptism – The Baptism of the Spirit'. They are not directly taught the new idiom but are told to submit to God, to relax and praise him in their own language, to wait until the new tongue comes. New members will usually acquire the gift only after a few meetings. The experience is interpreted as control of the organs of speech by the Holy Spirit, who prays through the speaker in a heavenly language.

Patterns of behaviour similar to Pentecostal glossolalia occur in such different settings as India, the Caribbean, Africa and Southern Europe. In each community it is believed to be a supernatural power entering into the individual. The participants tend to have their eyes closed, they may make twitching movements and fall; they flush, sweat and may tear at their clothes.

Although a psychiatrist might interpret glossolalia as an unusual or indeed abnormal mental state, it is nevertheless *social* behaviour.[2] Its benefits are supposed to be distributed to all, even though it is a personal experience. The pastor often decides when the congregation are ready to start and tells them to do so. Individuals in the congregation tend to speak for longer periods when they are engaged in interpersonal conflicts within the group, trying to win support or improve their status. Glossolalia is even used as a 'filler' in the service when enthusiasm flags. Speaking in tongues at unacceptable times is only done by newcomers. They soon learn how and when to use their newly acquired gift [55].

Participants often describe the power of the Spirit as a loss of voluntary control over their movements: 'You lose power over yourself when the Holy Ghost enters.' Pentecostalists describe how God is moving their limbs and his presence within can be felt controlling them. This sounds very similar to the passivity experience of schizophrenia in which the individual feels his own will replaced by that of an outside force or agency. The difference is that 'tongues' occur not in clear consciousness but in a dissociative state in which there is reduced attention to outside stimuli, that they are accepted as normal by a group and that they are usually experienced as enhancing the individual's will rather than diminishing it [441]. (Religious literature is, however, full of individuals who described themselves as having been possessed by God against their will. The Quaker George Fox found himself taking off his shoes in the snow; he tried to resist 'for it was winter: but the word of the Lord was like a fire in me. So I put off my shoes' [141]).

Can glossolalia precipitate mental illness? A pastoral counsellor, who had himself experienced psychotic episodes, could find no evidence of mental illness in members of a Holy Rollers church [39] and a number of other surveys have reached a similar conclusion [260]. Comparison between a group of schizophrenic patients from the Caribbean and West Indian Pentecostalists suggested that the worshippers believed that the patients were unable to control their dissociative behaviour sufficiently to conform with the highly stylized rituals of glossolalia in church [214]. The vast majority of Pentecostals have not been psychiatrically ill [367]. On the contrary, there is some evidence from a variety of cultures that, in any particular denomination, those members of it who speak in tongues are better adjusted that those who do not [215]. Among our Pentecostal West Indian patients a much *smaller* proportion speak in tongues than we would expect from seeing the congregation in action. It is claimed by those advocating glossalalia that, like jogging or meditation, it generates a sense of well-being which extends into other spheres of life. It has been suggested that glossolalia was common among migrants to the United States who had difficulty in speaking a new language. Speaking in tongues offered power by the supernatural asquisition of linguistic skills – a spiritualized metaphor of social aspirations – but also emhasized the importance of the Word in the everday world [312].

WEST INDIAN PENTECOSTALISM

What then of Evadne's church? Pentecostalism is the biggest church brought to Britain by West Indian immigrants. It started in the 1900s within the American Evangelical churches as a reaffirmation of the events at Pentecost described in the Acts of the Apostles. The 'gifts of the Spirit' are believed still to descend on a modern congregation as healing, prophecy and speaking in tongues. Although, like Jehovah's Witnesses, they daily anticipate the millennium, Pentecostals believe that God's dispensation of rewards has already begun to flow.

West Indians in Britain seldom join the existing white Pentecostal churches [55]. Their own Pentecostalism began in the churches founded after the abolition of slavery by black American Baptist missionaries, in association with an independent evangelical tradition and underground survivals of indigenous African religions.

Strict Pentecostalists see themselves as immediate successors to biblical figures, the intervening two thousand years being of little account. They call themselves 'saints'. Some groups believe that Christ was black, but most follow closely the teaching of the major denominations. In spite of their evangelical tradition, Catholic pictures and images are common in their homes; their anti-intellectual bias, their refusal to study 'the world' or cooperate with it more than is absolutely necessary results in indifference to and ignorance of other Christians and of their own historical relation to them. They are aware there is some similarity between themselves and other Protestant denominations and are prepared to use Baptist or Anglican clergymen for marriage or funerals (until recently few of their number being ordained). They may hire a local Baptist church to baptize by total immersion.

Their fundamentalism would be considered naïve by nonbelievers: the majority are not aware that the King James translation of the Bible is not the original version. Pentecostal representatives have recently accepted as authentic some rather dubious religious relics in the Holy Land. Interpretation of the Bible is the gift of God and is not subject to argument or discussion, but disputes within the churches reflect authority and status within each group. They are violently opposed to the Rastas for their matted hair, black nationalism and other *rude* ideas.

Depending on their strictness, Pentecostal relations with outsiders are ambivalent. While sinners are necessary to define the external boundaries of the sect and to emphasize the merit of being within, Pentecostals do engage in periodic missionary activity. They are not communalist; although members may live in the same house they do not work together. For some members work is a concession to a sinful world in which, like Evadne, they may be well integrated, even if, like many West Indians, they are employed below their original aspirations and abilities. There is no temporal conflict for most Pentecostals with the outside world. They eschew political activities but the New Year message of one group declared their opposition to 'drug addicts, murderers, demonstrators and unofficial strikers' [55].

An unworldly outlook is not common to all Pentecostal groups. In Latin America, the emphasis on the Book is used to promote literacy; co-operative farming and small-scale industry is common. Pentecostalism is seen as an opportunity to improve their standard of living by self-help, hard work, saving and the development of an educated opposition to the traditional alliance of church and landowner.

The Italian Evangelical church, composed of immigrants from rural southern Italy to the United States, is also characterized by adult conversion based on an individual revelation which is manifested by speaking in tongues. The Bible is held to be the revealed source of all doctrine and there is a belief in the literal existence of the devil and of evil spirits as his agents, and in the physical resurrection of the body. This group is a good example of Weber's suggestion that the asceticism and self-discipline of the Protestant ethic encourage saving and thus individual economic power [423]. Members have achieved significantly greater upward social mobility than have their fellow immigrants. 'I thank my saviour, Jesus Christ, that He has given me the will power to put my money in the bank instead of spending it every day on the useless frivolities of the world' [312].

There is no widespread practice of formal sorcery among West Indians in Britain, but a belief in *obeah* is common and various countermeasures are often employed. Caribbean Pentecostals may share a belief in their efficacy but it is not central to their doctrine. Physical and emotional illness can be caused by spirits, but the cure is more likely to be a laying-on of hands and prayer than any specific rite of exorcism or counter-magic. Local

Pentecostal preachers seem to be quite willing to allow their members to come to our hospital, but only after prayer has produced no therapeutic response. A Pentecostal who resorts to orthodox medicine is seen to be using a lesser method – faith alone ought to prove sufficient [55].

If thaumaturgical beliefs among white Britons are usually limited to isolated questions concerning everyday life or death (astrology, spiritualism, teacup reading), magic for some migrant communities may provide an explanation of a wider set of natural phenomena. Magic has a more limited place in the culture of the English-speaking Caribbean than in Catholic Latin America or the French islands because Protestantism made a great attempt to eradicate rather than assimilate indigenous beliefs and, unlike Catholicism, it does not itself contain thaumaturgical practices such as transubstantiation of the host. In Haitian *vodoun* or Trinidadian *shango* there is identification of West African gods with Christian saints (Ogun with St Anthony, Oxala with Christ) [386]; this is rare in the Protestant Caribbean tradition. Among immigrants to Britain witchcraft is seen as an embodiment of *evil* rather than as a morally neutral tool of sorcery which can be used either for good or evil.

The emphasis of Protestants on biblical interpretation and liberty of conscience has resulted in a proliferation of sects. (Jefferson remarked 'I am a sect myself'). Pentecostalism in the West Indies is not so very different from 'English' White Pentecostalism. However, in the Argentinian Chaco, Pentecostalism developed rapidly among tribes newly disorganized by contact with white colonization and it adopted various magical elements especially in healing [436]; the universal charisma of the Holy Spirit was seen as an extension to all the faithful of the contact with ancestral spirits previously limited to the shamans. The Pentecostal missionaries felt this new church diverged too much from orthodoxy and withdrew their support. There are in the West Indies a variety of other groups usually with an informal structure in a similar position whose beliefs and practices stretch from those of Pentecostalism to those of the syncretistic sects drawing on African and European sources, similar to *vodoun*. These groups are loosely known as *pocomania*. There is no evidence of pocomania having migrated to Britain and it is used by British West Indians as a term of abuse for sects more charismatic and 'enthusiastic' than that of the speaker.

Black Pentecostal sects tend to be volatile. Originally loosely associated with their parent churches in the United States, they are now largely autonomous, dividing and reforming, growing by a fifth each year. There are now over a thousand different groups. Their names, such as that of the Ransom Pentecostal African Methodist Episcopalian Zion church, reveal a number of influences. Often limited to a particular island group, some can now afford their own church but services might take place in rented halls or private houses.

Fifteen years ago the majority of members had been Pentecostals before coming to Britain but now about half are new converts. Probably a tenth of all West Indians are full members, but many more share their beliefs and attend meetings sporadically. A bigger proportion of West Indians coming to Britain were Pentecostals than in the non-migrating population because migrants were likely to be from the poorer section of the West Indian population: in Britain, however, Pentecostals seem to be slightly better-off than non-Pentecostal West Indians in spite of their belief in the materialistic world as a seductive but evil mirage.

Like most West Indians, Pentecostals usually work for a wage in factories or service industries. Many of their new converts give, as one of their reasons for joining, the response of the British churches they tried to join, which ranged from making them feel unwelcome to telling them 'their church was the one down the road'. Even when they were made to feel at home, difficulties over the degree of religious enthusiasm tolerated encouraged them to join 'their church', the Pentecostals [55].

Less than 4 per cent of all West Indian immigrants now attend a major denomination. White Pentecostals have sometimes welcomed their black co-religionists, but there are important doctrinal differences between the English Elim churches and the black American tradition: whether the tongues are interpreted afterwards (as they are in the Elim churches) or the significance of rituals such as 'washing the feet of the saints'. Theological differences do not of course exist independently of social context. It is possible to see the objections of the (white) Elim churches to black Pentecostalism as reflecting black-white racial stereotypes. The black churches consider that speaking in tongues contains within itself its own fulfilment; it is its own meaning and does not need to be interpreted. Glossolalia in black churches, although certainly not haphazard or without reference to the rest of the congregation, has an informal setting. It occurs usually within the context of music, singing or dancing and many may speak in tongues at the same time, rather than in strict rotation as among the whites with the congregation listening quietly to the speaker. For the Elim churches glossolalia is both more of a public demonstration and a technology whose *message* can then be used in everyday life. For the black immigrant, tongues, although occurring in a social context, are a personal event; they are their own justification; they are primarily an *experience*.

Rather than simply providing emotional release, black Pentecostalism is a significant way of perceiving the immigrant's world. It provides a justification of present misfortune and sin, and the guarantee of redemption by divine grace both immediately and in the future.

These churches would seem to provide a form of social integration for some West Indian immigrants in a situation of relative social and cultural anomie. They would seem to have a special appeal for an emotionally isolated group in an urban society because they provide a universal theme, a structured world view . . . The gifts of the Spirit compensate for the lack of material gifts and the gift of 'tongues' provides the inarticulate with an opportunity to speak . . . Religious status is substituted for social and racial status. [215]

HASIDISM

While the black Pentecostal churches in Britain represent a response to rejection and discrimination, they are still an attempt to seek acceptance into the mainstream of English social life. Contemporary ultra-Orthodox Judaism is by contrast a deliberate retreat into an isolated and self-contained bastion opposed to cultural assimilation [120].

When members come to a hospital the doctor or social worker is likely to be as perplexed as when he first encounters zealous Pentecostals. One psychiatrist we know, an intelligent and compassionate doctor, offered her hand in greeting to an Orthodox Jew, brought to her clinic by 'his family. His bland refusal to shake hands with her was however interpreted as 'catatonic negativism'. This young doctor did not realize that ultra-Orthodox Jews may not have any physical contact with women in case they are currently menstruating. Even within marriage a husband and wife may not be able to pass an object directly from one to the other without first putting it down. This prohibition applies during menstruation until the end of the following week, which is signalled by immersion in the *mikveh* or ritual bath.

In a street in North London, West Indian Pentecostals belonging to the Church of the Lord Jesus Christ of the Apostolic Faith live next door to members of another fundamentalist sect, the Hasidim. Many of these East European Jews are the survivors of Nazi persecution. They consist of six main groups each led by a hereditary leader, or Zaddik, and each with its characteristic Sabbath dress. Traditional formal clothing includes caftan, waist-band and fur hat. Residence, economic activities, family life and education are strictly determined by religious law and tradition. All daily activities, eating, bathing, conversation and even sexual intercourse are practised in conformity with established ritual. There is frequent correspondence and travel between the community and other members in New York and Antwerp but no contact with neighbouring non-members beyond essential economic transactions. Belief in *dybbukim* (evil spirits) is still common. While adhering strictly to the accepted body of Orthodox Jewish law and custom, the Hasidim, like the Pentecostals, are ecstatic, emphasizing the possibility of direct communion with God through prayer. A central Hasidic theme is the duty to be constantly aware of God in all daily activities and thoughts. There is encouragement of a practical mysticism which delights in the joys of shouting, singing, clapping and dancing in the prayer houses, punctuated by bursts of rapturous prayer [231].

This pietistic movement developed among the small Jewish communities of rural Poland in the eighteenth century and was preached by wandering traditional healers. It drew its original inspiration from the teaching of a humble lime-digger, Israel ben Eliezer, the possessor of the secret of the name of God which bestows healing powers. At first the Besht conformed to the conventional patterns of the local wonderworkers, writing amulets, exorcizing demons, prescribing medicine and healing the sick. His religious innovation was the emphasis on personal communion with God, either through ecstasy or through contemplation and an awarenes of the presence of the deity in all creation and in all human activity. He rejected both asceticism and traditional rabbinical scholarship pursued for their own sake. All men, however poor or ignorant, could communicate with God if they have enthusiasm and a warm trusting heart.

The Besht taught that simple everyday activities 'done for the sake of heaven' were equal in value to observing the 613 formal commandments, and that there was a duty to rescue the 'sparks' of divinity that, according to the Kabbalah, were trapped in the material world and were related to each man's soul. Communion with God could also take place through saintly intermediaries, the Zaddikim, whose charisma was transmitted through the several hereditary dynasties established by the disciples of the actual founder of the movement, Rabbi Dov-Baer. The Zaddik was a divinely elected intermediary with supernatural powers.

Hasidism spread rapidly during a period of Polish economic and political decline, civil unrest and endemic anti-semitism. The Hasidic emphasis on mysticism and joy provided a source of consolation in these harsh political and social conditions. As with other religious movements of the oppressed, communion with God endowed the persecuted and the poor with a sense of pride and dignity. The Besht's popular appeal, enhanced by his humble appearance and companionship with unsophisticated peasants, was due to his rejection of traditional values as being essential for redemption. Social protest by the poor against the wealthy communal leadership was inherent in his rejection of the legalistic scholasticism of Talmudic study. The movement has continued to flourish despite fierce opposition from Orthodox rabbis who rejected Hasidic pantheism, and the subsequent dispersal of the community from Eastern Europe to America and Britain. Millennial themes, always latent in Judaism as in Christianty, have appeared regularly. One Jacob Isaac of Lublin announced that the Napoleonic wars were the prelude to messianic redemption.

The various Hasidic sects have different traditions. Some still emphasize ecstatic experience and even attempt to gain converts, while others have lapsed into the hairsplitting textual criticism and arid formalism which the Besht had criticized. For all groups, however, life is constantly lived within the constraints imposed by a rigid system of classification, and a rejection of the culture of the modern secular state. At the same time messianic expectations lie close to the surface.

MORDECHAI LEVY

We have seen how difficult it is for an outsider to evaluate the significance of individual psychological difficulties in a tight-knit religious community. To distinguish zealousness from pathological scrupulosity is often impossible when religious ritual and observance are so highly valued and intensely integrated into all aspects of everyday life.

Mordechai Levy was born in a displaced person's camp in Germany in 1946. In a situation where children were extremely uncommon, his parents devoted a considerable proportion of their rations to their son. The only child among the remnants of the Hungarian Hasidim in the camp, his birth seemed a portent for the future. His parents came to Britain and joined the Hasidic community in London in 1949. All their relatives had perished.

Mordechai's education followed the traditional pattern of *cheder* and the *yeshiva*, where he learned to analyse the Talmud and its commentaries and how to reconcile apparent contradictions in the sacred texts. A quiet and conscientious student, he was not particularly successful and failed to live up to his father's hopes that he would become an outstanding scholar. Eventually his parents arranged a marriage in Antwerp with a girl from the same Hasidic community. He left to join her and, at the age of twenty-six, began work for the first time, helping in the family workshop. Although Mordechai met her father's criteria of lineage, Talmudic learning and Orthodox practice, the marriage failed because Mordechai was impotent, and he was divorced. On returning to London he appeared to his worried parents preoccupied and quiet, was unable to concentrate on his studies and failed in his attempt to earn a living in a small factory owned by a friend of his father.

Mordechai was brought to our hospital two years after his divorce by his understandably anxious mother after his weight had fallen to six stone as a result of extreme dieting. He was fasting for long periods, spending up to twenty hours daily in the study house and standing for hours immersed in the *mikveh*, the small rectangular pool in the basement, in order to 'disperse unholiness'. Family meals were a battle, as Mordechai politely but firmly refused to eat, his mother alternately cajoled and wept, while his father appeared strangely unconcerned. Communication with Mordechai was difficult – his knowledge of English was limited since he had never moved out of his Yiddish-speaking environment. He quietly told us that his mother was mistaken in her belief that he was *meshugge* (insane). When asked why he was fasting and what the religious sanction for it was, he remained silent and slightly supercilious. Did Mordechai believe that he had been specially chosen by God? He answered evasively. He refused to talk about his marriage, gazing past us into the distance.

His father, a figure out of a Chagall painting in black kaftan and broad-brimmed hat, was less dogmatic than the mother about Mordechai's behaviour and suggested that perhaps he was just 'very religious'.

It was difficult to accept that Mordechai's excessive religiosity and fasting were symptoms of a serious mental illness, despite his mother's insistent demands that he be admitted to hospital for 'treatment'. Lack of information about the marriage and what exactly was passing at home (an attempt to join a family meal proved unsuccessful) meant that we had little to go on apart from Mordechai's fasting and bathing. Both had religious sanction. We talked to members of his community who tended (especially the women) to share his mother's view, but a minority dissented. We tried to reassure Mrs Levy, who blamed her son's 'illness' on her own failure to fulfil scrupulously the requirement to separate and burn a small portion of dough when baking.

Psychiatric colleagues offered a variety of opinions and diagnostic labels. The refusal to eat and Mordechai's assertion that his weight was adequate were suggested by one doctor to be anorexia nervosa, with its characteristic distorted perception of body-image: Mordechai denied being thin even when severely emaciated.

A social worker interpreted his religiosity as Mordechai's understandable attempt to increase his status within the community. He had failed in his role as husband and scholar, and was perhaps striving to gain recognition by his ascetic piety. For another the ritual significance of food in Jewish family life, especially in a family who had survived near-starvation in concentration camps, was thought to offer Mordechai a powerful tool in some family dispute of which we were still unaware.

A nurse described as 'schizophrenic' Mordechai's explanation that he was simply carrying out God's command to fast and purify himself. He had heard these divine instructions during his long hours of prayer. Mordechai's feeling that he was being 'made' to carry out God's will appeared to resemble the schizophrenic experience of *passivity* (pp. 115–16).

Another psychiatrist suggested Mordechai was depressed even though he did not look dejected or miserable and denied feeling unhappy. He pointed out that Mordechai was unlikely to admit to depressive feelings and ideas since a melancholy attitude is anathema to devout Hasidim:

> At times the evil inclination misleads man into supposing that he has committed a serious sin when it was actually no more than a mere peccadillo or no sin at all, the intention being to bring men into a state of melancholy . . . But melancholy is a great hindrance to God's service. Even if a man has stumbled and sinned he should not become too sad because this will prevent him from worshipping God.

The diversity of medical opinion mirrored the conflicting attitudes to Mordechai's behaviour shown by his family and community. How acceptable were his ideas and ascetic practices by the standards of his own congregation? In a community in which all activity is guided by precedent and authority it appeared logical to do the same and look at the traditional teachers [161]. We turned for assistance to the works of Gershom Scholem [378] and to the contemporary British authority on Hasidism, Rabbi Louis Jacobs. According to Jacobs there has never been rabbinic advocacy of ascetic exercises which may endanger health. He quotes Rabbi Moses Hayim Luzzato: 'You may accept as a true principle that men should abstain from things in this world which are not absolutely necessary. But if, for any reason, a thing is physically indispensable, he who abstains from it is a sinner. To this there is no exception' [196]. On the other hand Mordechai himself appealed to the life of Rabbi Nahman of Brazlav. Nahman, great-grandson of the Besht, indulged in prolonged fasts, followed by immersions in an icy cold *mikveh*. 'The world imagines,' he said, 'that because I am a descendant of the Besht, I have attained a high status. It is not so. I have succeeded because I have afflicted my body . . .' [330].

Given the historic precedent for self-mortification we have refrained from diagnostic labels. Meanwhile Mordechai remains perilously underweight and we are far from certain that we have understood his predicament.[3]

A problem then for practising doctors seems to be to distinguish these two areas of religion and mental illness. Most contemporary churches make a clear distinction between healthy and unhealthy religion [301]. This was not always so. For the medieval church the power of 'the scandal of the Crucifixion' derived from its deliberate contravention of human reason [139]. The established churches now, however, avoid conflict with the area which modern science has defined for itself and accept the judgements of medicine. Although insanity may conceal the seeds of true religion, it is not itself believed to be a 'genuine' religious experience.

If the larger churches have achieved an accommodation with medicine, the smaller sects, frequently dismissed as unbalanced by their larger sisters, continue to regard the rationalism of medicine as a threat. One group has appealed to the Archbishop of Canterbury to intervene in the practice of psychiatrists who were diagnosing religious people as insane [169]. Some of the sects reverse the intrusion of medicine into their field by carrying out healing themselves. In doing this, they often take over many of the rituals of the medical establishment, such as wearing white coats and washing their hands before laying their hands on the next patient [387].

A solution to the problems of separating insanity from religious experience is to look at them, not as mutually exclusive natural states located in the physical world, but rather as being in particular domains of culture. The same biological events set up resonances in each system of reference. In the next chapter we shall look in this way at the different systems of medicine and religion and wonder whether the type of clear distinction we have been trying to make between the two is really an adequate framework.

NOTES

1 'And when the day of Pentecost was fully come, they were all with one accord in one place. And suddenly there came a sound from Heaven as of a rushing mighty wind, and it filled all the house where they were sitting . . . and they were all filled with the Holy Ghost, and began to speak with other tongues, as the Spirit gave men utterance' (Acts 2:1–4).

2 Although 'dissociative states' like glossolalia are socially patterned behaviour, they can occur out of context in stressful situations such as surgical operations or traffic accidents [278]. Their inappropriate use is not necessarily a sign of serious mental illness.

3 [1989] A paper written after the first edition of this book suggests some approaches (see Littlewood, 1983b in the references on page 318).

CHAPTER NINE

NORMAL
AND ABNORMAL

Ils ont dit: 'Cet homme est fou.' Qui dit que je suis fou? . . .
Un psychiatre français, un psychiatre qui ne connaît pas ma
personnalité, qui ne connaît pas mes mœurs, rien de mon
passé, rien du milieu dans lequel je travaille, qui ne connaît
pas ma langue maternelle. Ce monsieur dit: 'C'est un aliéné.'
Entre parenthèses, c'est un des beaux titres que j'ai eus:
'aliéné' veut dire 'qui a quitté le chemin' en latin, c'est-à-dire
que j'ai quitté le chemin de la stupidité dans le pays.

Le procès des Guadeloupéens – 18 patriotes devant
la Cour de Sûreté de L'Etat Français
(Co.Ga.So.D., Mourral, ? Paris, 1969)

Among certain South American Indians the absence of a
disfiguring skin disease – dyschromic spirochaetosis – was so rare
that some anthropologists once felt that it was regarded as
abnormal; people without the characteristic skin pigmentation
had difficulty in marrying [107]. That different societies have
different ideas of normality and abnormality is obvious. It is less
obvious how such abnormality is defined and recognized. We
have seen that some anthropologists suggest that the mentally ill
are those people in a particular community who fail to live up to
a very specific type of behaviour which is expected in the
community. The World Health Organisation project (p. 117)
found, however, that in widely differing societies there is a
pattern of experience and behaviour which is similar to our own
concept of schizophrenia; mental illness seems very similar
everywhere. Are these two points of view compatible? Do they
perhaps refer to two different things? Can we define a *delusion*?
Is it inevitable that what is a crazy belief in one community will
turn out to be a generally accepted truth in another?

This chapter proposes that we should not look at beliefs about
insanity in other cultures as if they were only more or less

accurate approximations to a 'scientific' description. Even in Britain the mentally ill are not recognized by procedures which bear any close resemblance to those of physical science.

We might hope that when psychiatrists get to know a particular ethnic group in Britain, they should easily be able to establish by sympathetic study what constitutes 'normal behaviour' for it. Considerations of normality and abnormality are not, however, 'innocent' or value-free – we have seen that European attitudes to insanity in non-Europeans have been closely tied to political values. Even inside small communities, tacit assumptions about abnormal behaviour reflect political considerations of various types. When we look at such groups as they change in relation to the wider community, the base-line of normality becomes increasingly elusive.

THE PERCEPTION OF MENTAL ABNORMALITY IN BRITAIN – BIOLOGY AND SOCIETY

Modern medicine is based on the assumption that physical illnesses are the same throughout the world. Tuberculosis, for example, may be found most frequently in association with certain patterns of poverty or of social life, including type of economic activity or household organization or beliefs about hygiene and the consumption of food. We can, however, describe its effect on the human body independently of culture. Psychological illnesses by contrast are defined and recognized only by looking at the total relationship of an individual to his or her community.

Physical disease itself may cause psychological disturbances: the organic psychiatric illnesses or even that vague malaise we recognize as part of feeling generally unwell. Fevers may induce disorientation and hallucinations; amphetamines can cause paranoia; syphilis affecting the brain may be associated with delusions of grandeur; brain damage during birth may be related to subsequent learning difficulties in children. Although they may be recognized as abnormal by reference to our usual beliefs and behaviour, these conditions are recognized as having a specific physical cause. Like tuberculosis, some of these physical causes are more common in particular social conditions – for these problems, certain patterns of sexual relationships, the availability of maternity services or social attitudes to the use of drugs. In these cases, we do have measures of physical abnormality – changes in body temperature or blood chemistry – which are similar to those available in general medicine.

Mental illness may be regarded as a spectrum ranging from organic psychiatric reactions of this type, which have a biological cause in the individual, to vaguer and more diffuse patterns of adaptive or maladaptive behaviour which can only be looked at in relation to the culture of a particular society: overdoses, suicide attempts, possession states or delinquency. The recognition of these conditions as abnormal depends solely on the norms of behaviour in a particular community at a particular time. The physical 'abuse' of children by their parents was once an accepted right in our own society but it has now become unacceptable, indeed pathological, behaviour. Although they involve society as a whole, we are more likely to perceive these reactions at the social end of the spectrum, as the consequence of free-will, than those at the biological end. We also tend to look at them as explanations of abnormal behaviour only after we have first eliminated as possible causes the organic reactions.

Psychological abnormalities understood as the consequence of biological changes	Psychological abnormalities determined by social standards alone

←———→

In the middle of this spectrum lies the most problematic area of mental illness. The psychotic mental illnesses such as schizophrenia or manic-depressive psychosis seem to have greater affinities with the biological end of the spectrum; the neuroses like phobias or anxiety states seem closer to the social end. On the whole, with a cultural emphasis in our own society on internal mental events, we usually think of psychotic illness as a disturbance solely within the individual himself; an abnormal perception such as hallucination or an abnormal mood like depression is a divergence from normal personal experience.

The central area between physical abnormality and social deviance is controversial. It has been the starting point for contemporary criticism of psychiatry, and indeed of medicine in general [195]. *Biologically orientated psychiatrists* emphasize genetic factors in the psychoses: we know for instance that a person with an identical twin who has schizophrenia is more likely than others to develop schizophrenia even if they have been brought up separately. The symptoms of psychotic illness seem also to fall into consistent patterns or syndromes reminiscent of those found in traditional physical illnesses.

The fact that some psychoses have been found to have a physical cause may suggest that this is likely for all psychoses; syphilis has been established by laboratory evidence as the cause of a syndrome called general paralysis of the insane (GPI), which had been recognized previously by clinical observation alone. (The nineteenth-century stereotype of mental illness – lunatic asylums full of pathetic figures claiming to be Napoleon or a member of the Royal Family – owes much to the grandiose delusions of GPI.) Biological psychiatrists point out that it may take a long time for the physical cause of some mental illnesses to be discovered: cretinism and pellagra, both associated with mental abnormality, were recognized as entities some two hundred years before their physical cause was finally established. Emotional causes tend to be emphasized particularly in illnesses whose nature is unclear (tuberculosis in the past and cancer at present [395]). Many illnesses which were once thought to have a supernatural or psychological origin have now been generally accepted as physical: epilepsy was for centuries believed to be of divine origin. It is claimed to be only a matter of time before the physical basis of schizophrenia is established: schizophrenia-like states are indeed found in certain types of epilepsy and drug intoxications.

Psychiatrists who see mental illness from the *social point of view* have suggested that mental abnormalities which have now been found to have a physical cause, such as GPI, always had an 'organic feel' about them – they are only found associated with easily recognized physical abnormalities of the body. The history of psychiatry has not always shown a movement towards biological explanation: since Charcot and Freud conversion hysteria, once 'organic', has been generally regarded as 'psychological'. Sociological theories emphasize that mental illnesses seem to form the clusters of abnormal behaviour we call syndromes only because we are already expecting them to do so: there are equally consistent 'syndromes' of behaviour, such as attempted suicide or possession states, which we do not believe to be biological in origin.

The presence of a genetic component in schizophrenia does not by itself make it an illness. Homosexuality, once considered an illness with genetic associations, is now accepted as an alternative pattern of sexual behaviour. A 'high genetic loading' for a particular condition suggests that it can occur in a wide range of environments: the comparatively low genetic loading found in schizophrenia suggests that the potentiality for it is only realized on comparatively few occasions. The environment in which it occurs, which includes family and social organization as well as the physical state of the body, is thus important. Genetic and biochemical associations appear to be more significant for manic-depressive psychosis than for schizophrenia, yet it appears to show greater variability across cultures (Chapter 3). The form of organic mental illness, unlike that of depression, is always very similar in quite different societies.

Psychiatrists sympathetic to sociological explanations point out that different cultures often have their own culture-specific types of mental illness. These were diagnosed as psychoses until the idea developed that all cultures had approximately similar rates of the same psychoses.

A single physiological change such as rapid pulse rate may be a feature of a variety of quite different subjective states: a biological change associated with altered mental experiences is not necessarily the cause of them, nor can it ever be identified with them (p. 71). In all societies mental illness is defined in terms of something other than itself, whether this is demonic possession, sin or biochemistry. It then tends to become identified with the explanation – insanity then *becomes* religion or biology.

Both frames of reference start from easily demonstrated positions at opposite ends of our spectrum, such as brain tumours at one end or possession states at the other. Their advocates then try to define the middle ground by means of techniques appropriate to their respective ends. We tend to explain the nature of things by the way we perceive and measure them: it is easier to perceive gravity as if it was the quality of an object rather than as a relationship between objects.

It is often assumed that psychiatrists who advocate what we have called the 'biological position' are more conservative politically than those taking 'the social position'. Both views may however be used either conservatively or radically. The

American Mental Health Movement, which follows psychoanalytical theory (at the social or 'radical' end), has proved to be
a medical apology for modern American values: suicides, strikes
and revolutions became 'mental health problems' [93]. The
biological school of psychiatry believes that the recognition of
mental abnormality as physical illness prevents the use of
psychiatric diagnosis for social coercion. We have seen that the
countries with the widest and most 'social' concept of 'schizophrenia' are those which have been most severely criticized for
using psychiatry as an agency of social control. If depression is
believed to be the product of certain types of family patterns,
then, if those patterns are characteristic of the dominant class,
depression itself becomes a mark of distinction.

The description of mental illnesses as each being located
somewhere along this biological–social spectrum is a little over-
simplified. (One can for instance occupy both ends of the
spectrum simultaneously without having a disturbed 'mental
state': a psychopath with brain damage does not normally have
hallucinations or delusions.) Psychological abnormality is always
recognized against a background of particular beliefs about
normality which are themselves cultural. Within given biological
constraints there is always a considerable variation in both the
presence and type of psychological expression. This variation is
socially determined.

Although the form of organic mental illness appears similar in
different communities, the actual content of the hallucinations
and delusional misinterpretations reflects the way a given
community structures its experiences [427]. Even the presence of
obvious organic features then does not necessarily mean that
mental illness should be considered from the 'medical' rather
than from the 'cultural' point of view: all aspects of physical
experience also have a social component. What is actually made
of this depends on the society. Male and female sex, hunger and
vomiting, are all located in the physical world, but masculinity
and feminity, fasting and ritual purging, are social institutions.
Societies select out as cultural entities different elements of the
physical world.

Not all cultures have concepts of mental abnormality similar to
our own. The Tembu, as we have seen, use a single category for
all hallucinations where we would classify them as either a healing
vocation or as insanity: in our own society the experiences of the

medical student are usually seen as rather different from those of the mental patient. The Hebrew word *shiggayom* refers in the Old Testament to both insanity and impulsive prophesying [161]. As late as the 1950s, mental illness among the monks of the Greek island of Cephalonica was characterized by extreme agitation and blasphemy. As it was regarded as a purely religious phenomenon, the treatment was imprisonment and exorcism. This treatment seems to us inappropriate because we include schizophrenia in the broad category of medicine rather than in that of religion.

CONCEPTS OF MENTAL ILLNESS, TREATMENT AND RESPONSIBILITY

Different ways of looking at mental illness pick out quite different patterns of illness as being important. A British doctor may diagnose depression in a man who moves and talks slowly and who tells us he has lost his energy and sexual interest, feels that life is not worth living and believes he has committed an unpardonable sin. A traditional healer in the Third World might feel that the important features in the same person were recent contact with his mother-in-law or unexpected good luck which has made his neighbours envious.

While one healer would be looking for certain key psychological symptoms to distinguish between schizophrenia and depression, the other would be principally concerned with distinguishing between the transgression of social customs and the influence of witchcraft. Internal mental experiences are significant for one doctor, but the other will be concerned to investigate the patient's relationships with his family and neighbours.

The urge to classify is not restricted to European science. The Hanunóo of the Philippines distinguish sixty different salt-water molluscs and have 150 names for different parts of plants [245]. Nor are complex differentiations of mental illness limited to the West. Traditional Yoruba healers in Nigeria distinguish a wide variety of psychological abnormalities which bear close parallels to western systems of classification. Among the psychoses they identify are chronic hallucinatory psychosis (*were*), acute psychotic episodes (*asinwin*), chronic withdrawn psychosis (*dindinrin*), regressed psychosis (*danidani*), psychosis with good preservation of the personality (*were alaso*), congenital psychosis (*were d'ile*) and psychoses associated with childbirth (*abisinwin*), old age (*were agba*) and epilepsy (*ipa were*) [326]. Concern with the exact diagnosis may be characteristic of communities with a specialization of roles: the Yoruba had a complex social structure with large towns, extensive trade networks, the working of metals by specialists and a monetary system.

Are the mentally ill in different societies identified by a clearly defined set of features or is mental illness merely a convenient rag-bag for a variety of unacceptable behaviours?

The answer depends in part on the healers' potential. If there are many psychiatrists offering treatment, as in the United States, it is not difficult to be diagnosed as mentally ill according to one or other theory; a broad concept of mental abnormality prevails involving most individuals who fail to reach an ideal type of behaviour. If a society has comparatively few healers, only the most conspicuously deviant can be classified as ill; criteria for inclusion are strict and may approximate to a particular pattern of abnormal behaviour, a syndrome.

Diagnosis also depends upon the efficacy of treatment – if exorcism or electro-convulsive therapy are successful in altering certain patterns of deviant behaviour, possession and depression are likely to be diagnosed frequently. It has been suggested that psychiatric illness in Europe and America can be classified as patterns of behaviour which are modified by particular pharmaceutical drugs [210]. Manic-depressive illness has been diagnosed particularly frequently in the last fifteen years with the introduction of the effective prophylactic treatment lithium.

Anthropologists used to believe that non-Europeans always classified illnesses in relation to their supposed origin, whether they were caused by malevolent witchcraft or something independent of human volition [70]. In fact many different types of classification are used. The Yoruba use clinical descriptions reminiscent of Western biomedical categories. Other African societies, such as the Ganda of East Africa, classify mental illnesses according to the part of the body believed to be affected. The Ganda say that temporary psychological changes (alcoholic intoxication or possession) are due to something *on* the head, permanent changes (chronic psychosis) as something *in* the head [308]. In Jamaica there is a similar distinction between permanent 'brain madness' and temporary 'mind madness': similar to biomedical 'genetically associated' versus 'stress associated'.

Diseases of the head, say the Ganda, result in violence and abuse: they include what Western medicine calls schizophrenia, mania, toxic confusional states and epilepsy. 'Heart diseases' include fright, insomnia and loss of appetite. Illnesses may also be classified according to their cause (sorcery, evil spirits or the breaking of certain prohibitions such as commiting adultery during pregnancy), subdivided into 'Ganda' or 'foreign' diseases, and into 'strong' or 'weak' illness. Illness of the 'head' type associated with violence usually results in the local police removing the patient to the psychiatric hospital. Men are traditionally more violent and dangerous and they are twice as likely to be admitted to hospital. The Ganda are embarrassed by psychiatric illness; the potential violence of sufferers from 'head diseases' is repeatedly stressed and they are immediately restrained [308].

Among four very similar rural East African societies the concepts of mental illness differ considerably [113]. In one community 60 per cent of people interviewed believed that psychosis was caused by witchcraft compared with only 1 per cent in another. While in some no one believed that psychosis was a disease, in another two thirds said it was an illness caused by a worm in the front of the brain accompanied by stress. No simple distinction can be drawn between those who feel that mental illness is due to malevolent forces and those who believe in an organic origin: people who believe that insanity is caused by sorcery also feel that God might be partly responsible for it or indeed that genetic factors play a part.

Madness in these communities is recognized by a sudden change of character and unusual behaviour, especially nudity. Unusual behaviour towards others is regarded as a better diagnostic criterion than altered subjective experience – only five people out of the six hundred who were interviewed mentioned hallucinations. How specific is this altered behaviour? In one of these four societies a benign withdrawn patient is believed to have a different type of illness from one who is aggressive. In another, withdrawal and aggression can alternate in the same illness. Interestingly, those communities which believe that mental illness is caused by witchcraft also believe it is curable and pursue a policy of treatment and care, while those who suspect an underlying organic cause leave the patient to starve or beat them; false accusations of insanity may even serve as an excuse for manslaughter of the accused [319].

Chronic mental illness in East Africa is always recognized, but acute episodes may provoke lengthy discussions, for people often feign mental illness to avoid payment of fines. Non-Western concepts of insanity are not rigidly imposed systems. There are frequent disagreements among the Ganda as to whether a person is mentally ill or merely eccentric. Diagnosis is negotiable. Societies use systems of diagnosis flexibly according to current social pressures. When the Spartan king Cleomenes became insane, the Spartans said it was because of heavy drinking while the Athenians insisted it was divine punishment for his politics. A Ganda proverb about one of the spirits states 'a Lubaale punishes with reason – providing it has not killed one of your relatives' [308]. Old Testament prophets were labelled mad when the implications of their prophecies were unacceptable [345]. Both Odysseus and David pretended to be mad to escape awkward situations.

The value of feigning mental illness depends on the benefits to be gained from the diminished responsibility which is attributed to the insane. The responsibilities and legal rights of deviant individuals are debated in small-scale communities just as they are in Britain. The Ganda regard sexual potency as such an important measure of normality that impotent men do not have to pay taxes [308]. The mentally ill in many cultures have, like the licensed jester, a certain 'extraterritoriality' which allows them greater freedom from social obligations than others. An Ashanti ruler wondered how responsible for their actions he should consider the mentally ill and the intoxicated [98]. He placed a psychotic and drunken man together inside a hut and then set it on fire; the psychotic walked out but his inebriated companion was severely burned. The king concluded that a man who is drunk should be deemed less responsible for his actions than one who is mad. In Britain the reverse is true – inebriation, unlike mental illness, is no excuse for homicide.

Every culture conceives of mental illness in relation to its dominant beliefs. To these, madness might well be seen as a challenge. Insanity was a sin in medieval Europe; then it became primarily a failure of self-sufficiency; later it was seen as an affront to man's basic rationality. Each conceptual framework has its own logic of explanation – the eighteenth-century theory that mania was caused by evaporation of the vital humours was validated by a series of experiments which apparently demonstrated that the brains of people suffering from mania were considerably lighter than usual [139].

The WHO study of schizophrenia (p. 118) suggested that patients in certain non-European countries, India and Nigeria, had a much better prognosis. Relatives of our own West Indian-born patients sometimes report that the patient has recovered surprisingly soon (to us) after a severe psychotic illness. It may be significant that certain cultures implicate a supernatural or physical cause and so an individual is not held responsible for his illness; if reparation is accepted immediately after the patient has been found to have 'broken a taboo', the sick role may also be shed more easily. Although the illness model of psychiatry, unlike psychoanalysis, relieves the patient of any personal responsibility for his illness, the popular stigma attached to mental illness still attributes personal blame [155].

Abnormal behaviour may be variously met with sympathy, persecution or exploitation. Japanese women used to be prone to *imu*, an episode of confusion and anxiety in which they imitated the gestures of those around and repeated their remarks. Women with *imu* were extensively used for entertainment and encouraged to parody the performance of professional actors. The theatre is often regarded as a contained space where the potentially dangerous stresses of the community can be safely acted out [375]. Actors are popularly considered to be unbalanced. In Java actors in certain roles in the epic drama frequently run *amok* and this can spread to the audience in a mass epidemic [148].

While schizophrenia in all societies may progress to a similar chronic end state, societies may differ in their ability to arrest or compensate this psychosis or to perpetuate it [87]. Some societies may be unable to tolerate experiences which are acceptable elsewhere. Hallucinations of any type are not a valid experience for industrial societies, partly because we have few occupations which can be pursued by someone who is hallucinating. Continual emphasis on the boundary between normality and abnormality may, in spite of the good intentions of conscientious after-care, confirm a patient in his role as a chronic psychotic. Schizophrenic patients about whose illness the relatives continue to express a good deal of emotion generally have a poor prognosis [417].

Tolerance of the unusual experiences of mental illness may also be related to the ability of members of a community to tolerate in themselves experiences such as vivid dreams or hallucinations. The suggestion by the anti-psychiatry movement in the 1960s that the experiences of schizophrenia were valid communications was associated with an interest in altered states of consciousness induced by psychedelic drugs or meditation, an interest comparatively rare in European history.

DEVIANCE AND MENTAL ILLNESS

Insane behaviour is often expected to invert the basic rules of society [16]. Among the Nyakysua who live in the north of Lake Nyasa, dirt and excrement are considered to be not only disgusting but dangerous. Insanity, the result of neglecting ritual obligations, is associated with eating dirt. Dirt and faeces, however, also represent the dead: mourners voluntarily accept being covered with rubbish. The voluntary acceptance of ritual impurities in a controlled setting may thus be a way of accepting those parts of the universe which are rigidly excluded from everyday life [104].

This is not to say that communities regard mental illness solely as undesired behaviour. As we have seen, undesirable behaviour is penalized, but this is done through rigorous classifications which may, like our own, be modelled on the idiom of physical illness. The different classifications we have looked at are not haphazard stabs at a 'scientific' approach which is value-free. They embody both a social function and a coherent theory. As the anthropologist Mary Douglas says, 'Through the classifications used, the furniture of the universe is turned into an armoury of control. In each social system human suffering is explained in a way that reinforces the controls' [105]. These theories are not merely social ascription or 'inaccurate' [cf. 439].

Under certain conditions, such as in the theatre or at carnivals, societies may freely tolerate behaviour which would normally be unacceptable [335]. It is as if the society tells the individual 'Don't do that – but if you must, then do it this way!' [257].

Deviance can be tacitly licensed by society which determines, as with normality, how it should be patterned. It may be a permanent institution. The Plains Indians had a heroic ideal of aggressive and warlike 'masculine' behaviour. Men who found that this was too much to live up to could opt out into a transvestite role called *berdache*. Transvestites were accepted halfheartedly: they were mocked, but could achieve distinction within certain prescribed occupations. Although allowed a certain licence, they were not regarded as capable of meeting full social obligations [96]. The ritual toleration of abnormal behaviour both limits tendencies which could otherwise threaten the whole society, and underlines the boundary between normal and abnormal.

It has been suggested that schizophrenia in our own society may have a similar basis [232]: 'Behave like this, but if you can't or won't, then we can find an approved role for you as a schizophrenic. It's not so good as being normal but at least we'll both know where you are and you'll be causing us less concern.' While deviant roles are themselves often punished, the person who steps into them soon finds that the options to act differently become increasingly limited [242].[1]

Every society has its characteristic mental illness, whether the Romantic longings of a Werther, the anxieties of a Kierkegaard or the self-conscious weirdness of Natty ('nutty') Dread, the Jamaican exile. Mental illness is a convenient peg on which a community may hang its feared preoccupations, accepting their existence but denying their validity. The mentally ill and witches (like foreigners and like the dead [16; 296]) may show us normal behaviour by doing the opposite. Psychiatrists have indeed equated witchcraft and mental illness [396]. Among the Ganda, as in Britain, epithets of insanity are freely used abusively or humorously. Popular terms like 'crazy' or 'barmy' continue to remind us of our basic assumptions. The company which advertises a sale with a sign saying 'Have we finally gone off our heads? Crazy prices!' confirms the pattern of behaviour in which each sane individual is expected to maximize his material advantages in all situations of exchange or production. The Kwakiutl *potlach* (p. 158) was made illegal as 'an insane use of resources'.

Those people who associate with and control the insane also become contaminated by their 'inverted' nature. Psychosis in

Haiti is believed to be caused by spirit possession and the *hungan* who has power over these spirits is regarded as homosexual [278]; compare this with the popular stories among doctors about the stability of their psychiatric colleagues – 'head shrinkers' and 'trick cyclists'.

The implicit goals of social conformity are frequently couched in the form of religious injunctions which are beyond question [106]. The definition of insanity serves the same goals, but this does not mean that it must always be regarded as a supernatural sanction. Sexual intercourse during menstruation, say the Mohave, leads to insanity – because the semen gets into the bloodstream. Physical illness too has a similar function; in Africa, leprosy is the consequence of marrying inside one's group, while in India, it is the consequence of marrying outside, in both cases the contravention of custom [252]. Although, unlike mental illness, the actual symptoms of the illness in the individual are not a function of the dominant ideology, leprosy provides a similar warning to the potential nonconformist. If epileptic fits are believed to be a consequence of possession, then all episodes of possession, including voluntary possession for the purposes of prophesying, are likely to be marked by fits.

Societies may sanction specific types of abnormal behaviour for the resolution of certain cultural conflicts: culture-specific patterns such as *koro* and *wild man* appear solutions to particular types of stress. They affect vulnerable individuals whose personal conflicts within the community serve as symbolic representations of the same conflicts within the community at large [98]. These conflicts are acted out and temporarily resolved in the individual reaction.

Among the Ojibwa Indians of Canada, some individuals, especially unsuccessful hunters, were described as developing a distaste for normal food and, after becoming possessed by the Witiko vampire, killing and eating their relatives [311]. This Witiko 'psychosis' was related to the male Ojibwa life experiences. After an indulgent childhood, the young boy is precipitated suddenly to adulthood by brutal tests of self-reliance and encouraged to fast in order to obtain supernatural power. Dependence on his parents is replaced by a precarious dependence on supernatural beings and solitary self-reliance in hunting. The mother, hated and feared for her violent rejection of the child, returns to possess him as the Witiko.˙ As we have suggested

(p. 168) this type of explanation may show us how such reactions are patterned but not why they occur. Indeed it has been suggested that the 'psychosis' has never occurred and that it is actually a misreading by whites of a traditional myth, to produce a mythical syndrome.

Koro is a reaction observed in the Far East; the affected man believes that his penis is withdrawing into his body. This belief is authenticated by the community, who may hang on to the penis to prevent this happening. Traditional treatment partially resolves the individual and social conflicts behind the symptoms, without invalidating the belief. *Wild man* behaviour in the Gururumba of New Guinea occurs among young men during the long betrothal period of their arranged marriages when they are faced with rapidly increasing social and economic obligations. They may suddenly start running around the village shouting and attacking their neighbours. They steal objects from other huts. They are tolerated but carefully watched, and the episode usually ends with their temporary disappearance into the forest. Subsequently it is generally accepted that they are less able to support their heavy obligations [298].

Among the Yugoslav partisans of the Second World War, engaged in a brutal conflict with the Germans, a draconian discipline prevailed: engaged couples were posted to different areas and love affairs between the guerillas were punished with summary execution. Episodes of hysteria frequently occurred among adolescent partisans, who would throw themselves to the ground wildly firing an imaginary machine gun.

Reactions of this type are a consequence of conflicts in particular individuals at specific times. The conflict may be so widespread that everyone is equally likely to develop the reaction, or it may be one which affects one group in particular; in these examples it is the men who are the vulnerable group.

'Culture-specific reactions' may be a means of social control by one group of another. The dominant belief system of the Somali nomads is Islam. They are liable to possession by the *sar* spirits in certain well-defined situations. Typically, a wife, struggling to bring up her children in a community in which her freedom is severely limited by men and continually enmeshed in the jealousies and tensions of a polygynous family, becomes convinced she is neglected by her husband, usually in favour of a younger and more attractive wife [251]. The spirits who possess her can be induced to leave only by presents of expensive clothes, perfumes, choice dainties and a lot of attention. Men grudgingly accept the existence of the *sar* spirits. They are torn between the necessity of placating them under public pressure, particularly from other women, and their own doubts as to the reality of the possession. Frequent possession is counter-productive: it is a game the spirits can play once too often. The existence of the *sar* spirits enables men to keep their authority over women without provoking a catastrophic revolt. The women gain short-term advantages without fundamentally changing their situation or even perceiving its reality.

Ninteenth-century Europe provided similar reactions, but within a medical rather than a religious framework: chlorosis, 'the vapours' and hysteria. Even now we need look no further than the 'housewife's psychosis' described by Freud or overdoses or shoplifting or depression in the mothers of young children (p. 133). Whatever the psychological and physiological basis of these reactions, they have a similar social function.

As with mental illness, society can use transient biological changes such as intoxication for its own purposes. Drinking is often an opportunity for temporary contravention of social norms [230]. The physiological consequences of taking alcohol – deadening of the senses, poor co-ordination and depression of male sexual performance – are universal in all cultures. The psychological structuring of drinking behaviour is more variable. Many societies report an increase in aggression amongst men when inebriated [193]: the Mohave by contrast become increasingly quiet and restrained [97]. We find that in no society do women get publicly drunk more often than men, and among nearly all ethnic groups in Britain men rather than women are admitted to hospital for alcoholism (Table 3, p. 90). The form in which alcohol is taken may determine the appropriate emotional and social response – compare the expected effects of champagne, beer and fortified 'British wine'.

A comparison of the drinking habits of fifty-six cultures showed differences in the significance of drinking [193]. While African beer-drinking tribes regard it as a food, the Abiquone, like Orthodox Jews, tend to limit alcohol to ceremonial functions only. In some communities it is a fundamental part of the local economy and the accompaniment to all social interactions outside the family or the traditional reward for cooperative group work.

Its use is restricted to married people among the Masai, to men in the Chaco tribes and in Bali to the elders. Consequences vary from prophesying to an increased licence for extra-marital sex. While the result in most communities is mild intoxication, for the Ainu complete stupor is the usual goal. Heavy drinking is common in communities where economic worries or rapid social change are recognized. In societies with an active belief in sorcery (and thus perhaps with a high level of inhibited aggression), drunken behaviour is frequently violent. It would be interesting to know whether these are also the communities in which insane people are also expected to be violent.

To what extent does culture actually structure the subjective experiences of biologically determined states?

Some experiences seem to be similar in different societies and may be closely related to brain physiology: the impression of a flight or 'trip' occurs with LSD in contemporary Britain, with the hallucinogenic drugs of the Cashinahua Indians of the Amazon – and may perhaps even be related to the broomstick flights of medieval witches [178]. On the other hand the delusions of people with brain damage tend to reflect cultural preoccupations [427]: even organic mental conditions among the Ojibwa were coloured by the Witiko theme. In classical Greece hallucinations of all types were usually ushered in by traditional flute music. People in delirium tremens cannot hallucinate small pink elephants if they come from a culture without a knowledge of elephants. Of two castes in an Indian village the Brahmins take cannabis and the Rajputs alcohol [59]. Both use their particular drug to the point of intoxication and both believe it induces highly valued experiences: boisterous sexuality for the hereditary rulers, the Rajputs, and mystical experiences for the priests, the Brahmins. In other societies these drugs have quite different effects [278]. Mescaline induces experiences in North American Indians completely dissimilar from those induced in whites [146]. While acute psychoses and hallucinations caused by smoking cannabis are frequently reported in Africa and Asia, they appear to be rare among European smokers.

Deviancy theory can be valuable, not in showing that psychiatry is a vast conspiracy, but as a way of demonstrating how, given the biological basis of some psychiatric disorders, society uses them as a model for coping with other awkward experiences. It is in addition applicable when talking about *psychopathic* behaviour rather than insanity. Psychopathy is defined as abnormal behaviour directed to other individuals in the absence of mental abnormality. Psychopaths differ from 'normals' quantitively not qualitatively. Barbara Wootton has suggested that we define persistent badness as a natural disorder – psychopathy – and then attribute this medical diagnosis to people who continually behave badly [448]. Antisocial behaviour becomes abnormal behaviour, and we then try to 'treat' it (unsuccessfully). Psychological techniques designed for the treatment of individual patients were used in the Special Control Units, and disquiet has developed over the use of psychiatric drugs in subduing potentially violent prisoners. The medicalization of the management of criminals is, by traditional criteria, seriously unethical. If all criminals are treated as mentally ill, mental illness itself becomes only another type of antisocial activity, as it was in the eighteenth century.

A single social group may contribute to apparently quite different types of deviance. Black Britons are over-represented both in the diagnosis of schizophrenia and in certain patterns of crime. Are they placed in two deviant categories because of two different types of behaviour, or are the two linked? Are blacks perceived as both madder and badder than whites? Black psychotic patients in our London hospital were twice as likely as whites to be there under Section 136 of the Mental Health Act (the clause which empowers the police to take people to psychiatric hospital). Black patients are also twice as likely as whites to have been sent to this particular psychiatric hospital from prison [258].

BELIEFS AND DELUSION

Europeans think of insane people as possessing peculiar beliefs which are nonsensical to others. These delusions may be 'grandiose' – the patient believes he is a friend of the Prime Minister; or fantastic – he believes he is in communion with extraterrestrial beings; or based on guilt – he tells us he has committed unbelievably terrible crimes; or of a persecutory nature – he is the victim of a conspiracy. We may sometimes be able to understand his delusions as an intelligible symbolic response to his feelings and experiences, but they remain beliefs which are idiosyncratic and not immediately meaningful to other people.

In many Third World countries mental illness is perceived as abnormal action rather than mistaken belief. Americans of Asian origin are more likely than those of European origin to recognize psychiatric disorder by unusual appearance or actions [400]. In Colombia both graduate nurses and untrained nursing aides are likely to perceive mental illness as being altered behaviour rather than as a psychological disturbance [280]. The beliefs of patients may well be shared by the family, although his or her behaviour will still be seen as abnormal [214; 289]. Accusations of sorcery against neighbours by a psychotic person may be perceived as initially quite acceptable, but they are then followed by maladaptive personal violence rather than employment of the accepted communal technique for dealing with sorcery [259].

It is particularly difficult to decide whether a person's belief is a delusion or not relative to the usual beliefs in his community when its culture is changing or when it contains a variety of conflicting belief systems. An immigrant from a rural society who has entered Britain adapts to new beliefs and values. If when under stress he momentarily reverts to sorcery accusations as a way of coping with particular difficulties, this does not make him mentally ill. A man from Trinidad who was under considerable stress from a disintegrating marriage told us he believed his wife was practising witchcraft against him. When interviewed she denied it and said that he was crazy. On a subsequent occasion we visited him at home and he showed us some of her books published by the De Laurence Company – the standard manuals of sorcery in the Caribbean. It appeared likely that his wife had been practising *obeah*. Because sorcery is now rare in Britain there is no accepted way of dealing with it and even to believe in its possibility is considered abnormal. A white Englishman who says he is the victim of sorcery is likely to be regarded as mentally ill because such beliefs and accusations are idiosyncratic in his milieu.

Delusions, then, are beliefs which are not empirically true and which are not sanctioned by a particular culture. Sometimes, as with folie à deux or folie à trois, the delusions of a psychotic person may be shared by one or more close relatives who are usually socially and emotionally dependent on the patient. Unusual beliefs may be shared by larger groups of people – flying saucer cults, extreme fundamentalist churches or utopian sects. These beliefs, and even religious beliefs in general, have been called delusions at times. We are dealing with a spectrum of belief:

Individual psychotic delusions	folie à deux	transient and obscure sects	psychic epidemics	widely held religious beliefs

←——————————————————————————→

The originator of individual delusions is a person who is considered by most people in his community to be abnormal. Towards the right of the spectrum a larger number of people (the 'lunatic fringe') share a belief, which is thus progressively 'less delusional'. Beliefs of small sects may vary from bizarre ideas shared by a small short-lived group such as those which await the salvation of the world by extraterrestrial beings, to larger, more established groups which are more obviously part of the shared cultural background, such as the groups that are preparing for the Second Coming of Christ.

A mass belief somewhat nearer the delusional end of the spectrum was that of socially and linguistically isolated groups of Japanese in Brazil after the Second World War. For a period of ten years or more, many of them believed that Japan had not surrendered but had emerged victorious from the war.

One interpretation of political or religious movements has been to suggest that they are initiated by a rather unstable individual who persuades a group of credulous people to follow him. This possibility becomes progressively less valid as we look at the right of the spectrum. A psychotic individual can rarely convince many others of the validity of his personal delusions.

Ex-President Amin of Uganda was described by a Professor of Medicine as suffering from 'grandiose paranoia, hypomania, probably schizophrenia, hypomanic paranoia, possibly GPI and the Jekyll and Hyde syndrome' [11]! To characterize political opponents as insane is unhelpful to those with psychological difficulties. It is also a facile abnegation of political responsibility. Amin could hardly have maintained power for nearly ten years if he were suffering from half a dozen psychoses. Insanity is a seductive explanation both of antagonistic societies (p. 28) and of political opponents. It is often difficult to resist; even in a book with the specific title *Illness as a Metaphor*, Susan Sontag says that cancer is a 'good metaphor for paranoids' [395]. By paranoids she means political extremists.

Insane *beliefs* taken in isolation may, however, rapidly become normative. During periods of social stress there is a greater acceptance of beliefs originating from the left of the spectrum; disturbed times are likely to bring forth progressively more unusual solutions. Individuals who at other times would be regarded as extremely bizarre may find a brief following. Two eighteenth-century Quakers were regarded by their American contemporaries as mad (they rolled about in the snow and produced books written 'in any order'). One of their beliefs was that slavery was immoral. Within a few years, perhaps because of the openness of the Society of Friends to unusual 'Workings of the Spirit', anti-slavery motions were passed by various Quaker meetings and Quakers were discouraged from owning slaves. The two pioneers do not seem, however, to have been regarded by their community as other than insane [92].

Beliefs or delusions from the left-hand side of the spectrum may thus be found to be meaningful by the community with a qualification: 'he's crazy but . . .' We believe, for instance, that Lautréamont, Hölderlin, Nietzsche and Artaud offer us more than medical case histories. Psychiatric patients have been insisting that God was an astronaut long before Erich von Däniken. One patient of ours, a highly intelligent Greek boy, used to counter objections to his belief that the earth was controlled from inside by a group of asteroids which possessed souls by reminding us that all new theories are greeted with incredulity: 'They said that Einstein was mad.' (His belief by itself is not of course ipso facto insane: beings in the centre of the earth have a respectable pedigree in Hermetic and Neo-Platonic philosophy.)

It has been suggested that societies which encourage greater contact with unconscious feelings can freely accept idiosyncratic beliefs and delusions from the left side of the spectrum but that they pay a price in economic and social inferiority [289]. Delusions occur in times of increased stress as if 'in relation to changing conditions a culture does call on individual members to sacrifice their mental health by the development of individual delusions which relieve communal anxieties'. It is the psychotics who structure the common experiences of the community because for them these same experiences are perhaps more overwhelming. The community can then use the statements of the psychotic as metaphors for their own experience. When we ask with Laing who is mad – a society prepared to use nuclear weapons or a girl who believes she has an atomic bomb inside her – we are affirming that individual delusions can be valid, albeit metaphorical, statements [232].

'Psychic epidemics' or psychic contagions occur when large numbers of people briefly hold beliefs or undergo experiences which they would at other times regard as abnormal [345]. One million people in America are estimated to have been involved in the disturbances caused by the radio broadcast of H.G. Wells's *War of the Worlds* [56]. The presentation of part of the play in the form of recordings on the spot of the Martian invasion, interspersed with government bulletins, resulted in widespread panic. In 1944 the Phantom Anaesthetist of Illinois was frequently to be seen on his nightly prowls, opening surburban bedroom windows and spraying the sleeping women inside with his mysterious gas [200]. After a major police hunt he was publicly declared imaginary and he ceased his visitations. The 'mass hysteria' of children's bands or of enclosed communities such as convents or schools are psychic epidemics [204].

Like the hallucinations induced by drugs or those found in psychosis, psychic epidemics take their themes from popular preoccupations. We see flying saucers in the skies where once celestial battles were fought [408]. During a period of millennial expectation in a German town, women

> tore their breasts, stretching their arms out so as to form a cross, whilst others lay upon their backs, foaming at the mouth, staring up at the sky with a look of anxious expectation. Then they would spring up raving, grinding their teeth and clapping their hands, invoking blessings and curses from Heaven at the same time. . . Some saw a great fire with blue and black flames descend from Heaven and cover the city; hysterical laughter and crying were heard on all hands. Ever and anon a group of men and women would be seen rushing through the streets shouting 'Repent and be baptized. Slay the unbaptized heathen.' Suddenly the rays of the sun struck a newly gilded weathercock . . . dazzling the eyes of those that looked that way. The assembled women

fell on their faces and, with folded hands, cried 'Oh! Father, Father, most excellent King of Zion, spare thy people!' (quoted in Worsley [447])

Occupying a convenient place between individual insanity and normative social behaviour, 'mass hysteria' has proved a useful term for invalidating undesirable political and religious movements such as the medieval 'dancing mania' and the anti-colonial 'Vaihala madness' in New Guinea [447]. The political phenomenon of Nazism has been conveniently digested as abnormal psychology – a result of 'mass hypnosis'. Again we have an example of applying the terminology of individual disorder to a group as a whole. 'Crowds' and 'mobs' become imbued with a personality of their own in an attempt to reduce the individuals of one particular group to a single organism which can, like the individual, develop an illness. For illness requires a surgeon . . . (otherwise known as the 'rotten apple' theory).

Madmen do not become sane when people accept slightly more idiosyncratic ideas as reasonable general propositions. While slightly broadening their perception of what reasonable belief is, they may reduce the tolerance extended to beliefs still regarded as unacceptable. One can tolerate a variety of beliefs regarded as abnormal or alternatively have a broad concept of acceptable behaviour while tolerating nothing outside it. Compared with the middle class, members of the American working class may have a much broader concept of what is normal, but they are less tolerant of behaviour outside it [101].

We have not considered two other characteristics of delusions. They contradict empirical reality and they are held with an unshakeable fervour which is usually inaccessible to argument. Religious beliefs, however, share these two features, and we have preferred here to emphasize the idiosyncratic nature of delusions and their place in a general picture of psychiatric illness which is itself partly determined by other criteria. In the last chapter we looked at some of the interrelations between religion and mental illness.

NORMALITY AND ABNORMALITY IN A
CHANGING CULTURE

If observations of mental illness across cultures are always biased by cultural preconceptions should psychiatrists only accept as mental abnormality that which a community itself recognizes?

Some years ago we were asked by a Hasidic couple to treat their fourteen-year-old son Chaim, who had apparently become insane. According to his parents he was able to appear quite normal to outsiders and had concealed his illness from school friends and teachers. We thought it best therefore to see him at home. The Weinberg household appeared very Orthodox – the men dressed in the traditional black clothes, their hair in ringlets with untrimmed beards; the women wore wigs. There was no radio, television or record player. The only books visible were various Talmudic texts. Along a table Chaim's brothers and brothers-in-law ignored us, bent over commentaries on the Torah.

Chaim was naturally embarrassed at the arrival of two psychiatrists but, at his father's prompting, took us up to his bedroom to talk. To our astonishment the walls were covered with posters of football stars and the table was a litter of rosettes, scarves and exercise books full of the analyses of football results. Some months before, while watching television illicitly with a school friend (whose family were rather less Orthodox), Chaim had seen a football match for the first time in his life. He was fascinated and surreptitiously started reading sports magazines and even by extreme cunning managed to see Saturday soccer matches. His parents had inevitably found out and the house for the last few months had been the scene of continual arguments. Insistence on filial obedience was countered by an open threat by Chaim to try to become a professional footballer. The family doctor was convinced the boy was developing schizophrenia. Allowing for the strain caused on the whole household by his outrageous ideas we felt there was no sign of mental illness in anybody.

If the community with its doctor (who as an Orthodox Jew presumably knew the limits of normality within the community) felt Chaim was mentally ill, could we disagree? Compared with the acceptance by his brothers of the society in which they had been brought up, Chaim was certainly behaving strangely. On the other hand the Weinbergs refused to accept that they were also part of a wider society, a society which offered a variety of different lifestyles. They saw doctors as supporters of their authority – indeed, their first request to us was to make Chaim obey them! Was the boy crazy in wanting to be a footballer or was the whole family crazy in expecting him to accept their rather narrow aspirations?

Societies are not static. As we are continually reminding ourselves, modern society is changing rapidly (although it is debatable whether it is changing 'more rapidly' than previously). For the immigrant, change of country is usually the major experience of his or her life. Migration which was originally embarked upon for economic reasons has unforeseen consequences in other directions. Traditional patterns lose their significance, the old systems fail and new crises define new groups of vulnerable people.

Standards of normality and abnormality change. Behaviour once accepted as desirable becomes unusual if not reprehensible. Individuals may be forced to use quite different standards of behaviour at the same time, resulting in a confusion of roles. Some West Indians who have recently joined fundamentalist churches in an attempt to deal with personal difficulties become depressed and accuse themselves of past sin, usually sexual activity tacitly accepted in their original community but now rigorously proscribed by their new church. Madeleine, a recent Jamaican convert to the Jehovah's Witnesses, hears two voices – a good one speaks into her right ear and a bad one into her left ear. The good voice exhorts her to live up to the standards of her church, while the bad one, the devil pours into her mind a series of lascivious temptations. 'Filthy and disgusting,' she tells us, 'if they would only leave me alone I would be pure, cleansed by the Blood of the Lamb.' At times the conflict between the two is so severe that Madeleine lapses into a stupor which is only broken by lucid periods in which she briefly requests both punishment and salvation – usually punishment from her doctors and salvation from her church, but sometimes the reverse. Having previously been given electro-convulsive therapy she continues to demand it again and again, for 'she has deserved it'.

For the family, adding to the financial and emotional stress of immigration, a psychologically disturbed relative comes as yet another burden. The loss of one person's wages threatens their precarious livelihood and reduces the small amount of money which is put aside to buy a shop or start a business. A solution frequently adopted is to keep 'the patient' at home, hidden away, often without consulting a doctor, in the hope that the situation will somehow resolve itself. Alternatively the family may try to get him or her labelled as insane as soon as possible and removed out of the way to a psychiatric hospital. Such stratagems are not of course specific to immigrants or to a particular ethnic group, but to keep a patient at home might be easier in large and cohesive families. A rigorous insistence on the mad role, accompanied by an offer to take the patient home 'when completely better', is frequent among West African men, whose career is often threatened by the demands of looking after a sick wife. The reaction of the family is related to the behaviour expected of mad people in their original culture: the Asian patient is supposed to be withdrawn, while the West African is expected to be aggressive and violent. The immigrant family, like the indigenous family, may progressively abandon the patient, particularly if there are lengthy stays in hospital.

The definition and recognition of emotional difficulties among immigrants gradually come to conform to that of British society. When there are a variety of different models of mental illness available, the one adopted is frequently the one which is apparently the least threatening in relation to personal adjustment – the medical model. Medicine promises control: we catch a disease rather than it catching us (possession).

Beliefs about the nature of mental illness are also changing among the middle classes in England and America. Sociology has replaced psychology as the source of fashionable theories. The rejection a few years ago of an American Vice-Presidential candidate after it was revealed that he had previously had psychiatric treatment suggests, however, that we are no more tolerant of emotional difficulties now than in the past.

One of the traditional ways in which doctors decide whether patients from different cultures are abnormal is to ask their relatives whether they have noticed anything strange in the patient's behaviour or emotions. We are only just beginning to appreciate how in the native white family penalization of one member as sick can be a convenient solution to everyone's difficulties. It would be surprising if the same process did not occur in other groups, and it is not unusual to meet families in which one person has been held responsible in this way for the family's failure to establish themselves successfully in Britain. Medical models provide a safe way for immigrants to structure personal difficulties. Sickness diverts attention from the realization of the unacceptable and may reduce anxiety all round, providing a solution which *strengthens* the group's attachment to British society by paradoxically using the concepts of the adoptive society (scientific medicine) to explain failure to become part of it.

Medicalization of family difficulties is a way of avoiding personal responsibility for decisions by concealing the real nature of the problem. The doctor only sees the reflection of the community's difficulties on to the individual. Frequently she too cannot penetrate further.

FATEMA KHAN

Fatema Khan came to London from a small village near Karachi. Her husband Ahmed had married the daughter of his paternal uncle fifteen years previously. Just before coming to Britain, he had also married Fatema, a young girl from a neighbouring village, and brought her with him. His small textile business was successful and he bought a house and car. Two children were born. Every year Ahmed would return to Pakistan for two months to visit his first wife, who still lived with his family on their piece of land. Fatema never accompanied him. We were never able to find out whether he was still legally married to his first wife or not. Fatema did not seem sure either, and Ahmed evaded the question, saying that his customs were too difficult for us to understand, and as busy doctors surely we were more interested in his wife's problem: his family life was not our concern.

What was the problem? While Ahmed was in Pakistan each year, Fatema looked after the children and the house as usual, and also successfully managed the shop with some help from a female cousin and her husband. Soon after Ahmed returned, the local hospitals started seeing a lot of Fatema who came up with emergency referrals from her general practitioner or (as is common in our area) from doctors working for a 'deputizing service'. She was having black-outs, pain in both her heart and her abdomen, episodes of violent trembling and vomiting and continual headaches. She became well known to the surgeons, physicians, cardiologists, and gynaecologists who, their tests and examinations proving negative, passed her on to us.

We frequently had to admit Fatema to the psychiatric ward, since her husband was seldom available for consultation. She slept poorly, wandering all night around the ward, but spent the day lying in bed. She grabbed anyone she could to talk to about her illness: she couldn't think, she had lost all feeling for her husband and her head was empty. Ahmed visited her infrequently and refused to be drawn into any discussion of her feelings about the domestic situation: 'She is happy; she has a house and a car and is much better off than people in Pakistan.' She had pains and we were her doctors – what were we wasting time for? Why didn't we just stop her pains? Fatema herself insisted that all was well at home; she just wanted a cure for her lost feelings. Psychotherapy was a failure and a variety of different tablets provided at Ahmed's insistence proved equally unavailing.

One day during one of her admissions, Fatema's husband came to the ward to find a young Indian patient sitting at the end of her bed talking excitedly to her. Sanjit's conversation was a curious mixture of the details of the examination requirements for entering different professions (a current personal concern) interspersed with obscenities. Fatema was sitting up in her bed placidly listening to him. Ahmed promptly removed his wife from the hospital. Appointments were not attended and visiting nurses were turned away. We never saw either of them again. While we can make a plausible guess about the problem, we doubt if it was resolved in the hospital situation.

So far in this book we have been concerned with fragmentary and isolated aspects of mental illness in ethnic minorities viewed from outside the individual's experience. We have looked at the effects of migration, of poverty and discrimination; the relationship between racism, medicine and the provision of psychiatric facilities; the difficulty for the doctor of diagnosing psychological disturbances in members of other cultures and the problem of differentiating cultural norms from personal idiosyncrasy. At the same time we have continually stressed two themes: (i) With a sympathetic knowledge of another's understanding and of their personal experience it is possible to understand much of what otherwise appears as inexplicable irrationality; (ii) there is always an interrelation between personal experience and cultural preoccupations which is not haphazard, which is related to the interests of the group as a whole (or certain dominant sections of it) and which can be understood historically. The relationship between the immigrant and psychiatry is a phenomenon of this nature. We shall now attempt to tie these themes together.

NOTE

1   It is difficult to see this as the sole explanation for all mental illness. People in widely differing societies may have the core features of schizophrenia, the First Rank Symptoms (p. 117). What is the universal cultural threat they present? If the potentially mentally ill everywhere pose a similar problem to all societies, we are nearly back to a biological explanation. Can these symptoms be the result of social invalidation when they are unknown to the general public?

CHAPTER TEN

THE ILLNESS
AS A COMMUNICATION

My mother bore me in the southern wild,
And I am black, but O! my soul is white;
White as an angel is the English child,
But I am black, as if bereav'd of light.
William Blake, 'The Little Black Boy'

In this chapter we shall look in detail at the experiences of a single patient to see how illness may be an intelligible response to certain difficulties. Rather than *explain* her illness from the outside by saying simply that it is the result of the stresses of migration or culture change, we shall try to *understand* how she herself feels.

Every society has characteristic ways of articulating experience. The Tembu, as we have seen, have a single word to denote that inner feeling of unease which may herald the development of a mental illness or the call to be a healer. This familiar experience is communicated to the rest of the community by a single pattern of behaviour.

We communicate with others around us by using symbols[1] with which they are familiar. Feelings of distress are communicated by our downcast gaze or our lack of interest in activities which we normally find enjoyable. Such characteristic behaviour may be amplified by a more specific symbolic behaviour – speech. Verbal communication of feelings also draws upon certain stock expressions which are familiar to our audience. Our distress is made apparent to others by such statements as 'I just don't feel like doing anything' or, more ominously, 'I want to end it all'. Both facial expression and words are messages directed to people around us. If they are already familiar with such messages they can respond appropriately. In a less dramatic way, what we decide to wear informs others symbolically about our personality, our social status or even the opinions we hold. The symbols chosen are usually well known to everybody in our community: in Britain an open shirt in a man suggests informality. External events may, however, alter the initial significance of the symbols: the hotter the weather the less does an open collar indicate informality. Alternatively, symbols may be drawn from our own private experience. We may habitually leave our shirt open to identify with some person whom we admire and who never wears a tie; if superstitious, we might omit a tie on Saturdays because on previous Saturdays on which we wore one our football team invariably lost. If we use this type of private symbolism we do not expect it to be immediately obvious to others. In fact we may be rather embarrassed about explaining it. We can normally easily distinguish between those public symbols which everyone understands and the private ones derived from our own experience.

Public symbols reflect the experiences of the community group as a whole. They may also tell us what experiences individuals in that community are likely to have had and a little about its history, social organization and dominant preoccupations. Some public symbols appear to be shared by many different communities throughout the world: in most (although not in all) a frown denotes anger. Symbols may have a different significance in different places. In Britain a tanned skin tells others that we are wealthy enough to have afforded a foreign holiday; in India it suggests that we are so poor that we work in the fields in the heat of the dry season.

To express adequately our experiences to others in our community we have to be able to perceive the world symbolically in a standardized manner. We may sometimes feel that this is a rather inaccurate representation. For the anthropologist Mary Douglas, 'physical nature is masticated and driven through the cognitive meshes to satisfy social demands for clarity which compete with logical demands for consistency' [106]. Sharing experiences with others in the same community enables us to learn the symbols by which we perceive the outside world and by which we communicate our experiences to others. Confusion in communication arises if we are trying to describe experiences for which there is no acceptable code or when we are uncertain which is the proper code to use. Other social groups may attach a different meaning to our signals or even fail to notice them. Those people we call mentally ill often use a private symbolism which is not readily accessible to others. A patient of ours who had been diagnosed as schizophrenic always wore his shirt open as a warning to others not to 'get him by the neck'. He believed that this message could be easily read by looking at him and did not accept our suggestion that it might be rather more difficult to understand. The more uncommon our experiences, the more difficult they will be to communicate to others, and schizophrenic patients usually employ highly idiosyncratic symbolic communication. Evadne Williams (p. 171) uses acceptable symbols in her own rather unusual way, but Elizabeth Ahyi (p. 119), who is schizophrenic, employs a much more personal and less accessible type of symbol. To symbolize is a cognitive process [397], and schizophrenic patients have been found to have unusual cognitive patterns (whether of biological or social origin). Symbols are always 'overdetermined' – they refer to many different things and we have to be constantly aware of their subtle ambiguities.

Mentally ill individuals do not always invent their own system of symbolic communication: they often employ the dominant system which others use – but they are likely to do so in a way which to others seems inconvenient and clumsy [427]. They use the system inflexibly. In the same way, members of cultural minorities (women, children, and ethnic and sexual minorities) have to use the dominant majority culture to articulate their concerns. The

dominant model may impede the free expression of alternative models of the world which subdominant groups may possess and perhaps may even inhibit the very generation of such models. Groups dominated in this sense find it necessary to structure their world through the model (or models) of the dominant group, transforming their own model as best they can in terms of the received ones. [10]

Their use of the dominant symbolism is likely to be 'rickety and cumbersome' [10].

When we move from one society to another we have to unlearn one pattern of expressing ourselves and learn another. Even moving to a new society which apparently speaks the same language may be difficult: nuances and meanings of particular words may alter, non-verbal gestures may be quite different. Confusion may in fact be greater than when we have to learn an entirely new language.

Mary Douglas has compared different societies by the extent to which their members are likely to share a common set of symbols [105]. In any social group an individual is subject to two pressures: (a) to use a shared system of categorizing the world, a shared symbolic system, and (b) control by others. She has produced a simple graph by which we can look at the relative contribution of these two forces:

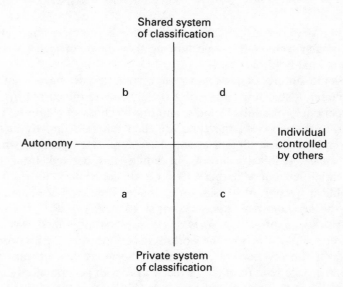

The more idiosyncratic the patterns an individual uses, the more he or she is likely to be located towards the bottom. In Britain the desired goal of 'self-individuation' is likely to be somewhere in the bottom left-hand quadrant (a), in which we might expect comparatively little public symbolism. We can conceive of a West Indian who before migrating uses a relatively shared system of symbols but has considerable autonomy (b). On moving to Britain he or she hopes to enter quadrant (a), availing themselves of the supposed options of a plural society. (We may doubt whether any individuals really exist in (a). This model is one of ideal subjective states considered independently of a particular political context.) While discarding some shared 'Caribbean patterns', black immigrants are, however, moved towards the right by the constraints of a racist society which limits the options of housing, education and employment. The first generation of immigrants appear to have responded with occasional episodes of idiosyncratic (psychotic) behaviour towards the bottom of the graph, while their children accept a position on the right: constrained by their blackness, they have accepted a black identity defined in opposition to white society.

THE ORIGIN AND POWER OF SYMBOLS

What determines the choice of symbols such as race in a particular community? And how do they maintain such a strong emotional hold over us?

Some anthropologists have suggested, as we have seen in Chapter 7, that the culture of a society is determined not by the experiences of adults in the group but by those of children. The early experiences of the child are then reflected directly in the group's political organization. The dominant symbols which articulate political concerns in adults are derived from the separate childhood experiences of all individuals [201]. The political symbols of Russia, for example, were seen as secondary to the *psychological* experience of swaddling (p. 160).

Durkheim offered a *sociological* explanation which was the reverse of this: the way the world is experienced by the individual reflects the way society is organized. Societies divided into two large groups tend to organize the world, both geographically and morally, in two contrasted segments [110]. Divisions of this type may be men and women, north and south, war and peace, hunting and agriculture. The binary opposition then appears in all aspects of communal experience. Members of one social division have particular social roles, are expected to be active at particular times of the year, to live in a certain area or part of the house, to eat particular food and even to have a particular personality. Alternatively we may find more than two basic divisions. Residues of this kind of typology are found in our astrological signs or in association with social distinction such as male/female or adult/child.

The symbols used reflect, then, the experiences, not of individual childhoods, but of adult social life experienced communally. The actual form the symbol takes may, however, be a metaphor drawn from the human body [296; 395]. Mary Douglas suggests for instance that concern with the entrances and exits of the body (eating and excreting) reflects communal anxiety about the precarious boundaries of the society [104]. She cites the Jews, always confronting the danger of assimilation (leaving the body politic), who carefully guard the entrances and exits of the physical body by restrictions on the food which may be eaten and on a variety of rules concerning menstruation.

The natural distinctions of the physical world provide us with a peg on which to hang a whole complex system of political and moral values. The slight biological tendency to right-handedness is often encouraged by society [296]: the 'Left Hand Path' is *sinister*. If fertility and death are traditionally represented by maternal milk and by the earth, then 'white' and 'black' will carry these symbolic associations [416].

The length and method of dressing hair can be described as representing the extent of social control [175; 238]. Institutions which especially value control over the individual by the community, such as monasteries, armies, hospitals, schools and prisons, have traditionally shorn the hair of their members. Long hair (like that adopted by the Rastafarians in distinction to the shorter hair of first-generation 'Pentecostal' Caribbean immigrants) within a particular society may represent independence or rebellion. Immigrant groups often have characteristic hair styles. Among the Hasidim, men wear part of their hair long, while married women, shaving the head, wear a wig, the *sheitl*. Male Sikhs wear their uncut hair under a turban. Though these might have an initial significance within the minority community, they may then take on a different meaning in articulating relations between the minority and the wider community.

Both psychological and sociological theories of symbolism are important. It is difficult to explain the overwhelming hold symbols possess over us unless they were learnt in association with powerful personal experiences. But symbols also refer to adult social life in a way which is not easily derived from infantile experiences [261]. They appear both to have a personal emotional or sensory pole and also to articulate general culture and social concerns [416]. The relation between the symbol and the sensory pole is likely to reflect the external form directly: blood = red flag = socialism. This association is a little more arbitrary – the blood shed refers to the blood of workers fighting for socialism, not to the blood of their opponents! Some (emotionally neutral) symbols, such as letters of the alphabet, appear to have a purely arbitrary relation to what they represent and lack altogether a 'sensory pole'. The symbolism of the insane may appear arbitrary to us initially but becomes less so as we get to know the mentally ill individual. In cultural life, we build up complex networks of symbols, associated with others by a direct equivalence or resemblance (metaphor: 'red material' to 'blood') or because they have a certain relation to them (metonym: 'socialism' to 'the blood of the workers').

STIGMATA

The external symbols which we exhibit to others are not always to our advantage. Our clothes or appearance may indicate that we hold unpopular political or religious beliefs or advocate unconventional sexual attitudes. The badges of identity of minority ethnic groups may cause friction with the wider British community, often on some apparently 'neutral' pretext: the long hair and turban of the Sikh community in Britain have twice been a point of controversy, ostensibly over the correct headgear of bus-conductors and the compulsory wearing of crash helmets.

What are symbols to others may well be aspects of our physical bodies we can do little about. We may be sexually attractive, or born with red hair or with a black skin. Those external physical symbols by which we are likely to be ashamed or oppressed result in our being *stigmatized*. The recognition of a particular physical sign by others as a stigma depends of course on their attitudes and beliefs. Facial scarring may lead to our being regarded as the unfortunate victim of an accident, as a failed suicide or as a courageous warrior. The interpretation may depend upon elaborate social fictions: the 'duelling scars' of nineteenth-century German students were often inflicted deliberately, although their significance resulted from the fact that they represented the 'accidents' of duelling.

If the code is not known or not acknowledged, symbols valued in one situation may become stigmata in another. To the white Englishman the facial scarring of certain West Africans is merely a sign of their 'primitiveness' (unlike his own practices of circumcision and ear-piercing), while to the bearer they indicate a particular status within his community. Westernized Chinese in the last century cut off their pigtails, but to the peasant community this represented the traditional shorn hair of the convict [155].

The search for physical stigmata continue *inside* the body. Ten years ago it was revealed that Asian women arriving in Britain were subject to vaginal examination to ascertain if their state of virginity or otherwise 'conformed' with their marital status. Private surgeons in London have offered 'hymen repairs' to women from Islamic societies who have to demonstrate physical virginity on marriage. In many Southern European societies the blood of the bride on the marriage bed signifies an 'honourable' marriage.

When we assume that individuals who bear a particular set of involuntary physical symbols are invariably of a certain psychological or moral type, we are *stereotyping* them. A man with a profusion of veins on his nose is likely to be suspected (often wrongly) of being an alcoholic. When we expect a woman with red hair to be a 'tempermental' red-head we are stereotyping her: whatever she does is interpreted as an example of her ready temper. We become confused or angry if the red-haired woman does not easily fit into our assumptions. We accuse her of hiding her real character. She might then find it easier to live up to her stereotype and joke about it; she begins to interpret her own behaviour in accordance with our expectations. It is safer to be 'a faithful black' than to aspire to middle-class goals – the colonial 'cheeky Kaffir'. The ambiguity of social mobility, like that of mixed ethnic origin (p. 43), is dangerous for the established order. If we are members of an ethnic minority it becomes difficult for us to adopt the gestures, mannerisms and opinions of those who are socially powerful. We can move up the social scale only at the cost of being considered untrustworthy. We are considered not 'successful' but 'forward'. Erving Goffman described how American black professionals had to apologize for their status: they used the back door when entering a client's house; black nurses found it easiest to be called domestics [154].

If we are to accept ourselves as stigmatized, we have of course to be aware of the external features by which we are recognized and the meaning which others place on them. There are various ways of minimizing the danger to our own integrity. We may use different strategies at different periods if one adaptation proves unsuccessful. First of all we can disguise ourselves. If to be black is undesirable we can at least make ourselves less black. We can use skin lightening cream or dye our hair. 'Blacks' have passed successfully as 'whites' [155]. While fully accepting the meaning of the social stereotype we try to avoid being taken for a member of the stigmatized minority. Even if we cannot change the way other people see us we can improve the image we present to ourselves – 'I'm not really red-haired but auburn'.

We can sometimes accept the view which others have and actually use it to gain some sort of advantage. We can be tolerated by the unstigmatized majority by becoming a mascot – 'our cripple', 'the token black', 'the creative homosexual'. We can then minimize the importance of our own stigma and pity or despise others who may be worse off than ourselves. We may even go out of our way to stigmatize other unpopular groups: 'I may be mad, but I'm not queer or anything dirty like that' as one patient from Trinidad told us. This is similar to the 'projection' which we have described in relation to racism (p. 53). Alternatively we may accept the stigmatized view others have of us but deny it much importance, asserting that other values are more important for us: it is not significant that we are black, what matters is whether 'in the last days we be saved'.

All these strategies collude with the views of those who regard us as defective. We may, however, accept the stereotyped view of ourselves but give it a desirable value. We may admit we are black or red-haired but maintain that this is a sign of beauty. We can gather around us other disadvantaged individuals who share our beliefs. In the case of minority groups, we have called this process 'ethnic redefinition'. We may employ symbols which have lost their original significance inside our community but help us to define ourselves 'positively' against the outside world. Irish workers in London continue the practice of Friday abstention from meat now abandoned by the Catholic Church [105]. Pork was only one of a large number of foods originally prohibited by the Jews, and the turban is not one of the five sacred personal emblems of the Sikhs.

The strategies which we adopt to deal with our disadvantage may at times be at variance both with our own experiences and the responses of others. We may have to move from one strategy to another. The problem of reorganizing the failures of our strategy may cause us great mental distress. The change of focus may involve changes to such a highly personal view of reality that we are seen as mentally ill.

BEATRICE JACKSON

Beatrice Jackson is the thirty-four-year-old daughter of a black
Jamaican Baptist minister. Her parents were both the children of
tobacco labourers who attributed their modest financial success to
an unswerving religious faith and a righteous life amidst a sinful
and depraved world. Family life was strict: self-control and a
horror of sensual indulgence were daily stressed to Beatrice and
her older brother and sister. Mrs Jackson died when Beatrice was
eight and she was brought up by her mother's sister, who came to
join in the household, a hard embittered woman whose own
marriage had broken down and whose strictness with the children
sometimes disturbed even the pastor. Daily life was a continual
battle against evil forces which swirled around the virtuous
family. At home and at school Beatrice was quiet and self-
effacing, working hard and methodically, but more and more
frequently lost in a daydream about the elegant ladies of Old
London who filled her history books.

To become a full member of the congregation to which her
father was minister one had to be 'born again', and be publicly
accepted by the whole congregation in a testimony of repentance
and a demonstration of the spirit of Christ within. As befitted the
children of the minister, her siblings were 'born again' when they
were only thirteen, the precocious children of a proud parent. By
the age of eighteen Beatrice had not yet testified and was causing
anxiety to her family. Her obvious indifference to spiritual
matters and the reluctance with which she attended prayer
meetings contrasted with her pleasure in displaying a new frock
at the church picnics and in the admiring glances of boys. Her
aunt repeated her warnings of demonic temptation and her father
forbade her to go out unless she was escorted by her sister. The
family atmosphere became strained. The next Easter service,
however, 'the Lord used my tongue' and she declared herself
born into the army of the righteous. Her father was relieved, the
atmosphere at home improved and her aunt found less occasion
to chastise her.

Soon after this the family agreed to send her on a typing
course, after which, with some parental misgivings, she was able
to fulfil her dreams and came to England. She found accommodation with a family friend in Notting Hill and soon afterwards
started work in a local travel agent. She was not disappointed in

London and, joining a local church and making friends, proceeded to enjoy herself. Her letters home did not mention her difficulties with the church, which did not offer her the affection and respect she expected. Nor did she mention that she had married when she was twenty-one until after a baby was born the following year.

Her husband was killed in an accident at work before she was able to visit Jamaica with him. Her family's letters clearly showed they were worried about her. Her aunt even hinted that she doubted that Beatrice had ever married at all. Her sister visited London the next year and reported back to Jamaica that it was unlikely that Beatrice had been married. Her father sent a letter indicating that she should cease to think of herself as being his daughter: communication between England and the Caribbean ceased.

Over the next ten years Beatrice's dream turned sour. She lost her job and could only find work in a dress factory in another part of the city. Her friends went away. Lonely and depressed, she reproached her family for the difficulties in which she found herself. She didn't blame the British, whom in fact she admired and envied more than ever. Life centred around her son John, with whom she spent all her non-working time. An Irish girl at work introduced her to the Catholic church, whose solemnity and ritual contrasted with the rather austere furnishing of her old church.

Beatrice and John lived in three rooms in a house in East London. The front room was carefully decorated; spotlessly clean, it was filled with glass-fronted cabinets full of china, cut glass and artificial flowers, while the papered walls were hung with religious pictures and a photograph of the Queen. John was not allowed in this room, which was reserved for the rare visitor. The other rooms were a small bedroom for John and the kitchen where Beatrice slept. Even when we got to know her well she never let us see the two back rooms, insisting they were dirty, although glances through the half-opened door suggested the reverse. One day, when she was about thirty, she was talking to a West Indian neighbour in the 'front room' when a quarrel started. Beatrice got angry and told the neighbour to leave, which she did, muttering under her breath.

Over the next few days Beatrice became uneasy – something

was wrong with her front room. It had become polluted and disturbed. She called in her Catholic priest, who rather reluctantly sprinkled some holy water around and said a prayer. Beatrice was not satisfied and demanded a full-scale exorcism. He refused, nor was he very impressed when a rather agitated Beatrice told him that her neighbour, who came from St Lucia (an island with a 'bad reputation' for her), was a witch, and that she, Beatrice, was being persecuted because she was an outstandingly religious woman: 'If God choose you, Satan don't let go.' Dissatisfied with his help, Beatrice left the church, confiding in us later that the priest 'was not a white priest but black inside'.

She now received news that her father had died in Jamaica and began to feel guilty, ruminating constantly about her life. She developed pain in her womb and, at her request, a gynaecologist performed a small vaginal operation. The pains continued, however, and after further appointments she persuaded the doctor to perform a hysterectomy, removing her womb and 'clearing all that away' as she put it. The pains now shifted to her back and the irritated gynaecologist referred 'this hysterical woman' back to her general practitioner. She continued to ask for further operations, which she felt would remove the trouble.

Last year,[2] after the Notting Hill carnival in London, her son John, who was now aged thirteen, returned home with an alarming story. Angry and upset, he told her of fighting between young West Indians and police. He talked in a way which Beatrice found new and disturbing. He told her that he thought the police had deliberately attacked the young blacks. Using ideas he had been introduced to that day, he told her that the immigrants had to stick together against white racism. Beatrice, horrified by his rejection of the British, argued with him, insisting that the fighting at the carnival was the fault of the blacks, who should have obeyed the police. West Indians should know better than to fight 'the government'. Tearfully the two went to bed, their argument unresolved.

Next morning, Beatrice's neighbours called the police after finding her naked on her balcony shouting down into the street that God had told her to kill herself. Taken to our psychiatric unit nearby, she fought with the police, talking incoherently, but at times could be understood to say that her son was not hers because he was black, that God was telling her to have sex with her social worker and that blacks were ugly people although *she* was not, as she was not black. Three days later she was less upset and told us that she had been made to come into hospital by Satan as a punishment. She could still feel him inside her wrestling with her spirit. All was going to turn out well, however, as she was now surrounded by God.

On the hospital ward it became apparent that Beatrice was much less attached to the black nurses and doctors than to the white ones, whom she frequently hugged and caressed. She continually argued with the West Indian staff, refusing to carry out for them requests to which she readily agreed if asked by a white nurse. She apparently enjoyed being in hospital, quickly became attached to the ward routine and announced her intention of becoming a nursing aide when she was completely recovered. She even tried to organize the patients who wanted to see the doctor in a queue 'as a sign of respect', instead of the comparatively casual approach we tried to encourage. In any disagreement between staff and patients she invariably sided with the staff and eventually the other patients refused to talk to her. At the same time she appeared depressed and complained of recurrent back pain, telling us she wanted to stay in hospital 'till the final operation'. She avoided the more relaxed atmosphere of occupational therapy, group therapy and casual meetings, while feeling more comfortable in the more medical and structured atmosphere of the ward. Informal approaches left her angry and feeling neglected and she took it as a slight if in meetings the doctor refused the largest chair which she had reserved for him. In many ways she was quite an embarrassing patient, revealing what a rigid and hierarchical structure lay behind the ostensibly informal hospital atmosphere.

THE WORLD OF BEATRICE JACKSON

Beatrice quite literally sees the world in black and white terms. Everything is either one or the other. Blackness appears to represent for her West Indians in general but also sin, sexual indulgence and dirt. Whiteness by contrast is associated with quite different qualities, with a white skin and with religion, purity and renunication.

We tend to see black and white as referring to two opposing universes. No other terms so clearly imply opposition. In the Western tradition, especially in Christianity, white stands for purity and joy: brides and angels are portrayed in white. Black, by contrast, 'was the color of death of the River Styx, of the devil; it was the color of bad magic and melancholy, of poison, mourning, forsaken love, and the lowest pit of hell. There were black arts and black humours, blackmail and blacklists, black-guards and black knights, the Black Death and "souls as blak as pykke"' [92]. Black signified negation, reversal, disorder, anon-ymity: insurrection was signalled by men colouring their faces black [16]. Ben Jonson wrote 'let's have the giddy world turned the heeles upward and sing a rare blacke Sanctus on his head, of all things out of order.' Black and white are contrasted in a variety of oppositions: evil and good, defilement and purity, ugliness and beauty, rage and calm, night and day, depression and joy, sickness and health, death and life, none and all, nature and culture, sensuality and renunciation.

We also use black and white in referring to skin pigmentation and by implication ethnic group. The off-pink skin of Europeans is contrasted with the black or brown of those of African descent.

Are these purely coincidental usages? Perhaps it is no accident that Christianity, primarily the religion of Europeans, values white as signifying desirable qualities. Black held for the European its sense of 'dirt, soiled, dirty, foul' before it was applied as a term of description to those of African origin. From the beginning of the colonial period whites made puns on its dual sense [203]. The stamp of the British Central Africa Protectorate bore as a motto: 'Light in darkness'. Africa, the dark continent, took on the qualities of blackness: 'Deeply stained with dirt, soiled, dirty, foul. . . Having dark or deadly purposes, malignant; pertaining to or involving death, deadly; baneful, disastrous, sinister. . . Foul, iniquitous, atrocious, horrible, wicked. Indicat-ing disgrace, censure, liability to punishment, etc.'[203]. This is of course a social not a 'natural' symbolism; in Africa black may represent something auspicious [416]. In classical Chinese opera, black-painted faces represent integrity, white faces evil.

The colonists saw themselves as heirs to the tradition of chivalry and its simplistic moral polarities [399]. 'In Europe the black man is the symbol of evil' [125].

It was the African's colour of skin that became his defining characteristic, and aroused the deepest response in Europeans. Though often designated as a 'Moor' or 'Ethiopian', he was also a 'negro' to Spanish and Portuguese, a 'noir' to the French, and a 'black' to the English; and in all four languages the word carried connotations of gloom, evil, baseness, wretchedness, and misfortune. Early in the seventeenth century a French traveller remarked, 'It might be properly said, that these Men came out of Hell, they were so burnt, and dreadful to look upon.' A century later John Atkins agreed that 'The Black Colour and woolly Tegument of these Guineans is what first obtrudes itself on our Observations, and distinguishes them from the rest of Mankind.' 'This gloomy race of mankind,' said Oliver Goldsmith, 'is found to blacken all the southern parts of Africa, from eighteen degrees north of the line.' . . . White, Herman Melville tells us, is the colour of purity and justice, of joy and sovereignty and holiness; it gave the European 'ideal mastership over every dusky tribe'. Yet there 'lurks an elusive something in the innermost idea of this hue, which strikes more panic to the soul than that redness which affrights in blood'. Only the most unimaginative minds could fail to see the moral ambiguities of colour. A black whale or white Othello would lose all meaning. [92]

This double meaning was thus consciously employed in literature: *Light in August*, *Heart of Darkness*. A recent critic has described the black harpoons attacking the white whale Moby Dick as representing the primitive instinctual parts of the mind [130].

After the abolition of slavery in the Caribbean, missionaries preached a Christianity in which this symbolism was predominant. By having their sins 'washed away' to become 'whiter than snow', by being born again into Christianity, the despised blacks were able to 'become white inside', even though it was of course physically impossible for them to become ethnically white, or indeed for them to enter the economically powerful class to which the white planters and officials belonged. By the experience of the European Christ within and by the adoption of Christianity, together with the virtues of obedience and patience, the blacks were offered a chance to become white in fantasy. Christianity stressed that purity within was infinitely more worthwhile than such mundane satisfactions as power or social advantage.

A lighter-coloured skin and its symbolic association with European supremacy is still a highly valued social asset in countries where many people trace descent from both Europe and Africa (such as in the Caribbean or Brazil). Black skin has long been devalued in Jamaica [420]. It is common in the Caribbean for a West Indian of partly African descent to use the word 'black' to describe those darker than himself. Lighter-skinned marriage partners have been favoured and paler children are spoilt [183]. As late as in the 1950s West Indian hotels operated an explicit colour bar. Black children both in the West Indies and in Britain score low on measures of self-esteem: this is particularly true of those who are *more* favourable to a black rather than a white identity. The social value of white physical attributes in the Caribbean and United States is attested to by pages of advertisements for skin-lightening creams and hair-straightening in popular magazines: to the extent that it was possible, blacks tried to become white in a real physical sense. Religion provided a less realistic but more attainable mode of becoming white. Millenarian movements in Jamaica promised that blacks would be reborn white. Franz Fanon recorded that 'It is in fact customary in Martinique to dream a form of salvation that consists of magically turning white' [125].

In both black–white systems, the moral and ethnic, Beatrice assumes a similar relationship of black to white: in both, white is superior and associated with the renunciations of civilization, in contrast with the more 'natural' and less valued black. Progression from black to white is possibly by self-denial and struggle, while the reverse is always a sliding back. We can conceive of the relation of black to white in each system as a *metonymic* one, while the relation of white in one system to white in the other (or black to black) is *metaphoric*:

Moral	*Ethnic*
White	White
↑	
Black	Black

Beatrice's family also saw the world in similar sharply divided terms. They considered themselves an oasis of purity in a sinful world. They had only succeeded in a material sense through righteousness in repelling the temptations represented by a personal devil. The rigid distinction of the world into spheres of black and white reflected the physical impossibility of black becoming white, although the adoption of 'white' virtues could, as with the Jacksons, occasionally lead to a modest approximation to a European life-style. Within West Indian society the lighter-coloured middle class are seen as heirs to the white tradition: educated and with desk jobs. The darker working class are the heirs to the slave tradition: uneducated and working outdoors. This black/white duality is often subsumed under an outside/inside opposition: 'outside' represents working-class employment, illegitimacy and black skin [15]. Migration to Britain has been described as an opportunity for the darker West Indians to move towards 'whiteness' [209].

Early confusion for Beatrice between the material benefits of being white (elegance, respect and fine clothes) and white as renunciation and austerity was solved by her religious experience. This allowed her to be accepted again by the congregation and her family, and also gave her greater freedom.

For her family the battle between good and evil was fought out on her body. Spiritual and material consummation could be gained only at the cost of sexual renunciation. Beatrice does not succeed in becoming completely 'white inside' and later feels part of her is still black, locating the trouble quite clearly in her sex organs. Her carnal feelings are in conflict with that part of her which seems to have managed to become white. The only solution is to remove her womb.

Her rigid distinction between physical experience on the one hand and socially approved behaviour on the other extends to her house. The part reserved for visitors is seldom used, untouched and peaceful, hung with the symbols of her values, occupied by unused furniture. The rooms of her physical existence, of cooking and eating and washing, and of her son, she believes are 'dirty'. The balance between the two is upset by the argument with her (black) neighbour in the (white) room. The clear categories are confused, the boundaries become ambiguous. She attempts to restore the balance with the priest. He fails, either because he does not perform the necessary expurgation, or because he tries to discredit her ideas. Just as Beatrice has tried to become white he changes too: although white he becomes 'black inside'.

Because she moves to Britain and tries to become white in a more real way, Beatrice's symbolic system is upset by the real world. It becomes clear that being white inside does not automatically correspond to becoming white socially. She deals with the discrepancies which arise in various ways. She emphasizes the importance of 'internal colour', so that respected whites may, as individuals, be spiritually black: this helps to explain why all white people do not conform to expectations. She denies the social reality of her situation and attempts to confront it on a symbolic level. Although concealing from her certain political realities, this device is adaptive. She is able to continue working and successfully bring up her son.

This strategy is, however, eventually threatened by her son's statements about his encounter with the police. To her astonishment John says that all the police, the representatives of white society, are bad. He challenges her complicated system with the simple statement that all blacks, by virtue of their skin, are treated unfairly, whatever personal efforts they make and whatever their morals. His central challenge to her system appears to shatter the precarious balance she has just achieved and, in a rather confused period, she repudiates her son altogether and actually perceives herself as having a white skin. The complexity of her system has eventually failed to cope with external reality and, in a simple restatement of her black/bad, white/good dichotomies, she identifies herself both ethnically and morally with the white/good side. This is too much at variance with the experience of others. In other words Beatrice has become insane. She is admitted to a psychiatric hospital.

To prove useful her symbolism needs continued validation: the social reality it mirrors must continue. When it does not, the system of classification collapses. Beatrice never discards altogether her original mode of perceiving the world. It is continually restated in new ways. In the course of her admission to hospital she returns to the view that whites are somehow superior and that by correct conduct she can become allied with them. Recovering from her psychotic episode she explains that it was due to the (black) devil. Although her illness was in many ways a more desperate restatement of her essential dichotomies, it enables her to become part of the white system. Being in a hospital in which most of the doctors were white and the nurses black gives her another chance of becoming white by identifying with the doctors.

Coming to Britain, Beatrice uses her symbolic system in a variety of social settings: in terms of physical illness, in a religious context and, when these fail, as a mental patient. Each time her private worries are clarified by adopting a particular role; as a sinner, a patient with abdominal pain or as a psychotic. Each of these roles has enabled her to communicate her difficulties in a form reasonably accessible to other people and also to provide her with a particular type of social support. Each change of status has involved new adjustments, new expectations by others, new obligations, but also new rights.

Even though she continually restates the black/white dichotomy, her position becomes increasingly maladaptive on each occasion. By seeing the Catholic priest as 'black inside', she eschews the social resources of the church. Her views even when she is in hospital are in direct opposition to those of the only person she is close to, her son.

Beatrice approached the medical profession twice. On the first occasion she saw a gynaecologist, on the second a psychiatrist. The events leading up to the psychotic episode seem a more accurate reflection of her situation than trying to locate all her difficulties in her womb. Her mental illness is, however, more socially disruptive, referring to and involving other people, compared with her original formulation in terms of her body alone.

Physical symptoms may often be used in this way to avoid greater psychological pain. Mary Hall is the twenty-year-old daughter of divorced black parents. We first met her one Saturday after she had been seen in four different hospitals on the same day complaining of abdominal cramps. At each hospital she was given a careful physical examination and then pronounced 'hysterical'. We saw her after she had taken sixty aspirin tablets 'to kill the pain'. When she was fifteen Mary had had a daughter, but after a traumatic court appearance had been judged incapable of looking after the baby, which was taken into care. Mary left home to live with the father, who treated her rather badly. After another pregnancy was terminated when she was eighteen, he left her. She then became reconciled with her mother, who allowed her to come home if she gave up her child for good and 'stopped misbehaving'. Mary agreed, her daughter was adopted, and she 'forgot the past and gave up men'. She behaved to the family's satisfaction, stopped going out except to evening classes and started attending the family church. In spite of her rather defiant statements that she was happy at this time we felt that she had probably been rather lonely and miserable. That year her mother remarried and became pregnant. Soon afterwards Mary developed abdominal cramps. It appeared that her mother's pregnancy signified her own unsatisfactory renunciations. In a similar way to Beatrice her womb became the focus for her sexual conflict.

CHANGING WAYS OF SEEING THE WORLD

If anything is constant in her adaptation, it is not Beatrice's own problems but the way she tends to see them. Initially she has to reconcile her own pleasure with family obligations and, later, her own sexual needs with her unmarried state and her beliefs about white social norms, her enthusiastic dreams of white society with its reality and her idealization of white people's motives with her son's political view. In trying to come to terms with these difficulties she continues to use her system of classification in an increasingly concrete way.

To help Beatrice to make a more accurate and possibly more satisfactory adjustment requires some interference with her way of seeing the world. We can help her to conceive of black and white as relative descriptive categories which because of her background she has used as absolute entities. This is difficult – we are asking Beatrice to discard one of the few things which has stayed constant in a changing and confusing world.

We can help her to differentiate between black and white in religious and political senses and suggest to her that some of her difficulties lie in confusing them. It is possible that as her categories become more relative and less absolute, Beatrice will be able to accept ambivalence and conflict in herself and in society. She may be able to accept that conflict in both is in fact inevitable.

It may be objected that her difficulties are inherent in a racist situation and that our intervention only helps her adjust to this rather than tackling the problem itself. If we can show her, however, the social origins both of her difficulties and also of the way by which she has tried to solve them, we are offering her a powerful way to adjust reality to conform to her needs rather than the reverse.

COMMUNICATIONS AND RESPONSES

Beatrice uses her black/white system not only to perceive the world but to communicate her experience to others. Communications express our emotions and demonstrate how we feel. When in a particular social situation we are also communicating in order to elicit a response from others.

How does Beatrice express her feelings during her psychotic episode (p. 229)? Her confusion certainly suggests an experience of helplessness, while her rather paranoid beliefs offer an explanation of the predicament she finds herself in. Identification with the deity is both an affirmation of meaning in an uncertain world and a claim to individual importance and value. She expresses anger at her situation; in directing this anger against blacks she continues to affirm her identification with the whites.

The difficulties Beatrice has experienced are common to most immigrant West Indians in Britain, and black/white symbolism is a major mode of perceiving the world for her generation. Not all West Indians who become mentally ill in Britain, however, articulate their preoccupations so overtly. It is likely that for her the polarities were clearer because of her religious background.

An American psychiatrist who has looked at the significance of the colours black and white as they occur in dreams suggests that, for a black patient, black primarily emphasizes her own negative feelings, her poor self-image and her sexuality [294]. Although he accepts that her skin is black, he fails to point out that the multiple references to this colour are already socially determined. He considers that the colour preoccupations of black patients with white doctors are secondary to difficulties within the treatment itself: 'For a long period . . . the patient continued to see her frustration by the analyst as being related to the color difference between us. She dealt with her rage against me at thwarting her sexual wishes by becoming increasingly involved with black militant groups. . .' Although relations between patient and doctor are of major significance and Beatrice does have important personal religious and sexual problems to resolve, we must never forget that they will always be located within a more general area of political and social symbolism.

Communications are also directed by individuals in specific roles at others who are expected to respond in a particular way. Beatrice expects that the solutions they offer, an operation by the gynaecologist or an exorcism by the priest, will prove useful. The psychotic episode is a rather less specific appeal to the community as a whole from her balcony. Unlike the later depressive period, it cannot be regarded as being addressed to psychiatrists.

Can we say that this last communication – depression – was in any way more useful or a better assessment of her situation than the psychosis? Depression is easily stated and can be described verbally to a sympathetic recipient in a letter or over the phone, unlike the more total behaviour of psychosis. Depression, though less dramatic, is a more flexible way of articulating specific difficulties. While it may lead to a more sympathetic discussion of her problems, it can also be more easily ignored.

In a society, however, where personal distress is often signalled by a short-lived psychotic reaction, this reaction may itself be a specific communication. An equivalent situation among whites might be that of an overdose of drugs; dissatisfaction is expressed and help is solicited by the individual attempting or threatening suicide. In Beatrice's case, her psychosis reflects not only the clash between the two different societies but also the clash between two different ways of seeing and acting on the world.

It is tempting to see depression as a more satisfactory way of getting help in Britain than an acute psychosis because it certainly seems more convenient and because it fits in with the way whites customarily experience difficulties. Although we are likely to give the public display of a psychosis more immediate attention, we are less likely to identify with psychotic experience. On the other hand, depression may not be an easy way of expressing difficulties for an isolated individual entering white society, for it requires the presence of someone else who is freely prepared to become involved.

Communication of course goes on in two directions. We have not considered the response of the doctor, his reception of the patient, the process of diagnosis and treatment, as symbolic statements about *his* social situation. With the conventional stereotype of black as emotionally labile and disturbed, Beatrice has perhaps to demonstrate these initially to the doctor and then, when contact is established, to discard them and try to obtain understanding. In the process she appears to become depressed – to develop feelings of guilt and a poor self-image. In the earlier psychotic episode she had blamed others for her misfortune.

Although beliefs of being deliberately persecuted are quite common among West Indians who break down in Britain, they are directed surprisingly not against whites but against fellow immigrants [259]. This paranoia is usually expressed in accusations of witchcraft: jealous neighbours are making the patient feel ill, preventing her finding a job or trying to take her husband away. Paranoia is a way of simplifying ambiguous situations, but it is not easy to explain why accusations of persecution should be directed against fellow blacks. It may be that like accusations of witchcraft they occur principally within communities which have a clear boundary between individuals inside and those outside, and yet have uncertain (and hence ambiguous) relations between the individuals inside [104]. While becoming part of white British society is virtually impossible, status inside the black British community fluctuates without clearly defined criteria. The ambiguous relations are the subject of persecutory beliefs even though real stresses come from outside the community.

It has also been suggested that witchcraft accusations are a form of aggression but an aggression which must be concealed [221]. Why should black immigrants feel aggressive towards their black neighbours who share the same problems? A possible explanation may be the difficulty for West Indian immigrants (coming to Britain with over-optimistic ideas of success) of changing their opinions and seeing their failure as the consequence of institutionalized racism. During the period of initial adaptation, identification by West Indians with the idealised values of British society appears common. It is perhaps easier for them then to use existing patterns of explaining misfortune and blame their fellow blacks for failing to live up to British standards, of practising witchcraft and being envious, and thus causing the white British to respond unfavourably. They can in this way preserve for a little longer the possibility of their eventual success in Britain. Indeed it seems to take over ten years for West Indian immigrants to become psychotic in Britain, compared with a much earlier pattern of breakdown for Africans, who have quite a different set of aspirations and experiences (p. 97).

Beatrice Jackson's son John, unlike his mother, accepts that he will never be part of white British society. He precipitates her psychosis by pointing out the real situation and thus the limitations of the system of classification. The children born in Britain of West Indian immigrants are discarding the assumptions of easy assimilation. Unlike their parents they are accepting realistically what it means to be black in Britain today.

Rastafari, to which many young West Indians bear nominal allegiance through wearing Rasta colours and dreadlocks, may seem more fantastic in its beliefs than the fundamentalist Christianity of the first generation: the African Emperor as God, the 'return' to Ethiopia. Dramatically counterposing black to white in the historical and political dimension, it does, however, reflect social reality more accurately. Unlike Pentecostalism, it does not share the symbolic system of the whites but elaborates new patterns which appear to be more relevant to the black experience. If God is black, then salvation lies in evolving a black system of values which examines the relationship between black and white, rather than by an adherence to the white God of the British.

NOTES

1   There is little agreement on the definition of sign, symbol, signal and so on. An elementary guide is to be found in Leach [239]. We are deliberately using *symbol* in the rather general sense in which 'symbols may be said to occur when some components of the mind's experience elicit activity and values ordinarily associated with other components of the mind's experience' [136]. That is, when one idea stands for or implies another. Among the sources drawn upon in this chapter are

contributions from the fields of sociology and anthropology [9, 10, 15, 32, 33, 92, 105, 106, 110, 148, 154, 155, 183, 203, 238, 239, 246, 254, 268, 272, 276, 277, 296, 340, 369, 371, 379, 393, 416, 425], semiotics and literature [16, 26, 115, 170, 372] and psychiatry [125, 198, 201, 223, 427].

2   1978

CHAPTER ELEVEN

SOME CONCLUSIONS

If mankind could dream collectively, it would dream
Moosbrugger.
Robert Musil, *Der Mann ohne Eigenschaften*, 1930
(*The Man Without Qualities*, Secker & Warburg, 1954;
Picador edn, 1979, p.85)

ANOMIE AND ALIENATION

An assumption running throughout this book is that all
individuals try to make sense of their predicament. They are
driven by a quest for *meaning*.[1] We believe that even the
mentally ill are making meaningful statements. Dismissing these
as totally 'mad' (meaningless) is characteristic perhaps of only a
few cultures, including Britain (Chapter 9).

If this is so, there is a problem. Why should the expression of
the illness so seldom be directly related to the events which
appear to have precipitated it? Situations which when viewed
'from the outside' appear intolerable or false do not always seem
to lead to emotional distress. Why do West Indians in Britain
who become paranoid, like Beatrice, direct their anger against
fellow blacks rather than against whites? Indeed, in a world of
racial violence and disadvantage why on earth should black
migrants be principally concerned with the *weather* (page 142)?

The answer usually given by medicine is that as mental illness
is biological there can never be meaningful associations between
the non-specific stresses which precipitate the illness and the
actual expression of it. A rather different explanation which we
have suggested is that the individual is seldom able to view his
situation 'from the outside'; the intellectual tools which are
available are not suitable for analysing what social scientists
might feel is the 'real' situation. Indeed, for Beatrice the

available tools are (perhaps deliberately) not intended to be used objectively: they are there to confirm the very situation which gave rise to the conflict. To resolve personal difficulties in the prescribed way serves to validate the social system, but these prescribed methods break down during social change, social mobility or in situations of overwhelming contradiction.

Part of the problem is a confusion between two rather different (but related) concepts – *anomie* and *alienation* [32]. Anomie is a dislocation between an individual and his or her community. It is experienced as subjective discomfort accompanied by feelings of isolation and a loss of personal purpose and meaning. We have talked a lot in this book about symbols. Symbols are important, not because they are somehow good in themselves [cf.105], but because they mediate between powerful personal experience and the political world of others (Chapter 10). A person without personal symbols is in a state of anomie, but he cannot resolve the situation by collecting them in the way an anthropologist or psychiatrist does: he has to live them. A symbol is not a *thing* but a *relationship* between experience and belief.

Alienation, by contrast, is not a state of which one is conscious. It can be recognized only from outside the experience of it and it is shared by all members of one's group. It is the type of false position that we have seen Beatrice in, a series of relationships with the outside world in which personal and social creations are mistaken for unchanging reality [32, 277].

What are the connections between anomie and alienation? Unlike anomie, alienation is often a most satisfactory experience. Indeed, it usually reduces the ambiguity of anomie by situating the individual in a concrete world and by providing 'meaning': a false series of relations between him and it.

When it is imposed by others alienation may, however, lead to anomie. The West Indian in Britain is both alienated and anomic; he lives in a world of social acts taken for reality which are not of his own making. Setting some people apart and alienating them from the dominant universe (Chaper 2) may reduce anomie for others (although they themselves become alienated by this very act) but it forces those who are alienated by others to live in a universe they have not constructed and which cannot satisfy their needs. If the European subjugates the non-European and then perceives him as inferior, not because of his (the European's) action, but because of the physical constitution of the non-

Europeans, then both are alienated but it is the non-European who experiences anomie.

The usual ways of reducing anomie often generate even greater alienation. One crude solution is to cut through the world of ambiguous roles by creating certainty within a rather limited area. Family discipline may be pointlessly rigid and individuals may choose to restrict their lives to situations where alternative thought is deliberately restricted, as it is in the armed forces or in authoritarian churches. Certainty produces security.

Religion is a typical example of alienation: personal wishes are mistaken for reality. It heightens the gap between subjective reality (possession by or communication with God) and objective reality (poverty and oppression) (p. 181). If psychiatry was solely concerned with suffering (anomie), it would perhaps welcome religion as a means of reducing anomie. It is, however, also concerned with its own concept of meaning (as it is in schizophrenia) and hence its own alienation; religion is a competitor for the same ground (Chapter 8).

We have suggested in Chapter 9 that the legitimation of social relations at different periods and in different communities will take different forms: religion, racism and psychiatry may all reduce anomie but they increase alienation. As they perform similar functions it is not surprising that they frequently overlap. Although the individual can sometimes 'choose' between these relations as Beatrice did or invert them as her son John did, to stand outside altogether is to risk anomie.

To reduce alienation is usually extremely unpleasant [32, 125, 143]. The dominant system is legitimated by countless everyday situations as well as by institutions which are more obviously ideological [121]. Any social system is supported by an inertia which prevents a search for alternative realities except sometimes in moments of crisis. To start to question even a little may lead to an unravelling of the whole system and a period of isolation from any reality before a satisfactory alternative position can be adopted.

The concept of insanity often represents for the community not only the ever-present fear of anomie but also certain types of belief recognized as alienated (Chapter 9). It is useless to look at how mental illness varies with culture unless we look at the social relationships which lie behind both. We may for example wish to examine the associations between witchcraft, paranoia and depression. In Britain paranoid beliefs are common in West Indian psychotic patients (Chapter 4), but this is a 'false' paranoia: it is directed against neighbours and fellow victims rather than against the agents of their alienation. In time this paranoia appears to be replaced by depression. By contrast, in the Caribbean, non-paranoid beliefs about personal religious experience and sorcery are common [427]. While they are related we must be careful not to identify sorcery with paranoia (as Lambo does [234]): the type of explanation we must develop will be one in which we can show how certain modes of adjustment which use sorcery accusations (functional for the community and adaptive for the individual) can in a rather different situation articulate first paranoia and then depression (e.g. Murphy [292]). Theories that quite simply equate depression with inhibited aggression (Chapter 2), or sorcery with concealed aggression (Chapter 10), are in themselves inadequate.

In addition to self-blame (depression) minority patients may, like Beatrice and Fatema, blame their bodies or their living conditions. Two thirds of disadvantaged American blacks and whites regard themselves as physically ill [430]. We have often worked with immigrant housewives who experience such bad bodily pains, insomnia and unpleasant dreams that they are unable to provide a secure domestic base for an ambitious husband to launch a career or business. They can be seen perhaps as protesting at their husbands' opportunities; he straddles the two cultures, while for them life does not seem to have changed from that in their home country (p. 215). While anger and frustration may occasionally be openly expressed, in the family they take the socially acceptable form of physical illness. As with *sar* (p. 203), the dominant political structure of the family can remain unthreatened.

On his last admission to hospital Calvin Johnson (Chapter 1) told us that he will continue to become ill unless he is found better housing. Although this is true as a partial and indirect reflection of his situation, by itself it does not provide a satisfactory way of solving all his personal difficulties, many of which are related to his relations with his wife. While such explanations are not deliberate evasions, we can regard them as 'false' solutions, solutions which are determined by the dominant welfare model but which confirm a helpless and disadvantaged self-image (p. 17).

Why have we talked so much of the importance of religious beliefs for the West Indian community? Religion is also a fundamental way of looking at the world in India, Pakistan and Bangladesh. For Asian immigrants and their children, however, it is becoming less significant. Originally poorer than the Caribbean immigrants and unlike them frequently acquainted with war and famine, they came to Britain largely for material reasons; these have usually been fulfilled. Religion for Gulden Ozchelick was a response to personal failure, as alcohol was for Rama Roy (pp. 145 and 110). For the West Indian community fundamentalist religion has been the centre of an attempt to acquire a British identity, an attempt whose failure has also been articulated in religious concepts (Chapters 6 and 8). This type of church may offer the possibility of spiritual redemption in the form of material success, but anomie and anxiety are the ever-threatening consequence of uncertain or impossible success [19, 145]. The mode of reducing anomie for the children of West Indian immigrants has been a redefinition akin to Rastafarian beliefs (Chapters 6 and 10).

Situations in which identity is ambiguous may lead to the alienated solutions of paranoia or of religion, but they may also generate an identity which lies outside the ambiguous options and which can transcend them. Rastafari may provide the basis for a de-alienation, not just of black, but also of white. De-alienation is, however, painful and in rejecting that accommodation we have characterized as the Pentecostal solution, the children of the Caribbean immigrants eschew the security and resources which identification with their parents might bring [119]. The children of Asian immigrants by contrast are moving in the same direction as their parents: conflicts occur by moving too fast rather than in challenging their parents' basic relations with white society.

We have suggested that racism alienates white as well as black. Rastafari, a response to the identity which white ascribes to black, holds up to white society a mirror of its own precon-ceptions. It has the potential to transcend racism not by ignoring it but by confronting it. For the liberal this very preoccupation seems to be black racism. The first Jamaican Rastas adopted many white racist themes, including repatriation and the idea that slavery was the consequence of the moral inferiority of the black. As the qualities ascribed to the black are seldom desirable ones, their ironical reflection is hardly likely to reproduce liberal ideals.

The self-image imposed on the young black is that of the criminal or the terrorist [411]; part of his reassertion is to play with this ascribed violence (as certainly the police, if not liberals, recognize). Ruth Benedict described how American blacks in the ghettos operated a sort of unconscious parody of the Stock Exchange by gambling on the last three digits of the daily turnover [29]. Pentecostal churches are only slightly less ironical in their literal acceptance of beliefs now held only metaphorically by the whites. Both an alienated false consciousness and a redefinition against it inevitably employ the dominant preoccupations although in rather different ways. For the middle-class liberal, black or white, who benefits from racism while consciously rejecting racist doctrines, this type of parody is offensive (and may be denied). It is a continual reminder that racism is not the unhealthy psychological state of a minority, but the mutual self-perception of white in black, of black in white.

At present it appears that the set of beliefs we have loosely termed Rastafari stands outside established political institutions. Can these themselves offer an alternative 'black identity?' Relations between immigrants and the labour movement have always been uneasy. In the 1950s a TUC advisory committe proposed that black workers should not be given supervisory powers and that they should be dismissed preferentially [64]. In spite of official statements to the contrary, it is difficult to escape the conclusion that, as in South Africa, white workers find blacks a convenient buffer between themselves and unemployment. There are few black shop stewards, and strikes by predominantly black workforces have been poorly supported by the trade unions. Whether such a temporary alliance as that between the West Indian 'rude boys' and the white 'skinheads' against Asian immigrants in the 1970s can develop into an alliance of the young unemployed of all ethnic groups remains to be seen [62]. An alternative identity for the black Briton may be, as for the Afro-American, that of being a member of the Third World, an identity with those Caribbean movements such as the Grenadan New Jewel Movement, which offered a synthesis of the Caribbean religious tradition with Marxism.

Intermarriage is frequently suggested as 'the solution to racial problems'. A new generation of half-black, half-white is believed to transcend the problem of 'race' – as if that problem was a biological one. The 8 per cent [78] of children with a black parent who also have a white parent are, however, regarded by white society as black. Indeed most 'black' West Indians who come to Britain already have some white ancestry. Although 'the problem of race' uses biology it is not itself a biological problem. Intermarriage is important, not because it removes 'racial problems', but because it signals the possibility that some people at least can try to build their lives without racism.

Intermarriage does not always imply a transcending of racism. In the Caribbean the preferred marriage partner has always been one of a light-coloured skin [183]. In Britain black men marry white women rather than the reverse; apart from its occasional associations with sex and race fantasies of the type we discussed in Chapter 2, this is a feature of all hierarchical societies: men, but not women, at the bottom can 'marry up' [42]. There are thus particular strains on the black woman which may be reflected in her mental health (p. 97). She is rejected sexually as black in the 'first generation adaptation' and yet as the principal culture carrier and 'stabilizing' influence of the 'white' Pentecostal ethos, she is rejected by her children. Rastafari is perhaps a male-oriented belief system for this very reason [436].

PSYCHIATRY, RACISM AND HISTORY

When looking at another group there is always a tendency to relate psychological difficulties to our own criteria of normality. We have seen that European doctors frequently regard as pathological some experiences such as religious possession which are common in other communities. To do the reverse and say that another community is so different that abnormal mental states in our sense cannot exist is no less prejudiced: earlier this century it was believed that 'the Negro cannot . . . be judged by the standards set for the white. Moral delinquency and emotional instability cannot be given a prominent place in the consideration of evidence to justify grouping under this heading, for the race as a whole is distinguished by these characteristics' [163].

It is only too easy to see others as pathological or deficient by our own criteria. If the white believes the black is 'instinctive' because he apparently lacks a future time sense, the black may regard the white as sick for treating experiences and people as though they were objects. Both assessments by black and white are meaningless without a consideration of the historical associations of both black and white. To practise slavery is of course to treat people as objects, while to be a slave is to have no future. The assessment of the black by the white is 'psychiatry', while that of the white by the black is 'only folk opinion' or a 'gut reaction'; the relations between the two groups determine the relative authority of what in both instances is folk-belief.

'Race', like so many other psychological and sociological conceptions, is derived from observations of individuals in society which are then abstracted, reified as an entity and then reinserted into the social world to serve as explanations. The strange equation between identity and equality legitimates injustice in the observation of human differences, differences themselves the product of inequality.

If racism is a political system rather than a product of scientific observations, we may expect to find 'inferior races' of all types having similar characteristics. In Japan the caste of 'untouch-ables', like minorities elsewhere, are characterized by poor health, unemployment, delinquency and low scores on IQ tests [133]. They are, however, physically and genetically indis-tinguishable from the general population and are kept segregated only by the scrutiny of family trees on marriage: to try to 'pass' is to court disaster. 'Inferior races', with their own undesirable psychological, cultural and moral characteristics, can thus be created in the absence of even such markers as skin pigmen-tation. 'Characteristic' patterns of illness in minorities, like the location of emotional difficulties in the body, are found not only in the black British (the 'Begum syndrome' [147]) but in other minorities, black and white. So we have the 'North African syndrome' (p. 70), the 'East Kentucky syndrome', the 'Puerto Rican syndrome' and so on [133]. Not to mention women in general ('hysteria').

If the mentally ill and ethnic minorities serve similar social functions, we can expect similarities between them. The 'inappro-priate affect' of the black or the schizophrenic, exaggerated irony and self-deprecation (p. 49), are perhaps related, not to their primary difficulties, but to a similar response to a similar situation (cf. Bleuler [36]). Like the schizophrenic, the immigrant must distance himself from his alienation, a distancing symbolized by an other-worldly identity: 'Why should I care if I get mashed and locked up? Jah is I and looking after I' [62].

To concentrate as we have done in this book on psychological difficulties in the black population offers the danger that their difficulties will be seen as the result of pathology, or alternatively that their primary identity is that of being disadvantaged. The black Briton has the same problems of everyday life as the white: economic security, a satisfactory personal and professional life and the need to make sense of his existence. His problems are, however, continually refracted through the experience of racism.

Psychiatry continually reinforces this flawed identity by its concern with the individual rather than the social and by its readiness to accept as primary the reflections thrown into it by other social phenomena. For 'preventative psychiatry' the use of 'the principles of psychiatry to resolve communication conflicts between Arab and Jew in Jerusalem is timely' [275]. The practice of psychiatry continually redefines and controls social reality for the community. Whatever the empirical justification, the frequent diagnosis in black patients of schizophrenia (bizarre, irrational, outside) and the infrequent diagnosis of depression (acceptable, understandable, inside) validates the stereotypes.

To avoid this bias by labelling the *racist* as insane (p. 52) is no solution. Indeed, it tries yet again to locate social institutions in individual biology. For ethnic minorities to describe anti-black politicians as clinically paranoid [411] is to ignore the political and economic causes of discrimination and to suggest that the solution lies in the 'treatment' of a few deviant but influential individuals. Responsibility for their opinions is removed, as we do not hold the insane accountable. And the community is not held responsible for the delusions of the few.

If racism is indeed a sickness we could expect to find that elderly white patients with delusions of persecution are paranoid against the black community. In our experience this is rare compared with the numerous relatives of these same patients, who, not openly expressing their guilt over leaving the patients in hospital, say that they are quite prepared to take them home when they are better, but that unfortunately close proximity to black patients has made them worse. (This is sometimes amplified by explaining that the illness of the black must be worse than that of the white and is perhaps 'contagious'.) Racism may be alienating but it none the less offers a highly adaptive social mechanism for the majority of the community. Like all successful social mechanisms it is maintained, not by being located solely in consciousness, but by its location in institutions. Its crystallization in neo-fascist political groups may bring its existence home to ethnic minorities, but they risk mistaking its clearest manifestation for its origin.

In Chapter 2 we considered the 'discovery' last century of what are called mental illness and race. *Insanity* was distinguished from criminal behaviour, and the mentally ill were isolated within particular institutions and theories. At the same time, as slavery came under attack, a new justification for it appeared: the biological concept of *race*. Acceptance of the moral equality of the slave together with his continued unequal treatment meant that the legitimation of this inequality had to be located in his body: he was inevitably inferior but through no fault of his own. In both areas cultural and moral explanations gave place to biology and psychology. The two groups, the non-Europeans and the mentally ill, were often linked to each other and even seen as variants of the same condition.

In a similar way the economic gains of migration to Britain from the Third World after the war were rationalized as *a price to be paid* for the loss of the Empire whose cultural benefits for black people were to be continued after independence. Identical patterns of immigration to other Northern European countries were perceived in more realistic terms [64]. The decline of the economy after the 1960s meant that a rationalization of the catastrophic social position of the ethnic minorities was needed. If they had not benefited from their cultural opportunities, the fault was not their own but located in their genes. (Through racism they could even serve as an explanation to the less well-off whites for failure to improve *their* standard of living.) The social *response* of minorities to discrimination was seen as the biological *cause* of their failure. This is particularly true for Caribbean immigrants and their families: Asians seem to have officially stayed 'Asian', while West Indians have become 'black' [e.g. 331]

After the last war there was a general international consensus that the idea of 'racial inferiority' was both politically immoral and scientifically nonsensical. In the last few years, however, we have found both a return to the cruder type of morphological physical anthropology mixed with cultural value judgements [e.g. 21] and work on racial genetics and intelligence such as that from the Department of Psychology at the Institute of Psychiatry. Racist periodicals discuss and give publicity to suitable results in cross-cultural psychology. It is not just that 'moderate' academics are naïvely giving legitimation to 'extreme' views; there is a close association between writers on genetics and race, sociobiology, physical anthropology and neo-facism [383].

The form psychological difficulties of ethnic minorities will take in the future depends upon the models they are offered, the roles ascribed to them and the response they themselves make. The diagnosis of schizophrenia may become less common as psychiatrists take more of an interest in the experience of their minority patients. They will perhaps be seen instead as having a 'situational reaction'. Such situational reactions are themselves likely to become less common, to be replaced by drug overdoses. It is probable that suicide among Afro-Britons will become more frequent; in the United States Southern blacks who move north have initially a low suicide rate which goes up some time after they have moved. We have seen how the second generation of Afro-Britons are developing a cultural response to racism. For the police: 'The first generation, you could always humour them, laugh and joke. . . But those days are gone. The new generation question everything. Those Rastas, they're boys trying to seek identity, hostile to everyone' (cited in Cashmore [62]). This search for identity will almost certainly be regarded as disquieting and pathological: 'There is no clear line within it between a criminal and a lunatic and a decent young person' [212]. We think, however, that 'delinquency' rather than 'insanity' will prove to be the popular diagnosis.

While medicine must of course be concerned with the mental health of minorities and the provision of better services, it must always remain conscious of its role in disguising disadvantage as disease and its tendency to offer an identity which is only that of the invalid. The dominant racism of our society is reflected not just in the theories and practices of psychiatry but in its very structure: white consultants, Asian junior doctors, black nurses and domestics. We must be wary of evolving special psychotherapies based on the 'need for authority' of disadvantaged groups [e.g. 133]. We need to develop a psychotherapy which takes into account the past and present relationship between European and non-European and which, while being sensitive to modes of expression such as religion, nevertheless does not regard minority mental illness as solely a 'cultural problem'.

Doctors are familiar with those academic papers which

conclude rather lamely with an urgent appeal for more research. Bearing in mind the record of psychiatry's relations with minorities we should perhaps be rather cautious about the motivations and application of research in this area. Future work will be worthless unless it takes into account the double reflection of black and white in our society, a reflection which sometimes crosses the mirror of psychiatry.

NOTE

1 It is doubtful that this is an innate human characteristic [cf. 32,148]. We appear to be entering an age in which the acceptance of an absence of meaning in certain domains has become possible, for instance in interpretations of the nature of the universe or of human existence.

CHAPTER TWELVE

THE DEVELOPMENT OF 'TRANSCULTURAL PSYCHIATRY' IN BRITAIN 1982–9

To hear them report at one of their modern conferences the results of their personal researches makes me blanch with terror.
Louis-Ferdinand Céline, *Journey to the End of the Night*,
1934. (New Directions edn., 1960, p.423.)

Over the last seven years we have noted a doubling of the number of papers in medical journals which have been concerned with the mental health of minorities in Britain. Whilst some of these provide brief overviews (for example, London, 1986), most continue to reproduce statistics of hospital admissions.

We can see that there has been an emphasis on two particular themes – overdoses among British Asian women and schizophrenia among Afro-Caribbeans, implicitly recalling the popular white stereotypes of Asian families as unassimilated, as being too autonomous, hidden from the medical gaze, whilst the West Indian family is perceived as too loose and disorganized, too exposed to public scrutiny (London, 1986, p.41). Doctors remain primarily interested in those minority groups which are not of white origin: the mental health needs of the Turkish and Greek communities are unexplored, whilst the Irish, who have the highest rates of psychiatric admission (p. 89), remain a matter of complete unconcern for British psychiatry, due perhaps to their lack of 'exotic' salience or maybe because of the traditional British inability to engage adequately with the Irish dimension of their own history (Brent Irish Mental Health Group, 1986; Bouras and Littlewood, 1988).

A popular book by a journalist about the life and mental illness of two black sisters is remarkable for the avoidance of the issue of race rather than for any consideration of its relevance to how they were sent to Broadmoor (Wallace, 1986). Three books besides the first edition of *Aliens and Alienists* have been produced by psychiatrists. *Race, Culture and Mental Disorder* by Philip Rack (1982) is expressly a handbook, emphasizing cultural variation in mental illness and offering the professional a guide to diagnosis and 'communication across cultures'. Whilst it is a humane and concerned work, Rack has been rightly criticized for his emphasis on 'culture' as something independent of political context and for what some have taken as a tacitly paternalistic approach. The book came out of his work in Bradford where Rack established a specialist service, the Transcultural Psychiatry Unit at Lynfield Mount Hospital, which provides psychiatric care for the local Mirpuri community and which has established close personal and research links with its centre of migration in Pakistan.

A collection of papers comes from members of the Trans-cultural Psychiatry Society, an informal grouping of largely medical origin (Cox, 1986). The book demonstrates the diversity of perspectives among the members, ranging from the traditional psychiatric focus on 'when is a delusion not a delusion' (the perception of an equivalence between a pathological belief among Europeans and analogous socially accepted beliefs in a non-Western society), through service provision and training in 'culture', to more critical perspectives on medical practice.

The neglect of the question of service provision and treatment has prompted a large number of justifiably concerned articles in the black and minority press (e.g. Skerritt, 1982). The finding that black patients receive higher doses of medication (p. 58) is frequently cited. A number of television programmes (Skin, 1981; Channel 4, 1986) have highlighted the issues without any substantive changes in medical practice. This may be in part because only about twenty psychiatrists in Britain would claim a special interest in minority mental health, and the contentious nature of the issue has led some well-meaning psychiatrists to follow Truman's dictum in another area: 'If you can't stand the heat get out of the kitchen'. Not surprisingly, it is social workers who are primarily involved with the issues, the medical profession restricting its own involvement to questions of diagnosis in the safe setting of the clinical ward round. Social work policy statements frequently represent the anxieties stemming from reliance on statistical medical articles plus a vague humanitarianism (e.g. British Association of Social Workers,

1982). The Commission for Racial Equality and the National Association for Mental Health have both set up groups to study minority mental health and have produced brief reports and some very general policy documents but no specific thesis (Ward, 1986, Rogers and Faulkner, 1987). The professional body of British psychiatrists, the Royal College of Psychiatrists, has recently set up a special committee to report on 'Ethnic Issues' but whether its eventual recommendations will add much to a mounting literature of banal policy directives and liberal self-doubt is open to question.

MORE STATISTICS

Given the dearth of testable hypotheses and the lack of an informed sociological approach, what do the recent papers on epidemiology show? They are essentially concerned with 'serious mental illness' which necessitates hospital admission (and thus easy collection of figures). There are no studies which look at why some minorities have a *better* level of mental health than the general population: a colleague of ours wished to find out why West Indians who have migrated to Britain were seldom admitted to hospital for alcoholism, compared with the high rates among other groups in Britain, especially the Irish or compared with the high rates in most Caribbean countries. She wanted to learn how the Afro-Caribbean communities had been able to avoid this problem, what strategies they had adopted to give them better mental health in this area: she was told by three major grant giving bodies that as 'there was no problem', there was nothing to find out. It is easy to see how an initial study which finds high admission rates for one problem develops its own momentum in terms of research and popular perception: it is a simple jump from perceiving a group as *having a problem*, then studying it exhaustively without any contextual knowledge, to then perceiving the group itself as *being a problem*. Overdose rates among some Afro-Caribbean age groups are lower than for white people (Merrill and Owens, 1988a and b): this does not prompt any study as to why they have better ways of adjusting to distress. South Asians in Britain have traditionally been said to have little alcoholism but recent medical observations that the Sikh community has high levels of attendance at alcohol treatment centres has prompted an interest in their drinking problems (Ghosh, 1984): this is now set to become a fashionable theme for research – 'Sikhs and alcohol'.

A few studies have been carried out on minor psychiatric illness and distress that were not severe enough to result in hospital admission. Burke (1986) examined the relationship between racism and this type of distress among West Indians in Birmingham with a commonly used psychiatric rating scale, the General Health Questionnaire, together with a less structured interview. He noted that they had higher rates of depression and somatic symptoms particularly when aged over 45 years. He has developed a theory which suggests that the model of 'loss' might explain these findings and relates it to his psychotherapeutic work with bereaved black families after the New Cross fire in South London. Burke found more physical symptoms among the West Indians and the old suggestion that non-Europeans experience and communicate distress through a bodily idiom (Chapter 3) has been examined by Bal (1984) in a study of white and Asian patients attending general practitioners, whom he interviewed immediately after they had seen their doctor. He found that Asians did present psychological and social difficulties through a language of physical complaints more often than did whites, and that these difficulties were not picked up either by Asian or white GPs. Rather than interpret these findings as due to an inability of Asians to have access to a verbal idiom of emotional distress (as does Leff, 1986), he examines the context of consultation. Working-class Asian patients are likely to use a mode of communication which they believe will be acceptable to the doctor, and one which does not involve blaming family members for their distress. Krause (1988) has examined in detail the personal meanings which physical distress holds for Punjabi patients in Bedford and she notes that such symptoms embody complex relations between external events, subjective experiences and personal selfhood, autonomy and control: the Punjabi 'sinking heart' articulates all these together in a similar way to popular white British notions of 'stress' or 'pressure' (Littlewood, 1988a).

All societies appear to have medico-psychological ideas which articulate distress and which are usually quite distinct from their ideas on serious mental illness, the lay person's 'madness'. Krause, and Moss and Plewis (1984) argue that the usual English language rating scales for distress might be quite inappropriate for non-European patients, whilst others (Watson and Evans, 1986), finding that there is reasonable agreement between different scales among Bengali-speaking women, argue the opposite. Currer (1984, 1986) finds some value in conventional scales used with Pathan women in Bradford, and concludes that the experience of racism as well as traditional conceptualizations affect their scores.

Johnson (1986) notes that Asians in Birmingham consult their doctors more often than do West Indians and whites, and suggests this is a consequence of their social class and income rather than any traditional Asian pattern of recourse to health services. Whilst the local white population appear more likely to consult for psychological reasons than do the Asians, he argues against the 'somatization' hypothesis and maintains that non-Europeans patients do not present psychiatric symptoms in the form of bodily complaints.

The meaning of rating scales of intelligence and social competence in mentally handicapped people has not been subject to the same scrutiny as measures of emotional distress, and the previous public concern over the labelling as mentally handicapped of large numbers of West Indian children (p.152) appears to have evaporated: indeed there are no recent figures and we conclude that workers in this area have downplayed or not published differential rates in order to avoid public scrutiny rather than examine the wider implications of their practice. We ourselves have had many informal reports from black colleagues which continue to express concern over diagnostic procedures and of the health care available for the mentally handicapped.

Theoretical explanations of the relationship between migration and mental illness remain an area of interest for mental health professionals. Rack (1982, 1986) argues that rather than look for overall patterns, we should examine in greater detail the reasons for migration and the patterns of settlement, differentiating between 'push factors' (reasons for leaving the country of origin) and 'pull factors' (perceived advantages in Britain). He distinguishes three general patterns of settlement – *Gastarbeiters* (migrant workers who intend to return), *exiles* (involuntary refugees) and *settlers* (those who voluntarily migrated to Britain intending to stay), and suggests that their experiences can be clarified by examining two sets of questions:

Questions Addressed to Immigrants

Is the new culture valued,
and to be adopted?

		Yes	No
Is the old culture valued, and to be retained?	Yes	Integration	Separatism
	No	Assimilation	Marginality

Questions Addressed to the Host Community

Are newcomers helped and encouraged
to adopt the host culture and
rewarded for doing so?

		Yes	No
Are racial differences and alternative lifestyles respected?	Yes	Integration	Separation
	No	Assimilation	Rejection

(from Rack 1986)

Cochrane and Bal (1987) present new data on the rates of first admission to British hospitals with a diagnosis of schizophrenia for white natives and the four largest foreign-born populations:

Table 6 Country of birth and hospital admission for schizophrenia.

	Men	Women
England	9	9
Ireland	18	22
Caribbean	39	35
India	11	18
Pakistan	19	12

Source: Cochrane and Bal, 1987.

Rates are of admissions per 100,000 of each population over fifteen years. The category of schizophrenia here includes paranoid psychoses. By contrast with Table 3 (p. 90), these figures are concerned only with first admissions (newly diagnosed patients), not all patients in treatment.

These figures are broadly consistent with those previously found (p. 90). As the authors argue, they have to be interpreted taking into account the figures for all admissions, not only schizophrenia, and not only for first admissions. They examine five different hypotheses to account for the rates.

(i) *Demographic differences* They point out that certain ages are particularly associated with the development of schizophrenia and that one ethnic group may have more people of this age than another. Allowing for age reduces the figures for the Asian groups but not for the Irish and West Indians.

(ii) *Higher rates in countries of origin* This appears to be true for the Irish but is probably not the case for the other groups.

(iii) *People developing schizophrenia are likely to migrate* What we know about the preparations for migration argues that this is not likely for the West Indies and South Asia.

(iv) *The experience of migration and conditions in Britain* They suggest that the more obviously stress related illnesses (depression, anxiety) seem lower in West Indians and would be shared by South Asians.

(v) *Misdiagnosis* This they feel is likely to explain the high rates in the West Indian patients, citing the arguments we discussed in Chapter 5.

A number of social scientists have pointed out that it is dangerous to base general conclusions just on hospital admission figures which come from inner-city areas, as these are not necessarily typical of one particular ethnic group, any more than we could draw conclusions about 'white mental illness' by concentrating on Tower Hamlets and ignoring Hampstead. A study in Nottingham showed that the rates of schizophrenia among minority groups differed more between different areas of the city than they did for the white English (Giggs, 1986), whilst in Bristol the highest rates for all groups were found in the areas with the largest proportion of immigrants (Ineichen, Harrison and Morgan, 1984). For black people, housing in the inner-city is the only choice but for long established working-class white communities, reasons of economic advantage and personal prejudice may lead them to move to the suburbs unless they are disadvantaged economically, particularly through being single parents or psychiatrically ill. Thus the reference group of black people, their white neighbours, is likely to include a greater .proportion of mentally ill people (p. 94).

Biological differences between ethnic groups in Britain have not been emphasized in the current debate except as much as a perceived different body shape or skin colour becomes the focus for negative social response and exploitation in the form of racism. Few believe that international variation in mental illness can be explained by population genetics, barring some rare neurological conditions and some causes of mental handicap. Nevertheless there have been suggestions that different groups in Britain respond differently to medically prescribed drugs and that antidepressant drugs are needed in smaller doses among Asians (Lewis *et al.*, 1980; Rack, 1982). The serious question of drug dosage as actually given by doctors to black psychiatric patients curiously remains unexamined since the study we cited on page 58; curiously indeed, given the concern raised by this study among black community groups and the widespread belief that black patients are invariably given higher dosages of drugs. Again medical concern focuses on the peculiarities of the patients and not on those of treatment.

Until recently, the debate among psychiatrists on ethnic minorities and mental illness was concerned with the young adult immigrant generation; in part because this avoided questions about British society through an emphasis on the culture of origin but also because there were relatively few elderly immigrants (Barker, 1984) or British born minority children. (Significantly, this generation is usually termed 'second generation immigrant' rather than black British or British Asian.)

Elderly black people have been widely ignored in the provision of day-care facilities and group homes, perhaps because of a comfortable assumption that they are all part of an 'extended family' network which, unlike the individual white family, continues to care for them (Barker, 1984, SCEMSC, 1985). Beyond this lies an uncertainty as to what constitutes 'age' in different ethnic groups: is it based on chronological age, social performance or work capacity? We do not know how the 'official' (chronological) definition interdigitates with popular perceptions. Is a Turkish immigrant deskilled more by compulsory retirement than a white Briton? Is the status of the elderly Indian woman maintained within her family by caring for her grandchildren and is this affected by welfare policies targeted on the child's mother? Later life is a period of reflection and assessment which often involves a return to traditional values (p. 145). If older people are less adaptable than those who are younger, we might expect that the organization of facilities which presume white English values would be particularly disorientating for the elderly (Bram, 1983).

Not surprisingly, the studies of the British born minorities have again examined rates of overdoses among Asians, schizophrenia among Afro-Caribbeans (and more recently eating disorders like anorexia nervosa: Lacey and Dolan 1988). In one study, Asians in Birmingham who took overdoses were more likely to be younger women and to be married than were whites (Merrill and Owens, 1988a); whilst rates for Asian women were higher than for white women, the reverse was true of men. The authors use the rather nebulous notion of 'culture conflict' to explain the findings: it is difficult to know what this really means. It is possible that 'parent–child differences' are called just that among white families, while for the Asian family these differences are perceived by medical staff (and perhaps also by the families themselves) as clashes over cultural values rooted in social change rather than in individual personality difficulties or in the everyday dynamics of family life. The ready association of Asians and 'culture conflict' is likely to reinforce the existing notion of Asian families as hidden: 'cultural' loci of pathology to be entered by the intrepid social worker intent on liberating the young adolescent from her patriarchial and sexist inheritance (Parmar, 1981; and page 155). Perhaps not surprisingly, Asian women's refuges are wary of researchers seeking to use them to demonstrate an association between arranged marriages and mental distress. As with another potentially sensationalist issue female circumsion in African Muslims – local community groups – have taken on the issues themselves. It would be unwise however to attribute the perception of overdose rates among young Asian women to medical stereotypes alone: the authors of this paper point out that the rate treated in casualty departments is now double that among young white women and seems to be increasing annually by 30 per cent (Merrill and Owens, 1988a). They note that the situation for the Afro-Caribbean community is quite different: for those under 25 the rates are about the same as for whites, for those who are older they are less.

Of all serious psychiatric difficulties among black people it is perhaps schizophrenia which has attracted the most interest. As we have seen, it appears to be diagnosed most commonly among West Indian immigrants and we surveyed the evidence, looking at the possibility that diagnostic practices may have led to an artificially elevated rate (Chapters 4 and 5: Table 3, page 90; Table 5, page 105).

Whilst concern has been expressed informally about the apparent high rates of schizophrenia in the children of West Indian immigrants, their age structure, weighted towards the lower end range of the population at risk (between 16 and 45 years old) has until recently precluded any epidemiological studies. Although migrants in a variety of situations may have high rates of mental illness, the consensus has been that their children have rates of a similar order to the general population. Recent studies suggest that for British-born Afro-Caribbeans this might not be true and indeed that they might have diagnosed rates of schizophrenia even higher than their migrant parents. (McGovern and Cope, 1987b, Harrison *et al*. 1988). Before accepting such figures as true reflections of the incidence of schizophrenia, a number of points have to be considered.

(i) The actual number of patients is so small that slight changes would have a disproportionate effect on the rates.

(ii) The numbers of black people in the local population (needed to calculate the rate) were not available in the last census and thus estimates are a likely source of potential error.

(iii) The black community is perhaps less likely to seek psychiatric help from predominantly white services and perhaps less likely to disclose any previous psychiatric treatment, thus inflating the number of 'first admissions' (which is the measure of the number of new cases.)

(iv) This may be accentuated by high residential mobility in search of work.

(v) The local black population are probably more likely to be admitted as emergencies under the Mental Health Act, whilst white schizophrenic patients may be preferentially treated by family doctors, thus decreasing the white rate which is used for comparison.

(vi) Considerable doubt has been shed on the diagnosis of schizophrenia in black people by white psychiatrists (Chapters 4 and 5 this volume; Adebimpe, 1984; Jones and Gray, 1986).

If we accept that these rates might really reflect the incidence of schizophrenia in the Afro-Caribbean British-born population, this is a matter of considerable concern. Disadvantaged and minority groups in a variety of countries in the world have high rates of schizophrenia. In any population a higher proportion are possibly vulnerable to developing schizophrenia-like patterns than actually do, depending on the social milieu. In British society, the black population are subject to continuing overt prejudice, to high levels of unemployment especially among young adults, and to poorer access to housing, welfare and health care facilities. It is for the Afro-Caribbean community in particular (for whom language, traditions and goals are similar to those of the dominant white population) that the ascription of inferior identity, together with the inability to achieve shared goals, presents a major psycho-social dislocation. We think it not unlikely that a major factor in the precipitation of what looks like schizophrenia in those vulnerable to it is the experience of racism refracted through subtle cognitive changes involving selfhood, autonomy and locus of control. 'Second generation strategies' such as ethnic redefinition (pages 143–5) may fail to improve this. Indeed they may make it worse.

Are we any nearer to clarifying the question of diagnosis – how white psychiatry perceives and classifies black people (Chapter 5)? We ourselves carried out a study to look at the possibility of misdiagnosis in the immigrant generation as resulting from a particular religious pattern of explaining personal distress. In a group of West Indian patients in a London hospital who experienced what medical staff would term 'religious delusions' we found that a high proportion were given a diagnosis of schizophrenia in the absence of the classic 'first rank symptoms' (page 16; Littlewood and Lipsedge, 1981), although other psychiatrists have come to the opposite conclusion – that white doctors mistake schizophrenia in West Indian patients for less serious illness (Richardson and Hendrik-Gutt, 1981).

One of the most extraordinary episodes in the area of diagnosis concerns the use of the term 'cannabis psychosis'. In 1986 one of us (R.L.) discussed possible research needs with the Birmingham Community Relations Council, members of the Wolverhampton Rastafarian Progressive Association and a number of West Indian churches and voluntary groups (Littlewood, 1988b). A matter of considerable local concern was the relationship between cannabis (*ganja*) use and psychiatric admission in

Birmingham. Whilst some black community workers did feel that cannabis was likely to precipitate psychiatric illness (a common belief in the Caribbean itself – Littlewood, 1988a), others suggested that the diagnosis of 'cannabis psychosis' was used to admit under the Mental Health Act a considerable number of young black men who had a personal or family crisis. A study at the time found that 27 per cent of the male Afro-Caribbean psychiatric patients in central Birmingham were diagnosed as suffering from 'cannabis psychosis' (McGovern and Cope, 1987b), a diagnosis given to only 1.2 per cent of white males: a 95-fold difference in terms of rates per each population. Ten years previously, however, the diagnosis was seldom used locally for any group (Royer, 1977). This relative prevalence did not seem to reflect the actual differential use of cannabis in the last two groups as it was extensively smoked by the local white working class. A short examination by one of us (R.L.) of a selection of some of the notes of these black patients suggested that 'cannabis psychosis' was often diagnosed without any evidence of cannabis being detected in the urine (the usual test). (Even finding it would, of course, be no indication that the diagnosis was 'cannabis psychosis' any more than the presence of alcohol in a patient's blood implies a mental illness is alcohol related.) The detection of an illegal substance by doctors in a patient has medico-legal implications, likely to switch the 'management' of a distressed young person from medicine to the penal system.

Increased salience was given to the issue by evidence offered to the Silverman Inquiry into the Handsworth riots by a prominent local psychiatrist who implicated cannabis use as a causative factor in rioting. This view was extensively (and critically) reported in the local black press. Concern was now expressed that, whatever the psychiatric consequences of cannabis might actually be (see page 23), 'cannabis psychosis' was a particularly vague term which was being employed in situations where psychiatrists had not taken enough time to understand the circumstances of personal difficulties. Because of the popular association of cannabis with the black community, the use of the diagnosis had, in addition, the effect of pathologizing black people: if West Indians used cannabis, and cannabis caused psychological difficulties, then the stresses black people in Britain experienced could be said to be, in part, a function of their own chosen way of life. A heavily publicized survey of local psychiatrists' attitudes showed that there was little general agreement on whether 'cannabis psychosis' existed and what its symptoms might be (Littlewood, 1988b). Attempts to have a joint psychiatrists/community workers meeting were unsuccessful but one possible consequence was that the diagnosis suddenly disappeared (Milner and Hayes, 1988).

To avoid the possibility of 'misdiagnosis' in the use of (often rather poor) past medical records, one of the studies on the rates of schizophrenia among British-born Afro-Caribbeans employed the methods used by the World Health Organisation in its study of schizophrenia (pages 117–19): interviews with each patient by the research team used an internationally standardized rating schedule (Harrison *et al.*, 1988). Doubts remain however as to the value of white administered interviews with black patients in Britain, and the schedule used (the Present State Examination) has been extensively criticized for being based on European symptomatology and thus missing the subtle differences between different groups in notions of the self and emotional expression (Marsella and White, 1982; Littlewood, 1986b; Fernando, 1988). Nevertheless, it remains the major international measuring stick for schizophrenia and is extensively used in Britain (Ndetei and Vadher, 1984).

A few studies have looked at other minority groups. The old question of whether manic-depressive illness is particularly common among Jews has been re-examined to suggest that this is indeed true but that they have lower rates of schizophrenia and alcoholism (Cooklin, Ravindran and Carney, 1983). The first study of the Greek Cypriot community in London compares them with mainland Greeks in Athens and with white English (Mavreas and Bebbington, 1987); the authors found minor psychiatric illness, especially anxiety, appears to be more common in both Greek groups than in the English (who are more obsessional). The authors suggest that the findings reflect different ways of expressing psychological distress, the Greek pattern being characteristic of Southern Europeans with an emphasis on shame rather than guilt and on the physical expression of distress (but see pp. 78–81).

By contrast with developments in medical anthropology in the United States which emphasize that the full range of local meanings and contexts must be taken into account before comparing symptoms of different groups (Kleinman, 1981; Marsella and White, 1982), British studies rely on traditional medical perceptions of symptoms based on the classical patterns described earlier this century (Littlewood, 1986b). A collection of essays, largely American in origin, has recently considered the question of the universality of depression (Chapter 3) and demonstrates brilliantly the ethnocentrism of the traditional medical approach when it ignores peoples' own contexts of illness and their patterns of recourse to help (Kleinman and Good, 1985). In another work, Arthur Kleinman has shown how, in the case of the Chinese Cultural Revolution, changes in political context rapidly alter the appropriate ways of expressing distress so that quite different medical syndromes emerge and disappear (Kleinman, 1986). In Britain, while there is some work on the use of 'traditional' therapeutic practices among minorities (Ballard, 1982; Chandrasena, 1983), we know little about the exact way in which they are used. For the Afro-Caribbean community, whilst there are descriptions of psychological categories of well-being and ill-health in the West Indies (Fisher, 1986; Littlewood, 1985; 1988a), their relevance to Britain is uncertain. Fernando (1988) criticizes the American anthropological approach for taking cultures as independent entities and for ignoring their construction through particular professional theories and perceptions.

A Japanese psychiatrist working with Afro-Caribbean patients in London found in a small survey that they only consulted alternative healers (herbalists, faith healers, etc.) after they had sought professional medical treatment and found it ineffective, inappropriate or unsympathetic (Suzuki, 1984). The only published study on popular attitudes to ill health held by British West Indians show that not only do they consider 'stress' a cause of illness, but they implicate unemployment and racism specifically (Donovan, 1986). The researcher in this study was white but it is interesting that when the interviewer is committed to an antiracist stance, whether they are themselves black or white, informants structure their experiences in a context of racial oppression (Donovan, 1986; Burke, 1984; Currer, 1984; cf. page 142).

A number of mental health professionals now work with overseas students (Babikeer *et al*, 1980; Cox, 1986; Furnham and Trezise, 1983) and with refugees (Baker, 1983; Bram, 1983;

British Refugee Council, 1984; Munoz, 1980; Perez, 1984). Here, whilst the explanations of depression and anxiety frequently do include some psychological understanding of the patient's own experience, and there has been a shift from purely psychological interpretations to a wider political context (compare Munoz, 1980 with Perez, 1984), we still have no knowledge of what constitutes 'stress' and 'support' for the individuals concerned. Too often our inadequacy in providing services is explained away by suggestions that one group or another 'stigmatize' mental illness more than do the white English. Therefore doctors say 'they' do not wish to use 'our' services and hide their severely mentally ill away: particularly the Asian community. Whilst high apparent rates of schizophrenia among West Indians are taken as valid, the relatively lower rates among Asians are seen as reflecting, not better mental health, but the presumed existence of patients kept hidden at home away from medical facilities. Severe mental illness may be more stigmatized by Asians than by other groups but there is no evidence one way or another. We ourselves strongly suspect that serious psychotic illness is stigmatized equally among all ethnic groups in Britain, black and white.

THE MENTAL HEALTH ACT

Assumptions about community attitudes to mental illness of this type are frequently cited to explain the greater proportion of black psychiatric patients who are compulsorily detained in hospitals under the Mental Health Act (Littlewood, 1986a). The current debate on the Act condenses many of the themes we have considered in this book and we shall look at it in detail.

Investigations of hospital records continue to demonstrate a disproportionate number of black patients, both born in Britain and in the Caribbean and West Africa, who are involuntary patients (see for example Ineichen *el al*. 1984). Some studies have found that Asian-born patients are also overrepresented. The degree of overrepresentation varies but most studies suggest that it is between two and three times the white UK-born rate; whereas about 8 per cent of white patients in psychiatric hospitals and units are involuntary, the figure for black patients is about 20 to 30 per cent. As far as we know this pattern is similar in different areas of Britain. To an extent the figures may be explained by an increased diagnosis of schizophrenia in the black community relative to other diagnoses (page 105), and which is more likely to be associated with involuntary admission. There is evidence however that the increase is independent of the diagnosis whilst the frequency of schizophrenia in minorities has, as we have seen, been called into question. Two broad groups of explanation have been offered: one implicates factors in the patients themselves and in the black communities, the other is concerned with the practice of psychiatry in a society permeated by racist assumptions.

Explanations orientated to the black patient
Not surprisingly these are the explanations offered by psychiatrists.

(i)   *The specific suggestion that psychiatric illness in black people is different* Among the quasi-medical terms which are commonly used is that of 'florid'; black patients are regarded as more antisocial and dangerous and thus legitimately more likely to be detained under the Mental Health Act, whilst the police are more often involved in the admission of black patients in general. Although there are few statistics on the numbers of black patients in prison hospital locked wards, secure units and special hospitals (presumably because of the reluctance of the Home Office and individual psychiatrists to be accused of racial bias) it appears that black patients are overrepresented in these settings too (Bolton, 1984). Why should the presentation of psychiatric illness in blacks be more anti-social than in whites? Amongst the arguments put forward (usually by analogy with suggestions made by colonial psychiatrists in Africa and elsewhere) is one that the illness is precipitated by organic factors such as anaemia or cannabis and therefore the symptoms are more 'toxic' and delirious with less responsiveness to social context. There is no evidence that this is the case, although the nutritional status of minority psychiatric patients in Britain has not been investigated, perhaps surprisingly given the medical preoccupation with the diets of Rastafarians and Hindus.

Different cultures do have different patterns of mental illness and another explanation has been that the illness in the black British community (which is regarded as a separate culture) represents a migration of the illness itself. (The majority of patients in Caribbean psychiatric hospitals are involuntary.) This offers a sort of acculturation model: black illnesses will, in due course, come to resemble indigenous white ones; or an evolutionary one – with industrialization psychopatholoy becomes more 'psychologized', private and internalized (Leff, 1986). A variant of this thesis is that illnesses are somehow shaped by the ambient culture and, as the Caribbean is regarded in general as akin to the image of West Kingston, the illness itself is more 'aggressive' and antisocial. This of course resembles similar models derived in the areas of law and education to explain prison statistics and examination results: in other words problems are seen to lie in the minority culture itself which is regarded as pathogenic if not pathological. Black patients of a variety of ethnic groups (including South Asians) are over-represented on Mental Health Act sections, some of whom are underrepresented on other measures of what may be termed 'social deviance'; nor are the various societies of the Indian sub-continent described by British professionals as 'anti-social' in the way the term Caribbean is perceived. In a small study we carried out of the offences which led courts to refer patients to psychiatric hospitals, mentally ill black patients were no more likely to have committed violent offences against others than were whites. However, transfer of patients to secure units is related to perceived 'unco-operativeness' and this is a more common experience for black patients (Bolton, 1984). What may be termed a 'liberal' variant of the same type of explanation locates the aggressive proclivity in the communities' response to racism in British societies. Similar patterns of compulsory treatment are found in other disadvantaged groups elsewhere in the world, independent of their own culture. In favour of this argument is the fact that the children of non-white migrants are as likely as their parents to be involuntary patients (McGovern and Cope, 1987a). Patterns of illness in migrants in any case quickly come to resemble the prevalent local patterns; teenage immigrants to Britain from rural South Asia may take an overdose after a few years of residence here.

(ii) *Community attitudes* Another, more general, explanation offered by psychiatrists of the figures is that the differences can be attributed less to the individual patient than to the minority communities' perception and conceptualization of psychopathology. According to this model mental illness is particularly stigmatized in minority communities, in part because of pre-migration folk models of mental illness, and in part because in the pre-migration culture there are anyway fewer and poorer psychiatric facilities which are reserved for the more severely ill and the anti-social. The presumed consequences are that: the potential patient is less willing to come into a mental hospital; the patient's own model of mental illness is more anti-social; the recourse to psychiatric facilities occurs later in the course of the illness when the patients are less likely to regard themselves as ill and thus accept treatment. Whilst it may be expected that the experience of being black in Britain is likely to lead to an increase in mental illness, the total rates of hospital admission are broadly similar in most groups, suggesting that perhaps only the most severely ill black patients are actually admitted. These are likely then to be disproportionately 'anti-social'.

In favour of the stigmatization argument is that black psychiatric patients appear to have a poorer relationship with doctors and to be more likely to miss appointments (page 57). However white migrants from countries with the same type of psychiatric facilities as those found in India or in the Caribbean are no more likely to be compulsorily detained than the white British-born. More significantly, although there are assumptions among psychiatrists of the stigmatization of the mentally ill by minority groups, there is no actual evidence for this (page 269). (Indeed we know little about popular conceptualizations of mental illness in any group including the white British.) There is evidence however that the prognosis of serious mental illness is actually better outside Europe; recent studies in rural India suggest that schizophrenic patients may be less excluded and invalidated by their families than in Britain (page 118). As to the prognosis of serious mental illness in different ethnic groups inside Britain, we again have no information. A more significant objection to this argument is that explanations based on pre-migration culture are infinitely elastic and of dubious validity to the situation here and now: over-representation under the Mental Health Act is as common in the British-born black community as it is among their immigrant parents.

Explanations which emphasize the role of the psychiatrist
A different set of explanations emphasizes the political role of

psychiatry or expresses the immediate subjective experience of being a black psychiatric patient in Britain. Many of the explanations here are strikingly similar to those suggested by professional psychiatry, with the distinction that the arrow of causuality is reversed; thus black psychiatric outpatients may indeed miss more appointments but this is because they receive an inferior service as in other areas of medicine (Mercer, 1986). A common suggestion is that the police are overtly racist and selectively pick out non-mentally ill black people in the streets, and take them to a psychiatric hospital under Section 136 of the Mental Health Act as an alternative to arrest. This did occur in our own clinical experience in East London and is commonly mentioned by the black community.

Black patients, however, are overrepresented on all types of Mental Health Act sections: not only from the police but those signed by general practitioners, psychiatrists and courts; for each this over-representation is of a similar order. This would fit in with the suggestion that, in a racist society, it is psychiatry which has a specific role as the social moderator of conformity, patrolling the uneasy borderline between illness and political dissent (Black Health Workers and Patients Groups, 1983). This is supported by the common assertion, not yet statistically substantiated but which is perhaps true, that members of Ras Tafari are particularly likely to be psychiatric patients, although a variety of studies show that (with the possible exception of Jehovah's Witnesses) membership of religious groups is usually associated with better mental health (page 171).

A more 'liberal' variant of this theory is that psychiatrists are just basically incompetent in diagnosis, and this is supported by the increased frequency of a change of diagnosis in patients from ethnic minorities (page 117). If depression in the black community is diagnosed as schizophrenia, patients are more likely to be compulsorily detained because of the perception of schizophrenia as inherently more anti-social.

Psychiatrists themselves would deny that they consciously and selectively penalize black patients whilst agreeing that they are dealing with the casualties of disadvantage. Wherever such practice is located it is not likely to be in conscious overt racism. In the only study which looked at the ethnicity of psychiatrists, admittedly one of limited scope (page 58), this did not appear to be associated with the treatment afforded to patients of different ethnic groups. Although a large proportion of junior psychiatrists are themselves non-white this does not seem to be related to the overall findings, suggesting again that racism does not operate at an overt, conscious level.

No one has attempted to deal with any degree of sophistication with how covert (institutional) racism operates in psychiatry. Is psychiatry 'a crucial . . . new operational method', a specific form of indirect control in a racist society (Black Health Workers and Patients Group, 1983), or is its use of the Mental Health Act merely part of the same package of oppression and disadvantage as unemployment and poor housing, such that to be an involuntary patient is merely on a par with the relative lack of access to psychotherapy or counselling and with higher doses of medication? Against this 'general racism argument' is the specific historical role of psychological and psychiatric theories in justifying slavery, colonialism and racism (Chapter 2). Supporting the argument that psychiatry merely reflects or represents general non-specific racism are the other indices of medical disadvantage, such as infant mortality and infectious diseases associated with poor nutrition, which demonstrate an over-representation of non-white groups; also in favour is the fact that the medical Sections (2, 3, 4) of the Mental Health Act have to be signed not only by doctors but also by members of the patient's family or by social workers. If a differential use of the Mental Health Act is located in conscious discriminatory practices, one might expect that black families would be reluctant to consign their relatives to mental hospitals and that more of the Sections for black patients would be signed by social workers than Sections for white patients. So far as we know this is not the case: a small examination by us of completed forms in Birmingham suggests that there is no difference. Families can, of course, be pressurized into signing by the professionals; however in the majority of cases when police have been called to a black person for psychiatric reasons, it has been at the request of neighbours or the family themselves (Rogers and Faulkner, 1987).

To what extent is it justifiable to explain the selective operation of the Mental Health Act in terms of racism? The idea that racism in Britain operates solely in terms of a policy of deliberate unequal treatment appears rather naïve. It is likely to be mediated by implicit assumptions of the type we have outlined earlier, part of a shared everyday view of the world, both on the part of those who benefit from the system but also of those who do not. We shall have to wait and see whether the appointment of three black health professionals to the Mental Health Act Commission (the new body set up to monitor the Act) will make any difference. Certainly the Commission has highlighted 'ethnic minorities' as a major issue (Mental Health Act Commission, 1987)

Both types of explanation appear inadequate in themselves: the psychiatrists' perception of violence as located in the patient and the perception of the psychiatrist as a simple agent of racism. Both are conspiracy theories which locate interaction between groups in British society in one element of it alone. Whilst that might seem a rather obvious conclusion, the explanations considered certainly do tend to fall discretely into one of these two groups. Some questions can be addressed relatively easily, such as the perception of potentially aggressive behaviours in black and white patients. American evidence suggests that black psychiatric patients are less violent than white patients (Lawson, Yesavage and Werner, 1984). On certain points then, further information is required, but such data need to be informed by a more developed theory. Rather than convergent data (comparing groups of independent sets of patients and locating the differences in these groups), we need divergent data through which we can perceive how different groups interact. Data, like the expression of mental illness itself, are not independent of constraining theories but are part of a total social context which includes such theory. An analysis of psychiatry's function of social control in the black community necessitates a consideration of its relations with other welfare agencies, courts, probation services, prisons and immigration control procedures; it is unlikely to be independent of policies and practices in such areas as social work and fostering. Objections to the first approach (page 276) are perhaps the most serious in that it may be reasonably questioned whether psychiatric theory and practice which themselves represent part of the interaction can provide an adequate tool for describing it. The second perspective too, particularly in its simplest conspiratorial form, is also partial, nor is there any reason to suppose that the immediate experiences of racism or the individual responses to it themselves comprise any type of privileged theory. What remains to be demonstrated is the nature of the social transaction whereby psychiatrists perceive their black patients as more dangerous (Fernando, 1988). We have yet to develop a criticial theory of the type so fruitful in women's studies, one which is independent both of psychological theories and personal experience, but which shows how both have originated historically and how they constitute each other.

PSYCHIATRY AS FETISHISM:
THE 'CULTURAL PATHOLOGY' OF THE RIOT

What of popular attitudes as reflected in the press and public policy? We have outlined earlier the tendency to deal with political relations between groups through explaining them as the characteristics of the culture or of psychological or anatomical defects of the subdominant group alone. By analogy with political theory, psychoanalysis and social anthropology we can characterize this type of 'condensation' and 'displacement' as *fetishism*: the substitution for whole areas of human relationships and history by objects which come to have a discrete existence of their own, and which then can be propriated or manipulated (Ellen, 1988). A popular reification of this type is 'black culture' taken as historically autonomous and inherently pathological (see Chapters 2, 3, 7–9).

Whilst earlier explanations of social disadvantage and mental illness in black people favoured biological theories, current opinion in the press, social work literature and 'race relations' now often attributes them to a social pathology of *culture* (Parmar, 1981; Lipsedge and Littlewood, 1985). Examples include repeated references to family structure, Jamaican 'subcultural violence', behaviour in court, poor English and poor attitudes to work. 'If the aetiology of these social problems is understood as cultural . . . then the culture itself becomes flawed and race becomes compounded as a disability' (Cross, 1982). Cultural explanations lead to 'welfare' solutions such as 'ethnic matching' the number of black social workers, thus minimizing the power of the marginal underclass as a potential disruptive force and providing a 'humane' solution. While clinical and scientific objectivity are claimed, the culture is discredited and reduced to both a symptom and the cause of pathology.

Medical staff presume that black lifestyle and diet are

responsible for high rates of still births and neonatal deaths (Brent Community Health Council, 1981). The organization of the black household is seen as the cause of these problems. The Select Committee on Home Affairs described homelessness as a 'cultural reaction' rather than as a direct result of poor housing or the need to seek work: 'family disputes lead young blacks to leave home'. The probation service suggests that whilst there may be a racial bias in the magistrates' sentencing practices, this is because '. . . . some black defendants behave impertinently, casually and inappropriately when before the court' (Central Council of Probation Committees, 1983). Overcrowding is attributed to the avoidance of contraception or to the 'extended family' whilst educational failure is related to the 'Victorian' educational values of black parents. Thus, obstructions to full social participation are located not in relations between black and white but in a fetishized black culture.

Moynihan's view of the pathological black American family (page 49) is echoed in Britain: 'a disturbing feature is the very large proportion of single parent families. . . This is not an isolated freak result. The author is aware of the high incidence of marital instability among West Indian households' (Ratcliffe, 1982). 'Slavery destroyed *conventional* family life leading to a poor sense of identity and poor self image. . . The lack of social control by the West Indian family due to fragmentation of the family in slavery led to youth problems with the police and subterranean values' (Cashmore, 1979, our emphasis). West Indian parents allegedly do not talk to their young children, and black youths become unemployable because they are lazy and ill disciplined. The welfare solution is to provide Youth Opportunity Schemes and to teach them social skills and docility.

A book by a British paediatrician suggests that

the sorriest, most downtrodden women in the world must surely be those from Bangladesh . . . a woman is treated like a chattel, secluded from contacts except within the family. The suicide rate is, not surprisingly, very high. [West Indian childbearing patterns are known] to be able to cripple a child's development [in] the curiously cold and unmotherly relationship between many West Indian mothers and their children . . . a distinct lack of a warm, intimate, continuous relationship. (Lobo, 1978, pp. 8, 34)

The maternally deprived black children grow into anti-social youths who

> are very fond and very good at sports, athletics and music. This is an area where their inborn physical and rhythmic talents help them win over the English competitors . . .Their rhythm, the noise and the flashing lights of the disco seem so much closer to the African culture. The physical co-ordination and sense of rhythm make the young West Indian superb dancers to pop music. They probably find in the music and dance a release of their frustrations and pent up emotions. (ibid, pp. 92–3)

Riots are seen by authority as threatening and irrational, 'a senseless, and wild orgy of destruction', formless, malign, incoherent and pathological. Participants are irrationally compelled into violence by a distorted perception of reality. In the nineteenth century Gustave Le Bon suggested the man in the crowd becomes a simple automaton; men are transformed into brutes by mental contagion and by the influence of 'agitators' (Le Bon, 1895). The contemporary British view of the riots of the 1980s emphasizes their uselessness, labels the participants as disordered and tends to offer psychological explanations for the phenomenon – a susceptible crowd manipulated by a charismatic and malign outsider.

Crowd behaviour however, is not a random, irrational, unfocused and destructive orgy. Rioters discriminate in their choice of targets. The traditional English mob 'did not riot as a protest, but because it expected to achieve something by its riot' (Hobsbawm, 1959). Riots have a recognized meaning to the participants and show selectivity and specificity in terms of the target chosen for damage. Historically, the mob was composed of a cross-section of the ordinary urban poor which aimed for collective bargaining as a deliberately selected technique of protest. The report on the Los Angeles Riots showed that these events were not caused by an atypical minority: nearly half of the residents of the area were involved (Sears and McConahay, 1970). The mob is traditionally represented by the establishment as the passive instrument of outside agents and thus the element of social protest can be minimized. The British riots of 1981 were blamed on 'social workers and allied people directly or indirectly inciting children to rebel not only against society but also against their parents' (Crawford, 1981). Probation officers however implicated manipulation of 'aggressive groups of young men . . . sometimes exploited by some of their elders for political, commercial or religious reasons' (Central Council of Probation Committees, 1983). The popular press blamed the riots on white ringleaders, 'sneering, denim-clad left-wing teachers' and, incredibly, on white 'witch doctors . . . the ghastly swirling figures of the Cloud of Unreason [who] belong to the same world as the messianic revolutionaries' (Kerridge, 1983).

Psychological and medical explanations of riots favour the 'frustration–aggression' theory (one has an innate tendency to attack the frustrating agent) and neglect the political context of the riot: a form of psychologization by which a certain complex of behaviours is modelled on the behaviour of laboratory animals and which thus both removes individual responsibility for the activity and proposes that a specific form of intervention is possible, one involving psychological or medical techniques. American physicians argue 'if slum conditions alone determined and initiated riots, why are the vast majority of slum dwellers able to resist the temptation of unrestrained violence? Is there something peculiar about the violent slum dweller that differentiates him from his peaceful neighbour?' (Mark, Sweet and Ervin, 1967). The same authors go on to cite evidence from the Neuro-Research Foundation to the effect that brain dysfunction related to a focal lesion plays a significant role in such violent and assaultive behaviour: 'We need intensive research and clinical studies of the individuals committing violence. The goal of such studies would be to pinpoint, diagnose and treat those people with low violence thresholds before they contribute to further tragedies'.

The equivalent British response was perhaps an article in the Police Journal advocating brain surgery for violent offenders (Hickmott, 1983). Other, stranger, explanations have been invoked. Meteorological studies indicate a curvilinear relationship between the likelihood of a riot and the ambient temperature at the time of the riot (Baron and Ransberger, 1978), whilst a British scientist observes that 'the type of uncontrolled riotous behaviour seen in Brixton accords accurately with the symptoms of lead intoxication, though social pressures can undoubtedly act to exacerbate the chemical effects of lead on the brain' (Bryce-Smith, 1981). Not to mention cannabis (page 226). Similarly, current historical studies of rebellions on the nineteenth-century slave plantations now favour, not a political understanding but one related to nutritional status at Christmas time: 'relief-induced agonism' (Dirks, 1987)

The British riots of the 1980s have much in common with the collective urban action of the American ghettos in the 1960s. There is the same perception of an inability to achieve shared aspirations and an awareness that traditional and legitimate channels for bringing about change and redressing grievances were blocked, the same hope of citizens that rioting could bring about changes by dramatically drawing attention to inner-city problems. The immediate catalyst is always an event which crystallizes the community's grievances, leading to the generation of a sense of outrage in the crowd directed against the collapse of acceptable relations between police and community. Popular riotous action reminds government of its traditional values and obligations – what E.P. Thompson has designated 'the moral economy of the crowd'. Collective violence is consciously and deliberately chosen only when other forms of protest have failed.

If riots are perceived as pathological aspects of 'West Indian culture' the more expressively theatrical representation of this culture, the annual Notting Hill Carnival, has continually balanced between a cathartic entertainment and an authentic riot. Like carnivals elsewhere (Littlewood, 1988a), whilst the participants' own experience is certainly cathartic, the event itself serves as a ritual theatre in which current political realities are enacted, less in the explicit themes of the bands and calypsoes than in the preceding articles in the popular press on anticipated violence, the masquerade overflowing into spontaneous action amidst the ambiguities of the debate on 'Whose Carnival is it anyway?' The carnival serves as a microcosm of the wider issues concerning black people, issues of 'cultural' definition, power and patronage, and the margins of assimilation, inherently ambiguous but seeking on all sides coherence and definition (see Cohen, 1980).

Riots are not meaningless pathology, but, amongst other things, pragmatic, if desperate, attempts to solve the problems faced by a group or an individual. It would be no wiser to offer a single unitary hypothesis of riots than for other psycho-political events medicalized by psychiatry (Littlewood and Lipsedge,

1987). Clearly no one is likely to riot in a heavy thunderstorm and the precipitating incident may be relatively trivial, but weather and provocation cannot be offered as the sole explanation any more than the participants' own anger. Incidentally, the most common reason given by young people interviewed on the causes of the 1981 riots was unemployment (Home Office, 1982). The Central Council of Probation Committees (1983) put the same notion rather differently: 'Perhaps the lack of employment left them with idle hands for mischief'.

THE DEBATE ON RACISM AND MENTAL HEALTH

Rather than attempt detailed analyses of the interrelationship of racism and mental health, British mental health workers who are active in black and ethnic minority issues have taken a pragmatic stance. Thus their only contribution on the riots were uncritical studies on health workers' perceptions and an examination of their effect on a local psychotherapy group (Bhat *et al.*, 1984a; 1984b). No one ventured to explore Fanon's suggestion that the violence might have a positive mental health function.

The closest to a general model is the work of Suman Fernando on racism and depression (1986, 1988). Reviewing the literature on the universality of depression (see Chapter 3), Fernando observes that we have to examine the analogous contexts of gender and class, for depression is a personal experience in a social context. He develops a thesis which emphasizes the 'learned helplessness' model. Depressed people perceive themselves as worthless, the outer world as meaningless and the future as hopeless. He notes that Jews as a minority in Britain have high levels of depression and that one's perceptions when depressed have analogues with experience of being in a minority, particularly a black minority in a white dominated society. Racism then is not just an added difficulty for black people, but a context and a control which specifically generates the symptoms of depression. He suggests that community responses which mobilize self-esteem and promote an ethnic identity in opposition to that of the dominant white group should both minimize the chance of depression and offer a coping strategy to help those who have become depressed – what we have termed above 'ethnic redefinition' (page 143).

Aggrey Burke, like Fernando a member of the Transcultural Psychiatry Society, in a chapter in a book written by members of the Society describes how a white professional emphasis on 'culture', with the perception of inappropriate childrearing patterns in a disturbed black mother as 'culturally normal', results in eventual recourse to punitive measures (Burke, 1986). The Society has moved however from a position in which 'cultural understanding' was all that was required to one in which the issue of racism has come to the fore. Given that an interest in 'transcultural psychiatry' is limited among British psychiatrists to the few members of the Society, it is perhaps ironical that much of its discussions have focused on why psychiatry should have this particular interest in black people (Littlewood, 1986b). Another member, S.P. Sashidharan, in the same volume, characterizes the whole area of comparative psychiatry as serving to control non-Europeans, 'a kind of medicine [and psychiatry] that embodies certain pernicious notions about black people and their lives and struggles' (Sashidharn, 1986). He notes correctly that 'culture' is only introduced into western medicine when the patient is not white. Indeed, 'western' psychopathology is usually taken by mental health professionals as if belief about illness, accepted patterns of expressing distress and childrearing patterns, were irrelevant to the illness experience: not so when the patient is black (Littlewood, 1986b; Littlewood and Lipsedge, 1987). Similar points have been made by the Black Health Workers and Patients Group (1983), the Campaign Against Racism and Facism (1983) and in the popular black press (Skerritt, 1982).

The most extensive critique of 'transcultural psychiatry' comes from a sociologist, Kobena Mercer (1987). Mercer suggests that the subject developed as part of the recent tendency within medicine to examine the doctor-patient communication and that desire for a knowledge of 'ethnicity' is part of an approach to medical practice which seeks to control the interaction more effectively (compare Armstrong, 1984). Though largely sympathetic to doctors and social workers who seek to view things from the clients' point of view he too notes that 'culture' itself becomes reified as a thing special to black people. He is critical of the attempt to redefine the experience of racism as purely psychological, and warns of the attempt to develop a psychotherapy which fails to take into account the question of power. Rackett (1987) takes a broadly similar view, emphasizing how 'transcultural psychiatry', independently of the overt aims of its practitioners, constitutes a particular type of knowledge embedded in contempory medical discourse.

In its various publications the Transcultural Psychiatry Society, whilst demonstrating considerable concern with the effects of racism and psychiatry on the mental health of black people, has proved unable to offer any clear understanding of the political issues. Much of its concern has gone into highlighting individual abuses (for example, Francis, 1985) and suggesting policy changes in limited areas couched in a rhetoric blended of outrage and liberal social administration with recourse to a rather diffuse understanding of 'racism' independent of its specific social formation and psychological representation, and an inability to place the issues in a particular political context. Nevertheless, the Society has done much to switch the perception of the psychopathology of black people as an *explanation* (of riots, family life or whatever) to an understanding of it as as *problem* (of black–white relations) (cf. Banton, 1988). Fernando (1988) alone provides a detailed programme for transcultural psychiatry but advocates a depoliticization of the issues with recommendations of managerial change in the National Health Service to make it more responsive to local communities. He suggests that research in the area should be carefully monitored and that medical journals and professional organizations should adopt an expressively anti-racist policy.

There is some evidence from the United States that black psychiatrists are less likely to diagnose black patients inappropriately than are white doctors (Adebimpe, 1982; 1984). Are black doctors in Britain in a similar position to affect clinical practices? One matter which has been of concern to the Transcultural Psychiatry Society is the poor career prospects available to those doctors who are not of European origin (page 12: Bhate, Sagovsky and Cox, 1986). Although first examined in the case of psychiatry (perhaps because psychiatrists, whether black or white, are more socially and politically committed than other hospital doctors, page 11), this seems true in all areas of medicine. The Commission for Racial Equality has carried out a detailed study of overseas trained doctors which confirms that they work especially in locum (non-permanent) jobs whilst those who are offered consultant positions tend to work in the unpopular specialities (geriatrics and psychiatry) whilst regarding general medicine and surgery as more appealing (Anwar and Ali, 1987). Interestingly, British-born minority doctors regard psychiatry as more popular than overseas graduates or British whites. Overseas doctors remain less likely to receive the lucrative and secret 'merit awards' and, compared with British trained doctors, are more prepared to see the Health Service as practising discrimination (58 per cent compared with 35 per cent).

Increasing restrictions on overseas doctors wishing to work in Britain are associated with a general contraction in the number of doctors produced by the British medical schools. What proportion of newly-qualified doctors are black? There are no established figures, for medical schools have not followed the CRE's recommendations for ethnic monitoring. Informal reports vary greatly but a general conclusion seems to be that British Asians do get into medical school but relatively few British Afro-Caribbeans. A chance finding which led to an inquiry (CRE, 1988) was that one of the prestigious London medical schools had a bias built into the computer program which dealt with student admission, a bias against accepting black students (and women).

The extent to which an underrepresentation of black medical students is due to bias at the point of interview, or because of a shortage of appropriately qualified candidates is not clearly given from the figures published. The earlier 'colour-blind' educational policies of the early 1970s were replaced by a specific focus on the educational underachievement of black children. Drawing on the American studies of the 'poor self-image' held by these children some educationalists advocated 'multiculturalism' in which positive images of black history and culture would be provided in schools. This was criticized for providing stereotyped images dating from the period of colonialism and for ignoring racism in comtemporary British society. The Swann Committee shifted from examining factors in the families of black children who did do well at school to considering the attitudes and expectations of the schools themselves.

The best known attempt to alter the behaviour of white teachers and other professionals was the introduction of a training devised by American psychologists, White Awareness Training, or, as it was called in Britain, Racism Awareness

Training. Known by the unfortunate acronym RAT it was modelled on group therapy processes and its advocates agreed that whilst the origins of racism were not individual and psychological, the 'sustenance and the practice of racism' (CRE, 1985 cf. page 54) could be understood in these terms. The technique of RAT (and to an extent its successor Anti-Racism Training) depended on a 'trainer' who encouraged the expression of anger and guilt by the white participants: emotions aroused in this way could be a powerful force for behavioural change (CRE, 1985). Opponents of RAT cited numerous cases reported in the press of whites who had 'broken down' during the session, whilst some supporters replied that these were only a replication of the historical experiences of black people with whites.

Critics on the left, particularly the Institute of Race Relations, denounced the whole exercise for ignoring issues of class and institutional racism, pointing out that even if black people did gain educational qualification they were less likely to be promoted than similarly qualified whites. Both left- and right-wing opponents noted that emphasis on behavioural change alone led to the groups becoming an end in themselves (Troyna and Williams, 1986): self-interested activity on the part of the 'race relations industry' and which in practice bore disturbing similarities to the conversion practices of certain religious sects. RAT trainers also appeared unwilling to evaluate the efficacy of the experience (CRE, 1985). It became apparent that the only white professionals who were required to undergo it were teachers, social workers and local government workers, members of poorly paid occupations with little political clout of whom a large proportion were women. Psychiatrists and directors of Social Services easily avoided any involvement.

By 1988 70 per cent of educational authorities had anti-racist policies of some sort or another and the issue of the murder in 1986 of an Asian boy at a Manchester school with an active policy of this type was widely used to attack any anti-racist initiative at all, RAT or otherwise (see, for example, Kerridge, 1988). Examination results are however now justifying some of the policies (Broom, 1988). A book criticizing anti-racist policies in general (Palmer, 1986) included both conservative opponents who argued that racism was a moral question which 'anti-racism' could only inflame and socialists who argued that to divorce race from class only psychologized issues of power, concealing their real base. The book prompted an extraordinary academic debate over eleven months in the *London Reveiw of Books* on the definitions of 'race', and on 'anti-racism' versus 'non-racism'. The issue of RAT demonstrates the impotence of concerned individuals to affect social practices at large or to alter the general population's attitudes, with recourse to developing 'training' packages for certain vulnerable professionals which then take on a momentum of their own. The identity of the black offered remains one which is created by whites, whether for good or bad, with black people reduced to elements in a group therapy theatre which continually rehearses whites' consciousness of their own power: a ritual of symbolic inversion.

PSYCHOTHERAPY

A recurrent theme throughout this book is that not only are political relations between social groups *fetishised*, turned into objects of analysis such as diseases or reifications of 'culture', but black people are considered in European medicine as more physical than psychological. The treatments offered to black people are more likely to be compulsory under the Mental Health Act or in Special Hospitals, but they also appear to be more physical: drugs or electroconvulsive therapy instead of the more socially valued psychotherapies (page 58). Emotional distress in blacks is seen as more somatic than in whites, expressed as aches and pains, disturbances of bodily function rather than as the 'real thing' – verbalized. Whilst exact figures on the numbers of black people offered formal psychotherapy have never been published by the Tavistock Clinic or the Institute of Psychoanalysis, the general impression has been that they are very small (Littlewood, 1988c). Training in psychotherapy or psychoanalysis remains restricted to the white middle classes. The black community mental health groups which have been established such as the Afro-Caribbean Mental Health Association or the Fanon Project's Day Centre in Brixton (Melville, 1985; Moodley, 1987; see Ward, 1986 for details of the different projects) offer support and advice or counselling rather than the sort of formal long-term intensive therapy developed by psychotherapists in private practice.

It may be argued that the major problem for minority patients who have been seriously psychiatrically ill is employment rather than therapy. One day hospital in Deptford has now developed a successful training project for unemployed black patients in information technology which helps them proceed to advanced courses in computing and thus proper jobs (Lipsedge and Summerfield, 1989)

Given that psychoanalytical therapy in Britain was effectively the creation of immigrants from central Europe with many of its classic papers based on intercultural work (Freud's famous case, the Wolf Man, was Russian), why did it not examine the question of therapy across cultures and race in this country? The social and economic history of psychoanalysis in Britain is still to be written but it is significant that many of the psychoanalytical immigrants were themselves Jewish and that they entered a society which was rabidly anti-semitic (page 12). At the same time this group, upper middle-class and cosmopolitan, formed links with the bourgeoisie of North London from whom a substantial number of its patients were drawn. Psychotherapy was a private contract between patient and therapist, and the issue of payment was integral to the therapeutic process: the personal contract allowed the therapist to avoid any question of the institutional politics of race.

A common statement, perhaps more muted recently, has been that psychotherapy is essentially culture-bound to the western middle-class milieu in which it was derived, practised by this class for themselves and that it is not appropriate for 'non-European' patients who are seen as less verbally sophisticated, less psychologized, preferring to express their distress through a different idiom – somatic, religious or whatever.

Let us consider these notions a bit further.

The question of 'non-European'   We are of course not talking of supposedly tribal societies but of groups within British society, which in part comprise British society. It would be surprising if the children of migrants to Britain, whatever their origins, who are living in western industrialized society, bound to its economic and social structures (with their everpresent representations in advertising, the media, and so on) remained unchanged, maintaining some type of autonomous prior system of personal identity, self-perception and social relations. The West Indies, one of the pre-migration cultures, is itself already a part of western society and the western political system, and one whose aspirations, ideas and notions of personhood are essentially the same as those of the United States or Britain. 'Asian culture' too is a product of interaction between European colonialism and its subject peoples.

The question of 'non-verbal' This has always been a common perception of subdominant groups, including women and the working class. The study of lay conceptions of personhood, distress and illness has now moved beyond the simple binary division between western societies (seen as psychologized and ego-centred) and non-western societies (seen as having a collective consciousness in which conflict is expressed through somatic experience, hysteria and hypochondriasis). We know from the work of critical psychologists like Rom Harrré (1983), or anthropologists like Kleinman and Good (1985), that there are many dimensions of personhood (including such parameters as public and private; external and internal; objective and subjective) which can themselves be combined in different ways to give a unique notion of the self, manifest as personal psychology, or indeed as physiology, perhaps as moralities and cosmologies, whether these are sorcery, psychoanalysis or dental appointments. Some of these 'sociology of knowledge' approaches seem to be entering the new psychotherapies, which use the patient's own explanatory models to generate therapy in an individual context.

These systems of popular psychology are not fixed and rigid for they are contingent on context. Different aspects of personhood are employed in different social situations. This suggests that we have to examine the particular patient–therapist interaction in more detail: what we might term the 'politics' of the therapeutic encounter. Whilst it seems true that patients born in South Asia do demonstrate psychosocial distress to general practitioners in somatic terms more often than do white natives (page 258), we have to bear in mind expressions of distress outside the consulting room, within which certain norms of appropriate self-disclosure and power, of responsibility and the possibility of future action are of course part of the patient's conception of what should happen. A working-class Asian patient is perhaps not aware of the possibility of formal psychotherapy and is neither likely to request it nor to present personal distress in such a way as to persuade the doctor, probation officer or social worker to consider psychotherapy as an option, particularly if such therapy is seen as only appropriate for those articulate in a white middle-class mode.

We should not underestimate the historical origins of psycho-analysis, and the dynamic psychotherapies in general, in European evolutionary theory of the nineteenth century (page 167). The innovation of Freud was to unite in a single idiom phylogenetic and individual history, generating a speculative evolutionary model which traced personal development in parallel with the conjectural psychohistory of humankind in general. Thus psychoanalysts inevitably sought analogies between the archaic and historical, the non-European, the child and the neurotic (page 157).

We should perhaps question then the particular notion of 'maturity' as used by psychotherapists. What does it connote? The Protestant ethnic? Bourgeois individualism? It is no accident that the therapies most successfully elaborated in work with minority or disadvantaged groups in the United States, such as Salvador Minuchin's family therapy, seems to eschew such individual development notions in favour of a systems theory approach (Minuchin, 1972). It is perhaps through family therapy that theories of personhood other than those of the middle class can be employed by therapists most successfully in facilitating change (but see Barot, 1988). Many individual therapists still rely on the evaluative rating of 'defence mechanisms', some of them perceived as inherently maladaptive. Certainly the somatic representation of distress is regarded with disapprobation. To an extent then certain theoretical notions of individuation or autonomy are Eurocentric or at least 'modern', industrial, bourgeois, western or whatever.

This however is a question which has achieved excessive prominence, for, to reiterate, we are not concerned in Britain with providing psychotherapy for some hypothetical Third World community. We are talking of a proportion of citizens in Britain now, a disadvantaged group certainly, but emphatically not one which has some sort of exotic system of psychological and personal development.

In the United States (Devereux, 1969) and in the French overseas territories (Gracchus, 1980; André, 1987) there has been a long tradition of using psychoanalysis, not only as a research tool with minority groups but as part of a practical everyday treatment. Many social anthropologists have used psychoanalysis as a way of approaching social institutions (Wintrob and Harvey, 1982; Devereux, 1969), a perspective which has often yielded results we have criticized as the pathologization of societies. In Chapters 2 and 3 we surveyed some of the American use of psychoanalysis among the black community and noted its ethnocentric assumptions. A recent French instance is the book by André (1987) which attempts to understand patterns of crime in Guadeloupe by emphasis on a black Oedipus complex.

Given the influence and prestige of psychoanalysis in the United States what now happens in practice? The identity of the United States is one of a society of different cultures of origin, whether they are seen as becoming assimilated ('melting-pot') or remaining distinct ('pluralism'). An emphasis in American social anthropology on 'culture' (as opposed to European anthropology which is closer to sociology) has led Americans to value more highly the healing practices of non-dominant groups, apart from the openness of the country as a whole to therapies developed in other traditions – Zen, Transcendental Meditation, yoga and Morita therapy. Coupled with this there has been a greater readiness on the part of American psychotherapists to respect the existing family networks, religious and traditional healing practices of their patients. Whilst in Britain much of the American work has been criticized for this preoccupation with the 'exotic' and for ignoring prejudices within the medical establishment, our own emphasis here on minorities simply as the victims of racism can lead to a perception of them as passive and deskilled, ignoring the considerable resources which as communities they possess (exceptions are Chandrasena, 1983; Perelberg, 1983). Indeed any proposal in Britain to encourage and help train Imams or black Pentecostal pastors as therapists is likely to be extensively criticized as an avoidance of medical responsibility.

American readiness to build on the existing resources of minority groups pioneered the notion of the 'culture broker', a member of the minority who worked with mental health professionals and who was able to mediate between lay and biomedical ideas and practice, particularly in the area of family therapy. At the same time there is a sensitivity as to why white therapists should especially be concerned with inter-cultural therapy (Wintrob and Harvey, 1982). General overviews of current Amercian practice with minority family therapy are provided in two recent books by McGoldrick, Pearce and Giardiano (1982), and Ho (1987). There is now a large research literature on *ethnic matching*: having therapist and patient from the same ethnic group (Marsella and Pedersen, 1981). Asian Americans, when offered a choice, seem to prefer a directive and active therapist who gives specific advice in contrast to the traditional passive therapist of psychoanalysis. Whilst this recalls white psychodynamic perceptions of black people as having an 'external locus of control' (feeling that decisions concerning them are made by others and that there is little they themselves can do), in practice different minorities in therapy seem equally prepared to take on personal responsibility for the future. Locus of control is perhaps less a psychological attribute rooted in personality and culture than a pragmatic realization of political reality. There is some evidence that minority patients in America initially prefer therapists of the same ethnic group irrespective of their therapeutic style. In terms of the eventual success or otherwise of the therapy, ethnic matching is possibly significant but this may be a function of the therapist's ability to understand and empathize with the client's personal experiences. Some American therapists argue that as the therapist–patient relationship is an unequal one anyway, any status differences (white–black, male–female, page 58) which increase this asymmetry tend to take on a particular prominence in the course of therapy.

The actual profession of the American therapist, whether they are doctor, social worker or nurse, does not seem significant in measures of outcome in intercultural therapy; nor, surprisingly, is their period of experience. What do seem important are the expectations of the patient in relation to what they believe to be the expectations of the therapist. A number of American centres now offer training in counselling and therapy which offer 'experience' of a particular minority culture for the therapist, including understanding of life situation, economic pressures, family patterns and ways of expressing distress (including the symbolism of physical symptoms, body language and patterns of science in communication), together with teaching appropriate ways of making eye contact, and physical closeness and bodily contact with the patient. If psychotherapy is a new experience for a particular group, the practice offered is based on appropriate existing models – clergy, traditional healer, or godparent. It is emphasized that 'cultures' are not monolithic entities and that different generations in America may have quite different patterns of response. Thus Ho (1987) shows how adaptation of first, second, third and fourth generation Japanese Americans (Issei, Nisei, Sansei, Yansei) have distinctive psychological and social expectations.

Whether patients of American or African origin constitute a separate 'culture' or whether they are a disadvantaged group of the mainstream Anglo group is a question of debate in the United States. Adebimpe (1984) notes that different therapeutic processes become highlighted not as a function of the internal development of psychiatric theory, but in relation to changing political relationships between black and white. As in Britain there has been concern about the overdiagnosis of schizophrenia, and the hyperkinetic syndrome in children, and of the use of personality tests which generated spurious pathology in normal black people (Jones and Gray, 1986). Therapy with black patients was once supposedly 'colour blind' or emphasized an indelible 'mark of oppression' (page 49). Block (1981) points out that after the passing of the Civil Rights Act it was suddenly accepted by therapists that anger and distrust of therapy, particularly with white therapists, could actually be an adaptive and healthy psychological defence rather than a denial of personal factors inside the particular therapeutic encounter (see pages 55 to 56, and Grier and Cobbs, 1968). By the late 1970s there was less emphasis in American psychotherapy on confrontation and unequal treatment, and a great emphasis on practical issues (Block, 1981). Research findings suggest however that a greater proportion of black rather than white clients drop out of therapy. On the question of ethnic matching, some evidence suggests that a black therapist achieves better results with a black patient; other studies find that it makes no difference. Examining the American studies however, it seems that few take into account other variables that are likely to be important: the training of the therapist in issues of race, the educational level of the client, the availability locally of other resources, the reasons for initially seeking therapy, and so on. All these are likely to be significant in success or failure of the therapy.

In Britain, the question of ethnic matching has come to prominence in the areas of adoption and fostering, counselling and therapy, and indeed more generally in social work (Owens and Jackson, 1983). It is a position which we certainly think needs to be taken more sympathetically by its critics than previously. It is perhaps less a solution to a complex situation than one possible option, one possible choice, analogous to that provided by women's therapy groups. It may however serve as a convenient excuse for white therapists not to confront their own racism and not to start working together with black clients.

Cultural pluralism of this type has an attraction in its simplicity, a false simplicity in our situation of muddled confusions, of coalescences and contradictions, in which we apparently still search for therapeutic encounters devoid of social constraints, devoid of power relations. Intercultural therapy is not some specialized psychotherapy presented to black people but simply therapy which takes into account these issues. By limiting itself to questions of formal psychiatric diagnosis and treatment, by its emphasis on statistics and epidemiology, anti-racist psychiatry in Britain has failed to provide an adequate critique of racism. Any system of dominance must involve not only overt power and violence but the problem of the consent of the dominated (Godelier, 1986).

In North London the Nafsiyat Inter-Cultural Therapy Centre, one of the recent developments in this area, and the only one conducting formal research, deliberately set itself against ethnic matching except where issues of language made it unavoidable (Accharya et al., 1989; Kareem and Littlewood, 1989). Funded jointly by the local health authority and Islington Council it offers formal psychotherapy of the psychoanalytical type in a set of consulting rooms off the local high street. Most of the clients are funded by their hospitals or social service departments but a small minority pay for their own therapy. Somewhat unexpectedly a large proportion of the clients who refer themselves have a serious psychotic illness; less surprisingly they come for therapy after dissatisfaction with medical treatment elsewhere. The clients, have, on average, high scores on various measures of 'neurotic' symptoms, largely anxiety and depression, again suggesting that a proportion of the black and ethnic minority population do have disabling psychological symptoms which are not recognized by or come to the attention of doctors (page 258). Arguing against classic psychotherapeutic dogma, black clients at Nafsiyat have good attendance rates even though they do not pay for their therapy and initial results suggest that therapy is highly effective in reducing their distress and enabling them to cope effectively and actively with their struggles in a racist society (Accharya *et al.*, 1989).

Many of us involved in these issues have been criticized for not presenting a detailed programme of action. In part this has been a recognition of powerlessness. In part it has been a deliberate eschewing of what Michel Foucault (1981) called 'prescriptive, prophetic discourse': 'What is to be done ought not to be determined from above by reformers, be they prophetic or legislative, but by a long work of comings and goings, of exchanges, reflections, trials, different analyses. . . The problem is one for the subject who acts.' Change occurs through the struggles of the people concerned, not because 'a plan of reform has found its way into the heads of social workers or doctors' (*ibid*). As Elaine Showalter (1987) remarks in her book on women and psychiatry, when women are spoken for but do not speak for themselves, even the most radical and sympathetic psychiatric theories 'become only the opening scenes of the next drama of confinement'.

Black people have experienced the harsher forms of psychiatric interventions, and we live in a period in which psychotherapy is perceived as uniquely empowering the 'client'. We cannot however assume that an adequate or appropriate goal is simply to provide access to 'therapy'. Psychotherapy or 'holistic' approaches are perhaps less innocent, less free of social and political ideologies than is biomedicine; they certainly have the potential to be far more insidious agents of social control than the Mental Health Act (see Baron, 1987; Sedgwick, 1982; Armstrong, 1984; Silverman, 1987; Littlewood, 1989). There is, of course, nothing inherently wrong with 'social control': it is the process by which all societies reproduce themselves through inculcating shared values and behaviour. The question is perhaps 'control of whom, by whom, for what end?'

Our aim then must be, not just 'therapy', but a self-reflexive practice which examines its own prejudices, ideology and will to power, which is aware of the ironies and contradictions in its own formation, and which is prepared to overcome them.

R.L., M.L. (1989)

REFERENCES

1 Ackernecht, E.H. (1943), 'Psychopathology, primitive medicine and primitive culture', *Bulletin of the History of Medicine*,14, 30–69.
2 Adorno, T.W., Frenkel-Brunswick, E., Levinson, D.J., and Sanford, R.N. (1950), *The Authoritarian Personality*, New York: Harper.
3 Alexander, F. (1950), *Psychosomatic Medicine*, New York: Norton.
4 Alexander, J. (1977), 'The culture of race in middle-class Kingston, Jamaica', *American Ethnologist, 4*, 413–35.
5 Allers, R. (1920), 'Über psychogene Störungen in sprachfremder Umgebung', *Zeitschrift für die gesamte Neurologie und Psychiatrie, 60*, 281–9.
6 Altschule, M.D. (1976), *The Development of Traditional Psychopathology*, Washington: Hemisphere.
7 Anumonye, A. (1967), 'Psychological stresses among African students in Britain', *Scottish Medical Journal, 12*, 787–803.
8 Anwar, M. (1979), *The Myth of Return: Pakistanis in Britain*, London: Heinemann.
9 Ardener, E. (1971), Introductory Essay in *Social Anthropology and Language*, London: Tavistock.
10 Ardener, S. (1975), Introduction in *Perceiving Women*, London: Dent.
11 Association of Psychiatrists in Training (1977), *Newsletter*, September.
12 Association of Psychiatrists in Training (1979), *Newsletter*, July.
13 Astrup, C., and Ødegaard, O. (1960), 'Internal migration and mental disease', *Psychiatric Quarterly, 34*, 116–30.
14 Augustine, Saint (1908), *Confessions*, Cambridge University Press.
15 Austin, D.J. (1979), 'History and symbols in ideology: a Jamaican example', *Man, 14*, 497–514.

16 Babcock, B.A. (1978), *The Reversible World: Symbolic Inversion in Art and Society*, Cornell University Press.
17 Babcock, J.W. (1895), 'The coloured insane', *Alienist and Neurologist, 16*, 423–47.
18 Bagley, C. (1971a), 'Mental illness in immigrant minorities in London', *Journal of Biosocial Science, 3*, 449–59.
19 Bagley, C. (1971b) 'The social aetiology of schizophrenia in immigrant groups', *International Journal of Social Psychiatry, 17*, 292–304.

20 Bagley, C., and Binitie, A. (1970), 'Alcoholism and schizophrenia in Irishmen in London', *British Journal of Addiction*, 65, 3–7.
21 Baker, J.R. (1974), *Race*, Oxford University Press.
22 Balfour, A., and Scott, H.H. (1924), *Health Problems of the Empire*, London: Collins.
23 Ballard, C. (1978), 'Arranged marriages in the British context', *New Community*, 6, 181–96.
24 Barrett, L.E. (1971), *The Rastafarians*, Kingston: Sangster.
25 Barth, F. (1969), *Ethnic Groups and Boundaries*, Boston: Little, Brown.
26 Barthes, R. (1967), *Elements of Semiology*, London: Cape.
27 Bateson, G. (1973), *Steps to an Ecology of Mind*, Frogmore: Paladin.
28 Bedford, E. (1967), 'Emotions', in Gustafson, op.cit.
29 Benedict, R. (1935), *Patterns of Culture*, London: Routledge & Kegan Paul.
30 Benedict, R. (1942), *Race and Racism*, London: Labour Book Services.
31 Benedict, R. (1946), *The Chrysanthemum and the Sword*, Boston: Houghton Mifflin.
32 Berger, P.L. (1969), *The Social Reality of Religion*, London: Faber.
33 Bernstein, B. (1971), *Class, Codes and Control*, London: Routledge & Kegan Paul.
34 Billingsley, A. (1970), 'Black families and white social science', *Journal of Social Issues*, 26, 127–42.
35 Binitie, A. (1975), 'A factor analytic study of depression across cultures', *British Journal of Psychiatry*, 127, 559–63.
36 Bleuler, E. (1924), *Textbook of Psychiatry*, London: Macmillan.
37 Bleuler, M. (1972), *Die Schizophrenen Geistesstörungen in Lichte Langjähriger Kranken- und Familiengeschichten*, Stuttgart: Thieme.
38 Bloch, S., and Reddaway, P. (1977), *Russia's Political Hospitals*, London: Gollancz.
39 Boisen, A.T. (1939), 'Economic distress and religious experience: a study of the Holy Rollers', *Psychiatry*, 2, 185–94.
40 Borrow, G. (1969), *The Romany Rye*, London: Dent.
41 Bourne, S. and Bruggen, P. (1979), 'Distinction awards for England and Wales 1977' *British Medical Journal*, March, 638–79.
42 Bowker, G., and Carrier, J. (1976), *Race and Ethnic Relations*, London: Hutchinson.
43 Brook, P. (1973), *Psychiatrists in Training*, Ashford: Headley.
44 Brook, P. (1974), 'Psychiatrists: background, career and career alternative, of a group of recently appointed consultants', *British Journal of Psychiatry*, 125, 1–9.
45 Brook, P. (1975), 'Training opportunities for overseas psychiatrists', *British Journal of Psychiatry*, 127, 179–84.
46 Brown, G.W., and Harris, T. (1978), *The Social Origins of Depression*, London: Tavistock.
47 Brown, G., Ni Bhrolchain, M., and Harris, T. (1975), 'Social class

and psychiatric disturbance among women in an urban population', *Sociology, 9*, 225–54.

48 Bruhn, J.C., and Parsons, O.H. (1964), 'Medical students' attitudes towards four medical specialities', *Journal of Medical Education, 39*, 40–49.

49 Buchan, T. (1969), 'Depression in African patients', *South African Medical Journal*, 23 August, 1055–8.

50 Burke, A.W. (1973), 'The consequences of unplanned repatriation', *British Journal of Psychiatry, 123*, 109–11.

51 Burke, A.W. (1975), 'Trends in Caribbean psychiatry – I', *West Indian Medical Journal, 24*, 218–22.

52 Burke, A.W. (1976a), 'Attempted suicide among Asian immigrants in Birmingham', *British Journal of Psychiatry, 128*, 528–33.

53 Burke, A.W. (1976b), 'Socio-cultural determinants of attempted suicide among West Indians in Birmingham', *British Journal of Psychiatry, 129*, 261–6.

54 Burke, A.W. (1980), *Aetiological Aspects of Depression – a Community Survey*, Transcultural Psychiatry Society Workshop, Edinburgh.

55 Calley, M.J.C. (1965), *God's People: West Indian Pentecostal Sects in England*, Oxford University Press.

56 Cantril, H. (1940), *The Invasion from Mars: A Study in the Psychology of Panic*, Princetown University Press.

57 Carkhuff, R.R., and Pierce, R. (1967), 'Differential effects of therapist, race and social class upon patient depth of self-exploration in the initial clinical interview', *Journal of Consulting and Clinical Psychology, 31*, 632–4.

58 Carothers, J.C. (1972), *The Mind of Man in Africa*, London: Stacey.

59 Carstairs, G.M. (1954), 'Daru and Bhang: cultural factors in the choice of intoxicant', *Quarterly Journal of Studies on Alcohol, 15*, 220–37.

60 Carstairs, G.M. (1973), 'Psychiatric training for foreign medical graduates', in *Companion to Psychiatric Studies,* ed. A. Forrest, Edinburgh: Churchill-Livingstone.

61 Carstairs, G.M., and Kapur, R.L. (1976), *The Great Universe of Koto: Stress, Change and Mental Disorder in an Indian Village*, London: Hogarth.

62 Cashmore, E. (1979), *Rastaman*, London: Allen & Unwin.

63 Castel, R. (1977), *L'Ordre psychiatrique*, Paris: Minuit.

64 Castles, S., and Kosack, G. (1973), *Immigrant Workers and Class Structures in Western Europe*, Oxford University Press.

65 Centro Studi Emigrazione (1976), *Rapporto di sintesi sulle caratteristiche del sistema religioso, sociale e personale deila seconda generazione italiana in Gran Bretagne*, Rome: CSE.

66 Charbonneau, B. (1978), 'Le Temple du Peuple, caricature de toute société, *Le Monde*, 5 December, Paris.

67 Chodoff, P. (1975), 'Psychiatric aspects of the Nazi persecution', in

Handbook of Psychiatry, ed. S. Arieti, New York: Basic Books.
68 Clare, A. (1976), *Psychiatry in Dissent*, London: Tavistock.
69 Clarke, E. (1972), *My Mother Who Fathered Me*, London: Allen & Unwin.
70 Clements, F.E. (1932), *Primitive Concepts of Disease*, University of California Publications in American Archaeology and Ethnology, 32, No.2.
71 Coard, B. (1971), *How the West Indian Child is Made Educationally Subnormal in the British School System*, London: New Beacon.
72 Cochrane, R. (1977), 'Mental illness in immigrants to England and Wales. An analysis of mental hospital admissions', *Social Psychiatry 12*, 23–35.
73 Cochrane, R. (1979), 'Psychological and behavioural disturbance in West Indians and Pakistanis in Britain', *British Journal of Psychiatry, 134*, 201–10.
74 Cochrane, R. and Stopes-Roe, M. (1977), 'Psychological and social adjustment of Asian immigrants to Britain', *Social Psychiatry, 12*, 195–207.
75 Cole, J., and Pilisuk, M. (1976), 'Differences in the provision of mental health services by race', *American Journal of Orthopsychiatry, 46*, 510–25.
76 Commission for Racial Equality (1978a), *Annual Report*, London: HMSO.
77 Commission for Racial Equality (1978b), *Looking for Work: Black and White School Leavers in Lewisham*, London: CRE.
78 Commission for Racial Equality (1978c), *Ethnic Minorities in Britain: Statistical Background*, London: CRE.
79 Community Relations Commission (1967), *Summary of PEP Report on Racial Discrimination*, London: CRC.
80 Community Relations Commission (1976a), *Refuge or Home*, London: CRC.
81 Community Relations Commission (1976b), *Aspects of Mental Health in a Multi-Cultural Society*, London: CRC.
82 Community Relations Commission (1977a), *Urban Deprivation, Racial Inequality and Social Policy*, London: HMSO.
83 Community Relations Commission (1977b), *Ethnic Minorities and Employment*, No.4, London: CRC.
84 Community Relations Commission (1977c), *Bulletin*, March.
85 Cooper, D. (1967), *Psychiatry and Anti-Psychiatry*, London: Tavistock.
86 Cooper, J.E., Kendell, R.E., Gurland, B.J., Sharpe, L., Copeland, J.R.M., and Simon, R. (1972), *Psychiatric Diagnosis in New York and London*, Maudsley Monograph No.20, Oxford University Press.
87 Cooper, J.E., and Sartorius, N. (1977), 'Cultural and temporal variations in schizophrenia: a speculation on the importance of industrialization', *British Journal of Psychiatry, 130*, 50–55.
88 Cooper, R.M. and Zubek, J.P. (1958), 'Effects of enriched and restricted early environments on the learning ability of bright and

dull rats', *Canadian Journal of Psychology, 12*, 159–64.

89 Copeland, J.R.M. (1968), 'Aspects of mental illness in West African students', *Social Psychiatry, 3*, 7–13.

90 Curtis, J.L. (1971), *Blacks, Medical Schools and Society*, University of Michigan Press.

91 *Daily Mail* (1978), 14 February, London.

92 Davis, B.D. (1966), *The Problem of Slavery in Western Culture*, Cornell University Press.

93 Davis K. (1938), 'Mental hygiene and the class structure', *Psychiatry, 1*, 55–65.

94 *Decennial Supplement on Occupational Mortality 1959–1963*, London: HMSO.

95 Deutsch, A. (1944), 'The First US Census of the insane (1840) and its use as pro-slavery propaganda', *Bulletin of the History of Medicine, 15*, 469–82.

96 Devereux, G. (1937), 'Institutionalized homosexuality of the Mohave Indians', *Human Biology, 9*, 482–98.

97 Devereux, G. (1961), *Mohave Ethnopsychiatry and Suicide*, Washington: Smithsonian Institute.

98 Devereux G. (1970), *Essais d'ethnopsychiatrie générale*, Paris: Gallimard.

99 De Vos, G. (1960), 'The relation of guilt towards parents to achievement and arranged marriage among the Japanese', *Psychiatry, 23*, 287–301.

100 Dicks, H.V. (1952), 'Observations on contemporary Russian behaviour', *Human Relations, 5*, 111–75.

101 Dohrenwend, B.P., and Chin–Shong, E. (1967), 'Social status and attitudes towards psychological disorder', *American Sociological Review, 32*, 417–33.

102 Donald, J.S. (1876), 'Notes on lunacy in British Guiana', *Journal of Mental Science, 22*, 76–81.

103 Donzelot, J. (1977), *La Police des familles*, Paris: Minuit.

104 Douglas, M. (1966), *Purity and Danger*, London: Routledge.

105 Douglas, M. (1970), *Natural Symbols*, London: Barrie & Rockcliff.

106 Douglas, M. (1973), *Rules and Meanings*, Harmondsworth: Penguin.

107 Dubos, R. (1965), *Man Adapting*, Yale University Press.

108 Dunham, H.W. (1965), *Community and Schizophrenia*, Detroit: Wayne State University Press.

109 Dunham, H.W., Phillips, P., and Srinvasin, B. (1966), 'A research note on diagnosis, mental illness and social class', *American Sociological Review, 31*, 223–7.

110 Durkheim, É., and Mauss, M. (1963), *Primitive Classification*, London: Routledge.

111 Du Sautoy, S. (1980), 'Register lists all offences by aliens', *Guardian*, 16 August, London.

112 Eaton, J.W., and Weil, R.J. (1955), *Culture and Mental Disorder*,

New York: Free Press.
113 Edgerton, R.B. (1966), 'Conceptions of psychosis in four East African societies', *American Anthropologist, 68*, 408–25.
114 El-Islam, M.F. (1969), 'Depression and guilt: a study at an Arab psychiatric clinic', *Social Psychiatry, 2*, 56–8.
115 Ellison, R. (1953), *Invisible Man*, London: Gollancz.
116 Engels, F. (1969), *Condition of the Working Classes in England*, London: Panther.
117 English, H.B. and English, A.C. (1958), *A Comprehensive Dictionary of Psychological and Psychoanalytical Terms*, quoted in Montagu, op.cit.
118 Enright, J.B., and Jaeckle, W.R. (1963), 'Psychiatric symptoms and diagnosis in two subcultures', *International Journal of Social Psychiatry, 9*, 12–17.
119 Erikson, E.H. (1967), *Childhood and Society*, Harmondsworth: Penguin.
120 Ettinger, S. (1968), 'The Hasidic movement', *Cahiers d'Histoire Mondiale, 2*, 251–66.
121 Evans-Pritchard, E.E. (1937), *Witchcraft, Oracles and Magic among the Azande*, Oxford: Clarendon.
122 Evans-Pritchard, E.E. (1940), *The Nuer*, Oxford University Press.
123 *Evening News* (1980), 21 May, London.

124 Fagin, L. (1979), 'The experience of unemployment', *New Universities Quarterly*, Winter, 48–73.
125 Fanon, F. (1952), *Peau noir, masques blancs*, Paris: Éditions de Seuil.
126 Fanon, F. (1965), *The Wretched of the Earth*, London: MacGibbon & Kee.
127 Fanon, F. (1970), *Towards the African Revolution*, Harmondsworth: Penguin.
128 Faris, R.E.L. (1924), 'Cultural isolation and the schizophrenic personality', *American Journal of Sociology, 40*, 155–64.
129 Faris, R.E.L., and Dunham, H.W. (1939), *Mental Disorders in Urban Areas*, University of Chicago Press.
130 Fiedler, L. (1967), *Love and Death in the American Novel*, London: Cape.
131 Field, M. (1958), 'Mental Disorder in rural Ghana', *Journal of Mental Science, 104*, 1043–51.
132 Figelman, M.J. (1968), 'A comparison of affective and paranoid disorders in Negroes and Jews', *International Journal of Social Psychiatry, 14*, 277–81.
133 Finney, J.C. (1969), *Culture Change, Mental Health and Poverty*, Lexington: University of Kentucky Press.
134 Firth, R. (1956), *Two Studies of Kinship in London*, London: Athlone.
135 Firth, R. (1961), 'Suicide and risk-taking in Tikopia society', *Psychiatry, 23*, 1-17.

136 Firth, R. (1973), *Symbols – Public and Private*, London: Allen & Unwin.
137 Fischer, S. (1943), 'The influence of Indian and Negro blood on manic-depressive psychosis', *Journal of Nervous and Mental Disease, 97*, 409–20.
138 Fortes, M., and Mayer, D.Y. (1969), 'Psychosis and social change among the Tallensi of Northern Ghana', in *Psychiatry in a Changing Society*, ed. S.H. Foulkes and G. Stewart Prince, London: Tavistock.
139 Foucault, M. (1967), *Madness and Civilisation*, London: Tavistock.
140 Foucault, M. (1973), *The Birth of the Clinic*, London: Tavistock.
141 Fox, G. (1978), *Journal*, New York: Baker.
142 Fox, R. (1967), *Kinship and Marriage*, Harmondsworth: Penguin.
143 Freud, S. (1930), *Civilisation and Its Discontents*, London: Hogarth Press.
144 Freud, S. (1979), 'Psychoanalytic notes on an autobiographical account of a case of paranoia', in *Case Histories – 2*, Harmondsworth: Penguin.
145 Fromm, E. (1941), *Escape from Freedom* (UK title: *Fear of Freedom*), New York: Farrer & Rinehart.
146 Furth, P.T. (1972), *Flesh of the Gods*, London: Allen & Unwin.
147 Galbraith, J. (1980), 'Begin the Begum', *World Medicine*, 14 June, 77–8.
148 Geertz, C. (1966), 'Religion as a cultural system', in *Anthropological Approaches to the Study of Religon*, ed. M. Banton, London: Tavistock.
149 Geggus, D. (1979), *The Slaves of British-occupied Saint Domingue: An Analysis of the Workforce of 197 Absentee Plantations 1796/97*, unpublished manuscript.
150 German, G.A. (1972), 'Aspects of clinical psychiatry in sub-Saharan Africa', *British Journal of Psychiatry, 121*, 461–79.
151 Ginsberg, H. (1964), *The Psychology of Society*, London: Methuen.
152 Glass, R. (1960), *Newcomers: West Indians in London*, London: Allen & Unwin.
153 Glass R. (1962), 'Insiders – outsiders', *New Left Review*, No.17, 34–45.
154 Goffman, E. (1959), *The Presentation of Self in Everyday Life*, London: Allen Lane.
155 Goffman, E. (1964), *Stigma*, Harmondsworth: Penguin.
156 Goffman, E. (1968), *Asylums*, Harmondsworth: Penguin.
157 Goldberg, E.M., and Morrison, S.L. (1963), 'Schizophrenia and social class', *British Journal of Psychiatry, 109*, 785–802.
158 Goodman, F.D. (1969), 'Speaking in tongues in four cultural settings', *Confinia Psychiatrica, 12*, 113–29.
159 Gordon, H.J. (1934), 'Psychiatry in Kenya Colony', *Journal of Mental Science, 80*, 167–70.
160 Gould, S.J. (1977), *Ontogeny and Phylogeny*, Harvard University Press.

161 Granek, M. (1976), 'Le Concept de fou et ses implications dans la littérature talmudique et ses exigèses', *Annales Médico-Psychologiques, 134*, 17–36.

162 Granville-Grossman, K. (1979), 'Psychiatric Aspects of Cannabis use', in *Recent Advances in Psychiatry – 3*, ed. Granville-Grossman, Edinburgh: Churchill-Livingstone.

163 Green, E.M. (1914), 'Psychoses among Negroes – a comparative study', *Journal of Nervous and Mental Disease, 41*, 697–708.

164 Greenless, T.D. (1895), 'Insanity among the natives of South Africa', *Journal of Mental Science, 41*, 71–8.

165 Griffiths, M.S. (1977), 'The influence of race on the psychotherapeutic relationship', *Psychiatry, 40*, 27–40.

166 Grosskurth, P. (1980), *Havelock Ellis*, London: Allen Lane.

167 *Guardian* (1967), 9 September, London.

168 *Guardian* (1978), 'Orthodox Jews plan "enclosure" in city', 9 February, London.

169 *Guardian* (1979), 16 August, London.

170 Guiraud, P. (1971), *La Sémiologie*, Paris: Presses Universitaires.

171 Gustafson, D.E. (ed.) (1967), *Essays in Philosophical Psychology*, London: Macmillan.

172 Haldane, J.B.S. (1938), *Heredity and Politics*, London: Allen & Unwin.

173 Haller, J.S. (1970a), 'The physician versus the Negro: medical and anthropological concepts of race in the nineteenth century', *Bulletin of the History of Medicine, 44*, 154–67.

174 Haller, J.S. (1970b), 'Concepts of race inferiority in nineteenth-century anthropology', *Journal of the History of Medicine, 25*, 40–51.

175 Hallpike, C.R. (1969), 'Social hair', *Man, 4*, 256–64.

176 *Hansard, 954*, No.161, London: HMSO.

177 Hare, E.H. (1956), 'Mental illness and social conditions in Bristol', *Journal of Mental Science, 102*, 349–57.

178 Harner, M.J. (1973), *Hallucinogens and Shamanism*, Oxford University Press.

179 Hart, J.T. (1971), 'The inverse care law', *Lancet*, 405.

180 *Health Trends* (1979), 'Medical staffing and prospects in the NHS 1978', 3, 53–6.

181 Healy, P. (1978), 'Ulster children suffer less from parental abuse', *The Times*, 6 September, London.

182 Hendin, H. (1969), *Black Suicide*, New York: Basic Books.

183 Henriques, F. (1953), *Family and Colour in Jamaica*, London: Eyre & Spottiswoode.

184 Hernton, C.C. (1969), *Sex and Racism*, London: André Deutsch.

185 Herskovits, M.S. (1941), *The Myth of the Negro Past*, New York: Harper.

186 Hilgard, E.R., Atkinson, R.C., and Atkinson, R.L. (1971), *Introduction to Psychology*, New York: Harcourt Brace Jovanovich.

187 Hill, C. (1972), *The World Turned Upside Down*, London: Temple Smith.

188 Hiro, D. (1971), *Black British, White British*, London: Eyre & Spottiswoode.

189 Hitch, P., and Rack, P.H. (1977), 'Paranoid symptomatology among Polish refugees in Britain', in *Fragen der Transkulturell-Vergleichenden Psychiatrie in Europa*, ed. A. Boroffka and W.M. Pfeiffer, Münster: Westfälische Wilhelms-Universität.

190 Hollingshead, A.B., and Redlich, F.C. (1958), *Social Class and Mental Illness*, New York: Wiley.

191 Home Affairs Committee (1980), *Race Relations and the 'Sus' Law*, HC 559, London: HMSO.

192 Home Office (1980), *Statistical Bulletin No.2*, London: HMSO.

193 Horton, D. (1943). 'The functions of alcohol in primitive societies: a cross-cultural study', *Quarterly Journal of Studies on Alcohol, 4*, 199–320.

194 Huillon, P., Hémery, J., and Houllion, G. (1977), 'Remarques à propos d'un révolutionnaire qualifie de psychotique', *Annales Médico-Psychologiques, 1*, 479–94.

195 Illich, I. (1975), *Medical Nemesis*, London, Calder & Boyars.

196 Jacobs, L. (1973), *What Does Judaism Say About. . . ?* Jerusalem: Keter.

197 Jarvis, E. (1971), *Insanity and Idiocy in Massachusetts*: Report of the Commission on Lunacy 1855, Harvard University Press, cited in B.P. Dohrenwend and B.S. Dohrenwend, 'Social and Cultural influences on psychopathology', *Annual Review of Psychology, 1974, 25*, 417–52.

198 Jaspers, K. (1962), *General Psychopathology*, Manchester University Press.

199 Jensen, A.R. (1969), 'How much can we boost IQ and scholastic achievement?', *Harvard Educational Review, 39*, 1–123.

200 Johnson, D.M. (1945), 'The "Phantom Anaesthetist of Mattoon"', *Journal of Abnormal Social Psychology, 40*, 175–86.

201 Jones, E. (1916), 'The theory of symbolism', in *Papers on Psychoanalysis*, London: Baillière.

202 Jones, P. (1980), 'Social factors in health – 2', *General Practitioner*, 14 March.

203 Jordan, W.D. (1968), *White over Black*, University of North Carolina Press.

204 Kagwa, B.H. (1964), 'The problem of mass hysteria in East Africa', *East African Medical Journal, 41*, 12.

205 Kalsa, S.S. (1979), *Daughters of Tradition*, Birmingham: Third World Publications.

206 Kamin, L.J. (1977), *The Science and Politics of IQ*, Harmondsworth: Penguin.

207 Kardiner, A. (1945), *The Psychological Frontiers of Society*, Columbia University Press.
208 Katz, M.M., Cole, J.O., and Lowery, H.A. (1969), 'Studies of the diagnostic process', *American Journal of Psychiatry, 125*, 529–538.
209 Katznelson, I, (1973), *Black Men, White Cities*, Oxford University Press.
210 Kendell, R.E. (1970), 'Relationship between aggression and depression', *Archives of General Psychiatry, 22*, 308–19.
211 Kendell, R.E. (1975), *The Role of Diagnosis in Psychiatry*, Oxford: Blackwell.
212 Kerridge, P. (1979), 'The myth of "black culture"', *Spectator*, 1 December, London.
213 Kiev, A. (1961), 'Folk psychiatry in Haiti', *Journal of Nervous and Mental Disease, 132*, 260–65.
214 Kiev, A. (1963), 'Beliefs and delusions of West Indian immigrants to London', *British Journal of Psychiatry, 109*, 356–63.
215 Kiev, Al (1964), 'Psychotherapeutic aspects of Pentecostal sects among West Indian immigrants to England', *British Journal of Sociology, 15*, 129–38.
216 Kiev, A. (1968), *Psychiatry in the Communist World*, New York: Science House.
217 Kiev, A. (1972), *Transcultural Psychiatry*, Harmondsworth: Penguin.
218 Kino, F.F. (1951), 'Refugee psychoses in Britain: alien's paranoid reaction', *Journal of Mental Science, 97*, 589–94.
219 Kitzinger, S. (1966), 'The Rastafarian Brethren', *Comparative Studies in Society and History, 9*, 34–9.
220 Klaf, F.S., and Hamilton, J.G. (1961), 'Schizophrenia – a hundred years ago and today', *Journal of Mental Science, 107*, 817–27.
221 Kluckholn, C. (1944), *Navaho Witchcraft*, Cambridge, Mass.: Peabody Museum.
222 Kluckholn, C. (1962), *Culture and Behaviour*, New York: Free Press.
223 Kovel, J. (1970), *White Racism: A Psychohistory*, London: Allen Lane.
224 Kraepelin, E. (1904), 'Comparative psychiatry', in *Themes and Variations in European Psychiatry*, ed. S.R. Hirsch and M. Shepherd, Bristol: Wright.
225 Kramer, J. (1980), *Unsettling Europe*, New York: Random House.
226 Krausz, (1971), *Ethnic Minorities in Britain*, London: MacGibbon & Kee.
227 Kreitman, N., Sainsbury, P., Morrissey, J. Towers, J., and Scrivener, J. (1961), 'The reliability of psychiatric assessment: an analysis', *Journal of Mental Science, 107*, 887–908.
228 Krupinski, J. Schaechter, F., and Cade, J.F.J. (1965), 'Factors influencing the incidence of mental disease among migrants', *Medical Journal of Australia, 2*, 269–81.
229 Krupinski, J., Stoller, A., and Wallace, L. (1973), 'Psychiatric disorders in East European refugees now in Australia', *Social*

Science and Medicine, 7, 31–49.
230 Kupferer, H.J. (1979), 'A case of sanctioned drinking: the Rupert's House Cree', *Anthropological Quarterly*, October, 198–203.
231 Kupfermann, J. (1976), *The Lubavitch Hasidim of Stamford Hill*, University of London, M. Phil. Thesis.

232 Laing, R.D. (1959), *The Divided Self*, London: Tavistock.
233 Lambert, J.R. (1971), *Crime, Police and Race Relations*, Oxford University Press.
234 Lambo, T.A. (1955), 'The role of cultural factors in paranoid psychosis among the Yoruba tribe', *Journal of Mental Science, 101*, 239–66.
235 Lambo, T.A. (1957), *A Report on the Study of Social and Health Problems of Students in Britain and Ireland*, Confidential Report for the Government of Western Nigeria, Microfilm.
236 *Lancet* (1977), 'Apartheid and mental health-care' (editorial), 3 September.
237 Laubscher, B.J.F. (1937), *Sex, Custom and Psychopathology: A Study of South African Pagan Natives*, London: Routledge.
238 Leach, E. (1958), 'Magical hair', *Journal of the Royal Anthropological Insitute, 88*, 147–64.
239 Leach, E. (1976), *Culture and Communication*, Cambridge University Press.
240 Lefî, J. (1973), 'Culture and the differentiation of emotional states', *British Journal of Psychiatry, 125*, 336–40.
241 Leighton, D.C., Harding, J.S., Macklin, D.B., MacMillan, A., and Leighton, A.H. (1963), *The Character of Danger*, New York: Basic Books.
242 Lemert, E.M. (1951), *Social Pathology*, New York: McGraw Hill.
243 Lenz, H. (1957), 'Der Wandel des Bildes der Depression', *Fortschritte der Neurologie, Psychiatrie und ihre Grenzgebiete, 23*, 58–67.
244 LeVine, R.A., and Campbell, D.T. (1972), *Ethnocentrism: Theories of Confiict, Ethnic Attitudes and Group Behaviour*, New York: Wiley.
245 Lévi-Strauss, C. (1966), *The Savage Mind*, London: Weidenfeld Nicolson.
246 Lévi-Strauss, C. (1968), *Structural Anthropology*, London: Allen Lane.
247 Lévi-Strauss, C. (1977), *Structural Anthropology 2*, London: Allen Lane.
248 Levy, D.M. (1947), *New Fields of Psychiatry*, London: Chapman Hall.
249 Levy, L. (1974), 'Social class and mental disorder', *Psychiatrica Clinica, 7*, 271-86.
250 Levy-Bruhl, L. (1910), *Les Fonctions mentales dans les sociétés inférieures*, Paris: Alcan.
251 Lewis, I.M. (1969), 'Spirit possession in Northern Somaliland' in *Spirit Mediumship and Society in Africa*, ed. J. Beattie and J. Middleton, London: Routledge and Kegan Paul.

252 Lewis, I.M. (1976), *Social Anthropology in Perspective*, Harmondsworth: Penguin.
253 Liebau, E. (1967), *Tally's Corner*, London: Routledge & Kegan Paul.
254 Lienhardt, G. (1961), *Divinity and Experience*, Oxford: Clarendon Press.
255 Lind, J.E. (1914), 'The dream as a simple wish-fulfillment in the Negro', *Psychoanalytic Review, 1*, 295–300.
256 Lindenthal, J.J., Myers, K.M., Pepper, M.P., and Stern, M. (1970), 'Mental status and religious behaviour', *Journal for the Scientific Study of Religion, 9*, 143–9.
257 Linton, R. (1956), *Culture and Mental Illness*, Oxford: Blackwell.
258 Lipsedge, M., and Littlewood, R. (1977), 'Compulsory hospitalisation and minority status, 11th Biennial Conference of the Caribbean Federation for Mental Health, Gosier, Guadeloupe.
259 Lipsedge, M., and Littlewood, R. (1979), 'Transcultural psychiatry', in *Recent Advances in Psychiatry – 3*, ed. K. Granville-Grossman, Edinburgh: Churchill-Livingstone.
260 Lipsedge, M., and Littlewood, R. (1981), 'Religion, culture and psychopathology', (manuscript).
261 Littlewood, R. (1980), 'Anthropology and psychiatry – an alternative approach', *British Journal of Medical Psychology, 53*, 213–25.
262 Littlewood, R., and Cross, S. (1980), 'Ethnic minorities and psychiatric services', *Sociology of Health and Illness, 2*, 194–201.
263 Lugard, F.D. (1929), *The Dual Mandate in British Tropical Africa*, Edinburgh: Blackwood.

264 MacFarlane, A.D.J. (1970), *Witchcraft in Tudor and Stuart England*, London: Routledge & Kegan Paul.
265 McLellan, D. (1976), *Karl Marx*, Frogmore, Paladin.
266 Malzberg, B. and Lee, E.S. (1956), *Migration and Mental Disease*, New York: Social Science Research Council.
267 Marcos, L.R., Alpert, M, Urcuyo, L., and Kesselman, M. (1973), 'The effect of interview language on evaluation of psychopathology in Spanish-American patients', *American Journal of Psychiatry, 130*, 549–53.
268 Marx, K., and Engels, F. (1955), *On Religion*, Moscow: Progress Publishers.
269 Maudsley, H. (1867), *The Physiology and Pathology of the Mind*, New York: Appleton.
270 Mauss, M. (1979), *Sociology and Psychology*, London: Routledge & Kegan Paul.
271 May, R., Angel, E., and Ellenberger, H.F. (1958), *Existence*, New York: Basic Books.
272 Mead, G.H. (1934), *Mind, Self and Society*, University of Chicago Press.
273 Mead, M. (1949), *Male and Female*, New York: Morrow.
274 Menninger, K. (1963), *The Vital Balance*, New York: Viking.
275 Menninger, K. (1980), quoted in advertisement for *Arab and Jew in*

Jerusalem, C. Caplan, Harvard University Press, in *New York Review of Books*, 17 July.

276 Merton, R.K. (1957), *Social Theory and Social Structure*, New York: Free Press.

277 Meszaros, I. (1970), *Marx's Theory of Alienation*, London: Merlin.

278 Métraux, A. (1959), *Voodoo*, Oxford University Press.

279 Mezey, A.G. (1960), 'Personal background, emigration and mental disorder in Hungarian refugees', *Journal of Mental Science, 101*, 618–27.

280 Micklin, M., and Leon, C.A. (1975), 'Images of mental illness and the mentally ill among nurses in a developing country, *Social Science and Medicine, 9*, 441–9.

281 Mill, J.S. (1965), *Principles of Political Economy*, New York: Kelley.

282 Minde, M. (1977), 'History of the mental health services in South Africa', *South African Medical Journal, 51*, 549–53.

283 Minuchin, S. (1974), *Families and Family Therapy*, Harvard University Press.

284 Montagu, A. (1974), *Man's Most Dangerous Myth: The Fallacy of Race*, 5th edition, New York: Oxford University Press.

285 Morice, R. (1978), 'Psychiatric diagnosis in a transcultural setting, the importance of lexical categories', *British Journal of Psychiatry, 132*, 87–95.

286 Moynihan, D.P. (1965), *The Negro Family*, US Dept. of Labor, Washington.

287 Muensterberger, W. (ed.) (1969), *Man and his Culture: Psychoanalytical Anthropology after 'Totem and Taboo'*, London: Rapp & Whiting.

288 Murphy, H.B.M. (1955), 'Refugee psychoses in Great Britain', in *Flight and Resettlement*, H.B.M. Murphy, Geneva: Unesco.

289 Murphy, H.B.M. (1967), 'Cultural aspects of the delusion', *Studium Generale, II*, 684–92.

290 Murphy, H.B.M. (1968), 'Cultural factors in the genesis of schizophrenia', in *Transmission of Schizophrenia*, ed. D. Rosenthal and S.S. Kety, Oxford: Pergamon.

291 Murphy, H.B.M. (1978), 'The advent of guilt feelings as a common depressive symptom', *Psychiatry, 41*, 229.

292 Murphy, H.B.M. (1979), 'Depression, witchcraft beliefs and, superego development in preliterate societies', *Canadian Journal of Psychiatry, 24*, 437–49.

293 Murphy, H.B.M., Wittkower, E.D. and Chance, N.A. (1967), 'Cross-cultural inquiry into the symptomatology of depression', *Transcultural Psychiatric Research Review, 1*, 5–18.

294 Myers, W.A. (1977), 'The significance of the colours black and white in the dreams of black and white patients', *Journal of the American Psychoanalytic Association, 25*, 163–81.

295 Nandi, D.N. (1980), 'Socio-economic status and mental morbidity in

certain tribes and castes in India', *British Journal of Psychiatry, 136,* 73–85.

296 Needham, R. (1977), *Right and Left,* Chicago University Press.

297 Nettleford, R. (1970), *Mirror, Mirror,* Kingston: Sangster.

298 Newman, P.L. (1964), '"Wild man" behaviour in a New Guinea highlands community', *American Anthropologist, 66,* 1–19.

299 *New Society* (1979), 'The immigrant numbers game', 22 November, London.

300 *New Society* (1980), 'Pakistan tops deportation league', 28 February, London.

301 Oates, W.E. (1957), *Religious Factors in Mental Illness,* London: Allen & Unwin.

302 Ødegaard, O. (1932), 'Emigration and insanity', *Acta Psychiatrica et neurologica,* Supp. 4.

303 Ødegaard, O. (1956), 'The incidence of psychosis in various occupations', *International Journal of Social Psychiatry, 2,* 85–104.

304 Commission for Racial Equality (1986) *Ethnic Minorities in Britain: Statistical Information on the Pattern of Settlement.* CRE: London.

305 Office of Population Census and Surveys (1980a), *Mid-year Population Estimates,* OPCS Monitor, MN 80/3, London.

306 Office of Population Censuses and Surveys (1980b), personal communication.

307 Okeley, J. (1975), 'Gypsy woman: models in conflict', in Ardener, op.cit.

308 Orley, J. (1970), *Culture and Mental Illness,* Nairobi: East African Publishing House.

309 Orley, J., and Wing, J.K. (1979), 'Psychiatric disorder in two African villages', *Archives of General Psychiatry, 36,* 513–26.

310 Parekh, B. (1974), *Colour, Culture and Consciousness,* London: Allen & Unwin

311 Parker, S. (1960), 'The windigo psychosis in the context of Ojibwa personality and culture', *American Anthropologist, 62,* 603–23.

312 Parsons, A. (1969), *Belief, Magic and Anomie,* New York: Free Press.

313 Parsons, T. (1952), *The Social System,* London: Routledge & Kegan Paul.

314 Pasamanick, B. (1963), 'Some misconceptions concerning differences in the racial prevalence of mental disease', *American Journal of Orthopsychiatry, 33,* 72–86.

315 Patterson, S. (1963), *Dark Strangers,* London: Tavistock.

316 Pines, J. (1977), 'The study of racial images: a structural approach', *Screen Education,* No.23, 24–32.

317 Pinsent, R.H.F. (1963), 'Morbidity in an immigrant population', *Lancet, 2,* 437–8.

318 Pinto, R.T. (1970), *A Study of Psychiatric Illness among Asians in the Camberwell Area,* M.Phil. dissertation, London University.

319 Plog, S.C., and Edgerton, R.E. (1969), *Changing Perspectives in Mental Illness,* New York: Holt, Rinehart & Winston.

320 Pollard, P. (1971), *The Formation of Social Relations among Jamaicans and Trinidadian Immigrants in a North London Borough*, M.Phil. Thesis, London University.

321 Pouget, R., Cirba, R., Chiariny, J.F., and Castelnau, D. (1975), 'Troubles psychiatriques chez les français musulmans immigrés', *Annales Médico-Psychologiques, 133*, 541–61.

322 Prange, A.J., and Vitols, M.M. (1962), 'Cultural aspects of the relatively low incidence of depression in southern Negroes', *International Journal of Social Psychiatry, 8*, 104–12.

323 Price, G.B. (1913), 'Discussion on the causes of invaliding from the tropics', *British Medical Journal*, ii, 1290–97.

324 Price, J.S. (1975), 'Genetics of the affective illnesses', in *Contemporary Psychiatry*, ed. T. Silverstone and B. Barraclough, Ashford: Headley.

325 Prince, G. (1967), 'Mental health problems in pre-school West Indian children', *Maternal and Child Care, 3*, 483-6

326 Prince, R. (1964), 'Indigenous Yoruba Psychiatry', in *Magic, Faith and Healing*, ed. A. Kiev, New York: Free Press.

327 Prince, R. (1968), 'The changing pattern of depressive syndromes in Africa', *Canadian Journal of African Studies, 1*, 177–92.

328 Pryce, K. (1979), *Endless Pressure: A Study of West Indian Lifestyles in Bristol*, Harmondsworth: Penguin.

329 *Psychiatric News* (1975), 'Racism said to be America's chief mental health problem', 16 April.

330 Rabinowicz, L. (1960), *A Guide to Hasidism*, Jerusalem: Yoseloff.

331 Raison, T. (1980), 'We're all in this together', *Guardian*, 16 July, London.

332 Rawnsley, K., and Loudon, J.B. (1964), 'Epidemiology of mental disorder in a closed community', *British Journal of Psychiatry, 110*, 830–39.

333 Ray, I. (1873), *Contributions to Mental Pathology*, Boston: Little, Brown.

334 Reader, C. (1958), 'The ecology of the medical student', *Journal of Medical Education, 33*, 164.

335 Reay, M. (1960), '"Mushroom madness" in the New Guinea highlands', *Oceania, 31*, 137–9.

336 Rees, T., Stevens, R., and Willis, C.F. (1979), *Race, Crime and Arrests*, Home Office Research Bulletin, No.8, London: HMSO.

337 Rees, W.L. (1973), 'The Candidates' background and the results of the M.R.C.Psych', in 'Examinations and the Training of Psychiatrists', Association of Psychiatrists in Training Symposium, Cardiff.

338 Reich, W. (1970), *The Mass Psychology of Facism*, Harmondsworth: Penguin.

339 Richmond, A.H. (1961), *The Colour Problem*, Harmondsworth: Penguin.

340 Rivers, W.H.R. (1920), *Instinct and the Unconscious*, Cambridge University Press.

341 Rogow, A.A. (1970), *The Psychiatrists*, New York: Delta.

342 Roheim, G. (1941), 'The Psychoanalytical Interpretation of Culture', reprinted in Muensterberger, op.cit.
343 Rose, E.J.B. (1969), *Colour and Citizenship*, Oxford University Press.
344 Rose, N. (1979), 'The psychological complex: mental measurement and social administration', *Ideology and Consciousness*, No.5, 5–68.
345 Rosen, G. (1968), *Madness in Society*, London: Routledge & Kegan Paul.
346 Rosen, G. (1975), 'Nostalgia: a "forgotten" psychological disorder', *Psychological Medicine*, 340–45.
347 Rosenhan, D.L. (1973), 'On being sane in insane places', *Science*, 179, 250–58.
348 Roth, C., and Wigoder, G. (eds.) (1972), *Encycolopaedia Judaica*, Jerusalem: Keter.
349 Roth, M., and Morrisey J.D. (1952), 'Problems in the diagnosis and classification of mental disorder in old age', *Journal of Mental Science*, 98, 66–80.
350 Rothman, D. (1971), *The Discovery of the Asylum*, Boston: Little, Brown.
351 Royal College of Psychiatrists (1979), 'Recent consultant appointments', *Bulletin of the Royal College of Psychiatrists*, January.
352 Royal College of Surgeons (1958), *Evidence on the Royal Commission on Doctors' and Dentists' Remuneration*, London: HMSO.
353 Royes, K. (1962), 'The incidence and features of psychosis in a Caribbean community', *Proceedings of the 3rd World Congress of Psychiatry*, 2, 1121–5.
354 Rozenburg, B.A. (1974), 'The psychology of the spiritual sermon', in *Religious Movements in Contemporary America*, ed. I.I. Zaretsky and M.P. Leone, Princeton University Press.
355 Rubin, V. and Comitas, L. (1975), *Ganja in Jamaica*, The Hague: Mouton.
356 Rush, B. (1974), *Medical Inquiries and Observations*, Philadephia: Dobson.
357 Russell, G.F.M. and Walton, H.J. (1970), *The Training of Psychiatrists*, Ashford: Headley.
358 Rutter, M., Cox, A., Tupling, C., Berger, M., and Yule, W. (1975), 'Attainment and adjustment in two geographical areas: 1 – prevalence of psychiatric disorder', *British Journal of Psychiatry*, 126, 493–509.
359 Rutter, M., Yule, W., Berger, M., Yule, B., Morton, J., and Bagley, C. (1974), 'Children of West Indian immigrants: I Rates of behavioural deviance and psychiatric disorder', *Journal of Child Psychology and Psychiatry*, 15, 241–62
360 Rutter, M., Yule, W., Morton, J., and Bagley, C. (1975), 'Children of West Indian immigrants: III Home Circumstances and family patterns', *Journal of Child Psychology and Psychiatry*, 16, 105–24.
361 Rwegellera, G.G.C. (1970), *Mental Illness in Africans and West Indians of African Origin Living in London*, M.Phil. Thesis, University of London.

362 Ryle, G. (1949), *The Concept of Mind*, London: Hutchinson.

363 Sabshin, M., Diesenhaus, H., and Wilkerson, R. (1970), 'Dimensions of institutional racism in psychiatry', *American Journal of Psychiatry, 127*, 786–93.

364 Saifullah Khan, V. (1979), *Minority Families in Britain: Support and Stress*, London: Macmillan.

365 Sainsbury, P. (1955), *Suicide in London*, London: Chapman Hall.

366 Sainsbury, P. (1975), 'Suicide and attempted suicide', in *Psychiatrie der Gegenwart*, ed. K.P. Kisker, J.E. Meyer, C. Muller and E. Stromgren, Berlin: Springer.

367 Samarin, W.J. (1972), *Tongues of Men and Angels*, New York: Collier/Macmillan.

368 Sanua, V.D. (1969), 'Immigration, migration and mental illness: a review of the literature', in *Behaviour in New Environments*, ed. E.B. Brody, California: Sage.

369 Sapir, E. (1921), *Language*, New York: Harcourt.

370 Sartorius, N., Jablensky, A., and Shapiro, R. (1977), 'Two year follow-up of the patients included in the WHO International Pilot Study of Schizophrenia', *Psychological Medicine, 7*, 529–41.

371 Sartre, J.-P. (1948), *Anti-Semite and Jew*, New York: Schocken.

372 Saussure, F. de (1916), *Cours de linguistique générale*, Paris: Payot.

373 Savitt, T. (1978), *Medicine and Slavery*, University of Illinois Press.

374 Scheff, T.J. (1966), *Being Mentally Ill*, Chicago: Aldine.

375 Scheff, T.J. (1979), *Catharsis in Healing, Ritual and Drama*, University of California Press.

376 Schiefen, A.E. (1961), 'A common defect in extrapolation: explaining psychic and social processes in terms of feeding', *Psychiatry, 23*, 143–52.

377 Schliefer, C.B., Derbyshire, R.L., and Martin, J. (1968), 'Clinical change in jail-referred mental patients', *Archives of General Psychiatry, 18*, 42–6.

378 Scholem, G. (1961), *Major trends in Jewish Mysticism*, New York: Schocken.

379 Schutz, A. (1944), 'The stranger: an essay in social psychology', *American Journal of Sociology, 49*, 499–507.

380 Searle, C. (1972), *The Forsaken Lover: White Words and Black People*, London: Routledge & Kegan Paul.

381 Seligman, C.G. (1966), *Races of Africa*, Oxford University Press.

382 Shapin, S. (1979), 'Homo Phrenologicus: anthropological perspectives on an historical problem', in *Natural Order: Historical Studies of Scientific Culture*, ed. B. Barnes and S. Shapin, London: Sage.

383 Sheehan, T. (1980), 'Paris: Moses and pantheism', *New York Review of Books*, 24 January.

384 Shepherd, M., Brown, A.C., and Kalton, G.W.(1966), *Psychiatric Illness in General Practice*, Oxford University Press.

385 Silverman, C. (1968), *The Epidemiology of Depression*, Baltimore: Johns Hopkins.

386 Simpson, G.E. (1962), 'The acculturative process in Trinidadian

Shango', 35th International Congress of Americanists, Mexico City.
387 Skultans, V. (1976), 'Empathy and healing', in *Social Anthropology and Medicine*, ed. J. Loudon, London: Academic Press.
388 Skultans, V. (1977), 'Moral order and mental derangement', in *Symbols and Sentiments*, ed. I. Lewis, London: Academic Press.
389 Skultans, V. (1979), *English Madness*, London: Routledge & Kegan Paul.
390 Slater, S.S.P. (1974), *The Employment of Non-English-Speaking Workers*, London: CRC.
391 Smith, D. (1977), *Racial Disadvantage in Britain*, Harmondsworth: Penguin.
392 Smith, D. (1979), *Overseas Doctors in the NHS*, London: Heineman.
393 Smith, M.G. (1963), *Dark Puritan*, Kingston: University of the West Indies.
394 Solien, N.L. (1960), 'Household and family in the Caribbean', *Social and Economic Studies, 9*, 101–6.
395 Sontag, S. (1979), *Illness as Metaphor*, London: Allen Lane.
396 Spanos, N.P. (1975), 'Witches in the history of psychiatry: a critical analysis and an alternative conceptualisation', *Psychological Bulletin, 85*, 417–39.
397 Sperber, D. (1975), *Rethinking Symbolism*, Cambridge University Press.
398 Sterba, R. (1947), 'Some psychological factors in Negro race hatred and in anti-negro riots', *Psychoanalysis and the Social Sciences, 1*, 411–27.
399 Street, B. (1975), *The Savage in Literature*, London: Routledge & Kegan Paul.
400 Sue, S., Wagner, N., Davis, J.A., Margullis, C., and Lew, L. (1976), 'Conceptions of mental illness among Asian and Caucasian-American students', *Psychological Reports, 38*, 793–808.
401 Szasz, T.S. (1971a), *The Manufacture of Madness*, London: Routledge & Kegan Paul.
402 Szasz, T.S. (1971b), 'The sane slave: an historical note on the use of medical diagnoses as justificatory rhetoric', *American Journal of Psychotherapy, 25*, 228–39.

403 Talmon, Y. (1968), 'Millenarianism', in *International Encyclopaedia of the Social Sciences, 10*, 349-62, New York: Free Press.
404 Tausk, V. (1948), 'On the origin of the "Influencing Machine" in schizophrenia', in *The Psychoanalytic Reader*, ed. R. Fleiss, New York: International Universities Press.
405 Teja, J.S., Nareng, R.L., and Aggarwal, A.K. (1971), 'Depression across cultures', *British Journal of Psychiatry, 119*, 253–60.
406 Temerlin, M.K. (1968), 'Suggestion effects in psychiatric diagnosis', *Journal of Nervous and Mental Disease, 147*, 349–53.
407 Thomas, A., and Sillen, S. (1972), *Racism and Psychiatry*, New York: Brunner/Manzel.

408 Thomas, K. (1971), *Religion and the Decline of Magic*, London: Weidenfeld & Nicolson.
409 *Times* (1976), 2 November, London.
410 *Times* (1977), 23 December, London.
411 *Times* (1980) (quoting a speech by Enoch Powell and various responses to it), 12 July, London.
412 Tobias, P.V. (1970), 'Brain size, grey matter and race', *American Journal of Physical Anthropology, 32*, 3–26.
413 Tonks, C.M., Paykel, E.S., and Klerman, G.L. (1970), 'Clinical depression among Negroes', *American Journal of Psychiatry, 127*, 329–35.
414 Toone, B.K., Murray, R., Clare, A., Creed, F., and Smith, A. (1979), 'Psychiatrists' models of mental illness and their personal backgrounds', *Psychological Medicine, 9*, 165-78.
415 Torrey, E.F., Torrey, B.B., and Burton-Bradley, B.G. (1974), 'The epidemiology of schizophrenia in Papua New Guinea', *American Journal of Psychiatry, 131*, 567–73.
416 Turner, V. (1967), *The Forest of Symbols*, Cornell University Press.

417 Vaughn, C.E., and Leff, J.P. (1976), 'The influence of family and social factors on the course of psychiatric illness', *British Journal of Psychiatry, 129*, 125–37.
418 Vint, F.W. (1932), 'A preliminary note on the cell content of the prefrontal cortex of the East African native', *East African Medical Journal, 9*, 30–55.

419 Wasserstein, B.M.J. (1979), *Britain and the Jews of Europe, 1939–1945*, Oxford: Clarendon.
420 Watson, J.L. (1977), *Between Two Cultures*, Oxford: Blackwell.
421 Watson, P. (1972), 'Can racial differences affect IQ?', in *Race, Culture and Intelligence*, ed. K. Richardson and D. Spears, Harmondsworth: Penguin.
422 Watson, P. (1973), *Psychology and Race*, Harmondsworth: Penguin.
423 Weber, M. (1930), *The Protestant Ethic and the Spirit of Capitalism*, London: Allen & Unwin.
424 Weightman, G. (1977), 'Poor man's Harley Street', *New Society*, 20 October.
446 World Health Organisation (1977), *Apartheid and Mental Health Care*, Geneva: WHO.
447 Worsley, P. (1968), *The Trumpet Shall Sound*, 2nd edition, London: MacGibbon & Kee.
448 Wootton, B. (1959), *Social Science and Social Pathology*, London: Allen & Unwin.
449 Wright, P. (1968), *The Coloured Worker in British Industry*, Oxford University Press.

450 Zilboorg, G. (1936), 'Suicide among civilised and primitive races', *American Journal of Psychiatry, 92*, 1347–69.

REFERENCES TO CHAPTER 12

Accharya, S. Moorhouse, S., Littlewood, R., and Kareem, J. (1989) 'The Nafsiyat Intercultural Therapy Centre', *Psychiatric Bulletin*.

Adebimpe, V.R. (1982) 'Psychiatric symptoms in black patients, in S.M. Turner and R.T. Jones (eds), *Behaviour Therapy in Black Populations*, New York: Plenum.

Adebimpe, V.R. (1984) 'American blacks and psychiatry, *Transcultural Psychiatric Research Review*, 21, 83–111.

André, J. (1987) *L'Inceste Focal Dans La Famille Noire Antillaise*, Paris: Presses Universitaires de France.

Anwar, M. and Ali, A. (1987) *Overseas Doctors: Experience and Expectations*, London: Commission for Racial Equality.

Armstrong, D. (1984) 'The patient's view', *Social Science and Medicine*, 18, 737–44.

Babikeer, I.E., Cox, J.L. and McMiller, P. (1980) 'The measurement of cultural distance and its relationship to medical consultations, symptomatology and examination performance of overseas students at Edinburgh University', *Social Psychiatry*, 15, 109–16.

Baker, R. (1983) *The Psychosocial Problems of Refugees*, London: British Refugee Council.

Bal, S. (1984) *The Symptomatology of Mental Illness among Asians in the West Midlands*, BA Dissertation, Dept. of Economics and Social Sciences, Wolverhampton Polytechnic.

Ballard, R. (1982) 'Ethnic minorities and the social services', in V. Saifullah Khan (ed.), *Minority Families in Britain*, London: Macmillan.

Banton, M. (1988) *Which Relations are Race Relations?* London: Royal Anthropological Institute.

Barker, J. (1984) *Black and Asian Old People in Britain*, Mitcham: Age Concern.

Baron, C. (1987) *Asylum to Anarchy*, London: Free Association Books.

Baron, R.A. and Ransberger, V.M. (1978) 'Ambient temperature and the occurrence of collective violence, *Journal of Personality and Social Psychiatry*, 36, 351–60.

Barot, R. (1988) 'Social anthropology, ethnicity and family therapy', *Journal of Family Therapy*, 10, 271–82.

Bebbington, P.E., Hurray, J. and Tennant, C. (1981) 'Psychiatric disorders in selected immigrant groups in Camberwell', *Social*

Psychiatry, 16, 43–51.
Bhat, A. *et al.* (1984a) 'The causes of and solutions for rioting in Britain in the summer of 1981', *International Journal of Social Psychiatry, 30,* 4–8.
Bhat, A. *et al.* (1984b) 'Psychiatric workers as emotional beings: the emotional reactions of staff following the Brixton Riots', *International Journal of Social Psychiatry, 30,* 9–14.
Bhate, S., Sagovsky, R and Cox, J. (1986) 'Career survey of overseas psychiatrists', *Bulletin of the Royal College of Psychiatrists, 10,* 121–3.
Black Health Workers and Patients Group (1983) 'Psychiatry and the corporate state', *Race and Class, 25,* 49–64.
Block, C. (1981) 'Black Americans and the cross-cultural counselling and psychotherapy experience', in Marsella and Pedersen, *op.cit.*
Bolton, P. (1984) 'Management of compulsorily admitted patients to a high security unit', *International Journal of Social Psychiatry, 30,* 77–84.
Bouras, N. and Littlewood, R. (eds) (1988) *Stress and Coping in the Greek Communities in Britain.* London: Guy's Hospital
Bram, G. (1983) 'Breakdown in elderly Polish refugees', in Baker, *op.cit.*
Brent Community Health Council (1981) *Black People and the Health Service,* London: BCHC.
Brent Irish Mental Health Group (1986) *The Irish Experience of Mental Ill-Health in London,* London: BIMHG.
British Association of Social Workers (1982), *Social Work in Multi-Cultural Britain,* London:BASW.
British Refugee Council (1984) *Refugee Health in the UK,* London: BRC.
Broom, D. (1988) 'Asian pupils beat whites in O levels', *Times,* 6 October.
Byrce-Smith, D. (1981) (Reported) *Daily Telegraph,* 18 April.
Burke, A.W. (1984) 'Racism and psychological disturbance among West Indians in Britain', *International Journal of Social Psychiatry, 30* 50–68.
Burke, A.W. (1986) 'Racism, prejudice and mental illness', in J.L. Cox (ed.) *Transcultural Psychiatry,* London: Croom Helm.

Campaign Against Racism and Fascism (1983) 'Racism and mental health', *Searchlight,* No.92, 16–17.
Cashmore, E. (1979) *Rastaman,* London: Allen & Unwin.
Central Council of Probation Committees (1983) *Probation: Multi-racial Approaches,* London: CCPC.
Chandrasena, R. (1983) 'The use of traditional therapies by ethnic minorities in the UK', Typescript. (Abstract in *Transcultural Psychiatric Research Review, 20,* 297–9.
Channel 4 (1986) *Mistaken for Mad.*
Cochrane, R. and Bal, S. (1987) 'Migration and schizophrenia: an examination of five hypotheses', *Social Psychiatry, 22,* 181–91.

Cohen, A. (1980) 'Drama and politics in the development of a London carnival', *Man*, *15*, 65–87.

Commission for Racial Equality (1985) *A Report on the Seminar on Racism Awareness Training*, London: CRE.

Commission for Racial Equality (1988) *Report of a Formal Investigation into St George's Medical School*, London: CRE.

Cooklin, R.S., Ravindran, A. and Carney, M.W.P. (1983) 'The patterns of mental disorder in Jewish and non-Jewish admissions to a district general hospital', *Psychological Medicine*, *13*, 209–12.

Cox, J.L. (ed) (1986) *Transcultural Psychiatry*, London: Croom Helm.

Cox, J.L. (1986) 'Overseas students and expatriates: sojourners or settlers', in Cox (1986) *op.cit.*

Crawford, J. (1981) 'Black leader attacks social workers', *Daily Telegraph*, 22 April.

Cross, M. (1982) 'The manufacture of marginality', in E. Cashmore and B. Troyna (eds.) *Black Youth in Crisis*, London: Allen & Unwin.

Currer, C. (1984) 'Pathan women in Bradford: factors affecting mental health with particular reference to the effects of racism', *International Journal of Social Psychiatry*, *30*, 72–6.

Currer, C. (1986) 'Concepts of mental well and ill-being: the case of Pathan mothers in Britain', C. Currer and M. Stacey (eds.) *Concepts of Health and Illness and Disease: A Comparative Perspective*, Leamington Spa: Berg.

Dean, G. and Bebbington, P. (1987) 'Depression in inner London', *Social Psychiatry*, *22*, 73;84.

Devereux, G. (1969) *Reality and Dream*, New York: Doubleday.

De Zulueta, F.I. (1984) 'The implications of bilingualism in the study of treatment of psychiatric disorder', *Psychological Medicine*, *14*, 541–57.

Dirks, R. (1987) *The Black Saturnalia: Conflict and its Ritual Expression on British West Indian Slave Plantations*, Gainesville: University of Florida Press.

Donovan, J. (1986) *We Don't Buy Sickness: It Just Comes: Health, Illness and Health Care in the Lives of Black People in London*. London: Gower.

Ellen, R. (1988) 'Fetishism', *Man*, *23*, 213–35.

Fernando, S. (1986) 'Depression in ethnic minorities', in Cox (1986) *op.cit.*

Fernando, S. (1988) *Race and Culture in Psychiatry*, London: Croom Helm.

Fisher, R. (1986) *Colonial Madness*, New Brunswick: Rutgers University Press

Foucault, M. (1981) 'The question of method', *Ideology and Consciousness*, *8*, 3–14.

Francis, E. (1985) 'Death at Broadmoor: the case of Michael Martin', *Bulletin of the Transcultural Psychiatry Society*, *7*, 7–11.

Furnham, A. and Trezise, L. (1983) 'The mental health of foreign students', *Social Science and Medicine, 17*, 363–70.

Ghosh, S.K. (1984) 'Prevalence survey of alcohol drinking and alcohol dependence in the Asian population in the Uk', in N. Krasmer *et al.* (eds) *Alcohol Related Problems*, New York: Wiley.

Giggs, J. (1986) 'Ethnic status and mental illness in urban areas', in T. Rathwell and D. Phillips, *Health, Race and Ethnicity*, London: Croom Helm.

Godelier, M. (1986) *The Mental and the Material: Thought, Economy and Society*, London: Verso.

Gorman, E. (1988) 'Notting Hill Carnival: armour squads fight crime', *Times*, 26 August.

Gracchus, F. (1980) *Les lieux de la mère dans les sociétés Afro-Americaines*, Paris: Care.

Grier, W.H. and Cobbs, P.M. (1986) *Black Rage*, Basic Books, New York.

Harré, R. (1983) *Personal Being: A Theory of Individual Psychology*, Oxford: Blackwell.

Harrison, G. *et al.* (1988) 'A prospective study of severe mental disorder in Afro-Caribbean patients', *Psychological Medicine, 18*, 643–58.

Hickmott, J.R. (1983) 'The essence of violence', *Police Journal, 56*, 15–17.

Hirst, P.Q. and Woolley, P. (1986) *Social Relations and Human Attributes*, 'Cultural relativity and psychiatric practices', London: Tavistock.

Ho, M.K. (1987) *Family Therapy with Ethnic Minorities*, California: Sage.

Hobsbawm, J. (1959) *Primitive Rebels*, Manchester: Manchester University Press.

Hobson, R. (1986) *Forms of Feeling: The Heart of Psychotherapy*, London: Tavistock.

Home Office (1982) *Research Study No.72: Public Disorder*, London: Home Office.

Ineichen, B., Harrison, G. and Morgan, H.S. (1984) 'Psychiatric hospital admissions in Bristol', *British Journal of Psychiatry, 145*, 600–11.

Johnson, M.R.D. (1986) 'Inner-city residents: ethnic minorities and primary care', in T. Rathwell and D. Phillips, *Health, Race and Ethnicity*, London: Croom Helm.

Jones, B.E. and Gray, B.A. (1986) 'Problems in diagnosing schizophrenia and affective disorders among American blacks', *Hospital and Community Psychiatry, 37*, 61–5.

Jones, J.H. (1981) *Bad Blood: The Tuskagee Syphilis Experiment*, New York: Free Press.

Kareem, J. and Littlewood, R. (eds.) (1989) *Inter-Cultural Therapy: Theory and Practice*, (in press) Oxford: Blackwell.

Kerridge, P. (1983) 'Myths that poison the minds of British blacks', *Daily Mail*, 1 July.

Kerridge, R. (1988) 'Never mind anti-racism: what about reality?', *London Evening Standard*, 4 June.

Kleinman, A. (1981) *Patients and Healers in the Context of Culture*, Berkeley: University of California Press.

Kleinman, A. (1986) *Social Origins of Distress and Disease*, New Haven: Yale University Press.

Kleinman, A. and Good, B. (eds.) (1985) *Culture and Depression*, Berkeley: University of California Press.

Krause, B. (1988) 'The sinking heart: A Punjabi categorization of distress (in press), *Social Science and Medicine*.

Lacey, J.H. and Dolan, B.M. (1988) 'Bulimia in British blacks and Asians', *British Journal of Psychiatry*, 152, 73;9.

Lau, A. (1986) 'Family therapy across cultures', in Cox (1986) *op.cit.*

Lawson, W.B., Yesavage, J.A. and Werner, P.D. (1984) 'Race, violence and psychopathology, *Journal of Clinical Psychiatry*, 45, 284–2.

Le Bon, G. (1895) *The Crowd*, reprinted 1947, New York: Macmillan.

Leff, J. (1986) 'The epidemiology of mental illness across cultures', in Cox (1986) *op.cit.*

Lewis, P. *et al.* (1980) 'Ethnic differences in drug responses', *Postgraduate Medical Journal*, 56, 46–9.

Lipsedge, M. and Littlewood, R. (1985) 'Social and cultural pathology', in P. Pichot *et al.* (ed.) *Psychiatry: The State of the Art, 8*, New York: Plenum.

Lipsedge, M., Summerfield, A.B. (1989) Teaching computing to psychiatric patients: the Speedwell Information Technology Project. British Journal of Health Care Computing. 14, 23–31

Littlewood, R. (1983a) 'The theory and practice of puzzlement: a reply to Murphy', *Transcultural Psychiatric Research Review,19*, 67–9.

Littlewood, R. (1983b) 'The antinomian Hasid', *British Journal of Medical Psychology, 56*, 67·78.

Littlewood, R. (1984) 'Correspondence', *Race and Class*, 25, 4, 86.

Littlewood, R. (1985) 'An indigenous conceptualization of reactive depression in Trinidad', *Psychological Medicine, 15*, 275–81.

Littlewood, R. (1986a) 'Ethnic Minorities and the Mental Health Act: patterns of explanation', *Bulletin of the Royal College of Psychiatrists, 10*, 306–8.

Littlewood, R. (1986b) 'Russian dolls and Chinese boxes: an anthropological approach to the implicit models of psychiatry', in Cox (1986) *op.cit.*

Littlewood, R. (1988a) 'From vice to madness: the semantics of naturalistic and personalistic understandings in Trinidadian local medicine', *Social Science and Medicine, 27*, 129–48.

Littlewood, R. (1988b) 'Community initiated research: a study of psychiatrists' conceptualizations of cannabis psychosis', *Bulletin of the Royal College of Psychiatrists 12*, 486–8.

Littlewood, R. (1988c) 'Towards an intercultural therapy', *Journal of*

Social Work Practice, Vol. 3, no. 3, pp. 8–19.

Littlewood, R. (1989) 'Science, shamanism and hermeneutics', *Anthropology Today 5*, 5–11.

Littlewood, R. and Lipsedge, M. (1981) 'Acute psychotic rections in Caribbean-born patients', *Psychological Medicine, 11*, 303–18.

Littlewood, R. and Lipsedge, M. (1987) 'The butterfly and the serpent: culture. psychopathology and biomedicine', *Culture, Medicine and Psychiatry, 11*, 289–335.

Littlewood, R. and Lipsedge, M. (1988) 'Psychiatric illness among British Afro-Caribbeans', *British Medical Journal, 296*, 950–1. *See also* correspondence following this: *B.M.J. 296*, 1333, 1260, 1671, 1538, *297*, 135, 1735.

Lobo, E. (1978) *Children of Immigrants to Britain: Their Health and Social Problems*, London: Allen & Unwin.

London, M. (1986) 'Mental illness among immigrant minorities in the United Kingdom', *British Journal of Psychiatry, 149*, 265–73.

Mark, V.H., Sweet, W.H. Ervin, F.R. (1967) *Journal of the American Medical Association, 201*, 895.

Marsella, A.J. and Pedersen, P.B. (eds.) (1981) *Cross-cultural Counselling and Psychotherapy*, New York: Pergamon.

Marsella, A.J. and White, G.M. (eds.) (1982) *Cultural Conceptions of Mental Health and Therapy*, Dordrecht: Reidel.

Mavreas, V.G. and Bebbington, P.E. (1987) 'Psychiatric morbidity in London's Greek-Cypriot immigrant community', *Social Psychiatry, 22*, 150-9.

McGoldrick, M., Pearce, J. and Giardiano, J. (eds.) (1982) *Ethnicity and Family Therapy*, New York: Guilford.

McGovern, D. and Cope, R. (1987a) 'The compulsory detention of males of different ethnic groups', *British Journal of Psychiatry, 150*, 505–12.

McGovern, D. and Cope, R. (1987b) 'First psychiatric admission rates of first and second generation Afro-Caribbeans', *Social Psychiatry, 22*, 139–49.

McNaught, A. (1988) *Race and Health Policy*, London: Croom Helm.

Melville, J. (1985) 'Mentally ill in Brixton', *New Society*, 15 November.

Mental Health Act Commission (1987) *Second Biennial Report 1985–87*, London: HMSO.

Mercer, K. (1986) 'Racism and transcultural psychiatry' in P. Miller and N. Rose (eds.) *The Power of Psychiatry*.

Merrill, J. and Owens, J. (1988a) 'Self-poisoning among four immigrant groups', *Acta Psychiatrica Scandinavica, 77*, 77–80.

Merrill, J. and Owens, J. (1988b) 'Correspondence', *British Medical Journal, 296*, 1260.

Milner, G. and Hayes, G. (1988) 'Correspondence', *British Medical Journal, 296*: 1333, *297*: 359.

Minuchin, S. (1972) *Families and Family Therapy*, Boston, Mass: Harvard University Press.

Moodley, P. (1987) 'The Fanon Project: a day centre in Brixton', *Bulletin of the Royal College of Psychiatrists, 11*, 417–18.

Moss, P. and Plewis, J. (1984) 'Mental distress in mothers of pre-school children in inner London', *Psychological Medicine, 14*, 541–57.

Munoz, L. (1980) 'Exile as bereavement: socio-psychological manifestations of Chilena exiles in Great Britain', *British Journal of Medical Psychology, 53*, 227–32.

Murphy, H.B.M. (1982) 'Review of Littlewood and Lipsedge, *Aliens and Alienists*', *Transcultural Psychiatric Research Review, 19*, 204–7.

Murphy, H.B.M. (1986) 'The mental health impact of British cultural traditions', in Cox (1986) *op.cit.*

Murray, J. and Williams, P. (1986) 'Self-reported illness and general practice consulations in Asian-born and British-born residents of West London', *Social Psychiatry, 21*, 139–45.

Ndetei, D.M. and Vadher, A. (1984) 'Frequency and clinical significance of delusions across cultures', *Acta Psychiattrica Scandinavica, 70*, 73–6.

Owens, G. and Jackson, B. (1983) *Adoption and Race: Black, Asian and Mixed Race Children in White Families*, London: Batsford.

Palmer, F. (ed.) (1986) *Anti-Racism: An Assault on Education and Values*, London: Sherwood Press.

Parmar, P. (1981) 'Young Asian women: a critique of the pathological approach', *Multi-Racial Education, 9*, No.3.

Perelberg, R.J. (1983) 'Mental illness, family and networks in a London borough', *Social Science and Medicine, 17*, 481–91.

Perez, M. (1984) 'Exile: the Chilean experience', *International Journal of Social Psychiatry, 30*, 137–61.

Pillay, H.M. *et al.* (1984) 'The concepts of "causation", "racism" and "mental illness"', *International Journal of Social Psychiatry, 3029–30*.

Proctor, R. (1988) *Racial Hygiene: Medicine under the Nazis*, Boston, Mass: Harvard University Press.

Rack, P. (1982) *Race, Culture and Mental Disorder*, London: Tavistock.

Rack, P. (1986) 'Migration and mental illness', in Cox (1986) *op.cit.*

Rackett, T. (1987) 'Policing the ethnic mind, nineteenth Annual Conference of the British Sociological Association Medical Sociology Group' (manuscript)

Rassaby, E. and Rogers, A. (1985) 'Ethnic bias and the use of section 136', Transcultural Psychiatry Society Conference, 'The Mental Health Act', Northampton.

Ratcliffe, P. (1982) *Racism and Reaction*, London: Routledge & Kegan Paul.

Rathwell, T. and Phillips, D. (eds.) (1986) *Health, Race and Ethnicity*, London: Croom Helm.

Richardson, E. and Hendrik-Gutt, R. (1981) 'Diagnosis of psychiatric illness in immigrant patients', *British Journal of Clinical and Social Psychiatry, 1*, 78–81.

Rogers, A. and Faulkner, A. (1987) *A Place of Safety: MIND's Research into Police Referrals to the Psychiatric Services*, London: MIND.

Roger, J. (1977) *Black Britain's Dilemma: A Medical-Social Transcultural Study of West Indians*, Roseau, Dominican: Tropical Printers.

Sashidharan, S.P. (1986) 'Ideology and politics in transcultural psychiatry', in Cox (1986) *op.cit.*

Sears, D.O. and McConahay, J.B. (1970) 'Breadth of riot participation in the curfew zone', in N. Cohen (ed.) *The Los Angelese Riots*, New York: Praeger.

Sedgwick, P. (1982) *Psychopolitics*, London: Pluto.

Showalter, E. (1987) *The Female Malady: Women, Madness and English Culture 1830–1980*, London: Virago.

Silverman, D. (1987) 'The discourse on the social', in *Communication in Medical Practice*, London: Sage.

Skerritt, S. (1982) 'Blacks and mental health', *Staunch*, May/June 6–8, July/August 8–11.

Skin (1981) *Mental Health*, London Weekend Television.

Standing Conference of Ethnic Minority Senior Citizens (1985) *A Seminar on Community Care for the Mental Health of Black and Ethnic Minority Senior Citizens*, London: SCE, MSC.

Suzuki, R. (1984) Personal communication.

Troyna, B. and Williams, J. (1986) *Racism, Education and the State*, London: Croom Helm.

Wallace, M. (1986) *The Silent Twins*, London: Chatto & Windus.

Ward, L. (1986) *Directory of Black and Ethnic Community Mental Health Services in London*, London: National Association for Mental Health.

Watson, E. and Evans, S.J.W. (1986) 'An example of cross-cultural measurement of psychological symptoms in post-partum mothers', *Social Science and Medicine, 23*, 869–74.

Wintrob, R.H. and Harvey, Y.K. (1982) 'The self–awareness factor in inter-cultural therapy', in P. Pedersen, J.G. Draguns, W.J. Lonner and J. Trimble (eds.), *Counselling Across Cultures*, (2nd edition), Honolulu: Hawaii University Press.

Zwingman, C.A. (1983) *Uprooting and Health: Psycho-social Problems of Students from Abroad*, Geneva: World Health Organisation.

INDEX